SHAKESPEARE'S IMAGERY

AND WHAT IT TELLS US

July, 1934.

E.

The 18th arch
Old Clopton Bridge
Stratford-on-Avon

The black line shows approximately the
movement of the current, with the eddy in front.

See p. 98

SHAKESPEARE'S IMAGERY

AND WHAT IT TELLS US

by

CAROLINE F. E. SPURGEON

And thus do we of wisdom and of reach,
With windlasses and with assays of bias,
By indirections find directions out.

HAMLET, 2. 1. 64.

CAMBRIDGE
UNIVERSITY PRESS

CAMBRIDGE UNIVERSITY PRESS
Cambridge, New York, Melbourne, Madrid, Cape Town, Singapore, São Paulo

Cambridge University Press
The Edinburgh Building, Cambridge CB2 8RU, UK

Published in the United States of America by Cambridge University Press, New York

www.cambridge.org
Information on this title: www.cambridge.org/9780521065382

First published 1935
Nineteenth printing 2005

A catalogue record for this publication is available from the British Library

ISBN 978-0-521-06538-2 hardback
ISBN 978-0-521-09258-6 paperback

Transferred to digital printing 2008

To the memory

of

LUCRETIA PERRY OSBORN

and

TO MY OTHER KIND FRIENDS IN AMERICA

whose practical and generous help

first made it possible for me

to begin writing

this book

ACKNOWLEDGMENTS

I wish to acknowledge, with thanks, the kind permission of the Council of the British Academy to use part of a lecture, 'Shakespeare's Iterative Imagery', delivered before that body in May 1931. I also desire to thank the Shakespeare Association for similar permission with regard to a lecture, 'Leading Motives in the Imagery of Shakespeare's Tragedies', given before it in 1930. I am also indebted to the editor of the *Review of English Studies* for permission to reprint some of my article on *The Use of Imagery by Shakespeare and Bacon* published in that paper in October 1933, and for allowing me to make use of the count of lines in Shakespeare's plays by Mr Hart, published in the *Review of English Studies*, Jan. 1932, p. 21.

Throughout this work I have met with so much kindness and have been given so much help that it is difficult in a short note to express in any sufficient way my deep sense of obligation.

I wish, however, specifically to record the encouragement and substantial financial aid so kindly given me, through the agency of the late Mrs Henry Fairfield Osborn, by a group of American friends and well-wishers, at a time when I had done little more than make a preliminary draft of my ideas and write one or two studies on this subject. This generous gift enabled me to take a year's leave of absence from my work in London, and to devote myself entirely to research on this subject. It has also made it possible for me to secure some very necessary secretarial help.

To the Council of Bedford College, London, I desire to express my warm thanks for having kindly granted me repeated leaves of absence from my active duties as Professor, so that I might carry on this research.

To my two successive secretaries, Miss M. A. Cullis and Miss Agnes Latham, I owe a great debt. If the facts in this book are accurate and the statistics to be relied on, as I believe they are, it is owing in large measure to their patient and careful work in sorting, checking, counting, classifying and cross-referencing my card catalogue of the images of Shakespeare and his contemporaries.

I am also indebted to Miss Lois Latham for her expert copying and drafting of some of my charts.

I am particularly grateful to my friend Professor Henry Fairfield Osborn for his keen interest in and approval of this bit of work in its very beginnings, for he gave me confidence to go on with it and strengthened my hope that it would prove worth the doing.

In the later stages of my work the enthusiastic interest and encouragement of my friend Mr A. W. Pollard have been an untold help and support to me, as has also his experienced and wise counsel. For all this I feel deep gratitude.

What I owe to my friend Dean Virginia Gildersleeve, of Barnard College, New York, from the very inception of this book to the final reading of the proof sheets, it is not possible, within these formal limits adequately either to describe or to acknowledge.

PREFACE

THE following study is an attempt to point out several directions in which the detailed examination of Shakespeare's images seems to me to throw new light on the poet and his work.

These are merely a very limited selection of literally dozens of directions which might be chosen, and along the lines of which I believe there is fascinating and most repaying work for scholars for years to come.

The richness and possibilities of the material I have been working with are so great that I have been forced strictly to limit the points I touch upon in this book, which is, as I hope and intend, the first only of three studies which I have planned, on various aspects of this subject.

This first study deals chiefly with suggestions as to light thrown by the imagery (1) on Shakespeare's personality, temperament and thought, (2) on the themes and characters of the plays. The other books will be chiefly concerned with questions of authorship considered in the light of this freshly collected evidence, and with the background of Shakespeare's mind and the origins of his imagery.

The material on which they are all alike based is the whole of Shakespeare's images, as well as—for the purposes of comparison—the images from a large number of plays by his contemporaries. These I have been gradually collecting, sorting and classifying during the last seven or eight years. When I have finished some of the deductions I am drawing from it, I hope eventually to publish the material itself, so that other students can check and perhaps extend it, in order that it may serve as data and starting-point for further research of various kinds.

I embarked on this task because it seemed to me that it might provide a new method of approach to Shakespeare; and I believe I have, by a happy fortune, hit on such a method, hitherto untried, which is yielding most interesting and important results.

It enables us to get nearer to Shakespeare himself, to his mind, his tastes, his experiences, and his deeper thought than does any other single way I know of studying him. It throws light from a fresh angle upon Shakespeare's imaginative and pictorial vision, upon his own ideas about his own plays and the characters in them, and it seems to me to serve as an absolute beacon in the skies with regard to the vexed question of authorship.

Shakespeare's images have, of course, constantly been picked out and drawn upon, to illustrate one aspect or another of the poet's thought or mind, but the novelty of the procedure I am describing is that *all* his images are assembled, sorted, and examined on a systematic basis, the good with the bad, the disagreeable with the pleasant, the coarse with the refined, the attractive with the unattractive, and the poetical with the unpoetical.

They are not selected to point or to illustrate any preconceived idea or thesis, but they are studied, either as a whole, or in groups, with a perfectly open mind, to see what information they yield, and the result comes often as a complete surprise to the investigator.

It seems scarcely necessary to say that the images form, when thus collected, a world in themselves, for they mirror the richest experience and the most profound and soaring imagination known to man. To deal with them adequately would call for very great powers, as well as a life-time of study and experience, for the problems to which they give rise and the light they throw on literary substance and technique are as profound and as brilliant as the mind from which they spring.

No one could study Shakespeare closely for years without being reduced to a condition of complete humility, and I am fully conscious of my boldness in venturing even to touch the subject, for I know well that I can only scratch the surface of what it is possible to find and reveal in the hitherto uncharted treasures of this rich and varied material. My excuse is that up to the present no one has attempted seriously or systematically to assemble or examine it at all. As it appears to me to open up an entirely new and illuminating vista of investigation, if what I say here leads others—better equipped—to study fresh aspects and garner further results from this vast and almost untilled field, my boldness will have been justified.

CAROLINE F. E. SPURGEON

ALCISTON, SUSSEX

JULY, 1934

CONTENTS

Part II

THE FUNCTION OF THE IMAGERY AS BACKGROUND AND UNDERTONE IN SHAKESPEARE'S ART

ILLUSTRATIONS

PLATES

CHARTS (*at end of book*)

All Shakespearian quotations are taken from *The Larger Temple Shakespeare* edited by Israel Gollancz, in twelve volumes (J. M. Dent, 1899). The shortened forms of the play titles used in reference are as follows:

Love's Labour's Lost	*L.L.L.*
Two Gentlemen of Verona	*Two Gent.*
Comedy of Errors	*C. of E.*
Romeo and Juliet	*R. and J.*
1st part of *Henry VI*	1 *H. VI*
2nd part of *Henry VI*	2 *H. VI*
3rd part of *Henry VI*	3 *H. VI*
Richard III	*R. III*
Richard II	*R. II*
Titus Andronicus	*Titus*
Merchant of Venice	*M. of V.*
King John	*K.J.*
A Midsummer Night's Dream	*M.N.D.*
All's Well that Ends Well	*All's Well*
Taming of the Shrew	*T. of Sh.*
1st part of *Henry IV*	1 *H. IV*
2nd part of *Henry IV*	2 *H. IV*
Merry Wives of Windsor	*M.W.*
Henry V	*H. V*
Much Ado about Nothing	*M. Ado*
As You Like It	*A.Y.L.I.*
Twelfth Night	*Tw. N.*
Julius Caesar	*J.C.*
Hamlet	*Ham.*
Troilus and Cressida	*T. and C.*
Othello	*Oth.*
Measure for Measure	*M. for M.*
Macbeth	*Mac.*
King Lear	*K.L.*
Timon of Athens	*Timon*
Pericles	*Per.*
Antony and Cleopatra	*A. and C.*
Coriolanus	*Cor.*
Cymbeline	*Cym.*
A Winter's Tale	*W.T.*
The Tempest	*Temp.*
Henry VIII	*H. VIII*

PART I

THE REVELATION OF THE MAN

Every secret of a writer's soul, every experience of his life, every quality of his mind, is written large in his works, yet we require critics to explain the one and biographers to expound the other.

Virginia Woolf, *Orlando*, pp. 189–90
(The Hogarth Press, 1928).

The real revelation of the writer (as of the artist) comes in a far subtler way than by...autobiography; and comes despite all effort to elude it;...For what the writer does communicate is his temperament, his organic personality, with its preferences and aversions, its pace and rhythm and impact and balance, its swiftness or languor...and this he does equally whether he be rehearsing veraciously his own concerns or inventing someone else's.

Vernon Lee, *The Handling of Words*, p. 109.

L'auteur dans son œuvre doit être comme Dieu dans l'univers, présent partout, et visible nulle part.

Flaubert (*Correspondance*, 1852, vol. ii, p. 155).

CHAPTER I (INTRODUCTORY)

THE AIM AND METHOD EXPLAINED

I know I am talking of a trite and threadbare theme—namely, figures of speech. But the trite we fight shy of because it is trite, is sometimes more shining than the upstart new, if we will but brush off the dust.
   Convention and Revolt in Poetry, John Livingston Lowes.

WHEN Polonius instructs his man Reynaldo how best to find out what kind of life his son is leading in Paris, he suggests various circuitous ways of extracting information from Laertes' friends, such as hinting that he games or drinks, and noting how they receive such hints, and so by the judicious use of these indirect methods to draw forth the truth.

He illustrates his meaning by a metaphor from bowls; a game Shakespeare was interested in, and in which the curious fact that the player does not aim directly at the jack, but sends his ball in a curve, trusting to the bias to bring it round again, greatly appealed to him.

Thus, says Polonius, characteristically, do we men of wisdom and capacity, with winding ways

> and with assays of bias,
> By indirections find directions out.

These lines describe so exactly what I propose to try and do in this book, that 'assays of bias' might well have served as title for it, could these words have been more easily understood by modern readers. I venture moreover to say I believe the game would have appealed to Shakespeare, for just as he was attracted by the subtle element in bowls, and the measure of skill and judgment needed to turn an indirect aim into a good and true hit, so would he have been interested in the working of the same method in the sphere of literature and psychology.

The first half of my theme is contained in the remarks of the two distinguished women writers quoted at the beginning of this chapter. I believe it to be profoundly true that the real revelation of the writer's personality, temperament and quality of mind is to be found in his works, whether he be dramatist or novelist, describing other people's thoughts or putting down his own directly.

In the case of a poet, I suggest it is chiefly through his images that he, to some extent unconsciously, 'gives himself away'. He may be, and in Shakespeare's case is, almost entirely objective in his dramatic characters and their views and opinions, yet, like the man who under stress of emotion will show no sign of it in eye or face, but will reveal it in some muscular tension, the poet unwittingly lays bare his own innermost likes and dislikes, observations and interests, associations of thought, attitudes of mind and beliefs, in and through the images, the verbal pictures he draws to illuminate something quite different in the speech and thought of his characters.

The imagery he instinctively uses is thus a revelation, largely unconscious, given at a moment of heightened feeling, of the furniture of his mind, the channels of his thought, the qualities of things, the objects and incidents he observes and remembers, and perhaps most significant of all, those which he does not observe or remember.

My experience is that this works out more reliably in drama than in pure poetry, because in a poem the writer is more definitely and consciously seeking the images; whereas in the drama, and especially drama written red-hot as was the Elizabethan, images tumble out of the mouths of the characters in the heat of the writer's feeling or passion, as they naturally surge up into his mind.

The greater and richer the work the more valuable and suggestive become the images, so that in the case of Shakespeare I believe one can scarcely overrate the possibilities of what may be discovered through a systematic examination of them. It was my conviction of this which led me to assemble and classify all his images, so as to have in orderly and easily accessible form the material upon which to base my deductions and conclusions.

I use the term 'image' here as the only available word to cover every kind of simile, as well as every kind of what is really compressed simile—metaphor. I suggest that we divest our minds of the hint the term carries with it of visual image only, and think of it, for the present purpose, as connoting any and every imaginative picture or other experience, drawn in every kind of way, which may have come to the poet, not only through any of his senses, but through his mind and emotions as well, and which he uses, in the forms of simile and metaphor in their widest sense, for purposes of analogy.

Such a picture can be so extended as to take up a large part of a scene, as does the symbol of the untended garden in *Richard II*; or it can be suggested by a single word:

Ripeness is all. *K.L. 5. 2. 11*

It may be a simple analogy from everyday things:

They'll take suggestion as a cat laps milk, *Temp. 2. 1. 288* or delicate fancy from the world of imagination:

R. and J.
2. 6. 18

> A lover may bestride the gossamer
> That idles in the wanton summer air
> And yet not fall; so light is vanity.

It may take the form of a personification drawn at full
T. and C.
3. 3. 165 length—time, the fashionable host, welcoming and speeding his guests; or it may be flashed on us in one vivid verb,

Mac. 2. 2. 42

> Glamis hath murdered sleep;

and it may be every kind of metaphor—Lady Macbeth urging her lord to 'screw his courage to the sticking-place', Duncan, after life's fitful fever, sleeping well, Donalbain fearing the 'daggers in men's smiles', and Macbeth wading in blood, or supping 'full with horrors'.

One could easily devote a volume to arriving at a definition of an image, elaborating, safeguarding and illustrating it, and to discussing what metaphor is and the philosophy which lies behind it.

But I do not propose to do this. In the first place, metaphor is a subject of such deep import that it calls for an abler pen than mine to deal adequately with it. For I incline to believe that analogy—likeness between dissimilar things—which is the fact underlying the possibility and reality of metaphor, holds within itself the very secret of the universe. The bare fact that germinating seeds or falling leaves are actually another expression of the processes we see at work in human life and death, thrills me, as it must others, with a sense of being here in presence of a great mystery, which, could we only understand it, would explain life and death itself.

The poet knows this is so, intuitively if not rationally; and he is a poet largely by virtue of the power he has, greater than other men, of perceiving hidden likenesses, and by his words, as Shelley says, unveiling 'the permanent analogy of things by images which participate in the life of truth'. Hence it is that great metaphor in great poetry moves and stirs us in a way impossible to account for purely rationally and logically. It stirs us because it touches or awakens something in us, which I think we must call spiritual, at the very roots of our being. For, as the poet well knows, as does also the seer and prophet, it is only by means of these hidden analogies that the greatest truths, otherwise inexpressible, can be given a form or shape capable of being grasped by the human mind.

But I am already being carried further than I wish to go here, for we must all agree with Mr Middleton Murry when he says that 'the investigation of metaphor is curiously like the investigation of any of the primary data of consciousness: it cannot be pursued very far without our being led to the borderline of sanity'.

Had Mr Murry not written his penetrating and satisfying little essay on 'Metaphor',[1] I might have been tempted to say more, but in that remarkable essay he seems to me to sum up all that can fruitfully be said on the subject. He points out that metaphor seems in part to arise out of the poet's strong and constant impulse to create life, or to transfer life from his own spirit, as Coleridge says, to things apparently lifeless. He draws attention to the way in which sensuous perception and spiritual intuition are both necessary to the great poet, and also to the fact that 'his constant accumulation of

[1] In *Countries of the Mind*, Oxford University Press, 1931.

vivid sense-perceptions supplies the most potent means by which he articulates his spiritual intuitions'. He shows how the subject he is contemplating stirs, for instance, in Shakespeare's imagination 'a picture, half visible, half spiritual' which gives rise to the imagery he creates to express and adorn it.

All these truths and others, we shall see illustrated in detail in Shakespeare's work.

Another reason why I do not propose to dwell at any length on the question of definition is that I am at present primarily concerned with the content rather than the form of images, which fact makes it unnecessary to enter on any discussion of formal classification. For my purposes at the moment I do not need therefore to distinguish and analyse the various kinds of image: the sunken, the decorative, the expansive and so on; or to dwell on the differences between metaphor, simile, personification, metonymy, synecdoche and the like.

This intensely interesting subject has already in part been treated by a good many writers, and any detailed study of the development of Shakespeare's art as seen through his images would naturally involve some close consideration of this kind, as would also any sustained investigation of his style. But if seriously embarked on as regards Shakespearian imagery, it would demand at least a book—if not a small library—to itself.

Finally, I feel that any elaborate discussion of definition would really be profitless here, because, however much one might discuss it, few people would entirely agree as to what constitutes an image, and still fewer as to what constitutes a poetic image.[1]

---

[1] Much has been written on these points, and none of the writers entirely agree. I would refer those interested to three books in especial:

But, as Burke wisely says, 'though no man can draw a stroke between the confines of night and day, yet light and darkness are upon the whole tolerably distinguïshable', so I believe, for practical purposes, and certainly for the purposes of the present study, we all know fairly well what we mean by an image. We know that, roughly speaking, it is, as I have already said, the little word-picture used by a poet or prose writer to illustrate, illuminate and embellish his thought. It is a description or an idea, which by comparison or analogy, stated or understood, with something else, transmits to us through the emotions and associations it arouses, something of the 'wholeness', the depth and richness of the way the writer views, conceives or has felt what he is telling us.

The image thus gives quality, creates atmosphere and conveys emotion in a way no precise description, however clear and accurate, can possibly do.

When, for instance, we hear that a young man's gaiety, wit and charm are such, that if he talks and jests, even

> aged ears *play truant* at his tales,   *L.L.L.* 2. 1. 74

those two metaphorical words call up a host of associations and emotions, and give us the picture of old grave men beguiled from their serious thought or labours by merry chatter of attractive and irresponsible youth, elders tempted from their grooves or their duty by fun and lightheartedness, as a boy is tempted to leave his lessons by the play of sunlight on a summer afternoon.

Poetic Imagery, by H. W. Wells, Columbia University Press, 1924; *The World of Imagery*, by Stephen J. Brown, S.J., Kegan Paul, 1927, especially chaps. II and VI; and *Intensifying Similes in English*, by T. H. Svartengren, Lund, 1918, especially Introduction.

We are conscious also of a certain slightly guilty feeling of erring and straying, and at the same time of an atmosphere of recklessness, and holiday making, all of which seems to throw up and accentuate the force of the attraction which causes this disturbance.

Again, when a soldier describes unexpected defeat in battle by saying of the weapons of the opposing host that they

3 H. VI,
2. 1. 129

like to lightning came and went;

and of those of his own side,

2. 1. 130

Our soldiers', like the night-owl's lazy flight,
Or like an idle thresher with a flail,
Fell gently down, as if they struck their friends,

in those three pictures, the one of the flash and deadly thrust of lightning, the other two of a quite peculiarly soft and silent downward motion, we have everything needful to conjure up in full what happened, and we see, on the one side, the swift and irresistible onslaught of glancing piercing steel, and on the other, the half-hearted, dispirited and ineffectual action of the beaten men.

So also, when we hear of a group of people, whose cheeks

Titus, 3. 1. 125

are stain'd, as meadows yet not dry,
With miry slime left on them by a flood;

again, the picture conveys, not only a number of facts and qualities, but a definite atmosphere, and we are conscious of the disturbing and ruthless nature of a flood, and its sodden and bedraggled after-effects, peculiarly depressing and disfiguring. Nothing could more fully describe the condition of the faces of those completely overwhelmed with sudden and appalling calamity, than the fact that they have not even given thought to wiping the stains of tears from their cheeks, and indeed, in this particular case, the chief sufferer has lacked hands wherewith to do it.

But these pictures do more than give us a swift illumination in the round—background, atmosphere, appearance, emotion—of the incident described, they tell us also that the writer of them had almost certainly seen and sympathised with schoolboys straying from school, that he had winced at the thrust of lightning and had roamed the country-side at night-time, that he was sufficiently observant and interested in birds, to note and register the peculiar characteristics of the small owl's flight, and had watched an idle or weary labourer at threshing time, and that he had, in all probability, at some period lived near a river where he would often have seen the meadows covered with the unprepossessing slime it leaves behind when it has overflowed its banks in spring.

It is this latter aspect of the images in which I am here primarily interested, that is in their stuff, and what this stuff or content tells us, and I use them from this point of view as documents, first as helping to reveal to us the man himself, and secondly as throwing fresh light on the individual plays.

CHAPTER II

SHAKESPEARE'S IMAGERY COM-PARED WITH THAT OF MARLOWE AND BACON

AS I have already explained, I believe we can draw from the material of a poet's images definite information about his personality.

In working out this line of thought, we are justified, I suggest, in assuming that a poet will, in the long run, naturally tend to draw the large proportion of his images from the objects he knows best, or thinks most about, or from the incidents, among myriads he has experienced, to which he is sensitive, and which therefore remain within his knowledge. For, as has often been pointed out, best of all perhaps by Bergson, memory is not a storehouse, it is a selecting machine—a sieve—and the fact that our instrument of memory selects certain things or aspects shows that they have a certain attraction for us, a certain suitability to our temperaments. Or it may work the other way, and we remember things because they are especially repugnant to us.

This reflection of the personality in the images can perhaps best be made clear by comparing those of different poets. Before describing and classifying the subject-matter of all Shakespeare's images and making certain inferences from them, I will therefore instance a few points drawn from the detailed analysis I have made of a dozen or so of the writers contemporary with him.

If, without such a comparison, I embarked on my

study of Shakespeare's figures, the reader might suspect that his subject-matter was merely the usual equipment of Elizabethan writers, and distrust my conclusions as to his personal peculiarities. My survey shows that, quite apart from style and method of forming the images (a study in itself), each writer has a certain range of images which are characteristic of him, and that he has a marked and constant tendency to use a much larger number of one or two kinds. Thus, to give the simplest kind of example, with Shakespeare, nature (especially the weather, plants and gardening), animals (especially birds), and what we may call everyday and domestic, the body in health and sickness, indoor life, fire, light, food and cooking, easily come first; whereas with Marlowe, images drawn from books, especially the classics, and from the sun, moon, planets and heavens far outnumber all others. (See and compare Charts I and II.) Indeed this imaginative preoccupation with the dazzling heights and vast spaces of the universe is, together with a magnificent surging upward thrust and aspiration, the dominating note of Marlowe's mind. He seems more familiar with the starry courts of heaven than with the green fields of earth, and he loves rather to watch the movements of meteors and planets than to study the faces of men.

No matter what he is describing, the pictures he draws tend to partake of this celestial and magnificent quality; whether it be soldiers on the road to battle,

> And with our sun-bright armour as we march,
> We'll chase the stars from Heaven;

1 Tamb.
2. 3. 620

the loveliness of a woman's face

> fairer than the evening air
> Clad in the beauty of a thousand stars;

Dr Faustus,
l. 1341

the conflicting emotions of a woman's heart, when

*Hero and
Leander, l. 361*

> like a planet, moving several ways
> At one self instant, she poor soul assays
> Loving, not to love at all, and every part
> Strove to resist the motions of her heart;

or the nature of man, and of his eager striving soul, one with the life force of the universe,

*1 Tamb.
2. 6. 876*

> always moving as the restless spheres

which

2. 6. 879

> Will us to wear ourselves and never rest.

Even when the image is of something quite other than the heavens, Marlowe clothes it naturally in this celestial and radiant light and imparts to it some touch of this terrific upward force.

If it is a soldier boasting of future victories, and the picture is of war, it takes this form:

*2 Tamb.
4. 1. 3875*

> I will persist a terror to the world,
> Making the meteors (that, like armed men,
> Are seen to march upon the towers of Heaven),
> Run tilting round about the firmament,
> And break their burning lances in the air;

if his lover dies, it is because

*2 Tamb.
2. 3. 3075*

> amorous Jove hath snatcht...[her]...hence
> Meaning to make her stately Queen of heaven;

and if he orders his artillery to fire, he does it thus:

*2 Tamb.
2. 3. 3072*

> with the cannon break the frame of heaven,
> Batter the shining palace of the Sun
> And shiver all the starry firmament.

With Shakespeare it is far otherwise. His feet are firmly set upon 'this goodly frame, the earth', his eyes are focussed on the daily life around him, and he misses no tiny detail of a bird's flight, a flower's growth, a house-wife's task, or the emotions written on a human face.

So is it that his greatest and most moving, as well as most vivid poetry, is often expressed by means of the simplest and homeliest metaphor:

> the long day's task is done,
> And we must sleep; *A. and C.* 4. 14. 35

> Scarf up the tender eye of pitiful day; *Mac.* 3. 3. 47

> Give not a windy night a rainy morrow; *Son.* xc

> Duncan is in his grave; *Mac.* 3. 2. 22
> After life's fitful fever he sleeps well;

> Hang there like fruit, my soul, *Cym.* 5. 5. 263
> Till the tree die;

> Peace, peace! *A. and C.* 5. 2. 308
> Dost thou not see my baby at my breast,
> That sucks the nurse asleep?

and he soars into the empyrean, not directly in one swift dart as does Marlowe, with a cold and lunar radiance, but indirectly and through the dusty ways of life, warmed and enriched by human experience, steeped in the homely atmosphere of this green earth.

Thus, by examining their imagery alone, we can see how entirely different were these two men, in mind, temperament and outlook. We see, among much else, that Shakespeare was intensely interested in and observant of everyday concrete things and events, especially in outdoor country life and the homely indoor routine, and that his senses were abnormally acute and responsive; while for Marlowe, concrete things had little interest; indeed, he hardly saw them, for he lived almost wholly in a world of ideas, so that his emotions were stimulated almost exclusively by *thought*, whereas Shakespeare's were stimulated by *feeling*.

I have, I must confess, largely indulged my own curiosity in my choice of the other writer I have selected for comparison with Shakespeare in this matter of their general use of imagery as a whole—Francis Bacon. Shakespeare and Bacon are the two greatest men of their day, and the claim that Bacon is in truth Shakespeare and wrote his plays is still held to be a serious and well-founded one by a large number of people. It is natural, therefore, that one should be eager to ask, 'What does an examination of their images tell us?'

For the purpose of this study I have analysed all Bacon's *Essays*, the *Advancement of Learning*, *Henry VII* and the first part of the *New Atlantis* on the same method that I have applied to Shakespeare's plays, and I compare the images thus obtained with those in the whole of Shakespeare.

We find, in the first place, that the proportion of the subject-matter of their images is entirely different. With Shakespeare nature images are always the most frequent, especially those relating to growing things in a garden or orchard: trees, plants, flowers and fruits; the weather: the sky, clouds, rain, sunshine, and the seasons. Next in frequency to these are animal images, and of these, especially images from birds. With Bacon (see Chart III), nature definitely takes the second place and his animal images are peculiarly few. Bacon's greatest number of images are drawn from subjects which may be grouped together under 'Domestic Life', that is everything touching the house and daily life indoors, such as light and fire, furnishings, hangings, textiles, needlework, clothes, jewels, marriage, birth, death, parents, children and human relations generally.

One reason why the 'Domestic Life' group of Bacon's images is so large is that it includes the many images drawn from light and darkness, the contrast between artificial and natural lights, and other 'light' effects, which constantly recur in his writings.

Thus, in Bacon's first essay alone, we find the three following light images: (1) 'This same truth is a naked and open daylight, that doth not show the masques and mummeries, and triumphs of the world, half so stately and daintily as candle-lights'. (2) 'The first creature of God, in the works of the days, was the light of sense; the last was the light of reason; and his Sabbath work, ever since, is the illumination of his spirit. First he breathed light upon the face of matter, or chaos; then he breathed light into the face of man; and still he breatheth and inspireth light into the face of his chosen'. Even when the image is really of something else, it is the 'light' aspect of it which attracts Bacon, as in this image (in Essay 1) of precious stones: (3) 'Truth may perhaps come to the price of a pearl, that sheweth best by day; but it will not rise to the price of a diamond or carbuncle that sheweth best in varied lights'.

When thinking of mental activity, some picture of light seems nearly always to come before him, as when (in Book I of the *Advancement of Learning*) he points out that the schoolmen, with their 'verbal points and niceties', broke up the solidarity of the sciences, and asks, 'For were it not better for a man in a fair room to set up one great light, or branching candlestick of lights, than to go about with a small watch candle into every corner?' And he further develops the simile when showing that the method of the schoolmen, in quibbling and arguing on every point, breeds 'one question as fast as it solveth another, even as in the former resemblance, when you carry the light into one corner, you darken the rest'.

Light, indeed, to Bacon, very noticeably represents all good things, enlightenment of every kind, both mental and spiritual: truth, virtue, knowledge, understanding, reason, and even the essence of God himself, *Adv. of L. II* 'the Father of illumination or lights'. Light, to him, is clear and unbiassed judgment ('dry light', not obscured by mists or humidity), and it is also the action of friendship, 'which maketh daylight in the understanding'.

It is not surprising, therefore, that his images drawn from light are, as a rule, very beautiful, and, for Bacon, unusually tinged with emotion. Such, for instance, is that in which the Governor of the New Atlantis when describing to the strangers the activities of the brethren of Salamon's House ('which is the lanthorn of this Kingdom') tells how some of their number are set apart to sail into far countries and bring back from there report of the progress of cultivation in all arts and sciences: 'thus', he says, 'you see we maintain a trade, not for gold, silver, or jewels; nor for silks, nor for spices; nor any other commodity of matter, but only for God's first creature, which was *Light*; to have *light* (I say) of the growth of all parts of the world '....These adventurers, he added, 'we call Merchants of Light'.

Shakespeare shows no sign of this great interest in light, nor of Bacon's almost passionate association of light with intellect, although in *Romeo and Juliet* we find a beautiful 'running' or constantly recurring image which shows that Shakespeare there imaginatively conceives of love as light in a dark world.

Just as Bacon seems continually to see and reflect on

human nature in the terms of light and shade, so Shakespeare seems to think most easily and naturally in the
terms of a gardener. He visualises human beings as
plants and trees, choked with weeds, or well pruned
and trained and bearing ripe fruits, sweet smelling as a
rose or noxious as a weed (pp. 86–91). Just as Shake-
speare, in the mouth of Iago, reflects that our bodies are *Oth. 1. 3. 323*
gardens and our wills the gardeners, so that whatever
is planted or sown in our own natures entirely depends
on the power and authority of our wills, so in the same
reflective spirit, Bacon characteristically pictures the
relationships of men in terms of light, when he writes in
the Essay *Of Envy*: 'Persons of worth and merit are
most envied when their fortune continueth long. For
by that time, though their virtues be the same, yet it
hath not the same lustre: for fresh men grow up that
darken it'. So also in speaking of the advantages of
adversity over prosperity as a training ground for man's
nature, he illustrates it thus: 'We see in needleworks   *Essay 5.*
and embroideries, it is more pleasing to have a lively   *Of Adversity*
work upon a sad and solemn ground, than to have a
dark and melancholy work upon a lightsome ground'.

Next to light and darkness, we find Bacon, in common with many Elizabethans, drawing most of his
images from the body and bodily action. Here he resembles Shakespeare; but where he once more noticeably differs from him is in the quantity and range of his
Biblical images, which are very numerous, and come
next in this respect to those of light and the body.
Bacon's mind is steeped in Biblical story and phrase in
a way of which there is no evidence in Shakespeare, and
there is a kind of what one may perhaps call sentimental
piety and pious phrasing in his work, unusual among

the thinkers of the time, which is indeed totally foreign to Shakespeare. Shakespeare's Biblical comparisons and references—which are few—are practically all to well-known characters and incidents, familiar to any grammar-school boy: Adam and Eve, Cain and Abel, Solomon, Job and Daniel, Herod, Judas and Pilate, the fall of Lucifer, the serpent in the Garden, the Flood, and the Red Sea.

Whereas the mind of Bacon, one feels, is absolutely at home in the whole of Biblical story, Old and New Testaments alike, and moves there naturally, drawing easily and readily for illustration upon lesser as well as generally known incidents, often visualised and pondered upon, and thus vivid and familiar to his imagination.

Thus, when speaking against the propagation of religion by wars, the forcing of men's consciences by sanguinary persecutions, he says that to put the sword into the people's hands tends to the subversion of all government, which is the ordinance of God. 'For this', Essay 3 he cries, 'is but to dash the first table against the second', and we realise that the mention of God's law has called up instantly before him the figure of Moses in the wilderness with the two tables of stone in his hands, one containing man's duty to God, the other man's duty to man.

Details of Biblical story are clearly very familiar to him, and he uses them constantly for illustration, sometimes rather strangely, but always appositely. Thus, in the same essay (III, *Of Unity in Religion*), he describes two false peaces or unities, the one grounded upon ignorance, the other, 'pieced up upon a direct admission of contraries in fundamental points', and continues,

'For truth and falsehood in such things are like the iron and clay in the toes of Nebuchadnezzar's image; they may cleave but they will not incorporate'.

A close examination of differences within various groups of images drawn from the same subject gives some interesting results; I can here only indicate one or two of these.

One set of images which reveal very definite differences between Bacon and Shakespeare are those on astronomy. Both writers are interested in the subject, both have a fair number of astronomical references; and the imagination of both men is held by the old Ptolemaic system, which so well corresponds to the testimony of our senses. I think it possible that the myth of Phaeton driving his horses across the sky, so dear to the Elizabethan poetic mind, was largely responsible for the unwillingness of the poets to give up the conception of the sun revolving round a fixed earth; and not the sun only, but also all the planets and stars, moving in fixed concentric spheres centred on the earth.

This latter idea, especially, fires Shakespeare's imagination, and his references to the movement of stars in their spheres, especially in imagery, are very many. Bacon does not refer to this, but he, on the other hand, is particularly attracted by the conception of the *primum mobile*, the great outer tenth sphere, which, according to Ptolemy, communicated its movement to all the lower spheres, as described in detail by Milton in a familiar passage in *Paradise Lost* (Book III, 481–3). Though Bacon was no poet, yet the idea appealed to him, as to Milton, and was apparently not displaced by the discoveries going on in his life-time, of these 'new carmen who drive the world about', as he calls Copernicus and

Galileo. He compares the organisation and action of the rulers of an earthly state to that of the heavens, and writes, 'For the motions of the greatest persons in a government, ought to be as the motions of the planets under *primum mobile* (according to the old opinion), which is that every of them is carried swiftly by the highest motion, and softly in their own motion' (Essay xv). And he likens the action of superstition, which 'hath been the confusion of many States', to that of bringing in 'a new *primum mobile*, that ravisheth all the spheres of Government' (Essay xvii). Shakespeare never once mentions the *primum mobile*, but the conception of the stars moving in their spheres, and straying from them only as a sign or result of great disturbance or disaster (not once referred to by Bacon), seems to be the most constant of astronomical ideas in Shakespeare's mind. Thus, the king in *Hamlet* declares his queen is

Ham. 4. 7. 14

         so conjunctive to my life and soul,
That, as the star moves not but in his sphere,
I could not but by her.

And Antony, when all is lost, declares that his 'good stars that were' his 'former guides',

A. and C.
3. 13. 145

Have empty left their orbs [spheres] and shot their
     fires
Into the abysm of hell.

Oberon, recalling to Puck the spectacle he had once seen, the beauty of the mermaid singing on a dolphin's back, says

M.N.D.
2. 1. 152

That the rude sea grew civil at her song
And certain stars shot madly from their spheres,
To hear the sea-maid's music.

Polonius reminds Ophelia that

> Lord Hamlet is a prince, out of thy star [sphere],   *Ham.* 2. 2. *141*

and this same idea forms a 'running' image throughout *All's Well*, to illustrate the unsurmountable difference of position of Helena and Bertram. It is summed up early in the play by Helena herself:

> 'Twere all one   *All's Well,*
> That I should love a bright particular star   *1. 1. 92*
> And think to wed it, he is so above me:
> In his bright radiance and collateral light
> Must I be comforted, not in his sphere.

The vividness and reality of the old Ptolemaic conceptions in Shakespeare's imagination are well illustrated by Cleopatra's cry of agony in the wildness of her grief, when Antony is borne in dead to the monument, and she, desiring darkness, calls out: 'O sun, Burn the great   *A. and C.* sphere thou movest in'. She is picturing the sun being   *4. 15. 9* whirled round the earth by the motion of a solid sphere in which it is fixed. Suppose this sphere were consumed, as Cleopatra wishes, the sun must wander in endless space, and the earth would, as a result, be plunged in darkness. That is an instance of the writer's imagination taken unawares, and betraying itself; for in a more prosaic passage, when Ulysses is making a definite statement about the ordering of the heavens, Shakespeare shows that his *reason* has fully grasped the new truth that 'the glorious planet Sol' is

> In noble eminence enthroned and sphered   *T. and C.*
> Amidst the other.   *1. 3. 89*

Their nature images are another group which have a very different character. Bacon not only draws far fewer images from nature than does Shakespeare, but these are of a different type: they are more general, dealing with larger tracts of country, the lie of the land, hills and valleys, coppices and woods; and they show little first-hand observation of *appearances*. As a whole, Bacon's interest, unlike Shakespeare's, seems to lie in the practical processes of farming rather than of gardening, and his reflections are noticeably often made from the point of view of the owner of the land, pondering how to preserve and improve it; as in the following image, where he is urging that in a country which aims at greatness, care should be taken that the nobility and gentry should not multiply too fast at the expense of the common people, who are the backbone of the land; *Essay 29. Of Kingdoms and Estates* 'even', he adds, 'as you may see in coppice woods; if you leave your staddles too thick, you shall never have clean underwood, but shrubs and bushes. So in countries, if the gentlemen be too many, the commons will be base'.

Essay 15. Of Seditions and Troubles 'Money is like muck, not good, except it be spread' is a remark peculiarly characteristic of Bacon, showing the farmer's practical care for the land, and the Lord Chancellor's interest in economics and finance, but it is unlikely that Shakespeare would have written it, for his interests lay in quite other directions.

The difference between the sea images of the two writers is the exact contrary of that between their nature images; Shakespeare's are the more general, Bacon's the more concrete and particular. Shakespeare's sea images are (i) chiefly of storms and shipwrecks. Mr Wilson Knight has shown recently how constant is the 'tempest' idea and symbolism in Shakespeare's thought, and with him the movements of the cruel, wild, ruthless, raging sea are frequently a symbol for the passions and emotions of men.

'But cruel are the times', says Ross to Lady Macduff,   *Mac. 4. 2. 18*
> when we hold rumour
> From what we fear, yet know not what we fear,
> But float upon a wild and violent sea
> Each way and move.

'My intents', cries Romeo, on entering Juliet's tomb,

>   are savage-wild   *R. and J.*
> More fierce and more inexorable by far   *5. 3. 37*
> Than empty tigers or the roaring sea.

I never once find this analogy in Bacon.

In Shakespeare's imagination, man is a 'fragile vessel' in 'life's uncertain voyage', and each human *Timon,* being launched into this world is as a frail bark set *5. 1. 204* afloat on the great and stormy ocean of his own passions; 'the bark thy body is', old Capulet tells Juliet, *R. and J.*
3. 5. 134

> Sailing in this salt flood; the winds, thy sighs:
> Who raging with thy tears, and they with them,
> Without a sudden calm will overset
> Thy tempest-tossed body.

This fairly obvious symbol is a constant one with Shakespeare; I only once find a similar, but not identical thought in Bacon, when, in Essay v, he speaks of 'Christian resolution that saileth in the frail bark of the flesh through the waves of the world'.

Shakespeare's other most constant sea images are (ii) the ebb and flow of tides, (iii) the action of currents, (iv) a tide rushing through a breach, (v) a ship being dashed on the rocks, and (vi) the infinite size, depth and capacity of the ocean (generally likened to love). These last three I never find in Bacon. But the great and constant difference between the sea pictures of the two writers is that Shakespeare's are chiefly concerned with the general character, quality or aspect of the sea, usually in storm, *as it might be viewed by a landsman*, whereas Bacon's are noticeably vivid little pictures of episodes or incidents on the sea *as experienced by a man in a ship or boat*. His practical and scientific mind is interested in the balance of boats on the water, and he is fond of the 'ballast' image: 'There must be some middle counsellors to keep things steady; for without that ballast, the ship will roll too much' (Essay VI). Shakespeare never once uses the word 'ballast'.

The over-laden boat, too, is a favourite with Bacon: 'When princes...make themselves as a party, and lean to a side, that is as a boat that is overthrown by uneven weight on the one side' (Essay XV). This idea never occurs in Shakespeare.

The incident of some of the crew or travellers on a ship in a storm, ignominiously fleeing and leaving it to its fate while saving themselves in the ship's boat, is never found in Shakespeare, but comes repeatedly into Bacon's mind, as when he is describing the baser kind of self-seeking politicians, 'never caring in all tempests what becomes of the ship of estates, so that they may save themselves in the cock-boat of their own fortune' (*Advancement of Learning*, I). Or again, in describing the actions of John Morton, archbishop of Canterbury, and his relations with Richard III and the Duke of Buckingham, he says the archbishop secretly incited Buckingham to revolt from King Richard, and continues: 'But after the duke was engaged, and thought the bishop should have been his chief pilot in the tempest, the bishop was gotten into the cock-boat, and fled over beyond seas' (*Henry VII*, ed. Lumby, Pitt Press Series, p. 182).

The images from sport and games form another sure

indication of a writer's tastes and individuality. Shakespeare has a great many, chiefly from falconry, shooting with bow and arrow, deer hunting, bird-snaring and fishing, and in games, chiefly from bowls, football and tennis, but his images from bowls, which he clearly knew and liked best, are about three times as many as from any other game.

In all the works of Bacon I have examined, I find three 'game' images only, one each from tennis, skittles and bowls, so there is no indication which game, if any, he himself preferred. His 'sport' images are comparatively few, and he draws upon archery, falconry, fishing, bird-snaring, wrestling, and rowing, in that order.

The differences of their attitude towards animals are also worth noticing. Shakespeare's attitude as seen in his images, is unique among the dramatists of his time, for he shows a sympathy with and understanding of the animal's point of view and sufferings which no one else in his age approaches. This is especially marked in the case of horses and birds, the two he loves best (pp. 105–8). His bird images are remarkable for the intense feeling they reveal for the trapped, limed or snared bird, which rouses in him a passion of pity and sympathy (pp. 105–6).

Of this sympathy for the trapped bird there is not a trace in Bacon, whose bird images are of the clipping of wings, scattering a flight of birds, the soaring of the lark and the hawk, and the action of birds of prey. His riding images are concerned exclusively with the need for and efficacy of the bridle, the rein and spur, and 'well managed' horses who know when 'to stop and turn'.

In addition to these marked differences in the ideas and pictures in certain groups of images used alike by Shakespeare and Bacon, we find some single images in Bacon which not only have no counterpart in Shakespeare, but which are in their essential idea the exact contrary of Shakespeare's view or belief. This type of difference, betrayed unconsciously or accidentally through individual or accumulated images, is the most subtle, and to my thinking, the most irrefutable proof of individuality of authorship that can be found. Such is Bacon's view of time, which, he says, repeatedly, 'seemeth to be of the nature of a river or stream, which carrieth down to us that which is light and blown up, and sinketh and drowneth that which is weighty and solid'. Clearly Bacon, in this artificial and rather forced analogy, holds that time, far from revealing truth, blurs and obscures it, passing on to us only that which is popular and superficial, while drowning that which is substantial and profound. Shakespeare, on the other hand, consistently thinks of time's function in quite opposite terms (see Chap. IX, p. 172 below), and pictures time as sorting out the important from the trivial, as a revealer and disentangler of truth, whose glory is 'to unmask falsehood and bring truth to light' (*Luc.* 940).

Adv. of L. 1, see also Preface to the Great Instauration

Another difference of opinion which is indicative, but which I cannot develop here, is shown in their several attitudes towards war.

Bacon. compared with Shakespeare, has very few 'war' images, but he definitely asserts that he strongly approves of war, and believes it to be as necessary to a State as healthy exercise to a man's body (Essay XXIX, ll. 259–64). Shakespeare hates war and condemns it through the mouth of Timon, 'contumelious, beastly, mad[1]-brain'd war', but a surer indication of his view is

Timon, 5. 1. 177

---

[1] This is the Folio reading. The Larger Temple edition reads 'man-brained'.

that he constantly symbolises it by and associates it with loud and hideous noises, with groans of dying men, with 'braying trumpets and loud churlish drums, Clamours of hell'. He speaks too of 'roaring war', 'the harsh and boisterous tongue of War', and to anyone who realises how intensely he hates all harsh, discordant and strident sounds, this is sufficiently indicative of his feeling. *K.J. 3. 1. 304*

Temp. 5. 1. 44

2 H. IV, 4. 1. 49

I could instance many other examples of significant differences between the two writers, but space does not permit. I have said enough however, I hope, to prove my point, which is this: that in addition to the very distinct differences in gifts and temperament easily to be seen in the matter and tenour of their writings, on a study of their imagery alone other noticeable differences emerge. We see, on examining their images, that the writers of these two sets of works viewed the world from a different standpoint, had had different experiences and were interested in and familiar with a different range of objects in everyday life, that even when interested in the same subject (as astronomy), different aspects of it appealed to their imaginations. We see that their tastes in sport and games were different, and that their attitude towards animals was entirely different, and that moreover, on certain abstract subjects (such as the action of time), they held diametrically opposite views.

These facts all point one way, and all seem to support the view that we have here, behind these two sets of writings, not one mind only, but two highly individual and entirely different minds.

CHAPTER III

IMAGERY OF SHAKESPEARE AND OTHER DRAMATISTS COMPARED

TO return from this general comparison with two single writers in which I have shown that certain general characteristics of a writer are reflected in his imagery as a whole, I will now make a more detailed examination of the subjects of certain groups or sections of images in Shakespeare and a number of contemporary dramatists. This will, I believe, show that such analysis throws light on each writer's individual tastes or experiences.

To illustrate this, I have worked out a chart (Chart IV) of the proportion and distribution of the group of images I assemble under 'daily life' (for notes on the classification of the images, see Appendix V, p. 371), as found in five plays of Shakespeare, and of five other Elizabethan dramatists, Marlowe, Ben Jonson, Chapman, Dekker and Massinger (for a list of these plays see p. 372, Appendix V, Note on Chart IV). Let us consider these for a moment, and see if, by looking a little closer, we can make anything out of them as a revelation of character.

To begin with, it is clear that the dramatists all vary considerably in the amount and proportion of their use of these different types of images.

With Shakespeare, the greatest number of images within this group are those drawn from 'sport' and he is the only one of the six with whom this subject comes first (see note on Chart IV), thus emphasising his love of country and outdoor life and occupations. He has more images of riding and of bird-snaring and falconry than of any other forms of outdoor sport, and in both these groups there is evidence of personal experience. His images from archery are also comparatively numerous, and read as if written by one who knew how to handle a bow. His fishing similes, on the other hand, are very ordinary, little more than the usual metaphorical meaning of 'angle' and 'bait', and show no sign of personal knowledge or interest. This is all characteristic, not only of these five plays here analysed, but of his work throughout, and, I believe, of his experience and interests (pp. 99–100).

It is worth looking at the sport images of all six dramatists together (see Chart IV). Marlowe has very few, and they show no sign of personal experience. Ben Jonson has a good many: hunting, fishing and snaring come first, but there is little sign of first-hand knowledge in them, except in the vivid touch of tracking *E.M.I.H.H.* a hare over the fields in the snow. His images from *3. I* fencing, however, do give one the feeling that he had himself used the foils. Chapman also has a good many: riding, hunting, archery and fishing come first, but only of archery does there seem a clear sign of personal knowledge. Dekker is the writer in this group whose proportion of sport images comes nearest to Shakespeare's. They are remarkable chiefly for the large number—nearly one half of the whole—he has from fishing, which was clearly his favourite sport, so easily and constantly does his mind run on baiting, letting out the hook and line, the fish's irritating habit of nibbling at the bait but refusing to swallow the hook, pulling the fish on shore or catching it in a net. Massinger's comparatively few sport images are absolutely conventional—fowling, hawking and hunting—and they show practically no sign of direct knowledge or observation; he is to be noted, however, as the only one of the six who draws an image from cock-fighting and from horse-racing.

On the whole we gather from this group of images that Shakespeare was accustomed to riding and was fond of horses, that he had first-hand knowledge of both hawking and bird-snaring, and clearly some personal experience of shooting with a bow. We see that neither Marlowe nor Massinger really cared for any outdoor sport. We note that though Ben Jonson and Chapman both had a large sporting vocabulary, which, as we know from Master Stephen, was the fashion,[1] yet they were neither of them really sportsmen,[2] but that Jonson had at some time probably enjoyed fencing, and that Chapman knew all about handling a bow. And it is clear that Dekker loved fishing above all other pastimes.

There is, however, one point in these images in which Shakespeare practically stands alone, and that is in the evidence of his sympathy with the animal hunted or snared, and in his understanding and feeling for the horse and his movements and response. It is he alone who suggests that kindly persuasion may achieve more *W.T.* *1. 2. 94* than the use of a spur, and that if you give a good horse *2. 3. 51* the rein and 'let her run, she'll not stumble'; he alone

---

[1] *Stephen:* '...an a man have not skill in the hawking and hunting languages now-a-days, I'll not give a rush for him. They are more studied than the Greek or the Latin'. *Every Man in his Humour,* 1, i.

[2] After I had written this, I was interested to find, in the section on 'Hunting' in *Shakespeare's England* (11, 335–8), a long quotation from Ben Jonson's *Sad Shepherd,* describing a deer hunt, and full of sporting terms, which Mr Fortescue (the author) pulls to pieces as giving clear evidence that Jonson knew nothing of woodcraft and must have copied the whole of the words out of a book of sport.

who thinks of the point of view of the 'poor bird' fearing
the net and lime, the pitfall and the gin, of the falcon
mewed up, and of the bear tied to the stake. In all the
sport images in these selected plays of the five other
writers we only once sense a glimmer of sympathy with
the victim hooked or snared, and that is in Dekker's
allusion to the 'poor salmon-trout...now in the net'. *The Honest Whore*, II. 5. 2

As regards games, which are included in this group,
it is characteristic that Dekker has nearly twice as many
images from games as anybody else, including five from
bowls, all showing a definite knowledge of the game.
Shakespeare happens to have two images only from
games in these five plays, although we know from his
total number of game images that he also was well
acquainted with bowls (see pp. 110–11).

Shakespeare's next largest number of images in this
little section is drawn from 'classes'. In this large group
from types of men and women, we at once see reflected
Shakespeare's love of humanity, his observation and his
quick eye for an oddity (pp. 142–5). We see also very
markedly his sympathy with the under dog (p. 142),
as nearly half these images are drawn from the poor
and oppressed, from prisoners, idiots or madmen, from
gipsies, beggars, pedlars and slaves. Even in this little
handful, from five plays only, we sense the writer's
sympathy with 'the poor and broken bankrupt', with
the inhuman treatment of the insane, with the village
idiot and with the 'poor prisoner in his twisted gyves'.
In this respect—the number of his images from the
poor and the width of his sympathy—he differs from
all the other writers here analysed. Indeed it is quite a
revelation of character to isolate this little group of
images from 'classes and types' in all six dramatists and

to study them. Ben Jonson and Chapman—except for a certain number of conventional references to slaves—have scarcely any from the poor or downtrodden but are chiefly interested in the fairly well-to-do town types, which interest Shakespeare comparatively little: courtiers, merchants, aldermen, fashionable city dames, gamesters, a politician, a poetaster, a puritan, a porter, a costermonger, a cook, a tailor and so on. With Jonson this group of 'classes' comes first, and he is the only one of the six of whom this is true. Like Shakespeare, though in a rather more formal and artificial way, he is —as we know from his plays—intensely interested in types of humanity, and this interest is repeated in the many vivid little thumb-nail sketches in his images of the 'humours' of his day: by means of which we can overhear the affected speech of waiting-women and the tedious talk of constables, or catch a glimpse of the

Cynthia's Revels, 4. 1 country lady 'ever in the rearward of the fashion' and
E.M.I.H.H. 1. 2 the milliner's wife arrayed in her wrought stomacher veiled in smoky lawn.

Chapman too, though this group does not come first
Byron's Consp. 2. 1 with him, gives us many little pictures of town 'cha-
All Fools, 2. 1 racters', such as the city dame and her jealous husband or the discreet waiting-woman.

Dekker's images from types of contemporary life are, like Shakespeare's, more varied, and anyone who knows his *Gull's Hornbook* is not surprised at the large number of them, nor at the vividness and humour with which he
The Honest Whore, 1. 5. 1 touches off their characteristics: the justice of the peace
ibid. 11. 4. 2 who talks on a thousand matters and to no purpose, the
ibid. 11. 4. 3 rank sweat of the bear-warder, the much tried baker on
ibid. 11. 2. 1 the day when he heats his oven, the deceitful apothecary
ibid. 11. 3. 1 and the cheating gamesters who 'will not win at first'.

Dekker has not anything like the same proportion of images from the poor or from rogues as has Shakespeare, but in his images alone of all these other five writers do I sense anything of Shakespeare's sympathy for the poor and unfortunate. He shows a touch of understanding about the mishandling of the insane,

Struggling with madmen, madness nothing tames,   *The Honest Whore*, II. 3. 1

and in a fine and well-known passage at the end of the first part of *The Honest Whore*, there rings out definite and tender sympathy with the prisoner and the beggar:

Patience, my lord! why, 'tis the soul of peace;   *ibid.* I. 5. 2

. . . .

'Tis the perpetual prisoner's liberty,
His walks and orchards: 'tis the bond slave's freedom,
. . . It is the beggar's music, and thus sings,
Although their bodies beg, their souls are kings.

Massinger has a certain predilection for drawing images from pages and grooms; otherwise his references of this kind to types of humanity are, on the whole, definitely more bookish and less from direct observation than any of the others, except perhaps Marlowe. Thus he has many from slaves: 'tanned galley-slaves', 'bond-slaves', 'slave unto a Moor', and he draws them from captives, pirates, giants and pigmies, a savage, a cannibal, and so on.

Marlowe's very small group of this kind is extraordinarily characteristic. The images are either general and rather vague, but imaginative and poetical, such as the stars compared to travelling pilgrims, or 'stand still,   *2 Tamb.* 3. 2
you watches of the element', which may connote the idea   *Ed. II,* l. 2050
of watchmen; or somewhat bookish—'nymphs and   *Hero and Leander*, II. 233
shepherds', the shepherd frolicking 'to see the paynted   *Ed. II,* 2. 2.
springe', 'a bold sharp sophister'. In all his work I find   *Hero and Leander*, I. 197

only four images drawn directly and vividly from types of the surging and varied life of humanity in the *Jew of Malta,* streets around him: a barefoot friar ducking low, a bash- *2, l. 786* ful puritan, 'curate-like' attire, and a 'dapper jack' or *Ed. II, l. 2390* young dandy. *Ed. II, ll. 769, 709*

To return to Shakespeare's images in this 'daily life' group—his images from 'trades and building' come next in number to 'sport' and 'classes', and of these the greatest number is drawn from carpentry (pp. 126–7), and after that from building, simple images of construction and foundation. Next come his war images, and in this selection of them I find nothing which indicates any direct knowledge of war or of fighting. They mostly belong to the usual common stock of Elizabethan war images, the explosion of powder and fire, the shot of cannon, the recoil of a gun, the cut of a sword or a dagger, the action of 'bruising irons', stabs and darts, a siege, an encampment, a barricade, a flag. The most vivid and individual of all this par- *R. and J.* ticular little group is perhaps the 'powder in a skilless *3. 3. 130* soldier's flask' which is set afire by his own ignorance, and he is thus dismembered with his own defence.

'Substances' come next in number, and at once, even in this small selection, we have ample indication of Shakespeare's extreme sensitiveness to touch and texture (pp. 82–3). Of this little group of seventeen images, only three are taken from the *appearance* of a substance ('their innocent alabaster arms', 'pale as lead', marble 'changed colour') and not from its feel. This seems to me significant, if compared, for instance, with Marlowe or with Ben Jonson.

The brittleness of glass, the softness of doves' down, the glutinous stickiness of blood, the toughness of leather, the absorbent quality of a sponge, the smooth wholeness of marble, the firmness of steel, the heaviness of lead, these are the qualities of substances which strike Shakespeare, and come at once to his mind. Many of these are of course commonplaces in Elizabethan imagery (glass, down, sponge, marble, lead) but they are by none of these other writers used so exclusively of feel, and the whiteness of marble, the pallor of lead, the sparkle of steel or of flint, the transparency of glass, the warmth of down, even the look of a sponge ('O, he looked somewhat like a sponge in that pinked yellow doublet, methought', Ben Jonson in *Every Man out of his Humour*, 2. 1) are qualities which strike the other dramatists more than they do Shakespeare.

Marlowe has, as compared with Shakespeare, and indeed as compared with all these other dramatists, a very small total number of 'daily life' images, and he is the only one with whom 'substances' form the largest group of these. This indicates his love of metals and of brilliance, for they are largely drawn from the sight—not the touch—of brass, gold, gilding, silver, steel and crystal, the appearance of silver springs and liquid gold, the hard sparkle of steel, and the clearness of crystal.

With Ben Jonson, four groups come very near together, classes and sport (already discussed), trades and substances. His 'trades' images are numerous, largely owing to the amount he has from building and allied crafts, such as painting, glazing, gluing, varnishing, nailing and the quality of timber. We may fairly argue that some traces of Jonson's apprenticeship to his stepfather's trade of bricklaying are to be found here, for of building there is every sign of first-hand knowledge, from the point of view of the craftsman. This peeps out in such a description as 'a well-timber'd fellow, he would ha' made a good column, an he had been thought on, when the house was a-building', or in similes drawn from the firmness of a wall, driving in something which loosens the whole fabric, a pile of building tottering down in a crash, fresh buildings springing from old ruins, pinnacles, pillars and so on.

And, like Marlowe, he has many images from 'substances', the large proportion from their appearance, their sparkle, clearness, glitter, lustre, and he loves metals, especially gold, silver, pewter and quicksilver.

His war images are not specially numerous (compared with Chapman, Dekker and Massinger), and, although we know he served in Flanders for a time, there is little sign in them of first-hand knowledge or observation.

With Chapman, on the other hand, 'war and weapons' are for his images by far the favourite topic, and with him and Dekker this subject heads the list within this group. Chapman is particularly fond of certain military terms like 'ensign' and 'hostage', also of images from armour, shields and bucklers, of shot from cannon and its effects, from explosives, firing trains of powder on ships and on shore, from sieges and the holding of a fort. Like Dekker and Massinger he is fond of using the warlike similes for love, and a large proportion of the war images of all three of these writers, and especially Massinger, are concerned with virtue besieged, the virgin fort assaulted, and the arrows of women's eyes. Except for the love-war similes in his two poems, and in *All's Well*, Shakespeare has surprisingly little of this particular and favourite Elizabethan imagery.

Chapman occasionally draws a war picture which has the ring of first-hand observation, such as

> . . . (like a murdering piece, making lanes in armies, *Bussy D'Ambois, 3. 1*
> The first man of a rank, the whole rank falling),

and he drops so easily into soldiers' language that, on the whole, these images bear out the passage in one of his poems which suggests that, like Jonson, he may have served in the Netherlands.

Dekker too, in his large number of war images, is very fond of the action of explosives, and one can conjecture some personal experience in being 'blown up with our own underminings'—though indeed that seems to have been the usual result of laying mines in Elizabethan times—in the quality of wild fire, and of sulphur, 'which being rammed up, more confounds'. His war images have, on the whole, some ring of first-hand knowledge, reinforced in this respect by some of his 'topical' images, such as the fighting of Dunkirk privateers, the 'low countries of black hell', shooting at Finsbury and so on.

Dekker resembles Shakespeare in the number of his images from the texture and feel of substances, but he also has quite a number drawn from their appearance, and he fully shares in the Elizabethan delight in the sparkle and glitter of metals.

It is worth noting that, in his 'trades' group, Dekker alone of these dramatists draws images from the shoemaker's craft, and this not only in *The Shoemaker's Holiday*, where it is in keeping with the speakers, but also elsewhere. Thus Matheo, in *The Honest Whore*, says

The Honest Whore, I. I. I

'if the duke had but so much mettle in him, as is in a cobbler's awl', and Bellafront, in the same play, accuses Roger of being ready to swear anything

ibid. I. 3. 2

As if thy soul were made of shoe-leather.

This bears out the evidence in *The Shoemaker's Holiday* and other plays of Dekker's first-hand knowledge of the daily work in a shoemaker's shop.

We have seen that Dekker, alone of these five other dramatists, shows in his images something of Shakespeare's sympathy with the poor and oppressed, especially with prisoners. There is one characteristic seen in another group of images altogether—that of birds—which I may just mention, as it emphasises this point. This is the quite remarkably large number of images he has from 'wings': soaring and riding on wings, being transported on the wind's swift wings, escaping by putting on 'winged feet', clapping on swift wings and the like. There are eleven such images in *Old Fortunatus* alone, besides many in other plays. Is it fanciful to imagine that this delight in swift, soaring, unfettered flight indicates a reaction from what such a nature must have endured in long years of an Elizabethan gaol? We know he was imprisoned for debt more than once, and for a long period, and we know from his tract 'The Misery of a Prison and a Prisoner' how bitterly he suffered.

The relation in his mind between 'wings' and incarceration seems to peep out in such a simile as

ibid. II. I. 2

I think she's poor; and more to clip her wings
Her husband at this hour lies in jail.

However this may be, there is no question that, next to those of Shakespeare, Dekker's images in this 'daily

life' group seem more alive and human, more charged
with his personality and direct experience than those of
any other of the dramatists here analysed. In especial,
in addition to those we have noticed, his little touches
of comparison with everyday things, such as,

He's more cold than a citizen's country house in *The Honest
Whore*, 1. 4. 4
Janivery,

They [the coins] jingle in my pocket like St Mary *The Shoemaker's Holi-
Overy's bells, *day*, 3. 1

How like a new cart-wheel my dame speaks, *ibid.* 3. 4

have a homely ring of personal feeling and experience
which only Shakespeare surpasses.

If Dekker's 'daily life' images are, next to Shakespeare's, the most personal and vivid, Massinger's are
the dullest and most general.

There is indeed little that is individual to note about
him, except that his largest group are the images from
trades and crafts. This is chiefly due to his fondness for
building similes, and to a distinct interest in machinery.
The building images are definitely more general and
less knowledgeable than Ben Jonson's, and are chiefly
of building on a sure or unsure foundation, propping a
falling tower, and raising or destroying a building. The
machinery ones, however, show a touch of real knowledge and observation, such as of the cog-wheel,

They being the greater wheels that move the less, *The Roman
Actor*, 3. 2

or of the action and movement of the crane,

An upstart, craned up to the height he has, *The Fatal
Dowry*, 3. 1
This is the man that carries *The Great
Duke of
The sway and swing of the court. *Florence*, 2. 3

There is much more that might be noted and that
forms part of the story these images tell of personal

characteristics, tastes and experiences unconsciously revealed by the individual writers.

Remember that with one exception (Dekker's images of 'wings') all I have said refers to one small group only, and if to this was added an examination of the images grouped under nature or animals, learning or domestic, the story could be greatly enlarged and enriched. I have, however, said enough here to illustrate my point, and to show the kind of way in which it is possible, legitimately, I believe, to deduce conclusions from evidence of this nature.

CHAPTER IV

THE SUBJECT-MATTER OF
SHAKESPEARE'S IMAGES

Since things in motion sooner catch the eye
Than what not stirs.
T. and C. 3. 3. 183

THIS little excursion into the writings of Shakespeare's contemporaries has helped, I trust, to support my suggestion that a poet's imagery reveals his own idiosyncrasies, and not only the usages of his period. Let us now look in more detail at the whole body of Shakespeare's images. With the aid of the chart (No. v), we can see my general classification of their subject-matter, and the proportion drawn from his various fields of interest. A consideration of these proportions will of itself throw light on his mind and interests.

The difference between references and images in this connection needs emphasising. We all know that lists of Shakespeare's references to various things, the law, school-books and learning, the Bible, religion, and so on, have been made out by enthusiasts who desire to prove from them that he at one time had been a lawyer's clerk or a schoolmaster, or that he was a Protestant or a Roman Catholic.

But mere references are quite different from images; and no computation of images only has, so far as I know, ever before been made out. A writer refers to a thing in quite a different mood and with quite a different poetic impulse from that which produces a simile or metaphor, which, in the case of Shakespeare certainly, comes usually with great spontaneity and under stress of heightened feeling. If a poet, then, continually draws upon certain classes of things, certain qualities in things and certain aspects of life, for his illustrations, we are justified, I suggest, in arguing that those qualities and those aspects specially interested him and appealed to him.

Now the great bulk of Shakespeare's metaphors and similes are drawn from the simplest everyday things seen and observed. Naturally there are others, facts learnt from books or hearsay, which he can never have seen or heard: a lion fawning over its prey, a tiger stiffening its sinews, high Taurus' snow, the basilisk's eye or the mandrake's scream; there are some purely fanciful and imaginative, such as wit made of Atalanta's heels, and a man plucking bright honour from the pale-faced moon, but the whole of these amounts to curiously few among the mass which are undoubtedly derived from direct observation by the senses.

The main body of his images falls, as I have said, practically into two groups, those from nature, and those from indoor life and customs. (See Chart v.)

Nature—the life of the English country-side, the weather and its changes, the seasons, the sky, sunrise and dawn, the clouds, rain and wind, sunshine and shadow; the garden, flowers, trees, growth and decay, pruning and grafting, manuring and weeding; the sea and ships, the river and its banks, weeds and grasses, pools and water, animals, birds and insects, sport and games, especially snaring birds, hunting and hawking; these are the things which chiefly occupy him and remain in his mind.

Daily indoor life comes next, especially the simple indoor occupations and routine, eating, drinking and cooking, the work of the kitchen, washing and wiping, dust, dirt, rust and stains, the body and its movements, sleep and dreams, clothes and materials, patching and mending, common handicrafts, the feel of substances, smooth or soft or sticky, fire, candles and lamps; sickness and medicine, parents and children, birth, death and marriage.

In addition there is a substantial number drawn from classes and types of men, kings, courtiers and soldiers, beggars, thieves, prisoners, servants and so on, a lesser number of classical images, somewhat fewer from war, weapons, guns and explosives, and about half as many from law and music. There are also small numbers from art in general (painting, sculpture, etc.), a similar small number from the theatre, from natural science and from proverbs and popular sayings.

The only remaining large block may be grouped as imaginative and fanciful, by far the greater number of these being personifications, chiefly of states, qualities and emotions.

The most marked omissions in this range of images, it will at once be noticed, are those from town life and scenes—taverns, shops, streets, marts, pageants and crowds; of these there are scarcely any; literary references other than classical or Biblical; exploration, travel and adventure in other countries, and what one may call philosophical or reflective—of each of these there are comparatively very few indeed.

Of all these images in the first section, nature and outdoor life, by far the greatest number is devoted to one aspect of nature, what one might call the gardener's point of view,[1] showing intimate knowledge and observation of growth, propagation, grafting, pruning, manuring, weeding, ripeness and decay. It is noticeable that Shakespeare's images from farming, the raising of crops and garnering of the harvest, are not only much more perfunctory and general, but are very small in number compared with those from the growth and life of a garden.

Next to gardening, the largest group of nature images is of those from the weather and its changes, the look and portent of the sky, the varying seasons, nipping frosts, clouds, spring-time, showers, sunshine, wind and storm, all revealing the practical knowledge and observation of the countryman, as well as the particular aspects of nature which most attract and delight the poet.

He notes with loving accuracy the sound of the different winds in our breezy island, 'the tyrannous breathing of the north' which 'shakes all our buds from growing', 'the southern wind' which 'by his hollow whistling in the leaves'

1 H. IV, 5. 1. 6   Foretells a tempest and a blustering day,

3 H. VI, 1. 4. 145 the 'raging wind' which 'blows up incessant showers' and the hush of the wind before rain, 'when the rage allays, the rain begins'.

He revels in delicate changes of light, especially at
Temp. 5. 1. 65 dawn, 'when the morning steals upon the night, melting
3 H. VI, 2. 5. 2 the darkness', and 'dying clouds contend with growing light', he delights in the changing effects of our spring
K.L. 4. 3. 19 weather, 'sunshine and rain at once', and he so loves the swift play of sun and shadow that when he seeks a

---

[1] In the chart, the blocks of 'growing things' and 'gardening' should, for this purpose, be put together.

comparison for the most exquisite of human experiences, young love, he can find nothing more beautiful in nature than 'the uncertain glory of an April day'. *Two Gent.*
1. 3. 85

The next largest section under 'nature' is the sea, ships and seafaring. The points which strike me about these images are that on the whole they are far more general than his nature ones, and the subjects which chiefly interest him are those which might be noted by any landsman: storm and wrecks and rocky shores, the boundless and fathomless depth of the ocean, the ebb and flow of the tide, the inrushing tide pouring into a breach or covering over muddy flats. Though they are generally a landsman's images, a few of them drawn from the management of a ship show that he had some knowledge of technical language and the sailor's craft, which indeed is sufficiently proved in the opening of *The Tempest*. Such touches as

> like a shifted wind unto a sail, *K.J. 4. 2. 23*
> It makes the course of thoughts to fetch about,

or

> as weeds before *Cor. 2. 2. 108*
> A vessel under sail, so men obey'd
> And fell below his stem,

look as if founded on sea experience, although they could, of course, be equally true of a sailing boat on a river.

One particularly vivid aural impression, derived surely at first hand,

> such a noise arose *H. VIII,*
4. 1. 71
> As the shrouds make at sea in a stiff tempest,
> As loud and to as many tunes,

comes in a part of *Henry VIII* generally thought not to be Shakespeare's, though I personally tend to believe it is either wholly or in part his.

My own impression, after carefully studying all his sea images, is that he had little, if any, direct experience of being on the sea, and that his knowledge of the sea and ships might well have been gained from books (Hakluyt, Strachey and others), from talk and from living in a great seaport.

He could not help seeing ships daily in the river, then London's main thoroughfare; and, in an age when national pride ran high in the exploits of our seamen and adventurers, he could not fail to meet and talk with the sailors who were then to be found in every street and tavern of the city.

Of the large animal group, the outstanding point is the great number drawn from birds. If we except the human body, its parts, movements and senses, Shakespeare's images from birds form by far the largest section drawn from any single class of objects.

His intimate knowledge of the life and habits of birds and his intense sympathy with them have probably often been pointed out, but I doubt if it has been noticed that the special aspect of their life which attracts him is their *movement*.

Not primarily their song, or their shape, or their colour, or their habits; but their *flight*, and their swift, accurate, easy movements when free; their fluttering, struggling movements when imprisoned; the soaring of the eagle and of the hawk, the 'fell swoop' of the kite, the wild geese flocking together or 'severed', 'scattered by winds and high tempestuous gusts', 'lagging before the northern blast', the plumed estridges (goshawks) that 'wing the wind', the swift flight of the swallow, the confident flight of the falcon, 'towering in her pride of place', the hungry eagle 'shaking her wings' or fluttering the dovecote, the turkey-cock swelling and jetting 'under his advanced plumes', the peacock sweeping his tail, stalking up and down 'a stride and a stand', the fairy-light hop of bird from briar, the tiny wren fighting the owl to protect her young, the terrified dove pecking the hawk, the 'new ta'en sparrow' 'fetching her breath' shortly, the woodcock struggling in the gin, the imprisoned bird in a cage or on a silken thread, hopping a little from his lady's hand, the cock strutting 'up and down', the Barbary hen swaggering, the lapwing running 'close by the ground', the dive-dapper peering through a wave, the swan with bootless labour swimming against the tide. All these and many more are the quick, graceful, characteristic movements of bird life which attract Shakespeare supremely, which he knows intimately and has registered with loving exactitude.

Of the images grouped under 'daily indoor life', by far the largest section is that taken from the body and its movements. Indeed, pictures drawn from the body and bodily action form the largest single section of all Shakespeare's images (see Chart v), and this apart from his very large number of 'personifications', which two groups it is difficult always clearly to separate. Certain types of bodily image belong to the common stock of Elizabethan imagery, especially parts of the body: face, eye, tongue, etc.; and particular actions, such as bearing a burden on the back, falling from a height, treading a path, climbing, swimming and so on. But even allowing for these, the proportion of Shakespeare's body images to the whole is considerably larger than that of any of the other dramatists examined. Ben Jonson comes nearest him as regards number, but it is significant that in the five plays of his examined there is no image of swift bodily action, save two of dancing, neither of which conveys any feeling of lightness or of quick movement. No one of the other dramatists approaches Shakespeare in the number and vividness of his images drawn from quick nimble action, such as jumping, leaping, diving, running, sliding, climbing and dancing.

This marked delight in swift nimble bodily movement leads one to surmise that there was experience behind it, and that Shakespeare himself was as agile in body as in mind, so that Fuller's famous description of his wit-combats with Ben Jonson might have been equally true of physical encounters, not only with the unwieldy Jonson, but with most of his fellows.

If this be so, Ben Jonson's memories of when he heard Shakespeare's 'buskin tread' 'shake a stage' would not be figurative language merely, and we should be confirmed in the belief that Aubrey had direct information from the son of Shakespeare's fellow-actor for his statement that 'he was a handsome well shap't man', and that when John Davies of Hereford picked out 'wit, courage, good shape, good partes', as characteristics of the player 'W. S.', he was choosing his epithets with care.

The more we study these main groups of images which constitute the greatest part of Shakespeare's imagery, the clearer it becomes that there is one quality or characteristic in them all which overpoweringly attracts him throughout, and that quality is *movement*: nature and natural objects in motion.

In other words, it is the life of things which appeals to him, stimulates and enchants him, rather than beauty of colour or form or even significance.

This fact of Shakespeare's love of movement is a good example of how a study of the subject-matter of his images may throw light on his poetic technique, for I believe it supplies a clue to one of the secrets of his magical style. Thus it leads us to note how constantly in description it is the aspect of movement or life he seizes upon and portrays; so that many of his most memorable and unapproachable lines are charged with this quality, often conveyed in a single word. How many epithets, for instance, have poets used for the moon —wan, silver, watery, inconstant, fruitful and so on— but has her particular quality of movement in relation to this planet, that of coming and going, ever been so magically caught as by Shakespeare in one word?

> And there is nothing left remarkable
> Beneath the *visiting* moon.

A. and C.
4. 15. 67

His use of verbs of movement is a study in itself, and one of his outstanding characteristics is the way in which by introducing verbs of movement about things which are motionless, or rather which are abstractions and cannot have physical movement, he gives life to the whole phrase:

> I *stole* all courtesy from heaven,
> And *dressed* myself in such humility
> That I did *pluck* allegiance from men's hearts.

1 H. IV,
3. 2. 50

> So weary with disasters, *tugg'd* with fortune.

Mac. 3. 1. 112

> I was never so *bethump'd* with words.

K.J. 2. 1. 466

> How he did seem to *dive* into their hearts.

R. II, 1. 4. 25

He continually in this way endows inanimate and motionless objects with a sense of life:

> that pale, that white-faced shore,
> Whose foot *spurns* back the ocean's roaring tides.

K.J. 2. 1. 23

And when such objects are in motion, by attributing to them human feelings and actions he supplies the sense of activity:

Mac. 1. 2. 49

> Where the Norweyan banners *flout* the sky
> And *fan* our people cold.

This 'giving life to lifeless things', as Aristotle puts it, is, it may be said, the ordinary method of poetry, but no poet before or since has made such constant and such varied use of it as has Shakespeare.

His love of movement is to be seen not only in his direct images from it, but also in the aspect of colour which most appeals to him, in his interest in the play of emotions in the human face (p. 58), and it accounts for his special delight in such words as 'peep' and 'peer', expressing swift, delicate and darting action. I believe that a great deal of Shakespeare's peculiar art consists in these rapid and constant substitutions of effect, especially as regards life and movement; one class of things being drawn upon to furnish an impression required for another.

It is the method of the greater number of his most distinctive and characteristic images, images which bear his hall mark on them and could not have been drawn by anyone else.

I will here instance three of these only: one from the movement of a human personality, one from movement in nature, and one from the animal world, all taken from the play in which this characteristic imagery abounds, *Antony and Cleopatra*. When the messenger is describing to Caesar the inroads of the pirates and their effect on the people living near the coast, who are panic-stricken and intimidated, while their young men rebel, for no vessel can put to sea without being immediately seized, Shakespeare expresses it in three lines of compressed vividness, by picturing the whole region as a human personality growing white with fear, the young men flushing with anger, while for the movement of the vessel he uses his favourite verb 'peep'—a human action—to convey the quick darting movement of an object desiring to escape unseen:

> the borders maritime
> Lack blood to think on't, and flush youth revolt:
> No vessel can peep forth, but 'tis as soon
> Taken as seen.

A. and C.
I. 4. 51

Or again, a little earlier, Caesar reflects on the instability of popular fame and approval, how the man in command is always desired as leader until he has gained leadership, while a public favourite who has lost popularity regains value when he is gone. Shakespeare transfers the whole idea into an image of a water flag and its movement, delicately discriminated, the whole suggested by two words in the second half of his statement.

> And the *ebb'd* man, ne'er loved till ne'er worth love,
> Comes dear'd by being *lack'd*.

I. 4. 43

'This common body', he continues,

> Like to a vagabond flag upon the stream,
> Goes to and back, lackeying the varying tide,
> To rot itself with motion.

What a picture it calls up of a particular kind of movement, exactly analogous to the fickle, uninformed action of the populace, and what force lies in the terms 'vagabond', 'lackeying', 'goes to and back', 'varying', conveying the idea of motiveless subservience changing

to and fro under pressure of the tide and leading nowhere save to self-annihilation.

So also when Cleopatra describes the intense vitality
of Antony, and his sheer joy in living, again it is by a
special kind of movement she conveys it to us:

A. and C.
5. 2. 88

> his delights
> Were dolphin-like; they show'd his back above
> The element they lived in.

Shakespeare possibly never saw dolphins at play, but
anyone who has watched, as has the writer, the spectacle
of a school of young porpoises plunging, diving and
leaping in mid-ocean, knows that by instinct, if not by
direct observation, he has hit upon the particular movement which of all others most completely expresses
sheer abandon of animal joy in life and exuberant
delight in play.

If we think of some of Shakespeare's great passages
we see how constantly this same characteristic holds.

T. and C.
1. 3. 83–136

Thus the whole idea, in Ulysses' noble speech on
order, is conveyed through movement, from the ordered
motion of the planets in their spheres to the earthquakes
and tidal waves which follow any change in this. In his
other great speech, in which he answers Achilles' hurt
3. 3. 145–69 query, 'What, are my deeds forgot?' again the oblivion
into which good deeds sink is seen in a series of swift
movements: men pursuing each other along so narrow
a path that if the foremost falters, the others inevitably
rush by him, leaving him hindmost; a tide bursting into
a breach; a fallen horse in battle overrun and trampled
on; a host simultaneously welcoming and bidding
farewell to his guests.

H. V, 3. 1 Henry V's incitement to his soldiers is in the terms
of the special actions of tiger and greyhound, Faulcon-

bridge's reflections on Commodity are translated into *K. J.*
the peculiar bias run of the bowl, Portia's on mercy into *M. of V.*
the movement of 'gentle rain' and Prospero's on life *Temp. 4. 1. 148*
and reality into the coming and going, the forming and
melting of clouds in the sky.

2. 1. 572–84
4. 1. 184

Indeed, it would almost seem as if a predominating
movement, which informs and vitalises the whole passage, is in part the secret of many of Shakespeare's
magical effects.

Think of Macbeth's soliloquy before the murder, and
how his desire for action and his recoil from it, his ambition and his fear are conveyed through the actions of
riding; and consider the part played and the effect
produced by various kinds of walking in his last bitter *Mac.*
summary of life. Look at the beautiful soliloquy of *5. 5. 19–28*
Henry VI on Towton field, and see how the battle and *3 H. VI,*
its changing fortunes are expressed by the movement of *2. 5. 1–11*
swaying to and fro, as seen in the successive pictures of
the dawn triumphing over the night, the mighty sea
combating with the wind and the two wrestlers fighting
'breast to breast'. And, above all, study the description *A. and C.*
of Cleopatra in her barge and compare it with its *2. 2. 194–221*
original in North's *Plutarch*, and see what it is that
Shakespeare has added: Movement, the elements
making obeisance to the beauty of the great queen.

This excessive susceptibility to movement, this passionate absorption in the life of things, Shakespeare
shares with two other great English poets. With Keats,
he seems especially sensitive to movement in the play
of light and shadow, the wayfaring of clouds and the
motions of the wind. This we know to be true of Keats,
quite apart from the evidence of it in his poetry, if we
read Joseph Severn's notes on his friend when on a

holiday. Severn tells us of the rapture it was to Keats to watch the passage of wind over a field of grass or young corn, and that he was so bewitched by the sight of the wind running over a field of oats or barley, that it was almost impossible to lure him away.[1] I feel sure that these notes of Severn's on Keats might equally well have been written of Shakespeare, had he, by a happy chance for us, possessed an artist friend who kept a diary; and this likeness is but one more illustration of the poetic and spiritual kinship of the two poets.

With Wordsworth also, but with a difference, less self-consciously and reflectively, but instinctively and spontaneously, Shakespeare seems to find in motion the very essence of life itself,[2] and, had he formulated such thoughts at all, he would, I believe, have agreed with Wordsworth that the highest principle we can conceive of is

> a motion and a spirit that impels
> All thinking things, all objects of all thought
> And rolls through all things.

[1] See *Life and Letters of Joseph Severn*, by William Sharp, 1892, p. 21; also *John Keats*, by Amy Lowell, vol. I, pp. 96–7.

[2] See a most delightful and suggestive article on 'Wordsworth's *Prelude*', by Helen Darbishire, in *The Nineteenth Century* for May 1926, in which Wordsworth's use of the word 'motion' is examined. It might fruitfully be compared in detail with Shakespeare's use of the same word.

CHAPTER V

SHAKESPEARE'S SENSES

Pour écrire en poète, pour peindre, il ne suffit pas d'avoir pensé, il faut avoir vu.   *Le Sentiment de la Nature*, V. de Laprade.

IN any analysis arrived at through his poetry of the SIGHT quality and characteristics of a writer's senses, it is possible in some degree to separate and estimate his senses of touch, smell, hearing and taste, but his visual sense is so all-embracing—for it is indeed the gateway by which so large a portion of life reaches the poet, and the registration, description and interpretation of things seen depend so completely on faculties of mind and imagination—that to deal with this sense at all adequately almost amounts to the same thing as to deal with the man as a whole and his work in its entirety.

All I propose to do here, therefore, is to point out some particular aspects of things seen which most attract Shakespeare, and are by him most fully and vividly recorded—for it is scarcely necessary to say that Shakespeare's sight must have been quick and penetrating beyond that of ordinary men, and that his memory of things seen was extraordinarily vivid and retentive.

We have already noticed his love of movement, and that it is this, above all else, that his sight most readily registers and remembers. Next we may notice one or two points about Shakespeare's colour sense, and his use of colour. He has curiously few colour images, that is, images which group themselves primarily under that particular heading. This is partly because he is interested in colour, not chiefly for its colour value, as is an artist, but rather as it appears in some definite object, and for the emotion which it thus arouses or conveys.

This accounts, probably, for the fact that what he notices about colour and what attract him supremely are *change* and *contrast*. His delight in shifting, changing colour is another manifestation of his delight in movement and life, and one would expect to find evidence of it all through his nature descriptions, but this is not so. He notices it almost exclusively in two phenomena only, which have apparently no relation to one another, yet which he constantly links together. These are the colour quickly coming and going in the human face, with the emotions it denotes, and the glory and changing colours of the rising sun.

Shakespeare's intense interest in the human face has never, I think, been adequately noticed: its frowns and wrinkles, smiles and tears, the tint and shape of the nose, the tension of the nostrils, the eye, its colour and character, 'in flood with laughter', sparkling, sun-bright, quick, merry, fiery, mistful, dim, lack-lustre, heavy, hollow, modest, sober, sunken or scornful; the peculiar beauty of the eyelid, the betrayal of the gnawing of a nether lip, the dimples on a child's chin, and, above all, the way in which he continually makes us *see* the emotions of his characters by the chasing changes of colour in their cheeks.

These he conveys through every kind of metaphor, which in each case carries with it the particular atmosphere of emotion which gives rise to the change, making it quite unnecessary, for the most part, to mention any specific *colour* at all. Thus we see the traitors whose

'cheeks are paper' as they glance at the documents *H. V*, 2. 2. 71
handed them by their king; the fair high colour of *R. II*, 3. 3. 62
Richard quickly coming and going, and in anger turn-
ing pale, as when Gaunt's outspoken words chase

> the royal blood *R. II*, 2. 1. 118
> With fury from his native residence;

we realise how flushed will be the faces of the soldiers
on the 'gaudy night' when Antony promises he will

> force *A. and C.*
3. 13. 190
> The wine peep through their scars;

we watch Bassanio, dumb with emotion before Portia's
surrender, the colour suffusing his face as he stam-
mers,

> Madam, you have bereft me of all words, *M. of V.*
> Only my blood speaks to you in my veins; 3. 2. 176

and we feel with Macbeth the horror and fear gripping
the servant who, with 'linen cheeks' and 'whey face', *Mac.* 5. 3. 16
rushes in to report disaster.

If we look at the opening lines of one scene only—
the immortal sheep-shearing feast—we note how life *W.T.*
and feeling are continually conveyed by these touches 4. 4. 1–161
of the colour coming and going on the speakers' faces:
Perdita's conscious blushes when 'most goddess-like
prank'd up' she meets Florizel, or her still deeper
blushes when her father chides her for not taking part
as hostess, recalling his old wife at such times, whom
we see through his eyes, welcoming all and serving
all, flushed with cooking and with repeated sips of
cordial,

> her face o' fire 4. 4. 60
> With labour and the thing she took to quench it;

SIGHT   the cheery countenances of the guests 'red with mirth',
the clear fair tint of Florizel which bespeaks his health
and youth, and the quickly moving colour in the exquisitely fair cheeks of the maid as she listens to her
lover's words,

W.T. 4. 4. 159
>   He tells her something
> That makes her blood look out: good sooth, she is
> The queen of curds and cream.

This interest in the shifting colour of the face and the
emotion it implies is one of the marked features of
Shakespeare's earliest poem, and a kind of running
colour symphony is there played on the shamed blushes
V. and A. 76   of Adonis, or his cheeks with 'anger ashy-pale', and the
35   flushed hue of Venus, 'red and hot as coals of glowing
fire', or with emotion so suddenly white that Adonis
believes her dead, and

468   Claps her pale cheek, till clapping makes it red.

We see him surreptitiously and reluctantly watching
her, his face beginning to glow

338   Even as a dying coal revives with wind;

and we note

345   the fighting conflict of her hue,
> How white and red each other did destroy.

Here and elsewhere, Shakespeare uses the most exquisite and delicate metaphors to convey the rare beauty
of the swift change of colour induced by emotion, such
as the two following, allied, yet quite different in effect,
the one conveying change, the other contrast, and both
alike painting the result of a sudden grip of fear in a
woman's face.

The first is the fear of Venus when she thinks of the
danger of the boar hunt:

> whereat a sudden pale, *V. and A. 589*
> *Like lawn being spread upon the blushing rose,*
> Usurps her cheek;

the second that of Lucrece, when dreading bad news:

> O, how her fear did make her colour rise! *Luc. 257*
> *First red as roses that on lawn we lay,*
> *Then white as lawn, the roses took away.*

Shakespeare is so conscious of the betraying change of colour in the face, as the signal flag of various emotions, fear, anger, astonishment, pleasure, and he so vividly and constantly describes it either directly or by means of an image, that I cannot help surmising he himself, like Richard II, was fair and flushed easily, and that possibly in youth he suffered from the ease with which, under stress of feeling, he betrayed his emotions through blushing or pallor.

The opening lines of *Venus and Adonis* exemplify Shakespeare's curious and constant association of the colour or expression of the face with the effect of sunrise, which is again more fully worked out in the eighty-first verse of the poem, when Venus, recovering from the faint which has so alarmed Adonis, softly lifts her eyelids, and

> The night of sorrow now is turn'd to day:
> Her two blue windows faintly she up-heaveth,
> Like the fair sun, when in his fresh array
> He cheers the morn, and all the earth relieveth:
>   And as the bright sun glorifies the sky,
>   So is her face illumined with her eye.

This association of idea is so frequent that it would be wearisome to cite too many instances, though I may perhaps quote two or three expressions of it of various

SIGHT

kinds. As in the first line of *Venus and Adonis*, the sun is constantly thought of as a *face*:

Titus, 2. 4. 31

> Yet do thy cheeks look red as Titan's face
> Blushing to be encounter'd with a cloud.

1 H. IV, 5. 1. 1

> How bloodily the sun begins to peer
> Above yon busky hill: the day looks pale
> At his distemperature.

It is also repeatedly described as an *eye*, perhaps most picturesquely—if somewhat fancifully—in Sonnet CXXXII, where it and the evening star are by the poet likened to the eyes of his mistress:

> And truly not the morning sun of heaven
> Better becomes the grey cheeks of the east,
> Nor that full star that ushers in the even
> Doth half that glory to the sober west,
> As those two mourning eyes become thy face.

These two ideas are united in one in the exquisite thirty-third sonnet, full of radiant beauty as the sunrise itself:

> Full many a glorious morning have I seen
> Flatter the mountain-tops with sovereign eye,
> Kissing with golden face the meadows green,
> Gilding pale streams with heavenly alchemy.

Here we have a sense of flooded colour rare with Shakespeare, combining his love of contrast ('golden' and 'green') with his enchanted delight in change, and a good example, in the fourth line, of his magical power of picturing that change without naming any colour at all.

It is a precisely similar pageant of changing beauty—over the sea instead of the meadows—which Oberon tells Puck he has so often watched:

M.N.D.
3. 2. 391

> Even till the eastern gate, all fiery-red,
> Opening on Neptune with fair blessed beams,
> Turns into yellow gold his salt green streams.

It is indeed clear that the spectacle of the rising sun seems ever peculiarly to inspire and delight Shakespeare. He connects it with youth and vigour, with strength, splendour, good cheer and renewal of life. The sight of the setting sun, on the other hand, depresses him; he sees in it, not the glory of its colour, or rest and quiet, or the promise of another day, but the end of things, old age, storms to come, sorrow, dangers, and approaching night (*J.C.* 5. 3. 60; *R. II*, 2. 4. 21; *R. III*, 2. 3. 34; *R. and J.* 3. 5. 127). This attitude he sums up concisely in the seventh sonnet, where he pictures men adoring the sun when he 'lifts up his burning head' and climbs the sky. The sun, he says, resembles strong youth in his middle age, but when 'like feeble age, he reeleth from the day', the watchers avert their eyes from the level rays which in setting he throws athwart them. Shakespeare's great fondness for the picture of changing colour, though not confined solely to the human face or to the sunrise, is very rarely found applied to anything else, and Macbeth's famous ejaculation—'making the green one red'—stands almost alone, forming in itself the most thrilling and dramatic use of changing colour ever made by Shakespeare or by any dramatist.

Shakespeare's other chief colour interest is contrast; and all his definite and simple colour images are of this kind, particularly of black and white, and red and white; such as Richard's impatience to see the white rose dyed 'in the lukewarm blood of Henry's heart'; Salarino's *3 H. VI,*
1. 2. 33
assertion that there is more difference between the flesh of Shylock and Jessica 'than between jet and ivory'; *M. of V.*
3. 1. 41
the hunted boar,

> Whose frothy mouth, bepainted all with red, *V. and A. 901*
> Like milk and blood being mingled both together,

and so on.

SIGHT

Shakespeare's keen sense of colour contrast is often connected with a dominant emotion or theme, and so runs throughout a play; as the thought of the befouling of the purity of Desdemona and the opposition of her colour and that of the Moor expresses itself in black and white all through *Othello*. It is kept before us in Iago's contemptuous use of 'black ram' and 'white ewe', or his rhyme,

Oth. 1. 1. 88

2. 1. 133

If she be black, and thereto have a wit,
She'll find a white that shall her blackness fit;

1. 3. 291
3. 3. 447

in the duke's summary of Othello's character, 'far more fair than black'; in Othello's call upon 'black vengeance', or his agonised ejaculation,

3. 3. 386

Her name, that was as fresh
As Dian's visage, is now begrimed and black
As mine own face;

and in the emphasis on the purity and fairness of Desdemona,

5. 2. 4

that whiter skin of hers than snow
And smooth as monumental alabaster;

5. 2. 272

O ill-starr'd wench!
Pale as thy smock!

and the contrast with Othello, as in Emilia's cry,

5. 2. 130

O, the more angel she,
And you the blacker devil!

In *Romeo and Juliet*, also, we find the general light and darkness symbolism reinforced by touches of both black and white, and red and white, the first bringing out the peerless quality of each lover in the other's eyes, the second enhancing the horror and the tragedy of the fate of youth in the play. Romeo, who, as Mercutio says,

R. and J.
2. 4. 13

was in his first love 'stabbed with a white wench's

black eye', was to find out that Rosaline, whom he
thought a swan, was but a crow, so that on his first sight *R. and J.*
of Juliet he exclaims,   *1. 2. 89*

> So shows a snowy dove trooping with crows,   *1. 5. 49*
> As yonder lady o'er her fellows shows:

Juliet, in her turn, with her finer imagination and more
exquisite diction, declares that Romeo will

> lie upon the wings of night   *3. 2. 18*
> Whiter than new snow on a raven's back.

So also the horror of the unnecessary death of Tybalt is
brought out by the nurse's ghoulish description of the
corpse,

> Pale, pale as ashes, all bedaub'd in blood,   *3. 2. 55*

and our fears for Juliet, repeatedly aroused, are thrice
subtly enhanced by colour touches. First when each
lover notices the other's pallor, and Romeo declares,
'Dry sorrow drinks our blood'; next when the Friar   *3. 5. 59*
describes the effect which the potion will have,

> The roses in thy lips and cheeks shall fade   *4. 1. 99*
> To paly ashes;

and finally when Romeo, thinking her already dead,
exclaims that

> beauty's ensign yet   *5. 3. 94*
> Is crimson in thy lips and in thy cheeks,
> And death's pale flag is not advanced there.

And are the flashes of green in the play pure chance?
I wonder. One is definitely conscious of them against
the background of light and darkness: the green, quick,   *3. 5. 222*
fair eye of Paris described by the nurse, and the contrast later, as Juliet in her anguish thinks of her other
lover, 'bloody Tybalt, yet but green in earth'; the sick   *4. 3. 42*
green 'vestal livery' of the moon; Capulet's coarse   *2. 2. 8*

description of Juliet's pale face, 'you green-sickness carrion!'; and the single touch of clear colour, 'green earthen pots', which stands out against the dark, musty, disorderly background of the vividly painted apothecary's shop.

Shakespeare is just as sensitive to the colour and tint of flesh, and the contrasts of the various shades which are called 'white',[1] as he is to the changing colour in the cheek. In his early poems this particular colour interest is, like the changing colour in the face, very marked, and he is for ever emphasising and illustrating the fairness of a woman's skin,

V. and A. 398   Teaching the sheets a whiter hue than white.

The whole of the sixty-first stanza in *Venus and Adonis*, for instance, is a play on various shades of white and a series of images to express them, so that when Venus gently takes Adonis by the hand it is

362   A lily prison'd in a gaol of snow,
             Or ivory in an alabaster band,

366   while the two lovers together show 'like two silver doves that sit a-billing'.

In describing Lucrece, also, there is constant play on her whiteness and fairness, and the poet uses, among other things, ivory, alabaster, snow, lilies, silver, wax and lawn to convey various shades of it; the most beautiful image of contrast, I think, being that of her 'fair hand'

Luc. 394   On the green coverlet; whose perfect white
              Show'd like an April daisy on the grass.

This delight in colour contrast is, like Shakespeare's joy in changing colour, but part of a larger and deeper

---

[1] As indeed he is also to the shades of black, 'lustrous as ebony', 'coal-black as jet', etc.

feeling, in this case an abiding consciousness of the strange, tragic, bewildering or beautiful contrasts which form human life.

It is this feeling, shared, alas, by so few of his commentators, which goes far to make him the supreme dramatist he is. The imagination which rejoices in the beauty of a woman's hand on a green coverlet, or of snow on a raven's back, is the same which exclaims in Hamlet's voice, 'What a piece of work is a man!', which inserts the Porter scene in *Macbeth*, or the exquisite boy's song after the prison scene in *Measure for Measure*.

His use of colour contrast adds greatly, in ways at first unperceived by us, to the beauty of his plays. Thus, in *A Midsummer Night's Dream*, the unusual number of bright colours that we find there freely contrasted, not only in Thisbe's love-song, or Flute's address to Pyramus, but throughout, as applied to fruit, flowers, birds, and maiden's eyes and lips, enhance the beauty of the play as does the flashing of light on jewels. There is in it, as we might expect, a great deal of green, intermingled with white and silver, purple, crimson and gold, and in the images especially, in Shakespeare's subtle and characteristic way, these contrasts are repeatedly brought out by suggesting rather than naming one at least of the colours; and so we have in them such gems of description as,

When wheat is green, when *hawthorn buds* appear,   M.N.D.
1. 1. 185
or

In their gold coats spots you see;   *2. 1. 11*
Those be *rubies*,

or   *hoary-headed frosts*   *2. 1. 107*
Fall in the fresh lap of the crimson rose.

This keen contrast consciousness expresses itself continually in every kind of way. One of the most perfect examples of it as regards colour, which includes and suggests the deeper and more subtle contrast, is Iachimo's soliloquy when gazing at the unconscious Imogen. He paints, in a series of images, an exquisite picture of the sleeping girl, as he watches her in the flickering light of the taper, and of her dainty setting in the perfumed room, giving or suggesting to us the colours of whites and reds, azure, pale yellow and crimson, with the background of rich tapestry and other adornments.

Cym. 2. 2. 14

> Cytherea,
> How bravely thou becomest thy bed! fresh lily!
> And whiter than the sheets! That I might touch
> But kiss; one kiss! Rubies unparagon'd,
> .   .   .   .   .   . the flame o' the taper
> Bows toward her, and would under-peep her lids
> To see the unclosed lights, now canopied
> Under those windows, white and azure, laced
> With blue of heaven's own tinct. .   .   .

2. 2. 37

> .   .   .   .   .   On her left breast
> A mole cinque-spotted, like the crimson drops
> I' the bottom of a cowslip.

And all the time, while we listen and look, the strange, mysterious, baffling contrast is ever being pressed upon us, between the freshness and delicacy of the senses which enable a man thus to enjoy and describe beauty, and the murkiness and foulness of his mind and intentions.

One has the feeling all through Shakespeare's use of colour that he is more interested in tone, contrast, character and emotion than in the colour itself. He gives us certainly many lovely colour groups, particularly in the Sonnets: violet, sable, silver, white and

green (XII), yellow, sunset, fire, ashes, black night
(LXXIII), violet, purple, lily, roses, red and white (XCIX),
or in his description of flowers: Marina's basket full of

> the yellows, blues,   *Per. 4. 1. 15*
> The purple violets, and marigolds,

she brings to strew upon the green; the

> emerald tufts, flowers purple, blue, and white   *M.W. 5. 5. 73*

of the fairies in the *Merry Wives*, or the daisies pied and
violets blue, the lady smocks and cuckoo buds of the
spring song. It is, however, significant that in the most *L.L.L. 5. 2. 897*
lovely and famous enumeration of all, when Perdita, at *W.T.*
the sheep-shearing, sighs for the flowers of spring to *4. 4. 116–28*
give her guests, in a passage which seems a very riot of
varied hues and beauty, *no single colour is named.*
'Violets *dim*', '*pale* primroses', '*bold* oxlips'; with the
aid of these well-nigh perfect epithets of tone and character, we ourselves supply the misty purples, faint
lemon and rich yellows which we *see* as Perdita be-
witches us with the ever-enchanted words.

As for his hearing, there can be little need to submit HEARING
any very detailed proof of the sensitiveness of Shakespeare's ear, or of his real musical knowledge, both
theoretical and technical. Ample evidence of this is to be
found all through his plays (see *Shakespeare's England*,
II, chap. xvii, 2), and his images from music are too
many and too familiar to be more than mentioned here.
The hastiest reader must notice their vividness, while
the student is assured of their peculiar accuracy (see
Shakespeare and Music, by Edward W. Naylor, 1896).

He uses with particularly penetrating analogy the
playing on a pipe and a viol, as in Hamlet's well-known

metaphor of the man easily swayed by emotion, a pipe
on which 'fortune's finger' sounds what stop she
pleases, or his satirical conversation with Guildenstern
about the recorder; and Rumour's characteristics have
surely never been so vividly and accurately portrayed as
in the picture of it as a pipe

> Blown by surmises, jealousies, conjectures,
> And of so easy and so plain a stop

that the

> *still-discordant wavering* multitude,
> Can play upon it.

How perfectly those adjectives convey the peculiar
sound produced by an unskilled yet eager player!

Among many other remarkable images from music
which throw fresh light on the subject handled, as well
as prove Shakespeare's own musical and technical skill,
are Iago's promise to lower the pegs on the viol and so
destroy the exquisitely tuned music of Othello's joy;
the perfect analogy (surely Shakespearian?) used by
Pericles between lawful love and lawless passion respectively and the right handling and disordered playing on
a viol; and Richard II's reflections on the broken time
in 'the music of men's lives'.

Quite apart from the evidence of Shakespeare's
general musical knowledge, his many references to
music and the part it plays in life, comforting, refresh-
ing, inspiriting, ravishing, soothing,[1] his unerring
touches describing the sound of special instruments—
the melancholy of a lover's lute, 'the vile squealing of
the wry-neck'd fife', the 'dreadful bray' of the trumpet,

---

[1] *Temp.* 5. 1. 58, 3. 2. 147–8; *A.Y.L.I.* 5. 4. 185–6; *Pass. Pil.* VIII,
5–6; *Oth.* 4. 1. 197; 2 *H. IV*, 3. 1. 14; *Temp.* 1. 2. 391; *M.N.D.*
2. 1. 152, etc.

Side notes (left margin):

Ham. 3. 2. 75

3. 2. 372

2 *H. IV*,
  Induc. 15

Oth. 2. 1. 201

Per. 1. 1. 81

R. II, 5. 5. 42

1 *H. IV*,
  1. 2. 81
M. of V.
  2. 5. 30
R. II, 1. 3. 135

the drone of a bagpipe, the thunder of the organ, the performance of a child on a recorder—and the opinions of his characters about those who are unmusical,[1] I submit that there is also clear evidence of a personal shrinking from discord and harshness, and great susceptibility, not only to 'sweet airs', but to sounds of every kind.

1 H. IV, 1. 2. 82
Temp. 3. 3. 97–8
M.N.D. 5. 1. 122

For example, surely no one who was not himself very sensitive to the tone and timbre of the human voice could have drawn so many characters who share this peculiarity as Shakespeare has done.

Among them we find people so different as Cleopatra (*A. and C.* 1. 1. 32, 3. 3. 15, 5. 2. 83), Troilus (*T. and C.* 1. 1. 54, 2. 2. 98), Emilia (*Oth.* 5. 2. 119), Trinculo (*Temp.* 2. 2. 90), Juliet (*R. and J.* 2. 2. 58), Mortimer (1 *H. IV*, 3. 1. 208), Quince (*M.N.D.* 4. 2. 12), Gertrude (*Ham.* 3. 4. 39), Edmund (*Lear*, 5. 3. 143), Caliban (*Temp.* 3. 2. 146), Romeo (*R. and J.* 2. 2. 167), Sir Andrew Aguecheek (*Tw. N.* 2. 3. 54), Henry V (*H. V*, 4. 1. 315), Tybalt (*R. and J.* 1. 5. 55), Othello (*Oth.* 5. 1. 28), Belarius (*Cym.* 4. 2. 105), Fluellen (*H. V*, 4. 1. 65, 81–2), Poins (1 *H. IV*, 2. 2. 52) and the boy in *Henry V* (4. 4. 68). The duke recognises Lucio, Lorenzo Portia, and Friar Laurence Friar John by the voice, Aegeon is aghast that his son fails to know his voice, Adonis knows and fears the 'deceiving harmony' of Venus' tongue 'bewitching like the wanton mermaid's songs', and Ferdinand confesses to Miranda that he has repeatedly fallen a victim to a woman's voice.

V. and A. 775–81

Temp. 3. 1. 41

Both Bassanio and Shylock notice and reprove Gratiano's loud voice, 'too wild, too rude, and bold', while Bassanio, talking of the deception of ornament, goes so far as to say that in law, if a tainted and corrupt

M. of V. 2. 2. 186; 4. 1. 140

---

[1] *M. of V.* 5. 1. 83; *J.C.* 1. 2. 204–10.

M. of V.
3. 2. 75

plea be 'season'd with a gracious voice' it obscures the show of evil. The blind Gloucester well remembers the 'trick' of Lear's voice, as Lear himself knows and loves Cordelia's, 'ever soft, gentle and low, an excellent thing in woman'.

K.L. 4. 6. 108

5. 3. 272

We note moreover the constant and exquisite discrimination in the quality of voices, largely expressed through images, such as the difference between the 'silver-sweet' sound of 'lovers' tongues by night', and the imperial voice of Antony 'propertied as all the tuned spheres', the harsh, hoarse call of the stricken Lucrece and the soft speech of her maid, the shrill refrain of the tapster, the 'care-tuned' tongue of Scroop, and Coriolanus's 'rougher accents', his 'throat of war' which he declares shall be turned

R. and J.
2. 2. 166
A. and C.
5. 2 83;
2. 2. 6
Luc. 1214, 1220

V. and A. 849
1 H. IV, 2. 4. 29
R. II, 3. 2. 92
Cor. 3. 3. 55

3. 2. 113

into a pipe
Small as an eunuch, or the virgin voice
That babies lulls asleep,

R. II, 5. 3. 75

the high-pitched 'eager cry' of the mother pleading for her son and Viola's 'small pipe', 'as the maiden's organ, shrill and sound', which Olivia places first among her claims to gentle blood, and to which she avows she would rather listen

Tw. N. 1. 4. 32

1. 5. 302

3. 1. 116

Than music from the spheres.

Quite apart from the absolute proof given by the fact that he was capable of writing his poetry, we can be quite sure, I think, from other sources of Shakespeare's 'daintiness of ear', and of his delicate susceptibility to tone, pace and pitch. It would seem equally certain that from youth up he disliked the speech of those who were 'ill-nurtured, crooked, churlish, harsh in voice', also that he shrank from noisy and acrimonious argument, and felt with Lepidus, when he urged Antony and

R. II, 5. 5. 45

V. and A. 134

Caesar to discuss their differences gently, and not by loud talking to 'commit murder in healing wounds'. *A. and C.* 2. 2. 19
In short, it is clear that those he most admired spoke 'low and tardily', 'with soft slow tongue'. *2 H. IV,* 2. 3. 26

Next to the human voice, there are three classes of *Luc. 1220; T.* sound which seem specially to interest or affect Shake- *of Sh., Induc. 1.* speare—echo and reverberation, the toll of passing or *114* funeral bell (both commented on elsewhere, see p. 325 below and Appendix VIII), and the song of birds.

For one so sensitive to sound, who is also such a bird lover, their song, the 'wild music' that 'burthens every *Son. CII* bough', is less often noted than one would expect.

He has however, and especially in the Sonnets, many exquisite and well-known descriptions of their song and its emotional atmosphere, showing the closest and most accurate observation: 'the lark at break of day *Son. XXIX* arising', the nightingale who

> in summer's front doth sing, *Son. CII*
> And stops her pipe in growth of riper days,

the robin-redbreast's love-song, the shriek of the *Two Gent.* 2. 1. 19–20
night-owl, the chirping of the wren and the 'dismal *R. II, 3. 3. 183*
tune' of the raven, 'the cock, that is the trumpet to the *2 H. VI,* 3. 2. 40
morn', the summer bird *Ham. 1. 1. 150*

> Which ever in the haunch of winter sings *2 H. IV,* 4. 4. 91
> The lifting up of day,

the 'bare ruin'd choirs, where late the sweet birds sang', *Son. LXXIII* and the dull cheer of the birds' song when winter is *Son. XCVII* near.

Even these are enough to prove how he noted and loved the sound and song of birds, but all the same it is not here, as we have seen (p. 48), that his chief interest lay; it is, as a matter of fact, another aspect of bird life which supremely appealed to and delighted him.

The general impression one gets on looking at Shakespeare's sound images, apart from his general delight in music and extreme sensitiveness to the human voice, is that he associates the purest emotion and the most spiritual condition known to man with music and with harmony, the most perfect earthly setting he can conceive is the hushed stillness of a summer day, and his picture of peace in death is a state in which

Titus, 1. 1. 155
                                                    are no storms,
            No noise, but silence and eternal sleep.

His attitude to stillness and silence throughout is well worth noticing, and one cannot but fancy the Countess of Rousillon's counsel would have been Shakespeare's own:

All's Well,
1. 1. 72
                                            be check'd for silence,
            But never tax'd for speech.

Would any other writer paint a husband welcoming
Cor. 2. 1. 184 the wife he loves as 'My gracious silence', and how many would have the delicacy of perception to realise, as
M. Ado, surely as Shakespeare does with Claudio, that 'silence
2. 1. 309 is the perfectest herald of joy'?

He definitely thinks of happy human love as music, 'the true concord of well tuned sounds':

Son. VIII
            Mark how one string, sweet husband to another,
            Strikes each in each by mutual ordering;
            Resembling sire and child and happy mother,
            Who, all in one, one pleasing note do sing,

while in Biron's noble description it is wholly through ear-charming sound that he conveys love's enchanting and magical quality:

L.L.L.
4. 3. 341
                                    as sweet and musical
            As bright Apollo's lute, strung with his hair;
            And when Love speaks, the voice of all the gods
            Make heaven drowsy with the harmony,

and the most exquisite setting Shakespeare can conceive for the great lovers of all time is a moonlit summer
night

> When the sweet wind did gently kiss the trees *M. of V.*
> *And they did make no noise.*   *5. 1. 2*

When his imagination is heightened, and on the rare
occasions when his characters speak directly of things
of deepest import, he tends naturally to fall into the
analogy of music, and the glorious words which describe
the 'harmony in immortal souls' may be Platonic in   *5. 1. 54–65*
origin but are surely Shakespearian in imaginative
belief and feeling.

So also in his latest play, in which, as I point out later
(p. 300), changing emotions and the movement of the
plot are expressed chiefly through sound, when Prospero at the close invokes the aid of 'heavenly music' to
resolve the discords, we are explicitly told in the
Epilogue that the agent of release and harmony is
prayer,

> Which pierces so, that it assaults   *Temp.,*
> Mercy itself, and frees all faults.   *Epilogue 17*

On the other hand, the things which Shakespeare
hates, or intends his characters to convey to us that they
hate, are constantly thought of in the terms of discord
and clamour.

There are certain things there can be no question
Shakespeare himself fears and hates, and one of these is
disruption of the social order, for the frame of human
society—the laws that bind man to man—seems to him,
as later to Burke, to have a mystical significance, to be
one with a higher law, and to partake of the same nature
as the mysterious agency by which the order of the

T. and C.
1. 3. 85

heavens, the stars, planets and the sun himself is determined.

It is natural but significant, therefore, that in his most impassioned exposition of this subject, the great speech

1. 3. 83–129

of Ulysses, he should at the apex of his feeling seize on the musical significance of 'degree' to point out that interval, succession and position are as essential to the universe and the ordering of human society as they are to the creation of music, and if they are ignored, in the one case as in the other, only chaos can result:

1. 3. 109–10

> Take but degree away, untune that string,
> And, hark, what discord follows!

Timon,
5. 1. 177

War—'contumelious, beastly, man-brain'd war'— was surely disliked by Shakespeare himself, and it is worth noting that the action of war is clearly associated in his mind chiefly with noise, whether he wants to convey dislike of it or delight in it on the part of his characters. (*R. III*, 4. 4. 152; *T. and C.* 1. 1. 92, 5. 2. 173; *K.J.* 5. 2. 164–9; *Oth.* 3. 3. 356; *T. of Sh.* 1. 2. 204–7, etc.) Those who like war and the soldier's life think of it in terms of sound and the association that particular sound brings with it; so Faulconbridge orders the battering cannon to be turned on Angiers,

K.J. 2. 1. 383

> Till their soul-fearing clamours have brawl'd down
> The flinty ribs of this contemptuous city,

and Othello, bidding farewell to

> the big wars
> That make ambition virtue!

Oth. 3. 3. 350

exclaims,

> O, farewell,
> Farewell the neighing steed and the shrill trump,
> The spirit-stirring drum, the ear-piercing fife,
> The royal banner and all quality,
> Pride, pomp and circumstance of glorious war!

And, O you mortal engines, whose rude throats
The immortal Jove's dread clamours counterfeit,
Farewell!

It is equally noticeable how often it is the sound
Shakespeare seizes on as abhorrent. Thus Richard II,
taking measures to keep the peace, thinks of war purely
as a hideous noise, and describes peace as an infant in
the cradle, gently asleep, which if

> roused up with boisterous untuned drums,   *R. II, 1. 3. 134*
> With harsh resounding trumpets' dreadful bray,
> And grating shock of wrathful iron arms,

may be frighted from his 'quiet confines'.

> The noise of battle hurtled in the air,   *J.C. 2. 2. 22*

says Calpurnia, describing her terrifying dream,

> Horses did neigh and dying men did groan,

and Blanch, begging that war be not renewed on her
wedding day, asks:

> What, shall our feast be kept with slaughtered men?   *K.J. 3. 1. 302*
> Shall braying trumpets and loud churlish drums,[1]
> Clamours of hell, be measures to our pomp?

Clamours of hell, so might a poet well write today, while
enduring the horrors of raucous sound in any great
modern city; but three hundred years ago, when man-
made noises must have been comparatively negligible
(except for bell-ringing, see Appendix VIII), it is more remarkable that this particular aspect of physical discomfort
should be selected to image the acme of pain. In Shakespeare's time and earlier, hell is commonly thought of
as a place of torment, as a very hot or a very cold or a

---

[1] There was no need for Shakespeare to have been in a battle to hear
these noises, for Hentzner (in 1598) remarks how fond the English
were 'of great noises that fill the ear, such as the firing of cannon, drums,
and the ringing of bells'. (For this latter, see App. VIII.)

very dark place (the three chief discomforts of life in the Middle Ages in Europe), but the torment rarely takes the form of its being pictured as a very noisy place.

Yet this is the conception which constantly recurs in Shakespeare's thought; hell is 'an age of discord and continual strife'; howlings, roarings and curses are its accompaniment. 'Foul devil', cries Anne to Gloucester,

1 H. VI,
5. 5. 63
R. and J.
3. 3. 47
3. 2. 44
R. III, 4. 4. 75
1. 2. 51

> thou hast made the happy earth thy hell,
> Fill'd it with cursing cries and deep exclaims;

1. 4. 58 Clarence's dream of hell was of a place where a 'legion of foul fiends' surrounded him and howled 'such hideous cries' in his ears that with the noise he awoke trembling, and the music the devils in hell, and they alone, dance to, is in reality a sound of harsh and terrible discord.

We are justified then in concluding that as in Shakespeare's imagination heaven is hushed stillness with 'touches of sweet harmony', and hell is a place of noisy strife, discord and clamour, he very much loved the one and hated the other.

SMELL   Shakespeare has clearly a very acute sense of smell, and is peculiarly sensitive to bad smells; the two he specially names and dislikes being the smell of unwashed humanity and of decaying corpses, both of them common enough in Elizabethan plague-stricken London. Coriolanus, in his words of supreme contempt for the fickle populace, gives expression to this dislike when he exclaims,

Cor. 3. 3. 120

> You common cry of curs! whose breath I hate
> As reek o' the rotten fens, whose loves I prize
> As the dead carcasses of unburied men
> That do corrupt my air.

3. 1. 66
J.C.
1. 2. 243–51

The disgust of Coriolanus for the 'rank-scented many' and their 'stinking breaths', Casca's fear of the

'bad air' of the crowd, Henry V's realistic picture of the
dead bodies of his soldiers, 'The smell whereof shall *H.V*, 4. 3. 103
breed a plague in France', or Constance's terrible apostrophe to Death, 'Thou odoriferous stench!' could have *K.J*. 3. 4. 26
been imagined only by one who was himself sensitive
to such odours; but did we need more proof of Shakespeare's own feelings, we could find it in the fact that
he expresses the height of disgust and horror through
the medium of revolting smells, and that to his imagination sin and evil deeds always smell foully.

We are definitely conscious of this in *Hamlet*, with
its underlying idea of a foul tumour, of rottenness and
corruption, offences that are 'rank' and smell to heaven;
in *Julius Caesar*, when Antony, vowing vengeance,
declares the murder of Caesar a 'foul deed' which

> shall smell above the earth *J.C.* 3. 1. 274
> With carrion men, groaning for burial;

in *King John*, where we hear the king's anger described
as a tumour breaking in 'foul corruption', and where *K.J*.
Salisbury, revolted on finding young Arthur dead, cries 4. 2. 79–81
out in horror,

> Away with me, all you whose souls abhor *4. 3. 111*
> The uncleanly savours of a slaughter-house;
> For I am stifled with this smell of sin.

We get touches of it also in other plays, and perhaps
nowhere is the startling quality of this swift transference
of feeling from the moral to the physical plane greater
than in Polixenes' cry that if what Leontes thinks of
him be true, then may his 'freshest reputation' be
turned to

> A savour that may strike the dullest nostril *W.T.* 1. 2. 421
> Where I arrive, and my approach be shunn'd,
> Nay, hated too, worse than the great'st infection
> That e'er was heard or read!

But it is above all in *Othello* that we are made conscious of the foul and horrible smell of evil, where Iago villainously suggests to the Moor that 'one may smell . . .

Oth. 3. 3. 232 a will most rank' in the very fact that Desdemona chose to marry a black man, and where the horror of the contrast between the fair looks of Desdemona and what he believes her deeds is made vivid by Othello entirely by means of smell. He laments,

4. 2. 67
O thou weed,
Who art so lovely fair and smell'st so sweet
That the sense aches at thee, would thou hadst ne'er
      been born!

and in answer to her piteous query,

Alas, what ignorant sin have I committed?

he gives her ample description of its character in his agonised cry:

What committed!
Heaven stops the nose at it.

As far as one can judge from his images, Shakespeare seems more sensitive to the horror of bad smells than to

Son. xcviii the allure of fragrant ones. Naturally he loves 'the sweet smell of different flowers' and also the sweet scents of spring, which he connects with sparkling

M.W. 3. 2. 66 youth who 'smells April and May'. He is susceptible
Mac. 1. 6. to the pleasant air where 'heaven's breath smells wooingly', he notes the sweetness of the violet, the eglantine (sweet briar) and the damask rose; but it is suggestive that in his most sustained and exquisite ap-

Son. liv preciation of the rose, what chiefly appeals to him is the fact that, unlike other flowers, roses even when faded never smell badly, but that

Of their sweet deaths are sweetest odours made.

What he shrinks from especially is a fair flower with

'the rank smell of weeds', or a sweet-smelling flower *Son.* LXIX
which turns very much the reverse when dead. We can
sense the repulsion in the words,

Lilies that fester smell far worse than weeds. *Son.* XCIV

It is also significant that anyone so sensitive to crude
town smells (the unwashed many, the unburied corpses,
the reek of a lime kiln by the Counter-gate), and so
susceptible to delicate flower scents, should almost
ignore the fashionable use of perfumes. It appears once
as an image of great charm, when poor Ophelia returns
Hamlet his gifts, which, she says, have lost 'their per- *Ham.* 3. 1. 98
fume' since he has proved unkind; Autolycus sells
fragrant gloves 'as sweet as damask roses', which was a
favourite scent of the time, probably also referred to by
Boyet in *Love's Labour's Lost* (5. 2. 296); there is mention of Borachio, as perfumer 'smoking a musty room', *M. Ado,* 1. 3. 58
and of Christopher Sly's hands being washed in a skin
basin full of rose water; but mostly one would fancy
Shakespeare had a contempt or even a dislike for
perfume.

He laughs at it in Mistress Quickly's immortal
account of Mistress Ford's suitors, 'coach after coach, *M.W.* 2. 2. 66
letter after letter, gift after gift; smelling so sweetly, all
musk'; or in the chaff of Benedick's friends who declare *M. Ado,* 3. 2. 49
he rubs himself with civet; and Falstaff speaks with
crushing disdain for the 'lisping hawthorn-buds' that *M.W.* 3. 3. 72
'smell like Bucklersbury in simple time'. One fancies
one may trace a hint of Shakespeare's own dislike for
the use of a strong artificial perfume to counteract or
cover an evil smell, in Lear's poignant cry when dis-
tracted by his most terrible and revolting thoughts,
'Give me an ounce of civet, good apothecary, to *K.L.* 4. 6. 132
sweeten my imagination'.

TOUCH   Next, let us consider touch. As we have already seen
(pp. 36–7), Shakespeare is fond, as are most of the
Elizabethan dramatists, of similes drawn from the texture
of substances, flint, iron, steel, wax, sponge and so
on, but one has only to compare their—mostly—very
obvious comparisons with his, to see how sensitive and
delicately discriminating he is in matters of touch.

There is one substance in especial to which he is
markedly sensitive, and that is the texture of the skin.
He notices it very closely, as he does the colour changes
Oth. 5. 2. 5   in the face. He describes Desdemona's skin, 'smooth
W.T. 4. 4. 368   as monumental alabaster', Perdita's hands, 'soft as
V. and A. 143   dove's down', Venus' 'smooth moist hand', Cressid's
T. and C.   'to whose soft seizure the cygnet's down is harsh', the
A. and C. 1. 1. 57   'flower-soft' hands of Cleopatra's maidens, 'a velvet
L.L.L. 3. 1. 197   brow', a 'smooth and rubious' lip, the hardness of the
Tw. N. 1. 4. 32   palm of a ploughman. (Note also Iachimo's sensitive-
T. and C.
1. 1. 59   ness to the texture of the cheek and hand of Imogen,
Cym. 1. 6. 99–107.) He is very conscious of and re-
sponsive to the feeling and quality of various substances:
K.J. 4. 2. 13   the smoothness of ice and oil, the cold hardness of stone,
1 H. IV, 1. 3. 7   the stickiness of blood and of slime, the soft furred sur-
Titus, 3. 1. 45
Mac. 5. 2. 16   face of moss, the peculiar roughness of bark, the malle-
Oth. 5. 2. 148   ability of wax when warm, the smooth imperviousness
Cym. 4. 2. 228
M.N.D. 4. 1. 48   of marble, and the pleasant, soft feeling of rain.
2 H. IV,
4. 3. 136   It is not surprising, therefore, that some of the most
M. for M.
3. 1. 236   vivid and striking of his similes are drawn from this
Titus, 3. 1. 16
M. of V. 4. 1.   sense of touch and substance.
185
A very curious one is Enobarbus' dying speech, in
which he apostrophises the moon and begs her to bear
witness to his deep repentance for having left his
master. It is drawn entirely from a vivid realisation of
the qualities of substances and their impact on each other,

moist, hard, soft, dried and powdered; yet could anything more poignantly convey hopeless grief, abject
remorse and the end of life and being?—

> O sovereign mistress of true melancholy, *A. and C.*
> The poisonous damp of night disponge upon me, *4. 9. 12*
> .   .   .   .   .   . throw my heart
> Against the flint and hardness of my fault;
> Which, being dried with grief, will break to powder,
> And finish all foul thoughts.

So also, as we watch Falstaff, can we not *feel* him manipulating the wax till he gets it to precisely the right
degree of softness, when he remarks complacently of
Shallow, 'I have him already tempering between my *2 H. IV,*
finger and my thumb, and shortly will I seal with him'? *4. 3. 136*
And is not Angus's satisfaction that Macbeth is reaping
the reward of his deeds expressed in what is surely one
of the most terrible and haunting pictures in a play
already replete with them, terrible, because of the substance *suggested by its texture*, but not named?—

> Now does he feel *Mac. 5. 2. 16*
> His secret murders sticking on his hands.

As regards taste, there is constant evidence, throughout TASTE
the images, of Shakespeare's delicate and discriminating
palate, especially when compared with his contemporaries
and their stock images of banquets, surfeits, a cloyed or
sharpened appetite, the taste of honey and spice. Shakespeare betrays again and again his appreciation of the
value of flavouring and the necessity of seasoning. 'There
were no sallets (nothing piquant) in the lines to make
the matter savoury', says Hamlet to the players, when describing—entirely in terms of food and taste—the speech *Ham.*
he remembers having heard one of them make, and *2. 2. 452–68*
the impression it left on him and others; 'it pleased not

the million; 'twas caviare to the general.' Lady Macbeth puts the palate's need for salt in food on the same plane as the body's need for sleep, when she tells her lord,

Mac. 3. 5. 141
> You lack the season of all natures, sleep,

and Pandarus does not hesitate to put seasoning in its relation to food on a level with all the finer qualities inherited or acquired in relation to a man's personality.

T. and C.
1. 2. 262
'Have you any discretion? Have you any eyes?' he cries to Cressid, when she suggests that Achilles is a better man than Troilus; 'Is not birth, beauty, good shape, discourse, manhood, learning, gentleness, virtue, youth, liberality, and such like, the spice and salt that season a man?' And Bassanio goes so far as to ask,

M. of V.
3. 2. 75
> In law, what plea so tainted and corrupt,
> But, being season'd with a gracious voice,
> Obscures the show of evil?

revealing not only how susceptible he, like his creator, is to soft and gentle diction, but also what value he attaches to seasoning and its effect on the attractiveness, and indeed on the essential goodness of food.

Shakespeare is especially sensitive to the feeling of revolt and the dulling of the palate on eating too much of any one thing, however good:

R. and J.
2. 6. 11
>   the sweetest honey
> Is loathsome in his own deliciousness,
> And in the taste confounds the appetite.

He is also obviously conscious of the softening, balancing and complementary effect of suitable sauces or condiments on food, and does not hesitate to compare this to things of highest import:

M. of V.
4. 1. 196
> And earthly power doth then show likest God's
> When mercy seasons justice,

says Portia, ending her great speech.

Shakespeare's own tastes in food, and the developments and change in these, are examined later (pp. 117–24). It is interesting to note that, just as with smell, his strongest feeling is reserved, not for sweet scents and fragrance, but for evil smells, which arouse in him a shudder of antipathy; so in this matter of taste, it is the loathsomeness of greasy, dirty, ill-cooked or ill-served food, and the intense feeling of repulsion which it arouses in him of which we are more conscious than we are of his undoubted appreciation of what is delicate and good. This is probably because he had had, on the whole, more opportunity of experiencing the one than the other.

CHAPTER VI

SHAKESPEARE'S TASTES
AND INTERESTS

(i) OUTDOOR LIFE

WE have already (in Chapter III) looked generally at the subject-matter of Shakespeare's images. From that survey it is clear what his main interests are. It would be wearisome to go into each of these at length, but I will now give a few examples of the way in which the facts can be worked out in detail.

We saw that one interest, above all others, stands out in Shakespeare's imagery. This is the life of the country-side and its varying aspects: the winds, the weather and seasons, the sky and clouds, birds and animals. One occupation, one point of view, above all others, is naturally his, that of a gardener; watching, preserving, tending and caring for growing things, especially flowers and fruit. All through his plays he thinks most easily and readily of human life and action in the terms of a gardener. This tendency to think of matters human as of growing plants and trees expresses itself in fullest detail in the central gardening scene in *Richard II* (3. 4), but it is ever present in Shakespeare's thought and imagination, so that nearly all his characters share in it. Thus, when Albemarle, in anger, sums up Goneril's deficiencies and inhumanity in character and action, he naturally sees her as the branch of a tree, and says,

K.L. 4. 2. 34
She that herself will sliver and disbranch
From her material sap, perforce must wither
And come to deadly use.

So also Malcolm cries,

> Macbeth
> Is ripe for shaking,

Mac. 4. 3. 237

and Juliet, when bidding Romeo good night, hopes that

> This bud of love, by summer's ripening breath,
> May prove a beauteous flower when next we meet.

R. and J.
2. 2. 121

In moments of stress and emotion this tendency of Shakespeare's mind is very marked, and he betrays how constantly he visualises human beings as the trees and plants he loved so well in orchard or garden. Thus the most moving moment in *Cymbeline* is when Imogen, at the end, throws herself into the arms of Posthumus, and he, looking down at her, mutters,

> Hang there like fruit, my soul,
> Till the tree die!

Cym. 5. 5. 263

The exclamations of Othello, in two supreme moments of agony, are equally characteristic. First, when finally persuaded of Desdemona's guilt, he cries out to her,

> O thou weed,
> Who art so lovely fair and smell'st so sweet
> That the sense aches at thee, would thou hadst ne'er
> been born!

Oth. 4. 2. 67

and then later, when gazing at her in bed, asleep, he soliloquises:

> When I have pluck'd the rose,
> I cannot give it vital growth again,
> It must needs wither: I'll smell it on the tree.

5. 2. 13

Shakespeare is particularly interested in the processes of growth and decay, and, as he expresses it in the fifteenth sonnet ('When I consider everything that grows'), in the likeness between men and plants in coming painfully and with many struggles and checks to perfection, to stay there but for a moment and then begin to decay.

He is repeatedly impressed, as all gardeners must be, by the vitality and strength of seeds, especially of weeds, and their power, if unchecked, of overgrowing and killing all else, and he is continually conscious of a similar strength and power in the weeds and faults in human character, so that when describing the pride of Achilles, the following language is natural to him:

T. and C.
1. 3. 316

>   the seeded pride
> That hath to this maturity blown up
> In rank Achilles must or now be cropp'd
> Or, shedding, breed a nursery of like evil,
> To overbulk us all.

He has a great number of images drawn from grafting —a new process in his time—and was clearly immensely interested in its possibilities and results, being led to wonder, with Polixenes (*W.T.* 4. 4. 79–97), if such marvels of control and improvement may be achieved by scientific cross-breeding in plants and flowers, why not also in the human race?

Like all English gardeners, too, he is keenly conscious of the disastrous effects of spring winds and frosts on tender buds and flowers. To quote many instances of this would seem superfluous, for such images are among his best-known lines, for example:

Son. XVIII

Rough winds do shake the darling buds of May,

and

T. of Sh.
5. 2. 140

Confounds thy fame as whirlwinds shake fair buds.

L.L.L. 1.1.100

Biron is like an envious sneaping frost,
That bites the first-born infants of the spring,

and on Juliet, death lies

> like an untimely frost
> Upon the sweetest flower of all the field.

R. and J.
4. 5. 2

Diseases in plants too—especially canker in roses—he sees with the gardener's eye, and resents their destruction of beauty. In his imagination the disease is continually affecting and damaging the plant exactly as evil passions or repressions destroy the human being. Jealousy is the 'canker that eats up Love's tender spring',

V. and A. 656

Gloucester bids his duchess to

> Banish the canker of ambitious thoughts,

2 H. VI,
1. 2. 18

Prospero describes Ferdinand as

> something stain'd
> With grief, that's beauty's canker,

Temp. 1. 2. 415

and Viola lets

> concealment, like a worm i' the bud,
> Feed on her damask cheek.

Tw. N.
2. 4. 113

The hopes and despairs of the gardener are expounded in detail by Lord Bardolph, when he is being pressed to say whether the rebels' side is strong enough to have hope of success. He is very cautious, and points out in a gardener's simile how misleading even good grounds for hope may be:

> Indeed the instant action—a cause on foot—
> Lives so in hope as in an early spring,
> We see the appearing buds; which to prove fruit,
> Hope gives not so much warrant as despair
> That frost will bite them.

2 H. IV,
1. 3. 37

It might be argued that these gardening similes are of common Elizabethan stock, and it is true that certain ones—ripe fruit being shaken from the tree, thorns in a rose, the sticking qualities of burs, and grafting—are

common to, and some of them are favourites with, other
Elizabethan dramatists. One may therefore discount
the peculiar and personal significance of some of these
of Shakespeare's. On the other hand, nothing more
brings out his close and loving knowledge of growing
things than a comparison of his gardening images with
those of his contemporaries.

In the first place he has a great many more—propor-
tionally—than they; the idea or conception is more
constant with him; and secondly, he shows much closer
knowledge of the growth and care of plants. I find
practically no sign of first-hand gardening knowledge or
observation in the images of the other writers, nothing
of the type of the constable's rebuke to the Dauphin,
telling him Henry V is not the hare-brained, shallow
youth he takes him for, but a very great king

> terrible in constant resolution,

and these vanities and humours which he notices are

H. V, *2. 4. 37*
> but the outside of the Roman Brutus,
> Covering discretion with a coat of folly;
> As gardeners do with ordure hide those roots
> That shall first spring and be most delicate.

The similes of the other dramatists are chiefly of the
most obvious kind: 'rooting', 'planting', 'cutting',
'sowing', 'springing up', 'weeding', 'lopping', 'pruning', with sometimes a display of real ignorance, as in
this of Beaumont and Fletcher's:

Valentinian,
5. 6
> In whom thou wert set
> As roses are in rank weeds.

Roses are not in the habit of growing in the midst of
rank weeds.

The one exception to this very general and super-

ficial use of gardening similes without real knowledge is
Bacon, who really cared about a garden, and was particularly interested in the question of soil; so we find
him writing that philosophy as a study is not idle, because all professions are served from it. 'For if you will
have a tree bear more fruit than it hath used to do, it is
not anything you can do to the boughs, but it is the *Adv. of L.* II
stirring of the earth and putting of new mould about
the roots that must work it.' Or again, later, he says,
'Notwithstanding, to stir the earth a little about the
roots of this science...as we have done of the rest...'. *ibid.* II

I do not find, in all my search of the other dramatists,
any single image of frosts and sharp winds nipping buds,
which is so common with Shakespeare, and not a trace
of love or care for the plant, so characteristic of him. The
difference in feeling between Shakespeare and Marlowe
in this respect, for instance, is well exemplified in old
Capulet's ejaculation on seeing Juliet dead, quoted
above:

> Death lies on her like an untimely frost
> Upon the sweetest flower of all the field,

and Don Mathias' description of Abigail becoming a
nun:

> A faire young maid scarce fourteen yeares of age,   *Jew of Malta,*
> The sweetest flower in *Citherea's* field   *621–4*
> Cropt from the pleasures of the fruitfull earth,
> And strangely metamorphis'd Nun!

Another of the chief interests of Shakespeare's mind   THE RIVER
was the river. The man who had spent his boyhood
by the banks of the Avon never forgot its appearance in
fair weather or in foul, in winter or in summer. He has
sauntered by the river in its peaceful mood, when the

Two Gent.
2. 7. 25

Luc. 1667

Cor. 5. 4. 49
current glides 'with gentle murmur', he has leant over Clopton Bridge and watched the 'violent roaring tide' swirling and eddying through its arches, he has seen the river oftentimes in flood, and it is this last aspect of it which, above all others, has impressed itself for ever on his memory.

We know that the Avon was, then as today, often and regularly in flood, both in winter and summer; that, as Leland tells us, Sir Hugh Clopton built his famous bridge at the end of the fifteenth century, because, before his time 'there was but a poor bridge of timber and no causey to it, whereby many poor folks and other refused to come to Stratford when Avon was up; or coming thither, stood in jeopardy of life';[1] that in July 1588, the wet and stormy Armada summer, this comparatively new stone bridge was broken at both ends by flood, imprisoning on the middle portion three men who were in the act of crossing it; and that on this occasion the water 'rose a yard every hour from eight to four'.[2] There can be no question that the flooded river, swollen and raging, overflowing its banks and bearing all before it, was one of the—probably recurrent—sights of boyhood which made the most indelible impression on Shakespeare's imagination.

Three pictures of it in especial he draws in simile again and again: the irresistible force of a river in flood, Oth. 1. 3. 55 which suffers nothing to stop it, but 'engluts and swallows' all it meets, and how this force is increased by R. II, 3. 2. 106 any stoppage or interference; the heavy rain on 'an unseasonable stormy day', which accompanies the flood and aggravates it; and the appearance of the meadows

---

[1] Leland's *Itinerary*, ed. Toulmin Smith, ii. 48.
[2] Memorandum in Welford Register.

after a 'bated and retired flood', rank and 'stain'd... *K.J. 5. 4. 52*
with miry slime'.   *Titus, 3. 1. 125*

I find fifty-nine river images in Shakespeare, and I
include in these seven wading images, which I feel sure
apply to a river, though only four do so as obviously
as Macbeth's:

I am in blood   *Mac. 3. 4. 136*
Stepp'd in so far that, should I wade no more,
Returning were as tedious as go o'er.

Of these fifty-nine, twenty-six are of different aspects of
a river in flood. Eight of these are of the river overflowing its banks, such as:

a proud river peering o'er his bounds,   *K.J. 3. 1. 23*

a gentle flood,   *Luc. 1118*
Who, being stopp'd, the bounding banks o'erflows;

eleven are of the impetus, force and overbearing
nature of a raging flood, when the wild river drowns its *V. and A. 331*
shores and 'swells' with 'rage', and especially of the *R. II, 3. 2. 106*
rending fury of 'interrupted waters', 'vex'd with...im- *K.J. 2. 1. 335*
pediment', which then 'impatiently' do 'rage'

and o'erbear   *Cor. 3. 1. 249*
What they are used to bear.

Five are of general reference to a flood of waters, or a
statement such as 'no flood by raining slaketh', and two *Luc. 1677*
are vivid pictures of the river after flood, withdrawn into *K.J. 5. 4. 52*
its banks again, leaving behind its mark on the meadows *Titus, 3. 1. 125*
it has submerged.

His interest in the image is largely psychological, for
he sees in this picture of a river overbearing its boun-
daries a perfect analogy to the result of stress or rush
of emotion in men, as when Brabantio, distraught on

hearing Desdemona has left him for Othello, cries to the
duke,

Oth. 1. 3. 55

> my particular grief
> Is of so flood-gate and o'erbearing nature
> That it engluts and swallows other sorrows,
> And it is still itself.

This is therefore one of Shakespeare's most characteristic
similes, and he uses it no less than nineteen times, on
five of which it is definitely likened to rebellion or in-
subordination, as when Scroop, speaking of the uprising
of Bolingbroke, compares the state of things to

R. II, 3. 2. 106

> an unseasonable stormy day,
> Which makes the silver rivers drown their shores,
> As if the world were all dissolved to tears,
> So high above his limits swells the rage
> Of Bolingbroke.

This large number of river similes is unusual in other
Elizabethan dramatists, and this marked interest in a
river in flood is quite peculiar to Shakespeare. The river
images of Peele, Greene, Heywood and Kyd are few and
negligible ('streams', 'spring', 'torrent', etc.). Lyly (in
two plays) has none, and Marlowe, characteristically, has
only images of the ocean and no river images throughout his work. Dekker, though a fisherman, and a maker
of vivid pictures, has only a few most perfunctory and
general river images, a current or river frozen up (three
times in two plays), 'crystal banks', 'golden current'
and so on. Massinger's are equally general and colour-
less: 'torrents', 'crystal rivers' flowing into one another,
a rivulet, a brook flowing into a river, 'a silent stream
shaded with night and gliding softly'.

Ben Jonson's are more numerous (seventeen in five
plays), but, with one exception (a curious simile, apparently of the city's sewage running into the Thames

and infecting the purity of its 'silver' waters, in the Epilogue to *Every Man out of his Humour*), they are of the slightest and most general nature, showing no sign of direct observation. Thus we find a current, a torrent that carries all before it, a stream—'to be carried to and fro, with the stream of her humour'—a river running into the 'boundless ocean', and 'a pure and sprightly river', *E.M.O.H.H. 2. 1* *ibid. 4. 2* *E.M.I.H.H. 5. 1*

> That moves for ever, and yet still the same. *E.M.O.H.H. 2. 2*

Beaumont and Fletcher, among a number of ordinary river images—'a purling stream', 'torrents', and so on —have three rather remarkable images of a river in flood, clearly taken from direct observation. One is of a rotten bridge which cracks in a current 'when he is swelled and high', one of a torrent, fed by the 'moist south', drowning 'the ripe corn and weeds', and one of a 'wild overflow', carrying with it 'a golden stack', shaking down bridges, cracking strong-rooted pines, taking whole villages on its back, and laying desolate *Valentinian, 5. 4* *Faithful Shepherdess, 3. 8*

> Strong towns, towers, castles, palaces. *Philaster, 5. 3*

Of this group of writers, outside Shakespeare, Chapman's river images are much the fullest and most interesting. But they give entirely different pictures from those Shakespeare draws. Chapman writes of the winding course of 'a subtle river' twisting about in open flat country, gliding 'slyly by', the 'little rivers' drinking up the brooks as they run to the ocean, the 'shallow streams' *Byron's Consp. 3. 1; 1. 1*

> That make themselves so many heavens to the sight, *ibid. 5. 1*

the streams

> that run below the valleys and do yield
> To every molehill, *Byron's Trag. 5. 1*

but when torrents come, are swollen, mad and troubled, and the

Byron's Consp.
2. 1

> black torrent, that bears all things down,
> His fury overtakes, his foamy back,
> Loaded with cattle and with stacks of corn.

All these pictures are vivid, and some are beautiful, but Shakespeare draws nothing like them. He has not been struck by the damage done by a river in flood, breaking bridges, uprooting trees, and carrying along in its torrent stacks and cattle; nor by rivers, as they wind to the sea, being fed and swollen by tributary brooks, nor by the exquisite reflection of the sky in a clear shallow stream, but he is interested almost exclusively in the *life* of the current itself, its course and movement, how violently, and like a living thing, it resents impediment, 'chafes' and is 'provoked', swells, rages, overflows its bounds, drowns its shores and floods the neighbouring meadows. That is a kind of composite summary of his chief picture, and in none of the other dramatists do we find these particular points emphasised.

I feel as sure as I can be of anything that these many pictures drawn by Shakespeare of the movement and behaviour of a river in flood are all boyhood memories of the Avon at Stratford. This, I believe, is peculiarly true when he compares the movement of the waters to the emotions and passions of men.

I had an interesting confirmation of this belief on one visit to Stratford recently, when I made the acquaintance of Captain William Jaggard, the owner of the old print and book shop in Sheep Street, and descendant of the William Jaggard, who, in 1599 and 1612, printed and published the *Passionate Pilgrim*, and from whose press, in 1623, the 'First Folio' was issued.

I was telling Captain Jaggard that I was very anxious
to see the river in flood, and particularly to stand on old
Clopton Bridge and watch the movement of the current,
as Shakespeare often referred to it. 'Oh yes!' he said,
'and you should stand on the eighteenth arch[1] of the
bridge (the one nearest the London side), for when the
river is in flood, the force of the current under the
adjoining arches, combined with the curved shape of
the bank on to which it is driven, produces the most
curious effect. I have often stood there and watched the
current being forced beneath the narrow Tudor arch,
on to the right bank at an angle which produces a
swirling eddy, so that the water is then forced back
through the arch equally swiftly and in an exactly contrary direction to that in which it has just come.' 'I
have', he added, 'sometimes hardly been able to believe
my eyes when I have seen sticks or straws, which
I have just noticed swirled on the flood downward
through the arch, being brought back again just as
swiftly in the opposite direction and against the flood
weight.'

Captain Jaggard, as he said this, was at the further
end of his shop, searching among its piled-up masses of
books and papers for some prints he wanted to show me,
and his voice, coming thus somewhat muffled from the
distance, gave me the most curious thrill and start, as if
it were a voice from the dead.

For here was a present-day Stratfordian describing
to me in prose, in minute detail, exactly what a Stratford

---

[1] Sir Hugh Clopton's stone bridge, built about 1490, consists of
eighteen arches, of which today only fourteen are visible, because four
of them sustain the approach-road from the town, originally swamp and
bog, and are completely hidden from sight, beneath the causeway.

man had thus set down in verse nearly three hundred and fifty years ago.

Luc. *1667–73*

As through an arch the violent roaring tide
Outruns the eye that doth behold his haste,
Yet in the eddy boundeth in his pride
Back to the strait that forced him on so fast,
In rage sent out, recall'd in rage, being past:
    Even so his sighs, his sorrows, make a saw,
    To push grief on and back the same grief draw.

I at once called out to Captain Jaggard asking him to write down what he had just said, which he kindly did, and I then said, 'Can you find me a copy of Shakespeare's Poems?' and he laughingly answered, 'I think perhaps I can', and returned to me bringing back a volume along with him. I turned up the above quotation and showed it to him. He had not previously noticed it and was extremely interested.

Later, I went down myself to the river bank and stood looking under the eighteenth arch. The river that day was perfectly calm and smooth, but, even so, on watching closely, I could easily follow the characteristic movement of the current, even though it was slow and gentle. There happened to be a big tuft of grass on it which sailed under the arch at an acute angle straight on to the bank, as in the sketch (frontispiece), then swirled round in an eddy, and proceeded to return under the arch in the direction whence it had just come. There is a sort of little hook or bend in the bank just below where the current strikes it after coming under the arch, which produces the eddy and helps to send the water back again (see sketch). Just because, when I saw it, it was quite gentle, this unusual and unnatural movement of the water was perhaps more curious and marked than it would have been in furious flood. But there was no question that here was the very spot where Shakespeare must often have stood as a boy, and this was the very phenomenon he had noticed and described with such meticulous accuracy. Years ago, before I knew Shakespeare's ways as well as I do now, I had—rather carelessly—always thought this image probably referred to the current under one of the arches of old London Bridge, which, we read, was very swift, so that at times it was quite a feat to shoot through it in a boat; but closer knowledge of his habits and methods convinced me that Stratford was the place to seek for the original of it, with the result just described.

As regards river sports, such as swimming and fishing, he was clearly, in boyhood at any rate, a keen and strong swimmer, and had probably, with schoolfellows, often plunged and buffeted in the angry waters of the Avon, as did Cassius once with Caesar in the Tiber. Only one who was himself an experienced swimmer could have written,

> Doubtful it stood;   *Mac. 1. 2. 7*
> As two spent swimmers, that do cling together
> And choke their art;

or

> Like an unpractised swimmer plunging still   *Luc. 1098*
> With too much labour drowns for want of skill,

to select two only out of his varied swimming similes. His many vivid images from wading, diving, plunging, and his pictures of reeds and river weeds moving with the stream or falling below a boat, must surely also be the result of personal experience and observation.

But, although he was fond of the river and of river sports, he was no fisherman, and seems to have had little real knowledge of the art. I find twenty-four fishing images in Shakespeare[1]—that is, little more than half the number of the falconry or bird-snaring ones, and considerably less than those drawn from either hunting or archery. Of these twenty-four, seven are a simple metaphorical use of the word 'angle', such as

1 H. IV,
4. 3. 83

                            did he win
     The hearts of all that he did angle for;

and eight are an equally obvious use of the word 'bait'. There is no evidence in any of them of a knowledge of fly-fishing. For the rest, he alludes to trout being

2 H. IV,
3. 2. 350

groped for or taken by tickling, to the 'young dace' being 'a bait for the old pike', to the easily deluded

M. of V.
1. 1. 102

'fool-gudgeon', to the wary nature of the carp,

Ham. 2. 1. 63

     Your bait of falsehood takes this carp of truth,

and the only metaphorical allusion which seems to indicate personal experience in handling a rod, is when Leontes, having sent Hermione and Polixenes out into the garden alone, remarks,

W. T. 1. 2. 180

                       I am angling now,
   Though you perceive not how I give line.

When we realise how vivid and particular are Shakespeare's images drawn from the things he knows well, we may safely assume therefore that he had little personal knowledge of or interest in the sport of fishing.

    Perhaps the fact that he specially delighted in swift nimble movement, and that, although acutely observant, he was not of a meditative nature, may partly explain his lack of interest in fishing.

    Next to the river, the most constant outdoor back-

---

[1] Twenty-five, if we include the rather obscure one in *Macbeth*, 1. 7. 1–7, which is primarily of a fisherman handling a net or 'trammel' on the edge of a pool.

ground in Shakespeare's mind is hunting of various kinds. As regards the popular sport of deer hunting, I do not believe he cared for it. His *knowledge* of it needs no demonstration from me. It has already been proven in fullest detail by Madden (to name one book only) in his well-known *Diary of Master William Silence*. Shakespeare's images are alive with technical and sporting terms, culled, not from books, but from personal and accurate observation, and there is constant reference to and description of the sport throughout his plays. In the forest of Arden the wounded stag seeks the brook, in the King of Navarre's park the princess takes careful aim—to kill and not to wound—in the northern English forest the keepers with crossbows discuss coverts and the best way to shoot, and the 'musical discord' of hounds and horn re-echoes through the wood outside Athens as in the forest near Rome. And in most of these descriptions and references, put into the mouths of others, we get strongly the feeling of the zest and joy of the chase, which has led Shakespeare's commentators to assume that he himself loved it. But— and herein lies the whole point of these investigations —if we look at his *images* only, we get an entirely different picture. We get the picture of an extremely sensitive man, whose sympathy is scarcely ever with the hunters, but consistently and obviously on the side of the hunted or stricken animal (as in 1 *H. VI*, 4. 2. 45; *J.C.* 3, 1. 204–10), and we are ever conscious, if we group these similes together, not of the joyous abandon of the sportsman, but of the 'fell and cruel hounds' pursuing the 'moody-mad and desperate' stag, 'hunted even to falling'. So much is this the case, that out of thirty-nine hunting images, I only once find the hunt

Tw.N.
1. 1. 22
1 *H.VI*,
4. 2. 50
A. and C.
4. 1. 7

pictured as a gay and joyous pastime, and described from the point of view of the sportsman. This one time is when the image is used quite deliberately by the English herald to hearten the citizens of Angiers and to encourage them to open their gates to John and his victorious army. He tells them that

K.J. 2. 1. 321

> like a jolly troop of huntsmen come
> Our lusty English, all with purpled hands,
> Dyed in the dying slaughter of their foes.

But this image, in tone and attitude, stands alone in Shakespeare's work. From his hunting images generally, we gather that he clearly had often seen a deer hunt, and had enjoyed the clamorous echo of hounds and horn, but that although he knew all about driving the deer into nets ('into a toil'), and shooting them with a crossbow, he had probably not much experience of hunting deer with hounds only. He had certainly seen the stag at bay, surrounded by the yelping dogs, stained with the blood of their prey, but he himself shows little enthusiasm for the sport.

What he did like was to watch the deer, unseen by them, in their native forest, and he must often, in the woodlands of the Warwickshire Arden, have seen them

All's Well, 1. 3. 57
L.L.L. 5. 2. 309
V. and A. 236
A.Y.L.I. 2. 7. 128

'jouling' horns together, running swiftly 'o'er the land', or grazing on 'sweet bottom grass'. He had watched the mother deer going to find her young and give it food, the 'milch doe'

V. and A. 876

> Hasting to feed her fawn hid in some brake,

and he had seen and felt with

Luc. 1149

> the poor frighted deer, that stands at gaze,
> Wildly determining which way to fly,

V. and A. 561
Titus, 3. 1. 88

the 'fleet-foot roe that's tired with chasing', and the deer mortally wounded, 'straying in the park, seeking to hide

herself'. He was well versed in woodcraft, and being a
true woodman, would have scorned to 'bend his bow'   *Luc. 580*

    To strike a poor unseasonable doe;

he knew about the 'unruly deer' that   *C. of E.*
                                                2. 1. 100

                  breaks the pale,
    And feeds from home,

he could sum up the qualities of the 'rascal' or worth-   *1 H. VI,*
                                                4. 2. 49
less deer, he knew the ways of the 'hound that runs   *Cor. 1. 1. 162*
counter and yet draws dry-foot well', and the fact that   *C. of E. 4. 2. 39*

                                 coward dogs   *H. V, 2. 4. 69*
    Most spend their mouths when what they seem
        to threaten
    Runs far before them.

Indeed, he liked watching the dogs almost as much as
watching the deer, and knew all about their skill and
shortcomings, on a hot or cold scent 'keeping' or 're-   *Tw.N.*
                                                2. 5. 124
covering' the wind, crying on a 'false trail' or, in their   *3 H. VI,*
                                                3. 2. 14
eagerness, outpacing the other dogs and having to be   *Ham. 3. 2. 353;*
                                                4. 5. 109
restrained, to be 'trashed for over-topping'.   *Oth. 2. 1. 311*
                                                Temp. 1. 2. 80

    These are the kinds of images he lets fall by the way as
it were, in considerable numbers (twenty-one of the
deer,[1] fifteen of the dogs), and by far the larger number
of what may be grouped under his hunting and woodcraft similes are concerned with the habits and be-

---

[1] It is worth noting that, with one exception—the comparison of
Antony to the stag who, in snow, browses on the barks of trees (the diet
of the barks of trees is taken from North's *Plutarch*, but Shakespeare adds
the stag simile, *A. and C.* 1. 4. 65)—all the images of the habits of deer
come in the early plays (and the two poems), *As You Like It* (1599)
being the latest play in which one of them occurs. The hounds and
hunting similes, on the other hand, occur chiefly in the later plays. I can
suggest no explanation for this, because although the knowledge of deer
was doubtless gained in boyhood, almost certainly that of dogs and
hunting was also, and in any case, Shakespeare never forgets his early
impressions.

haviour of the deer and the eager skill of the questing
hounds, rather than with the actual chase. His comparatively few images of the chase or the kill are introduced, so it seems to me, more consciously and in more
rhetorical form. Such are Antony's apostrophe of the
murdered Caesar,

J.C. 3. 1. 204

> Here wast thou bay'd, brave hart;
> Here didst thou fall, and here thy hunters stand,
> Sign'd in thy spoil and crimson'd in thy lethe;

and Talbot's description of his soldiers as

*1 H. VI,
4. 2. 46*

> A little herd of England's timorous deer,
> Mazed with a yelping kennel of French curs!

whom he adjures to

> Turn on the bloody hounds with heads of steel
> And make the cowards stand aloof at bay.

He was certainly a good shot, and very possibly he may
himself as a boy, with his crossbow, have

Titus, 2. 1. 93

> full often struck a doe,
> And borne her cleanly by the keeper's nose,

keenly enjoying the latter part of it at any rate; but it is
hard to believe that anyone who so clearly shrank from
L.L.L. wounding an animal ('not wounding, pity would not let
4. 1. 27 me do't'), and so hated to think of their sufferings, could
greatly have enjoyed the chase.

I should imagine from his images that he knew personally much more about the Cotswold sport of coursing
and of hunting the hare generally than he did of deer
hunting (as apart from his knowledge of deer, hounds
and woodcraft). The well-known description in *Venus
and Adonis* (673–708) of the hunted hare doubling and
crossing to put the hounds off his scent is sufficient to
prove that he knew all about it; but here again it is

noticeable that the intensity of his feeling is for the victim, rather than for the fun of the chase. He has many images from the hare, its timidity and quick movement; he gives us a picture of

> a brace of greyhounds
> Having the fearful flying hare in sight—

3 H. VI,
2. 5. 129

but in only one image do we find conveyed a feeling of enjoyment in the sport, and that is when Scarus, thinking the enemy are beaten, cries, like a boy, to Antony,

> Let us score their backs
> And snatch 'em up, as we take hares, behind:
> 'Tis sport to maul a runner.

A. and C.
4. 7. 12

Another boyhood sport which has made a profound impression on him is the trapping and snaring of birds. His bird images are remarkable for the intense feeling and sympathy they reveal for the trapped, limed or snared bird, which to him symbolises the greatest pitch of terror and agony mortal creature may endure. So Claudius, at his prayers, realising that he is so hopelessly besmirched and involved in the results of his crime, that he dare not even pray for forgiveness, cries,

> O wretched state! O bosom black as death!
> O limed soul, that struggling to be free
> Art more engaged!

Ham. 3. 3. 67

So, in the most moving scene in *Macbeth*, when Lady Macduff and her little son realise the imminence of their danger, she compares her boy to a poor bird in peril of 'the net', 'the lime', 'the pitfall' or 'the gin'. So Othello, when at the end, in an agony he realises how he has been

Mac. 4. 2. 34

duped, uses the same metaphor to express Iago's treatment of him, and asks Cassio to

Oth. 5. 2. 302
> demand that demi-devil
> Why he hath thus ensnared my soul and body?

So also Lucrece, escaped from Tarquin's brutality,

Luc. 456
> Wrapp'd and confounded in a thousand fears,
> Like to a new-kill'd bird she trembling lies.

Of this sympathy with the trapped bird I find not a
trace in other Elizabethan writers, nor indeed do I find
the image itself at all, except in Marlowe, who, somewhat perfunctorily, thus describes Hero in Leander's
arms,

H. and L.
2. 289
> Even as a bird, which in our hands we wring,
> Forth plungeth, and oft flutters with her wing,
> She trembling strove.

How different this from the passionate feeling of
sympathy for the bird which we sense in

3 H. VI,
5. 6. 13
> The bird that hath been limed in a bush,
> With trembling wings misdoubteth every bush,

or the horror of the sense of the limed twigs in the death
scene of Beaufort, as he remembers the murders of
Gloucester,

2 H. VI,
3. 3. 14
> He hath no eyes, the dust hath blinded them.
> Comb down his hair; look, look! it stands upright,
> Like lime-twigs set to catch my winged soul.

In short, Shakespeare's intense sympathy with the
feelings of animals is illustrated again and again in his
similes, and most especially his feeling for and love of
birds, and his horror of their sufferings when limed or
snared. But this sympathy is more remarkable if we
choose something less obviously appealing than the
snared or netted bird, and look at what he says about

snails, and how much it reveals of that outstanding quality of his, the capacity to enter into the being and feeling of other creatures.

He concentrates on the qualities and characteristics of the snail so unerringly that, as Keats says in commenting on it, 'he has left nothing to say about nothing or anything'.

Most people, asked suddenly to name the outstanding quality of the snail, would answer 'its slow pace'. Not so Shakespeare, who assigns that second place only. The snail seems to him an example of one of the most delicately sensitive organisms in nature; it is 'love's feeling' only that

> is more soft and sensible   *L.L.L. 4. 3. 336*
> Than are the tender horns of cockled snails.

The marvellously sensitive simile in *Venus and Adonis*, describing this peculiarity, also incidentally reveals the poet's acute appreciation of the point of view of the other person, when he describes the feelings of the

> snail, whose tender horns being hit,   *V. and A. 1033*
> Shrinks backward in his shelly cave with pain,
> And there all smother'd up in shade doth sit,
> Long after fearing to creep forth again.

Notice how he emphasises the greater poignancy of mental than physical pain, even in a snail, and remember how appositely he applies the same sensation and action years afterwards when describing Aufidius,

> Who, hearing of our Marcius' banishment,   *Cor. 4. 6. 43*
> Thrusts forth his horns again into the world;
> Which were inshell'd when Marcius stood for Rome,
> And durst not once peep out.

Had we nothing but these three similes to guide us, we should realise that the author of them had the most exquisitely sensitive apprehension of the feelings of others, not only of men but of the humblest animals. As we know, because he himself tells us so, that Keats took part in the existence of a sparrow when it came and picked in the gravel before his window, so surely do we know, because Shakespeare tells us so in another way, that he took part in the existence of the snail and its feelings when he inadvertently touched it on the garden path.

Shakespeare's love of the horse and of riding must not pass unnoticed. Here again he differs from his contemporaries, who, although they draw images from horses and riding, show none of the tender intimate knowledge of the horse and its feelings, or of the close sympathy between horse and rider which Shakespeare does. They are more concerned with the characters of different kinds of horses, an old mare, a stallion, a wanton jennet, a lusty courser, a footcloth nag, a traveller's hackney, mill-horses, young colts; and the use of the rein, bridle, spur and bit. We never with them meet with little touches of love and sympathy such as these two Shakespearian images convey:

M.N.D. 3. 1. 98 As true as truest horse, that yet would never tire;

T. and C. Or, like a gallant horse fall'n in first rank,
3. 3. 161 Lie there for pavement to the abject rear;
O'er-run and trampled on.

No one of his contemporaries could have written the carriers' talk in the Rochester inn yard, with their complaints about the bad quality of Cut's food, and their thought of softening and padding her saddle, to make *1 H. IV, 2. 1. 5* it more comfortable for the 'poor jade...wrung in the withers out of all cess'.

Shakespeare thinks of the tired horse and its uncom-
plaining endurance, 'though patience be a tired mare, *H. V*, 2. 1. 24
yet she will plod', and he alone, of all writers of his time,
so far as I have read, seems aware of the cruelty and folly
of undue use of the spur—'how fondly [foolishly] dost *R. II*, 4. 1. 72
thou spur a forward horse', cries the eager Fitzwater to
Surrey, who is goading him to trial by combat; and in
A Winter's Tale he notes how much better is kindly
persuasion than castigation,

W.T. 1. 2. 94

> you may ride 's
> With one soft kiss a thousand furlongs ere
> With spur we heat an acre.

As regards other outdoor activities, in common with
most Elizabethan writers, Shakespeare shows a knowledge of archery and has many images from it, not
general ones only about taking aim, and hitting with
Cupid's arrow, but little pictures which have a ring of
personal experience, such as Bassanio's acceptance of
Antonio's offers of help in the opening scene of the
Merchant of Venice (1. 1. 141):

> In my school days, when I had lost one shaft,
> I shot his fellow of the self-same flight
> The self-same way with more advised watch,
> To find the other forth; and by adventuring both,
> I oft found both.

So, he adds in effect, 'I owe you much', and 'that which
I owe is lost', but if you please to shoot another arrow
the same way you sent the first, I believe if I watch the
aim carefully, I will either find both,

> Or bring your latter hazard back again.

In other words, Bassanio would have Antonio believe
this to be one of the few occasions when it is worth
while sending good money after bad.

From bear-baiting, too, Shakespeare draws a number of pictures; this, curiously enough, is unusual among the Elizabethan dramatists; indeed, in my search I have not found a single bear-baiting image except in Shakespeare. His most vivid and effective use of it is in Macbeth's despairing cry at the end:

Mac. 5. 7. 1　　They have tied me to a stake; I cannot fly,
　　　　　　　But bear-like I must fight the course.

Gloucester, when hard driven, caught, bound and baited, just before his eyes are put out, has the same feeling of helplessness, and when pressed as to why he has sent Lear to Dover, answers:

K.L. 3. 7. 54　　I am tied to the stake, and I must stand the course.

There is a fuller account of the sport in the vivid little picture Richard Crookback draws of his father York, surrounded by his enemies:

3 H. VI, 2. 1. 13　　Methought he bore him in the thickest troop
　　　　　　　. . .as a bear, encompassed round with dogs,
　　　　　　　Who having pinch'd a few and made them cry,
　　　　　　　The rest stand all aloof and bark at him.

It is noticeable that in every one of Shakespeare's bear-baiting similes, his sympathy is wholly on the side of the bear, and he accentuates his bravery and the horror of his position.

Of all the games and exercises Shakespeare mentions —tennis, football, bowls, fencing, tilting, wrestling— there can be no doubt that bowls was the one he himself played and loved best. He has nineteen images from bowls (besides other references, such as *Cym.* 2. 1. 1–8; 50–1), or more than thrice as many as from any other game, and these all show close knowledge of the game and of the peculiar run of the bowl. Although we know the game of bowls was popular in Shakespeare's day (see Gosson's complaint in his *School of Abuse*, 1579, and Stowe's in his *Survey*), yet this image cannot be classed as a commonplace of Elizabethan writers. For in an examination of the work of eleven other dramatists, forty-nine plays in all, we find, if we except Dekker,[1] only one image from bowls, and that is in Ben Jonson,[2] and reveals no particular knowledge of the game. So that Shakespeare's interest in it is unusual, and is a personal characteristic.

His images include the long metaphorical soliloquy in which the world is thought of as a bowl and Commodity as the bias, an image suggested to Richard II's queen 'to drive away the heavy thought of care', three rather difficult and strained images in *Troilus and Cressida* (1. 3. 13; 4. 5. 8–9; 168–70), apt and discriminating ones like Petruchio's comment on Katharine's improved temper,

K.J.
2. 1. 574–86

R. II,
3. 4. 1–5

> Well, forward! forward! thus the bowl should run,
> And not unluckily against the bias,

T. of Sh.
4. 5. 24

or Menenius' description of his tendency, in his zeal, to over-praise Coriolanus,

> Like to a bowl upon a subtle ground,
> I have tumbled past the throw,

Cor. 5. 2. 20

and oft-quoted ones, such as that on the title-page of this book (*Ham.* 2. 1. 64), Gloucester's summary of Lear's state, 'the king falls from bias of nature', or Hamlet's well-known ejaculation, 'Ay, there's the rub'.

K.L. 1. 2. 119

Ham. 3. 1. 65

---

[1] Dekker, like Shakespeare, is clearly a player of bowls, and draws five images from them in three plays.

[2] The image is in *Every Man in His Humour*, 3. 2, where the rustic compares Sordido's tears when they 'trilled' to 'master Vicar's bowls upon the green'.

CHAPTER VII

SHAKESPEARE'S TASTES AND INTERESTS

(ii) INDOOR AND OTHER INTERESTS

SHAKESPEARE'S images from indoor life, which are very numerous, reflect in the most marked and interesting way the life and activities in a simple, or as we might say today, a farm-house kitchen, where we would surmise, when indoors, he spent a good part of his boyhood. Nothing there has passed unobserved, and some things which entail unpleasantness, especially to the sense of smell, are very vividly remembered.

Among these a 'stopped oven' is especially noticeable, and the fierce burning, smoke and cinders which ensue. It is the same quality in it as in the overflowing and dammed up river which attracts him, that is, the life in it, and the likeness of fire to human passions, which, when suppressed, become more fierce and unruly.

V. and A. 331
> An oven that is stopp'd...
> Burneth more hotly...
> So of concealed sorrow may be said;
> Free vent of words love's fire doth assuage.

Titus, 2. 4. 36
> Sorrow concealed, like an oven stopped,
> Doth burn the heart to cinders where it is.

The smoking, ill-burning lamp, short of oil, dry of wick, and consequently evil smelling, the short length of candle, going out when most wanted, are other household inconveniences which have left a deep impression on Shakespeare.

It might be thought that the ill-ventilated fire, the guttering candle, and oil-dried lamp form a common stock of material for Elizabethan imagery. This, however, is not so, for in a search of my other twelve dramatists I do not once find an allusion to a 'stopped oven' or a badly burning lamp. Ben Jonson speaks of the 'fierce burning of a furnace...whose vent is stop't'. Chapman once refers to a lamp going out:

> The lamp of all authority goes out,
> And all the blaze of princes is extinct,

Byron's Trag.
3. 1

and to a smoky fire on a winter's morning (see below). Massinger once refers to making use of

> The counsel of our servants, that oil spent...
> Like snuffs that do offend, we tread them out.

Duke of Milan,
5. 1

Beyond these I find nothing in the least analogous to Shakespeare's constant awareness of the inconvenience and discomfort of ill-fed and ill-cared-for fire and light. The other dramatists have many 'fire' images; ashes, embers, sparks and flames, cooling, flaming and flashing, but only once outside Shakespeare do I find so vivid a little picture of an actual and homely experience as this of Chapman's:

> Indeed, such love is like a smoky fire
> In a cold morning; though the fire be cheerful,
> Yet is the smoke so sour and cumbersome,
> 'Twere better lose the fire than find the smoke:
> Such an attendant then as smoke to fire,
> Is jealousy to love.

All Fools, 1. 1

Characteristically Marlowe's 'lamp' images are all applied to the planets in the heavens, as,

> *Apollo, Cynthia,* and the ceaseless lamps
> That gently look'd upon this loathsome earth,
> Shine downwards now no more.

Certain 'domestic' images are common to all the Elizabethan dramatists; such are 'mirror', scales and weighing, locks, keys and coffers, clocks, dust, rust, stains and washing. But in none of their work except that of Shakespeare do we find this constant and acute consciousness of what must have been the very common discomforts in a small house in the sixteenth century, connected with faulty light and smoky fire, so that we are justified in arguing that these things were felt by him more acutely than by his fellows.

Indeed, as far as I myself am concerned, it was his insistence on it which first made vivid to my mind what must have been the constant discomfort from which people in humble life suffered before matches were invented. For the difficulty and chanciness of striking a light on flint and steel made it of course a really serious inconvenience when lamps went out and candles guttered.

In addition to the 'light' and 'fire' images, Shakespeare has an unusually large number drawn from the daily work and occupations of women in a kitchen and living room: washing glass and knives, breaking glass and cracking china, scouring, wiping, dusting, sweeping, removing spots and stains, preparing food, knitting, patching, lining, turning and remaking clothes (pp. 124–6 below). Notable among these are the analogies drawn from the various processes of washing: steeping, scouring, wringing, sponging, wiping and hanging out in the sun to dry, the constant references to stains and spotted garments, things 'besmeared' or 'soiled', especially the 'gloss' of a new material spotted or sullied. Various objects to be found in a kitchen are a favourite source of imagery: a dishclout, a bellows, a sieve, a skillet (coal-scuttle), scales and the action of weighing, a jug full of sack or other liquor; indeed vessels of all sorts, but particularly those filled to the brim or running over; as when the queen in *Hamlet*, without naming any object at all, so accurately describes the unfortunate result we have all experienced when trying with the utmost care to carry an overfull jug or bowl:

> So full of artless jealousy is guilt,   *Ham.* 4. 5. 19
> It spills itself in fearing to be spilt.

This work-a-day kitchen is, next to the orchard or garden, the atmosphere in which Shakespeare's mind moved most easily, this is the concrete background from which he most readily selects objects for comparison or analogy, as the eye of his memory lights upon them.

One need only run through a few of them, and one sees a picture gradually built up:

Their ragged curtains poorly are let loose,   *H. V,* 4. 2. 41
And our air shakes them passing scornfully.

                    thy counsel,   *M. Ado,* 5. 1. 3
. . .falls into mine ears as profitless
As water in a sieve.

And is become the bellows and the fan   *A. and C.*
To cool a gipsy's lust.   1. 1. 9

Yond same black cloud. . .looks like a foul bombard *Temp.* 2. 2. 20
[black jack] that would shed his liquor.

I do think him as concave as a covered goblet.   *A.Y.L.I.*
                                        3. 4. 23
                  The cloyed will,   *Cym.* 1. 6. 47
That satiate yet unsatisfied desire, that tub
Both fill'd and running.

Foul cankering rust the hidden treasure frets.   *V. and A.* 767

Wipe off the dust that hides our sceptre's gilt.   *R. II,* 2. 1. 294

The dust on antique time would lie unswept.   *Cor.* 2. 3. 124

Mac. 2. 2. 38   Sleep . . . sore labour's bath.

Ham. 3. 4. 34   Leave wringing of your hands: peace! sit you down,
And let me wring your heart: for so I shall,
If it be made of penetrable stuff.

Tw. N. 3. 2. 24   The double gilt of this opportunity you let time wash off.

M.W. 5. 5. 139   Have I laid my brain in the sun and dried it . . . ?

A. and C.   It's monstrous labour, when I wash my brain
2. 7. 102   And it grows fouler.

Luc. 1701   How may this forced stain be wiped from me?

C. of E.   My wasting lamps [eyes] some fading glimmer left.
5. 1. 315
R. II, 1. 3. 221   My oil-dried lamp and time-bewasted light
Shall be extinct with age and endless night;
My inch of taper will be burnt and done,
And blindfold death not let me see my son.

1 H. VI,   These eyes, like lamps whose wasting oil is spent,
2. 5. 8   Wax dim, as drawing to their exigent.

Cym. 1. 6. 109   Base and unlustrous as the smoky light
That's fed with stinking tallow.

The composite picture made by running together a
number of similar images of other writers drawn from
the house indoors is quite a different one, and conveys
the impression of a larger house, of more consequence.
Thus in Dekker we find, on taking a bundle of such
images at random, 'bright mirror, ruby coloured portals,
set open the windows, golden bowl, trunks, sieves,
yellow silk curtains, lead or latten casements, common
sink, glass [mirror]'; in Massinger, 'locks, rust, washed
off, key of cabinet, a strong cabinet, rusted sword, down
pillows, keys, magazine [storehouse], mirror'; in Chapman, 'stain, clear glass, sink, lock, footstool, open doors,
rust, mirror, set open all doors, sets gates open, bar
doors, mirror, strew the chamber like a rush, our rooms

of state kept like our stables, great vessels never emptied into less, dull piece of wainscot, rust, little specks on sides of glasses, two stairs, lowest and highest, sift, sieve, white pillows, key, lock, a plummet that sways a door' [swing door].

As regards Shakespeare's interest in food, and especially in its preparation and cooking, we have ample evidence of this in his imagery, and if we study in approximately chronological order groups of his food images we get some light on Shakespeare's own development, experience and tastes in this respect.

Let us examine those on food, taste and cooking. In his early work, up to about 1594 or 1595, the images of food, of which there are many, are of the most obvious, elementary and general kind; in the *Sonnets*, *Lucrece*, *Love's Labour's Lost*, and the *Two Gentlemen*, they are almost wholly confined to the simple states of hunger, starvation, famine, appetite, fasting, feasting, gluttony, gorging and surfeit, used much as in *Sonnet* LXXV. The possibly proverbial remark 'unquiet meals make ill digestions', in the *Comedy of Errors* (1592), should however be noted. Two of the three food similes in *A Midsummer Night's Dream* are of the general nature characteristic of this early period, one of fasting, *C. of E. 5. 1. 74*

> we must starve our sight *M.N.D.*
> From lovers' food till morrow deep midnight; *1. 1. 222*

the other, of the unhappy experience of youth after eating too many good things,

> a surfeit of the sweetest things *2. 2. 137*
> The deepest loathing to the stomach brings.

There are a few exceptions in the early work to these generalised images of hunger and surfeit, and five of these would seem to argue personal experience. These are Mercutio's scurrilous comparison of the Nurse to R. and J.
2. 4. 134 a mouldy hare in a lenten pie, Demetrius's reflection that food, natural and pleasant to us in health, is M.N.D.
4. 1. 178 loathsome in sickness, the statement that sweet things Luc. 867; R. II,
1. 3. 236 turn acid or sour in digestion, and the reference to a substance being mixed with 'seconds' in *Sonnet* cxxv. We may assume this refers to flour of a poor quality, 'unbolted' or unsieved, for Shakespeare is interested in this, as he is altogether in good bread, the right quality of material and proper baking (*T. and C.* 1. 1. 14–26, 5. 1. 5; 1 *H. IV*, 2. 4. 480, 3. 3. 77; *All's Well*, 4. 5. 1; *T. of Sh.* 5. 1. 137, 1. 1. 109). His most vivid use of the unsieved flour as a simile is in Menenius's plea for Coriolanus, who, he urges,

Cor. 3. 1. 321

> is ill school'd
> In bolted language; meal and bran together
> He throws without distinction.

About the time of writing the *Merchant of Venice* and *All's Well*, however (1594–6), we begin to find more concrete and individual references to food, with some hint of personal preferences and dislikes on the part of the writer. Thus, he notices that seasoning is useful in M. of V.
3. 2. 75 obscuring the taste of tainted meat, he touches discriminatingly on salads, and the herbs which are good All's Well,
4. 5. 17
1. 1. 169 in them, of which sweet-marjoram was not one, he thinks poorly of the 'French withered pears', for they M.W. 4. 5. 101 'eat drily', he shows acquaintance with custard pie T. of Sh. 4. 3.
81; 4. 3. 89
2. 1. 257 and apple tart, and loves the sweet kernel of the hazel nut, he hates saffron and unbaked doughy bread or All's Well,
4. 5. 1 cake, and he has a horror of greasy food. The last we might guess as early as Dromio's description of his C. of E.
3. 2. 95 kitchen wench, who is 'all grease', but it is in the

Merry Wives that we first find a simile that makes
it clear, when Falstaff, describing his horrors of heat
and suffocation in the evil smelling clothes basket,
declares he was 'more than half stewed in grease, like a   *M.W.* 3. 5. 118
Dutch dish'.

By 1599, when he was five and thirty, Shakespeare
has probably experienced heartburn as the result of
acidity, and realises that musty food needs a good   *M. Ado*, 2. 1. 3
stomach to digest it, also that one's taste in food alters   1. 1. 48
with age, and it is now we get the first indication of his   2. 3. 239
extreme sensitiveness to nicety and cleanliness at table
and his dislike of food ill kept and ill served of which we
are so conscious a few years later, especially in *Troilus
and Cressida*.

The number of food and taste similes in *As You Like
It* (1599) is remarkable, and it is in keeping with
Touchstone's educated and fastidious taste that he
should share his creator's sensitiveness to the cooking,
the flavour and the presentation of food. Thus it is
natural to him to assure Corin he is damned, 'like an   *A.Y.L.I.*
ill-roasted egg all on one side', or to tell the dazed   3. 2. 38
Audrey that although honesty coupled to beauty is to
have 'honey a sauce to sugar', yet to cast away honesty   3. 3. 30
upon a foul slut is to 'put good meat into an unclean dish'.   3. 3. 35

It is in *Troilus and Cressida*, however, that we realise
in full Shakespeare's feeling of disgust at 'greasy relics'   *T. and C.*
and his shrinking from dirty ill-served food, and we see   5. 2. 158
that 'fair fruit in an unwholesome dish', as far as he
is concerned, is 'like to rot untasted'.   2. 3. 123

His interest in and acute observation of cooking
operations are very marked all through his work, from
Love's Labours Lost to *Henry VIII*, as in Moth's picture
of the rabbit on a spit, Richard II's description of the   *L.L.L.* 3. 1. 19

R. II, 3. 2. *152* making of a covered pie, Parolles' knowledge of how
All's Well, a pasty is 'pinched', or Gremio's disgust at the failure
  4. 3. *131*
T. of Sh. of the cake that is 'dough on both sides'. He knows
  1. 1. *109*
  4. 1. 5 how quickly a little pot heats, has watched the operation
M.W. 4. 6. *14*; of larding, the washing of a sheep's heart, the making
1 H. IV, 2. 2.
A.Y.L.I. *112* of savoury sauce, the sugaring or icing of a cake or
  3. 2. *434* sweet, the sudden curding of milk in a posset, and the
Tw. N.
  3. 4. *154* distillation of a substance to jelly. But it is in *Troilus*
Ham. 3. 1. 46
  1. 5. 68 *and Cressida* that we see how extraordinarily close is
  1. 2. *204* his knowledge of different kinds of cooking—the kneading, baking, boiling, mincing, broiling, stewing, frying,
stuffing, larding, basting and distilling he must often
have watched taking place in his own kitchen at home.

Later we have evidence of his understanding of how
Cor. 4. 5. *192* to score a beefsteak for broiling, and also that he has
watched with interest the strange phenomenon of the
sudden boiling over of a saucepan of milk:

H. VIII,   Know you not,
  1. 1. *143*   The fire that mounts the liquor till't run o'er
             In seeming to augment it wastes it?

As regards table habits, Shakespeare seems to accept
as a matter of course the accident of choking through
R. II, 2. 1. 37 eating too greedily ('With eager feeding food doth
choke the feeder') which throws a side-light on the
manners of the time; but his disgust at over-eating,
which was probably even more common, is clearly to
be seen in his many images from surfeit and its results,
as in Emilia's coarse but forcible description of the
Oth. 3. 4. *104* ways of men with women, or the archbishop's vivid
comparison of the fickle populace to a 'beastly feeder',
who having greedily eaten too much, is forced like a
2 H. IV, 'common dog', to disgorge it; and it is worth noting
  1. 3. 95 that his earliest distinction between love and lust is that

'Love surfeits not, Lust like a glutton dies', and that *V. and A. 803*
the adjective which Troilus chooses at the height of his
passion and disillusionment to describe the broken faith
of Cressid is 'o'er-eaten'.

It would seem fair to argue that Shakespeare's extreme sensitiveness about the quality, cooking, freshness and cleanliness of food developed rather late—
possibly after experience of more delicate fare than that
of Stratford, at the tables of his London friends. Up to
about the age of thirty, we get little sign of it, and his
references to hunger, appetite and surfeit are such as
might be made by any healthy youth. From thirty
onwards there is increasing evidence of fastidiousness,
of sensitive digestion (*M. Ado*, 1. 1. 48, 1. 1. 119, 2.
1. 276, 2. 3. 239), of disgust at over-eating, of *T. and C. 5. 2.*
revolt from greasy food and 'morsels unctuous' which *157; Oth. 3. 4. 104*
culminates in the strange play of *Troilus and Cressida*, *Timon, 4. 3. 195*
written probably when he was about thirty-eight or
thirty-nine, at which period it would seem he suffered
from some deep perturbation, shock and revulsion of
nature, emotional, moral and spiritual, which translated
itself into terms of physical appetite and its disgust. We
get echoes of this in *Othello* and *Measure for Measure*
(*Oth.* 3. 4. 104, 2. 1. 235, 1. 3. 354; *M. for M.* 2. 2. 165,
1. 4. 40, 1. 2. 125), as also in *Antony and Cleopatra*,
although it seems to me Antony's cry when he thinks
himself betrayed,

> I found you as a morsel cold upon *A. and C.*
> Dead Caesar's trencher, *3. 13. 116*

and later,

> this false soul of Egypt! this grave charm,... *4. 12. 25*
> Like a right gipsy hath at fast and loose
> Beguiled me,

never touches the piercing personal note of passionate rebellion and disgust which rings in the bitter cry of Troilus, beginning,

T. and C.
5. 2. 153

      Cressid is mine, tied with the bonds of heaven

and ending,

> The fragments, scraps, the bits and greasy relics
> Of her o'er-eaten faith, are bound to Diomed.

After *Antony and Cleopatra* we get no further similes of revolt of physical appetite, and indeed very few food images at all.

Some of Shakespeare's images of cooking or the preparing of food are extraordinarily apt and vivid, and leave us with an unforgettable picture: Falstaff who

1 H. IV,
2. 2. 112

>   sweats to death,
> And lards the lean earth as he walks along;

Grumio, sent ahead to make a fire, and worn out with Petruchio's mad ways, grumbling,

T. of Sh.
4. 1. 5.

> Now, were not I a little pot, and soon hot, my very lips might freeze to my teeth,...ere I should come by a fire to thaw me;

T. and C.
2. 3. 187
Ham. 1. 2. 204

Achilles, who 'bastes his arrogance with his own seam [lard]'; Horatio's report on the appearance of the soldiers of the watch when they saw the Ghost,

>   distill'd
> Almost to jelly with the act of fear;

2 H. IV,
3. 2. 328

L.L.L. 3. 1. 18

T. and C.
1. 2. 22

Falstaff's wicked description of old Shallow 'like a forked radish, with a head fantastically carved upon it with a knife'; Moth's rude words to Armado, 'with your arms crossed on your thin-belly doublet, like a rabbit on a spit'; and Alexander's account of Ajax, as 'a man into whom nature hath so crowded humours that his valour is crushed into folly, his folly sauced with discretion'.

All through, Shakespeare shows evidence, as we should expect, of a keen discriminating palate, as in *Sonnet* cxviii, which runs on his favourite metaphors of food and sickness, and opens with the description of what to modern ears sounds curiously like a cocktail,

> to make our appetites more keen,
> With eager compounds we our palate urge,

going on to assert to her who has been unfaithful, that

> being full of your ne'er-cloying sweetness,
> To bitter sauces did I frame my feeding.

The simple seasonings of salt and sugar are constant as similes, occasionally we find vinegar, pepper, mustard, spice, saffron and nutmeg, and one may note that the idea of a sauce as a corrective, contrast, complement or digestive to food comes naturally to him. 'Thy wit', says Mercutio, 'is a most sharp sauce', 'And is it not well served in to a sweet goose?' retorts Romeo. 'Folly sauced with discretion', 'praises sauced with lies', 'I'll sauce her with bitter words', meat 'sauced with... upbraidings', and

Tw. N.
3. 4. 154
2 H. IV,
2. 4. 252
T. and C.
1. 2. 264
All's Well,
4. 5. 1
H. V, 3. 7. 20
R. and J.
2. 4. 81
T. and C.
1. 2. 24
Cor. 1. 9. 53
A.Y.L.I.
3. 5. 69
C. of E. 5. 1. 73
J.C. 1. 2. 303

> rudeness is a sauce to his good wit,
> Which gives men stomach to digest his words
> With better appetite,

are examples of this underlying idea. We know that contrasted sauces were more usual in Elizabethan England, as they still are on the continent, than in our country today, which rejoices so contentedly in its one entirely tasteless condiment of 'melted butter'.

Shakespeare's own individual tastes, so far as we can gather them, have already been indicated. We may sum up by saying he seems to dislike stale or dry tasteless things, dry biscuits, dried pears, stale dry cheese, musty

A.Y.L.I.
2. 7. 38
All's Well,
1. 1. 169–71
T. and C.
5. 4. 11

T. of Sh. 1. 1.
109; 5. 1. 137
Cym. 5. 4. 152

or tainted meat, ill-baked doughy bread, sodden or greasy food, a carelessly boiled egg or an over-roasted joint; that he appreciates green salad and the sharp

Ham. 2. 2. 460
T. of Sh.
    2. 1. 256
T. and C.
    5. 1. 5
    5. 2. 56

savoury tang of herbs, the sweet kernels of nuts, the taste of honey, well-baked crusty bread, and looks on beefsteak and fried potatoes as a luxury. If we add to this, what we all know, that skim milk struck him as

1 H. IV,
    2. 3. 35
Tw. N.
    2. 3. 118
R. III, 2. 1.41;
H. VIII, 3. 1.
105; Temp. 2.
    1. 10

a poor drink, while cakes and ale seemed good to him, that ginger and a cordial appeared to him of more comfort than cold porridge, it is but one more proof of how completely he shared in the tastes and weaknesses of our common and suffering humanity.

Shakespeare also noticed the women's sewing and mending which he saw going on round him, and there is clear evidence of his observation of and interest in needlework in the many images he draws from it and

L.L.L. 5. 2.613

things pertaining to it, such as a bodkin, a silken thread,

M. Ado,
    5. 1. 25
Cor. 5. 6. 95
T. and C.
    5. 1. 30
K.L. 2. 1. 121;
K.J. 5. 4. 11
T. and C.
    2. 1. 82

a twist of rotten silk, or an 'immaterial' skein of sleave or floss silk and needles, threaded and unthreaded. The tiny size of the eye of the latter is used with effect by Thersites when he declares—in spite of Achilles—that Ajax has not so much wit 'as will stop the eye of Helen's needle, for whom he comes to fight', and the sharpness of its point lends vividness to Imogen's assertion that she would have watched Posthumus waving farewell on his ship

Cym. 1. 3. 18

till the diminution
Of space had pointed him sharp as my needle.

He shows knowledge of knitting, mending, ripping up an old garment, remaking an old cloak into a new jerkin, trimming, facing, lining, and of the loose light stitching called 'basting'. His men have as much knowledge of all this as his women, indeed one of the most

detailed of these metaphors is used by Benedict the
bachelor, after a bout of wit with Don Pedro, in which
both have been fencing, and Don Pedro has been
quoting from old plays. Benedict leaves him saying in
effect, 'Don't mock me any more. Your conversation
is sometimes adorned with very poor, worn out stuff,
and very slightly attached too; before you flourish any
more of these antiquities, examine yourself and see if
they don't apply to you', which he clothes thus:

The body of your discourse is sometime guarded *M. Ado,*
[ornamented] with fragments, and the guards [orna- *1. 1. 285*
ments] are but slightly basted on neither: ere you flout
old ends any further, examine your conscience:

showing a knowledge of trimming a garment, and the
way a needlewoman or tailor would set about preparing
it, which is somewhat unusual. Knitting he has often
watched, and uses it metaphorically with great exactitude, as when Prospero complacently reflects that his
'enemies are all knit up in their distractions' or Mac- *Temp. 3. 3. 89*
beth in 'Sleep that knits up the ravell'd sleave of care' *Mac. 2. 2. 36*
draws his wonderful picture of knitting up the loose,
fluffy all-pervading substance of frayed-out floss silk,
thus reducing it in bulk and changing its texture to
something firm and definitely finished off. His pictures
of mending and patching ('anything that's mended is *Tw. N. 1. 5. 47*
but patched') show the same close observation of the
homely art, as when Menenius, realising the seriousness of the breach between Coriolanus and the people,
declares 'this must be patch'd with cloth of any colour', *Cor. 3. 1. 252*
and the fact that the patch of a small hole, if not very
well done, actually calls attention to the worn-out place
is aptly used by Pembroke when he shrewdly reminds

King John that the excusing of a fault often makes 'the fault the worse by the excuse',

K.J. 4. 2. 30

> As patches set upon a little breach
> Discredit more in hiding of the fault
> Than did the fault before it was so patch'd.

There is little reference to fancy work. The mention of Titus, 2. 4. 38 Philomel's sampler is due to Ovid. However Timon's Timon, 3. 6. 95 words, 'who stuck and spangled you with flatteries' are certainly suggestive of some sort of embroidery.

Shakespeare shows, as we should expect, a knowledge of numbers of trades or crafts and their processes, and draws upon many of them repeatedly for his similes— the smith shaping the hot iron in his forge, the butcher in his slaughter-house, the potter tempering clay and whirling his wheel, the tailor cutting out by his pattern, the weaver at his loom, the glover, the printer, the solderer and the dyer. But few readers, I think, would at once guess which is the craft that he seems much the most familiar with, and in terms of which he thinks most often and most easily. It is carpentering—the work of a village carpenter, which includes operations like coopering, and the making of carts and wheels. The number of Shakespeare's images drawn from screwing, nailing, riveting, hooping a barrel with ribs of metal, the action of wedges, the tendency of wood to shrink and warp, and general joinery and carpentry, is remarkable, as well as the number of those from specific tools, such as the hammer, mallet, handsaw, file, auger or vice and the sharpening of knives and implements on a whetstone.

Many of these carpentering images are very vivid, and show a close knowledge of the action of tool or material, as when Jaques dissuades Touchstone from

being married by Sir Oliver 'under a bush like a beggar'. *A.Y.L.I.* 3. 3. 82
'Get you to church', he tells him, 'and have a good priest that can tell you what marriage is: this fellow will but join you together as they join wainscot; then one of you will prove a shrunk panel, and like green timber warp, warp.' He knows precisely the result of dovetailing, and how important it is for the success of that particular job that the wood should be perfectly dry and well-seasoned.

The action of wedges gives some striking similes, as when Troilus tells the inattentive Pandarus that when he is sitting at Priam's table and Cressida comes into his thoughts, then it seems as if his heart 'as wedged *T. and C.* 1. 1. 34 with a sigh, would rive in twain'. Or when Ulysses bethinks him of administering a good snub to Achilles by sending Ajax to answer Hector's challenge, a strong measure taken to meet an intolerable situation, the overweening pride and insolence of Achilles, he sums it up perfectly in the carpenter's phrase 'Blunt wedges rive hard knots'. 1. 3. 316

The hooping of a barrel with bands of metal is a favourite image with Shakespeare and serves him to express vividly various ideas of binding, strengthening and embracing. Such are pictures of two people being held firmly together in the well-known advice of Polonius with regard to tried friends, 'Grapple them to thy soul with hoops of steel', or in Caesar's heartfelt *Ham.* 1. 3. 62 wish to Antony, 'if I knew what hoop should hold us *A. and C.* 2. 2. 115 stanch'. Reinforced strength is conveyed in Lady Percy's advice to Northumberland that if the nobles are successful, he should join

> with them, like a rib of steel, *2 H. IV,* 2. 3. 53
> To make strength stronger,

or in Leonato's cry when fresh evidence appears of
Hero's guilt,

M. Ado,
4. 1. 151

> Confirm'd, confirm'd! O, that is stronger made
> Which was before barr'd up with ribs of iron!

W.T. 4. 4.
442–4

and the feeling of holding a person closely is vividly
pictured in Polixenes' threat to Perdita, 'if ever hence-
forth thou...hoop his body more with thy embraces'.

All's Well,
2. 2. 24
Two Gent.
2. 4. 192

The images from nails are probably some of them
merely proverbial, 'as fit. . . as the nail to his hole', 'as one
nail by strength drives out another', but those from the
use of the screw and the rivet are peculiarly individual
and vivid, and when Iachimo gazing at Imogen asleep
in bed asks,

Cym. 2. 2. 43

> Why should I write this down that's riveted,
> Screw'd to my memory?

Tw. N.
5. 1. 121

Mac. 1. 7. 60

Ham. 1. 2. 20
Mac. 3. 2. 16

Cym. 2. 2. 41;
5. 4. 8

we feel that has been written by one who has known
the satisfaction of the finishing touches of driving a
screw well and truly home. So also when the duke,
thinking of Viola, tells Olivia he knows the instrument
that screws him from his true place in her favour and
Lady Macbeth urges her lord to 'screw' his 'courage
to the sticking-place' we have the same sense of the
knowledge of the use of a special tool. The general idea
of something 'disjoint and out of frame' we find in both
Hamlet and *Macbeth*, and picking locks and bolts twice
in *Cymbeline*; the first one probably suggests to Iachimo
his image of the screw quoted above.

The small deep hole made in wood by a carpenter's
auger serves Shakespeare as an image of a tiny space,
as when Menenius tells the citizens their franchises are
'confined into an auger's bore', or an infinitesimally
small hiding place, as when Donalbain after Duncan's

Cor. 4. 6. 86

murder whispers to Malcolm that they had best get
away quickly from the spot where

> our fate, *Mac. 2. 3. 126*
> Hid in an auger-hole, may rush, and seize us.

And one of the best known philosophical reflections
of Shakespeare is in the form of a rough carpentering
simile, used with close exactitude and knowledge of the
subject. This is Hamlet's remark to Horatio that

> There's a divinity that shapes our ends, *Ham. 5. 2. 10*
> Rough-hew them how we will,

which we know applies specifically to the cutting and
shaping of wool-skewers, which Shakespeare, in view of
his father's trade, doubtless knew all about. (See Steevens'
note in Boswell Malone's *Shakespeare*, vol. VII, p. 487.)

A study of Shakespeare's images of sickness and
medicine shows that he had throughout his life a distinct
interest in the treatment of disease and the action of
medicine on the body, but that this interest became
stronger in middle age.

It seems also that one can trace a certain change of
attitude towards sickness in the tone of the images. The
early ones are, on the whole, somewhat perfunctory,
and such simple remedies as salve for a sore wound,
purgation or blood-letting are constantly used as similes
in a somewhat detached and obvious way, as when
Warwick, hearing the bad news of the escape of
Edward of York, turns to the king and says:

> But let us hence, my sovereign, to provide *3 H. VI,*
> A salve for any sore that may betide, *4. 6. 87*

or when Henry, puzzled by his people turning their
allegiance to Edward, pathetically says:

> My pity hath been balm to heal their wounds. *4. 8. 41*

Later, when dramatic as well as, possibly, personal feeling runs high, and it would seem that bitter pain has been experienced, this same type of image, here so mild and ordinary, is used, with a vividness that hurts, to express excruciating agony, when Troilus, 'mad in Cressid's love', finding Pandarus matter-of-fact and unresponsive, cries

T. and C.
1. 1. 61

> instead of oil and balm,
> Thou lay'st in every gash that love hath given me
> The knife that made it.

I do not think it too fanciful to suggest that the development of Shakespeare's feeling about sickness and disease is reflected in his similes. If we examine, for instance, those drawn from the plague, we notice that many of his early ones give us rather a shock by their extraordinary lack of feeling and even of good taste. When we reflect what the tragic horrors of the repeated plague epidemics must have been, the use of these experiences by Biron as a jesting simile jars and offends us.

But we have to remember that Biron was a light-
L.L.L. 5.2.846 hearted youth 'replete with mocks', who sorely needed the training imposed on him by Rosaline to visit the sick and use his gaiety and wit to cheer them, so that his sympathy and feeling for others should be developed. Hence his comparison of his three love-sick companions to men infected by the plague, caught of their ladies'
5. 2. 419 eyes, who should have 'Lord have mercy' written on them, and his assertion that he sees 'the Lord's tokens' [plague-spots] on the ladies also, is possibly in keeping with his character as a clever, high-spirited, but some-
5. 2. 847 what shallow and thoughtless jester, 'full of comparisons and wounding flouts'.

However that may be, it is worth noting, though it may be pure coincidence, that all Shakespeare's images from the plague up to the year 1600 are light, and, with one exception, show a certain lack of feeling; whereas after 1600 every one of them is serious, and is used in such a way that the gravity and horror of the disease are emphasised. Thus Speed laughingly assures Valentine he knows he is in love by 'special marks', one of which is that he walks alone, 'like one that had the pestilence'; Beatrice avers that Benedick 'is sooner caught than the pestilence, and the taker runs presently mad'; Olivia, taken aback by her sudden infatuation for Viola, reflects that 'even so quickly may one catch the plague'; but a sense of real feeling of the menace and horror of the infection is implied in the Duke's cry of love at first sight which gives us what would seem almost a contradiction in terms, a metaphor from this subject full of charm and poetry: *Two Gent.* *2. 1. 20* *M. Ado,* *1. 1. 84* *Tw.N. 1.5.305*

> O, when mine eyes did see Olivia first,   *1. 1. 19*
> Methought she purged the air of pestilence!

But after *Twelfth Night* (c. 1600), it so happens that the plague images have a different tone and are used in a graver context. Antony, in his passionate soliloquy over dead Caesar's body, gives us what would seem to be a side glimpse of the horrors of London streets in time of plague, when he cries,

> ...this foul deed shall smell above the earth   *J.C. 3. 1. 274*
> With carrion men, groaning for burial;

Ulysses declares Achilles is so

> plaguy proud that the death-tokens of it   *T. and C.*
> Cry 'No recovery';   *2. 3. 179*

Lear, at the height of his rage and disgust, calls Goneril a 'plague-sore'; Scarus, in order to bring home to *K.L. 2. 4. 227*

Enobarbus how utterly and tragically they are defeated,
A. and C. tells him that the fight on their side is 'like the token'd
3. 10. 9 pestilence, where death is sure'; the tribune Brutus, at
the moment of highest feeling against Coriolanus, when
they are inciting the people to kill him, pictures him
as one plague-stricken, and cries, let us 'pursue him to
his house', and

Cor. 3. 1. 309
> pluck him thence;
> Lest his infection, being of catching nature,
> Spread further;

and the climax of Bishop Gardiner's bitter and deadly
H. VIII, indictment of Cranmer is that he is 'a pestilence that
5. 1. 45 does infect the land'.

We have already noticed Shakespeare's disgust at
surfeit, and many of his earlier similes reflect his
curiously modern belief that we bring about a great
deal of our own ill health ourselves by ill regulated
living, and especially by over-eating, and are then in-
clined to lay the blame on an unkind fate; or, as Edmund
K.L. 1. 2. 129 expresses it, 'when we are sick in fortune—often the
surfeit of our own behaviour—we make guilty of our
disasters the sun, the moon and the stars'. So that we
may, I believe, take the Archbishop of York's description of the state of England,

2 H.IV, 4. 1. 54
> we are all diseased,
> And with our surfeiting and wanton hours
> Have brought ourselves into a burning fever,
> And we must bleed for it;

and the remedy,

> To diet rank minds sick of happiness,
> And purge the obstructions which begin to stop
> Our very veins of life,

as expressing pretty fairly Shakespeare's own view of the cause and cure of the sickness of the ordinary healthy man. (Cf. also *V. and A.* 803; *All's Well*, 3. 1. 17; 2 *H. IV*, 1. 3. 87; *Mac.* 5. 3. 50; *M. of V.* 1. 2. 5; *M.N.D.* 2. 2. 137; *Tw. N.* 1. 1. 1.) All through the many images of this kind in 2 *H. IV*, chiefly arising out of the idea that the kingdom is 'sick with civil blows', the attitude is generally to be found that 'distemperature' of the body is a thing for which we are ourselves responsible, that it is brought about by excess and unwise living, and that excess in either direction is to be avoided, starvation as well as surfeit, for, as Nerissa sagely remarks, 'it is no mean happiness to be *M. of V.* 1. 2. 5–8 seated in the mean'. We may hazard therefore that Norfolk's advice to Buckingham would be Shakespeare's own:

> Ask God for temperance; that's the appliance only *H. VIII,* 1. 1. 124
> Which your disease requires.

But at the turn of the century, in *Hamlet*, we find in the 'sickness' images a feeling of horror, disgust and even helplessness not met before (save for a touch of the first two in Jacques' bitter moralising and the duke's answer, *A.Y.L.I.* 2. 7. 58–61, and 67–9); and the general sense of inward and unseen corruption, of the man helplessly succumbing to a deadly and 'foul *Ham.* 4. 1. 19 disease', which feeds 'even on the pith of life', is very strong. This is accompanied by the impression that for such a terrible ill the remedy must be drastic, for

> diseases desperate grown *4. 3. 9*
> By desperate appliance are relieved,
> Or not at all,

and that anything short of this is but to

Ham. 3. 4. 147
> skin and film the ulcerous place,
> Whiles rank corruption, mining all within,
> Infects unseen.

This is, as we shall see later, the general symbolic trend of these images in the play, and Hamlet and the others pay the price demanded for the necessary cleansing of

A.Y.L.I.
2. 7. 60
the 'foul body of the infected world'.

But Shakespeare's use of these symbolic pictures here reveals incidentally a graver conception of disease, and a peculiar horror of tumours, ulcers, abscesses, cancer and the like, never found before or later. We get, however, an echo of it in Lear's terrible description of Goneril in his agony of rage and disillusionment,

K.L. 2. 4. 226
> thou art a boil,
> . . . an embossed carbuncle,
> In my corrupted blood;

and we find in *Coriolanus* a reiteration of the need of drastic remedy for serious disease, and the opinion that the preventive and disciplinary measures, enjoined in 2 *Henry IV*, might be not only useless, but even, in cases of gravity, harmful:

Cor. 3. 1. 220
> those cold ways,
> That seem like prudent helps, are very poisonous
> Where the disease is violent.

In *Troilus and Cressida* and in *Coriolanus*, where these 'sickness' images are numerous, though they are some-

T. and C.
1. 1. 53
times painful, as in Troilus' description of the 'open ulcer of my heart', they are never so serious as in *Hamlet*, and the sense of the disgusting aspect of certain bodily ills is more lightly touched on, as when Thersites

2. 1. 30
desires to make Ajax 'the loathsomest scab in Greece', or Coriolanus contemptuously tells the citizens that in

rubbing the 'poor itch' of their opinion, they make *Cor. 1. 1. 168*
themselves scabs.

Shakespeare's interest in the compounding and action of drugs, healing or noxious, and in medical theories, is to be seen in the story of many of his plays, such as *All's Well, Cymbeline*, or *Romeo and Juliet*. In the images also we find indications of this very early, when Tarquin assures Lucrece that

> The poisonous simple sometime is compacted *Luc. 530*
> In a pure compound; being so applied,
> His venom in effect is purified,

which would seem to mean that a small amount of poison can be used medicinally with other compounds with good effect. So Northumberland, in 2 *Henry IV*, 1. 1. 137, points out the curative action of poison under certain circumstances, comparing it with the stimulating effect of bad news on a sick man.

Various medical facts and theories are made use of for images, such as the well-known one that mental trouble drives out physical pain, and

> where the greater malady is fix'd *K.L. 3. 4. 8*
> The lesser is scarce felt,

or that greater pain cures the lesser,

> Great griefs, I see, medicine the less; *Cym. 4. 2. 243*

the good effect of counter irritation,

> Take thou some new infection to thy eye, *R. and J.*
> And the rank poison of the old will die; *1. 2. 50*

and the principle of inoculation, which, had Shakespeare known it, is described even better than purgation, when he writes,

> As, to prevent our maladies unseen, *Son.* cxviii
> We sicken to shun sickness when we purge.

In general medical knowledge and theory, such as belief in 'humours' and in vital spirits in the arteries, and so on, Shakespeare was naturally of his time, and his views have been examined by experts. There is one image, however, which might possibly be interpreted as showing a comprehension far beyond his time, and *A.Y.L.I.* that is when Rosalind declares, 'Love is merely a mad-*3. 2. 411* ness; and, I tell you, deserves as well a dark house and a whip as madmen do'. Does she just accept the ordinary view that madmen should be thus treated, or is there an underlying suggestion that, if the right treatment for madmen is darkness and the whip, then so it certainly is for lovers, for both are equally ir-responsible and blameless, and therefore neither should be thus harshly treated?

However this may be, Shakespeare was greatly ahead of his time in such questions as the relation of temperate living to health, and his dislike of over-eating and drunkenness, and this is clearly to be seen even in the images.

His sensitive understanding of the influence of mind on body is what, however, puts him nearest to modern expert opinion, and this is as marked in his early as his later work. Thus the whole story of the cause and development of madness in a brain over-strained with exasperation and anguish is sketched in the *Comedy of Errors*, fifteen years before the full portrait of it is drawn in *King Lear*; even the detail, so tragic in the story of the old king, when the sorely needed sleep *K.L. 3. 6. 101* which might have 'balm'd' his 'broken sinews' is denied him, is stressed by the Abbess when she says,

C. of E. 5. 1. 83   In food, and sport, and life-preserving rest
To be disturb'd, would mad or man or beast.

But apart from the great pictures of mind acting on body in such plays as *King Lear* and *Macbeth*, the detailed knowledge of how this interaction works peeps out in unexpected touches in the images, as when Lucrece laments,

To see the salve doth make the wound ache more, *Luc. 1116*
R. and J.
1. 1. 201

or when Romeo points out the ill effect on a sick man of urging him to make his will. Shakespeare must have greatly enjoyed talking with his son-in-law, Dr John Hall, and exchanging views on these matters which so much interested him, as they strolled round his garden on summer evenings.

Last among the interests of Shakespeare which I propose to examine, I have placed what I have called classes and types of people. It is, of course, entirely unnecessary to draw on the evidence of the images to prove that Shakespeare was interested in various types of human beings, but this intense interest is so strikingly illustrated in the imagery, that I cannot let it pass unnoticed.

To begin with a specific type—children; Shakespeare's interest in and observation of children and child nature from babyhood are remarkable, and the many pictures he draws of them in his images in just a line or two are amply sufficient to show how intense are his sympathy and understanding.

M.W. 5. 5. 56;

The healthy babe in its cradle, sleeping the sound *R. II, 1. 3. 132* sleep of 'careless infancy', rocked by night and day, *V. and A. 1185;* *2 H. IV, 3. 1. 20* 'the froward infant still'd with dandling', 'not yet out *V. and A. 562;* of his swaddling clouts', the nurse's song which pleases *2 H. VI, 1. 3. 145* *Ham. 2. 2. 399;* her babe, the lullaby which puts it to sleep, her tender *1 H. IV, 3. 2. 112* care, the wayward 'testy babe', who scratches and beats *V. and A. 974* *Titus, 2. 3. 29* *Son. XXII;* *R. III, 4. 1. 102*

Two Gent. 1. 2.
57; *M. for M.*
1. 3. 30
Cor. 5. 6. 97
Ham. 3. 3. 71
Temp. 1. 2. 484
T. and C.
1. 1. 12
4. 2. 5
W.T. 5. 3. 27
the nurse, who whines and roars, the soft sinews of the new-born babe, the feebleness of infants, 'skilless' and 'unpractised', their emptiness of all thought, their tender grace, all this and more he draws upon for comparison and illustration.

The many pictures of mother and child are well known, such as the 'long-parted mother with her child', who

R. II, 3. 2. 9
Plays fondly with her tears and smiles,

1 *H. VI*, 3. 3.
47; 2 *H. VI*,
3. 2. 391
2 *H. IV*,
4. 1. 210
the mother looking on her dying babe, the curious picture of the wife who has enraged her husband, and egged him on to strike her, and 'as he is striking, holds his infant up' to shelter herself and to stop his blow, and the amazingly vivid one (in *Sonnet* CXLIII), which he must surely have watched, just as he describes it, in actual life, of the mother setting down her babe in order to catch an escaped chicken, and the neglected child crying, and in turn chasing its mother, who is wholly taken up with the pursuit of the feathered creature 'which flies before her face'.

Unquestionably the two most dramatic uses of Shakespeare's intimate knowledge of mother and babe
Mac. 1. 7. 54
are Lady Macbeth's terrible words and Cleopatra's marvellous image in the simple query with which she
A. and C.
5. 2. 307
checks Charmian's lamentations at the sight of the asp at her breast.

The many pictures of children and their parents look as if the children were spoilt and parents were kind and easy-going, much as today; on any ocean steamer or in any big hotel we can still see the

T. and C.
3. 2. 126
unbridled children, grown
Too headstrong for their mother;

the 'unruly children' who

> make their sire   *R. II, 3. 4. 29*
> Stoop with oppression;

the impatient parent, who, weary of arguing, bids the
child go whip his top; and, if whipping were still the *L.L.L. 5. 1. 65*
fashionable corrective, we should have now, as then,
'fond fathers', who

> Having bound up the threatening twigs of birch,   *M. for M.*
> Only to stick it in their children's sight   *1. 3. 23*
> For terror, not to use, in time the rod
> Becomes more mock'd than fear'd.

We get many vivid touches by the way, of quick,
eager, restless, impressionable child nature, 'wanton', *L.L.L. 5. 1.763*
'skipping and vain', 'fond', 'testy' and 'wayward', *Luc. 1094*
longing for everything that he can come by, doting on *Two Gent.*
3. 1. 124
'an idle gaud', impatient and delighting in his new *M.N.D.*
4. 1. 172
clothes; it is an unkind and tantalising thing, says Don
Pedro in effect, 'to show a child his new coat and forbid *M. Ado, 3. 2. 6*
him to wear it'; and Juliet anxiously awaiting Romeo,
could not better describe the slow passing of time than
when she declares,

> so tedious is this day   *R. and J.*
> As is the night before some festival   *3. 2. 28*
> To an impatient child that hath new robes
> And may not wear them.

Shakespeare's especial interest in small boys is clear
enough from the tiny but extraordinarily vivid sketches
of boys when they appear for brief moments as characters
in his plays, where they seem like delicate but bril-
liantly-hued little water-colours, drawn nearly always
against the murky background of tragedy. Such are
young Macduff, plying his mother with questions, the *Mac.4.2.30–63*
'gallant and precocious' Mamillius bandying words

with his mother's ladies, but becoming a very child in
W.T. 2. 1. 1 his appetite for a good tale, the sturdy little Marcius
Cor. 1. 3. 60–9 persistently chasing the butterfly and venting his spleen
on it, Robin, who has the makings of a courtier, and
M.W. 3. 2. 8; William, as his mother begins to hope, of a scholar,
4. 1. 80
or the two little princes, entirely different, the elder so
dignified and thoughtful, the younger wayward, spoilt
and sharp-tongued, yet when he chooses, full of ready
and princely tact,

R. III, 3. 1. 155   Bold, quick, ingenious, forward, capable.

This delight in boy nature is evident also in the many
images Shakespeare draws from it, and the little vignettes
he gives us continually of the boy in his daily life and
H. V, 4. 1. 204 play are of great interest. We catch glimpses of him
A. and C.
3. 13. 91 at his games, shooting somewhat ineffectually with his
M. Ado, 2. 1.
223; R. and J. elder-gun, rushing forth into a 'muss' or scramble,
2. 5. 74 bird-nesting, chasing 'summer butterflies', learning to
Cor. 4. 6. 94
H. VIII, swim, and playing at football and pushpin, going re-
3. 2. 358
C.of E. 2. 1. 82; luctantly to school 'with heavy looks' and rushing away
Ham. 3. 3. 93
K.L. 1. 4. 88 from his books with joy when, the school breaking up,
R. and J.
2. 2. 157–8
2 H.IV, 4. 2. 105   Each hurries toward his home and sporting-place.

We sympathise with the boy who sighs because he has
Two Gent. 'lost his A.B.C.', with him who is whipped till
2. 1. 21

A. and C.   you see him cringe his face,
3. 13. 100   And whine aloud for mercy,

1 H. IV,
2. 4. 435 and with the truant who successfully escapes for a
R. III, 4. 2. 29
1 H.IV, 3. 2. 66 day's blackberrying. We see careless, gibing, peevish,
J.C. 5. 1. 61
M.N.D. waggish and impudent boys as well as the cruel wanton
1. 1. 240
M. for M. boy who tortures and kills flies for his sport.
1. 3. 29   The complete and perfect picture of the mentality
K.L. 4. 1. 38 of happy care-free youth, with its entire lack of perspec-

tive, living absolutely in the joy of the moment, is seen
in Polixenes' description of himself and Leontes:

> Two lads that thought there was no more behind,   *W.T. 1. 2. 63*
> But such a day to-morrow as to-day,
> And to be boy eternal.

We find also in images, little sketches thrown out by
the way, which show how completely Shakespeare knew
and sympathised with various aspects of boy nature, as
when Caesar, deploring Antony's self-indulgence, declares he is behaving just like a boy who ought to know
better,

> 'tis to be chid   *A. and C.*
> As we rate boys, who, being mature in knowledge,   *1. 4. 30*
> Pawn their experience to their present pleasure,
> And so rebel to judgement,

or when Antony, in two lines, sums up the whole
essence of the keen and resolute boy who intends to
succeed,

> This morning, like the spirit of a youth   *4. 4. 26*
> That means to be of note, begins betimes.

Shakespeare gives us, of course, many pictures and
descriptions of the boy of older years, the devoted page
and servant or the fashionable, wayward, affected youth.
Although there are no images to illustrate this, it is
worth just noting here how often he associates with
them inconstancy and changeableness, especially in love
or affection.

Rosalind's summary of the character of the 'moonish   *A.Y.L.I.*
youth...changeable...proud, fantastical, apish, shal-   *3. 2. 421*
low, inconstant', the Fool's remark that 'he's mad that
trusts in the tameness of a wolf, a horse's health, a boy's   *K.L. 3. 6. 20*
love', and the disappointed bitterness of Lucius when
he believes that Imogen has failed him,

Cym. 5. 5. 105

> The boy disdains me,
> He leaves me, scorns me: briefly die their joys
> That place them on the truth of girls and boys,

all show how readily this aspect or quality of character comes to the surface when Shakespeare is thinking of a charming, attractive, high-spirited boy in his teens, such as Rosalind and Fidele appear to be.

To pass from children to their elders, we realise that the mass of varied figures, clear-cut and vivid, which we catch sight of in Shakespeare's imagery, is drawn from every type and class in Elizabethan society, and throws many side-lights on the customs of the day, as well as incidentally at times on Shakespeare's own sympathies.

In this moving mirror of images, alight with colour and life, we catch glimpses, as if through a pierced lancet window, of a rich and motley company passing before us in their rags or homespun or their gay and gorgeous coats; the shifting, changing, momentary reflection of the people of Shakespeare's world as he saw it; pilgrims and hermits; beggars, thieves and prisoners; pirates, sailors and serving-men; pedlars, gipsies, madmen and fools; shepherds, labourers and peasants; schoolmasters and pupils; heralds, ambassadors, messengers, officers of state, spies, traitors and rebels; burghers, courtiers, kings and princes.

Mingling here and there with these, are the members of definite trades and professions, tinkers and tailors, tapsters and ostlers, as well as groups of human beings in their domestic and everyday relation and setting, nurses and babes, women and children, mothers, lovers, parents and schoolboys. Thus we find similes drawn from every sort and type of person, but as we should expect,

Shakespeare is particularly fond of the humblest and least respectable: beggars, thieves, prisoners and servants.

We sense his sympathy with the 'silly beggars' *R. II, 5. 5. 25* sitting shamefaced in the stocks, but taking refuge in the reflection

That many have and others must sit there;
And in this thought they find a kind of ease;

or with the bankrupt beggar wailing his case

        with lank and lean discolour'd cheek,   *Luc. 708*
With heavy eye, knit brow, and strengthless pace;

and we get little vignettes of the beggar woman bearing her brat on her shoulder; the 'poor beggar' who *C. of E. 4. 4. 39* 'raileth on the rich'; the one at Hallowmas who speaks *K. J. 2. 1. 591* 'puling'; or he who is ignored by the miser who passes *Two Gent.* him by in the street giving him neither 'good word nor *2. 1. 25* look'. *T. and C.* *3. 3. 142*

There are a great many images from thieves, robbers and cutpurses, and we have glimpses of them, rough customers, ranging 'abroad unseen' at night time 'in *R. II, 3. 2. 39* murders and in outrage', 'loose companions', such

        as stand in narrow lanes,   *R. II, 5. 3. 7*
And beat our watch, and rob our passengers;

and when caught and desperate,

        all hopeless of their lives,   *3 H. VI, 1. 4. 42*
Breathe out invectives 'gainst the officers.

Shakespeare's sympathy would seem to be with the prisoners, as with the beggars; we hear of the 'polluted *Luc. 1726* prison', the gaoler who is 'dull unfeeling barren ignorance', and we can see the poor prisoner in his *R. II, 1. 3. 168* 'twisted gyves' 'wildly overgrown with hair' wondering *R. and J. 2. 2.* how his *180; H. V, 5. 2.* *43*
        vain weak nails   *R. II, 5. 5. 18*
May tear a passage through the flinty ribs

of his prison walls; and finally, the 'wretches' who
Two Gent.
4. 2. *132*
'o'ernight' 'wait for execution in the morn'.

We see also flashes of reflection, as it were, in the
images, of the army of retainers in a great house,
domestics ready to serve the will of their lord as it
H. VIII,
2. 4. *115*
pleases him to 'pronounce their office'; we realise the
use of servants in carrying out the simple Baconian
stratagem for provoking murder or violence while dis-
claiming any responsibility for it (exactly Henry IV's
procedure with Exton, *R. II*, 5. 4; 5. 6. 30–42):

J.C. 2. 1. 175
> as subtle masters do,
> Stir up their servants to an act of rage
> And after seem to chide 'em.

We catch glimpses, in this living mirror, of the servant
M. of V.
3. 2. *103*
H.V, 4. 1. *281*
who is a 'pale and common drudge', the lackey who
sweats all day from rise to set of sun, and all night
H. VIII,
5. 3. *139*
H.V, 3. 5. *51–2*
'sleeps in Elysium', the 'lousy footboy' waiting 'at
chamber-door', the lord who is free to 'spit and void
his rheum' on his 'low vassal', and the fine chamber-
Timon, 4. 3. *221*
lain, putting the warmed shirt on his master, while his
page skips at his bidding.

So on the road, through these side windows of
A.Y.L.I.
5. 3. *14*
L.L.L. 4. 3. *185*
Shakespeare's mind, we catch sight of 'two gipsies on
a horse' 'both in a tune', the butter-woman ambling
on her nag to market and the galloping post, we note
the determined gait of the harvestman

Cor. 1. 3. 39
> that's tasked to mow
> Or all, or lose his hire,

H.V,5 Prol. 12
we meet the 'mighty whiffler' preparing the way before
Two Gent.
2. 7. *9–10*
the king, and the weary pilgrims with 'feeble steps'
helped by the good fellowship on the road, when
Luc. 790
'palmers' chat makes short their pilgrimage', while

years before Autolycus was born we have a glimpse
of the 'wit's pedler' who

retails his wares *L.L.L.* 5. 2. 317
At wakes and wassails, meetings, markets, fairs.

In the village we stop and watch the 'drivelling' *R. and J.*
2. 4. 92
'natural', who runs 'lolling up and down to hide his
bauble in a hole', the 'worthless peasants' bargaining
for their wives ('for wealth and not for perfect love')

As market-men for oxen, sheep, or horse; *1 H.VI,* 5. 5. 53
the pedant that 'keeps a school i' the church', and the *Tw. N.* 3. 2. 78
pupil who takes 'correction mildly', kissing the rod; *R. II,* 5. 1. 31
the pulpiter with his 'tedious homily', wearying his
parishioners, and never even crying 'Have patience, *A.Y.L.I.*
3. 2. 158
good people!', and the unlettered clerk who cries
'Amen' to every hymn. *Son.* LXXXV

In the city and court, we come across the 'sour *V. and A.* 655
informer', 'bate-breeding spy', the 'scurvy politician'
who seems 'to see the things' he does not, and the fickle *K.L.* 4. 6. 174
turncoat courtiers,

favourites, *M. Ado,* 3. 1. 9
Made proud by princes, that advance their pride
Against that power that bred it.

In London streets we meet the rich and portly burghers,
with proud and dignified gait, staring blandly un-
seeing over the heads of the lesser folk, the

petty traffickers *M. of V.* 1. 1. 12
That curt'sy to them, do them reverence;

the gay and brilliant ambassador or 'fore-spurrer' of
a great lord, the hurrying messengers sent on an 2. 9. 93
Son. XLV
M.N.D. 2. 1. 10
embassy, and the tall and gorgeous gentlemen pen-
sioners gay and glittering in their gold coats, moving in
attendance on their great queen.

CHAPTER VIII

EVIDENCE IN THE IMAGES OF SHAKESPEARE'S THOUGHT

Shakespeare seems to do his very thinking in metaphor.
Shakespeare in the English Men of Letters
Series, by Walter Raleigh, p. 224.

THOSE who have followed my argument so far will, I hope, agree that I have grounds for believing that a study of Shakespeare's imagery throws light on his physical equipment and characteristics—in short, on his personality. I suggest, however, that we can go even farther than this, and that we can obtain quite clear glimpses into some of the deeper thoughts of Shakespeare's mind through this oblique method, the study of his imagery.

If, for instance, we look carefully at the pictures aroused in his mind by certain abstractions, by emotions, such as Love, Hate and Fear, conceptions such as Evil and Good, Time and Death, we cannot escape gaining at least a glimmer of light on Shakespeare's own attitude towards them.

LOVE

Take Love, for example. We see at once that he has a large number of merely conventional images of love; it is a fire, a furnace, a blaze and lightning; it is an arrow, a siege and a war; it is a food, a drink and a banquet; it is a plant, a fruit, a sickness, a wound, a fever; it is a building on firm or frail foundations, fair and strong or in ruins; it is constant as the sun, false as water, musical as Apollo's lute.

All these we find in one form or another in contemporary dramatists, while fire, war and food are common to them all. Several of these writers have each one special aspect which chiefly appeals to him; thus Marlowe tends to connect love with music, Fletcher with fire, Massinger with food and so on. But there are touches even in this ordinary range of images, specially Shakespearian. Thus in his view love is a food, but it is also a hunger, an aspect I do not find brought out by others:

> she makes hungry
> Where most she satisfies.

A. and C.
2. 2. 240

> So are you to my thoughts as food to life,

Son. LXXV,
ll. 1, 9–10

> Sometime all full with feasting on your sight
> And by and by clean starved for a look.

Cp. M.N.D. 1.
1. 222; Son.
LVI, etc.

The bitter-sweet character of the food of love is emphasised by Shakespeare as by no one else. It is luscious and bitter, sweet and sour, delicious and loathsome, 'a choking gall and a preserving sweet'. It is indeed an unconscious realisation of its twofold nature which prompts Troilus' bitter reproaches to 'injurious time' when he parts the lovers,

Cp. A.Y.L.I.
4. 3. 102; Son.
CXVIII; T. and
C. 2. 2. 142
Oth. 1. 3. 354
Luc. 867
R. and J. 2. 6.
11
1. 1. 193

> And scants us with a single famish'd kiss,
> Distasted with the salt of broken tears.

T. and C.
4. 4. 47

Shakespeare's very definite distinction between love and lust in the terms of this image is, so far as I have found, also confined to him alone; he affirms very early that

> Love surfeits not, Lust like a glutton dies,

V. and A. 803

and it will be noted how many are the images of surfeit and its results, applied to lust as distinguished from love (cf. *Luc.* 703; *Cym.* 1. 6. 43; *Oth.* 2. 1. 235, 3. 4. 104, etc.).

Perhaps the best way to arrive at a glimpse of Shakespeare's individual conception is to look at some of his images which are definitely different from those of his contemporaries. These seem to me to consist mainly in pictures which bring out four qualities or aspects of love: its wayward, uncertain and consequently attractive character, its swift and soaring nature, its shaping and transforming power, and its infiniteness.

Its wayward and uncertain qualities, seen mostly in the early comedies, are conveyed chiefly by likening it to a child, spring time, and a shadow.

Love is impulsive, headstrong, undisciplined, it is

Two Gent.
3. 1. 124
> like a child
> That longs for every thing that he can come by;

1. 2. 57
> how wayward is this foolish love,
> That, like a testy babe, will scratch the nurse,
> And presently, all humbled, kiss the rod!

Love grows, changes, and develops; it is impossible, therefore, at any given time, to tell what it may become, to be 'certain o'er incertainty', for 'Love is a babe', and

Son. cxv
> one cannot 'give full growth to that which still doth grow'.

Love is a spring time, showers and sunshine, made up of changing emotions, hope and despair, tears and smiles.

V. and A. 799
> Love comforteth like sunshine after rain;

A. and C.
3. 2. 43
> The April's in her eyes: it is love's spring,
> And these the showers to bring it on,

says Antony, watching Octavia's emotion on parting from her brother; the freshness of love's 'gentle spring' is contrasted with 'lust's winter'; and Proteus, when at the beginning only of his perplexities and troubles, likens love to that time of year we believe Shakespeare himself best loved, and sighs,

Two Gent.
1. 3. 84
> O, how this spring of love resembleth
> The uncertain glory of an April day.

The intangible and elusive as well as fleeting qualities
of love are brought out in likening it to a shadow,

> momentany as a sound,   *M.N.D.*
> Swift as a shadow,   *1. 1. 143*

and when Ford sums up his experience of love in the
terms of the old emblem, comparing it to a man's
shadow which flies from him when chased, and pursues *M.W. 2. 2. 212*
him when he runs away from it, he has certainly caught
one of its salient characteristics.

The images of the swift and soaring quality of love
arise out of the old myth of Cupid and his wings, but,
as is so often the case with Shakespeare, he takes a
hackneyed idea or image, plays with it and delights in
it, and finally by some magic touch, a difference of
setting, an intensification of feeling, some slight shift
of words, he recreates and entirely transforms it. Notice
for instance how the use of this image grows in depth
and feeling in *Romeo and Juliet* alone. Mercutio and
Romeo play with the idea in the old fashion, and
Romeo, before he knows what love is, declares he is
so oppressed with it he has a soul of lead. Mercutio,
teasing him, answers,

> You are a lover; borrow Cupid's wings,   *R. and J.*
> And soar with them above a common bound,   *1. 4. 17*

to which Romeo replies he is

> too sore enpierced with his shaft
> To soar with his light feathers.

But when he has met Juliet, far from being weighted,
he finds that it is 'love's light wings' which enable him
to climb the high orchard wall,

> For stony limits cannot hold love out.   *2. 2. 67*

Juliet in her impatience, suffering the swift urge and movement of love, which floods the being with life as does the blood coursing in young veins, which sweeps over and transforms the whole world as do the sun's beams

R. and J.
2. 5. 6

Driving back shadows over louring hills,

declares with sudden full realisation of the real meaning of the symbol,

2. 5. 7–8

Therefore do nimble-pinion'd doves draw love,
And therefore hath the wind-swift Cupid wings.

Finally, yet another lover, Troilus, in the moment of his highest tension and impatience, when stalking about Cressid's door,

T. and C.
3. 2. 9

Like a strange soul upon the Stygian banks
Staying for waftage,

turns to Pandarus in despair and in the intensity of his feeling lifts the image entirely out of the realm of light badinage when he begs,

3. 2. 13

O gentle Pandarus,
From Cupid's shoulder pluck his painted wings,
And fly with me to Cressid!

It is this conception of the swift soaring resistless flight of love which lies behind touches such as Hamlet's

Ham. 1. 5. 29

desire for 'wings as swift as…the thoughts of love' to

Cym. 3. 2. 50

sweep to his revenge, Imogen's exclamation, 'O, for a horse with wings!', the queen's suggestion that

3. 5. 61

wing'd with fervour of her love, she's flown
To her desired Posthumus,

Ham. 2. 2. 132

Polonius's perception of Hamlet's 'hot love on the

Two Gent.
2. 7. 11

wing', Julia's certainty that 'she that hath Love's wings to fly' will never weary, and many others.

The transforming quality of love as well as its

stamping or shaping power is suggested sometimes by imagery; indeed the whole of *A Midsummer Night's Dream* is but a fantasy on this subject, and Helena's reflections prepare us for what is coming when she says,

> Things base and vile, holding no quantity, *M.N.D.*
> Love can transpose to form and dignity. *1. 1. 232*

But there is a serious meaning in the lover's assertion that love has taught his eye

>   this alchemy, *Son.* cxiv
> To make of monsters and things indigest
> Such cherubins as your sweet self resemble,

or in the countess' reflection on the seal or 'impress' *All's Well,* of 'love's strong passion' in youth, or Hero's belief *1. 3. 137* that Beatrice cannot love, because she is of too proud or hard a stuff to take the 'shape' and 'project of *M. Ado,* affection'. *3. 1. 54*

The 'infinity' of certain emotions or qualities is recurrently suggested in Shakespearian imagery, especially with regard to love and honour, neither of which, it is implied, is capable of being bounded or weighed by common, or rather one might say, business, measures or values.

But we cannot always be sure that this view is not just that of the character speaking, as in Troilus' argument with Hector, who maintains that Helen is not worth the terrific sacrifice of Trojan lives, and should be let go. Troilus passionately disagrees with this common-sense and eminently 'reasonable' attitude, and declares that the king's honour is greater than any 'reasons', and cannot be weighed 'in a scale of common ounces', asking,

T. and C.
2. 2. 28

will you with counters sum

.   .   .   .   .

And buckle in a waist most fathomless
With spans and inches so diminutive
As fears and reasons? fie, for godly shame!

But although we feel tempted to think that Shakespeare also believed 'honour' and 'fears and reasons' to be incommensurable, and that he is with Troilus rather than with Falstaff in his view of honour, this image here expresses purely Troilus's point of view, and Hector argues with equal cogency on his side that

2. 2. 56

'tis mad idolatry
To make the service greater than the god.

The infiniteness of love, however, is suggested or implied so constantly, and by so many different contexts, that one cannot but believe that here Shakespeare unconsciously reveals his own intuitive view.

This quality is merely suggested in the imagery of love in its relation to time, where we see (p. 177 below) that alone of many precious things, youth, beauty, strength, life itself, love does not come under the dominion of time, but seems to elude and transcend it, for the infinite cannot be imprisoned by the finite.

Elsewhere, the boundless timeless character of love is constantly suggested by the imagery, especially in its definite comparison and association with the unplumbed depths of the sea. The grounds of this comparison are definitely stated in two of Shakespeare's earliest works:

V. and A. 389

The sea hath bounds, but deep desire hath none;

Two Gent.
2. 7. 69

A thousand oaths, an ocean of his tears,
And instances of infinite of love,
Warrant me welcome to my Proteus.

It is played with by Rosalind,

O coz,...that thou didst know how many fathom deep *A.Y.L.I.*
I am in love! But it cannot be sounded: my affection   *4. 1. 2*
hath an unknown bottom, like the bay of Portugal,

as well as by Celia, who gives it a turn towards the waste
of unlimited love on an unworthy or unresponsive
object, when she answers,

Or rather bottomless; that as fast as you pour affection
in, it runs out.

This thought is expressed in all seriousness by
Helena, when she acknowledges that she knows she
loves in vain:

> Yet, in this captious and intenible sieve,   *All's Well,*
> I still pour in the waters of my love.   *1. 3. 207*

Orsino confidently affirms that the capacity of love *Tw. N. 1. 1. 11*
'receiveth as the sea', and that his love in especial,
particularly as compared to a woman's, 'is all as hungry   *2. 4. 102*
as the sea, and can digest as much'. Juliet declares,

> My bounty is as boundless as the sea,   *R. and J.*
> My love as deep,   *2. 2. 133*

and both 'are infinite'. Othello's great love, when
thwarted, turns into vengeance 'like to the Pontic sea', *Oth. 3. 3. 453*
and in the opening lines of the greatest love drama of
them all, the earthly sea no longer suffices as symbol
for the depth and vastness of the passion it paints, and
Antony tells Cleopatra that if she sets 'a bourn how   *A. and C.*
far to be beloved', then must she 'needs find out new   *1. 1. 17*
heaven, new earth'.

On the whole, there is in Shakespeare very little HATE
imagery of Hate, and there are scarcely any personifications of it at all. Shakespeare has, it is needless to say,
portrayed in his dramas the emotion of hate with great

vividness, as for instance in the latter part of *Timon*
of Athens, when, deceived and disillusioned, 'sick of
man's unkindness', Timon, in his sudden and bitter
revulsion of feeling, believes that mankind is utterly without love, and therefore rotten and worthless, and so he
curses men and calls down upon them disease, disorder,
disintegration and extinction. Here and elsewhere, in
the mouths of Shakespeare's characters, hate is painted
as a very definite and vivid force; but it is significant
that in most of the imagery, on the contrary, hate seems
to be negative, empty, inert, restrictive and twisted,
rather than an active and piercing emotion, and in this
connection the adjectives used of it are indicative: such
as 'barren', 'sour', 'deadly', 'blood-drinking', 'grudg-
ing', 'cankered', 'misbegotten'.

I find hate twice only in an image definitely contrasted with love, once when the king reproves Bertram
for his casual slackness with regard to Helena, and his
avowal of love that comes too late, saying,

Our own love waking cries to see what's done,
While shameful hate sleeps out the afternoon,

and once when Othello, finally convinced of Desdemona's guilt, cries,

Yield up, O love, thy crown and hearted throne
To tyrannous hate!

The truth is that the real opposite of love in the Shakespearian vision is not hate, but fear.

FEAR   Fear, the opposite pole from love, 'of all base passions,
fear is most accursed'. The words may not be Shakespeare's, but it is quite certain that they express his
sentiments; that in his view a state of fear is the worst
kind of evil, leading to every other kind of evil, and that

Timon, 4. 3. 6

All's Well,
5. 3. 65

Oth. 3. 3. 448

FEAR
1 H. VI,
5. 2. 18

it is therefore the most remote from a state of love. For if there is one line in the Bible above any other of which Shakespeare—probably unconsciously—consistently demonstrates the truth and importance, it is that 'perfect love casteth out fear'.

This opposition is quite clear in the imagery: love is a flame, a hot fire; fear is cold and freezes the veins; *R. and J. 4. 3. 15; V. and A. 891; R. II, 1. 2. 34* kindliness and cheerfulness thaw 'cold fear', for love and fear cannot subsist together, a fact recognised even *H. V, 4 Prol. 45* by the basest natures:

Against love's fire fear's frost hath dissolution.   *Luc. 355*

Love is a lord and sovereign, fear is a low vassal: *2 H. VI, 4. 1. 129*

Let pale-faced fear keep with the mean-born man,   *3. 1. 335*
And find no harbour in a royal heart.

Love is wingéd, fear is base, 'leaden servitor to dull *Tw. N. 5. 1. 145* delay'; love is a binding or knitting together, a strong *R. III, 4. 3. 52* cement, fear is disintegrating, annihilating;

                 distill'd   *Ham. 1. 2. 204*
Almost to jelly with the act of fear,

says Horatio of the scared officers of the watch at Elsinore; love is strong and unshaken, fear is weak, *Son. cxvi* pale-faced and pale-hearted, shuddering, trembling, *1 H. IV, 4. 3. 11* *2 H. VI, 3. 1. 335* and so on. *Mac. 4. 1. 85* *M. of V. 3. 2. 110*

It has been pointed out[1] that the most terrible part *Luc. 511* of *Macbeth*, 'Shakespeare's most profound and mature vision of Evil', is the stifling, baffling, murky atmosphere of fear in which everyone moves; the mystery, darkness, doubt on every side, the horrible rumours, the still more horrible murders, all tending to produce the state of tense irrational fear that we connect with nightmare.

---

[1] In a most interesting chapter, 'Macbeth and the Metaphysic of Evil', in *The Wheel of Fire*, by G. Wilson Knight.

The whole play of *Macbeth* may indeed be regarded
in one sense as an 'image' of fear, and I believe no man
could have written it just as it is, had he not believed
fear to be the most evil and life-draining of all emotions,
constricting, withering, paralysing, and so the very opposite of love, which is expansive, fruitful and vitalising.
It is certainly indicative that there are only two plays
in which the word 'love' occurs so seldom as in *Macbeth*,
and no play in which 'fear' occurs so often; indeed
it occurs twice or thrice as often as in most other
plays.

The opposition of fear and love is poignantly brought
out at the climax of the tragedy in the little scene (5. 3)
which opens in a quiver of fear, when suddenly Macbeth
sees that in spite of everything he has done to gain
power and happiness, he is actually bereft of all that
matters most in life, for he is sick at heart, broken and
old,

Mac. 5. 3. 24   And that which should accompany old age,
As honour, love, obedience, troops of friends,
I must not look to have.

Too late he realises that all pervading fear has inevitably
cast out love, that, as Angus says earlier,

5. 2. 19   Those he commands move only in command,
Nothing in love,

and all that is now left him is to drop all pretence,
range himself boldly on the side of evil, so that, his
courage being no longer sapped by secrecy and duplicity,
he is enabled to die fighting bravely.

This constrictive weakening character of fear as well
as its opposition to love is brought out repeatedly in
the imagery, and it is worth while to look at one or two
of the pictures of fear in this tragedy of fear.

Those with occult vision tell us that one of the most pitiful objects in nature is a man in the grip of fear, and that they can see him, when in this state, throwing out round himself a kind of cage of livid and vibrating grey bars. However this may be, certainly it is this sense of constriction, of stifling, paralysing imprisonment which is so vividly pictured by Macbeth, when he cries,

> . . . I am cabin'd, cribb'd, confined, bound in   *Mac.* 3. 4. 24
> To saucy doubts and fears,

and how amazingly his sensitive, quivering, craven condition of mind is portrayed by the use of one word in his answer to the apparition who bids him beware of Macduff,

> Thou hast *harp'd* my fear aright.   4. 1. 74

Macbeth's fear is repeated in the other characters; Banquo is caught in it, and feels it as a weight of lead   2. 1. 6 lying on him; Lady Macbeth, when all is over, is shattered by it and dies of it; Lady Macduff declares her husband's flight was madness—prompted by fears which have made him traitor, he loves nor wife nor babes,

> All is the fear and nothing is the love.   4. 2. 12

In startling contrast to the behaviour of the man, she draws the picture of the tiny mother wren in an ecstasy of courage defending her young against the owl. So also Ross, trying to excuse Macduff, points out the utterly demoralising effect of fear of the unknown,

>   when we hold rumour   4. 2. 19
> From what we fear, yet know not what we fear,

and pictures him as a man buffeted from every side and helpless, afloat 'upon a wild and violent sea'.

In yet one other play we may note in a curious image the definite opposition of love and fear, when Troilus asks Cressida why she checks her wish to the gods, what does she fear?

T. and C.
3. 2. 70

Fears make devils of cherubins; they never see truly.... O, let my lady apprehend no fear: in all Cupid's pageant there is presented no monster;

a thoroughly Shakespearian way of saying that fear is a blinding, distorting, debasing emotion, and that in perfect love there exists no place for it.

Evil in Shakespeare's imagination is dirty, black and foul, a blot, a spot, a stain; and some sixty examples could be quoted of this, as well as many of the reverse and rather more obvious uses of spotless, stainless and so on. This constant habit of his imagination gives rise at times to vivid touches of description, as when Lucrece, studying the mild and fair seeming of Sinon in the Troy picture, refuses to believe that

Luc. 1517

False-creeping craft and perjury should...
...blot with hell-born sin such saint-like forms.

It adds realism to such a statement as Gloucester's crafty shifting of responsibility to the citizens for his acceptance of the throne:

R. III, 3. 7. 231

But if black scandal or foul-faced reproach
Attend the sequel of your imposition,
Your mere enforcement shall acquittance me
From all the impure blots and stains thereof;

and it lends a startling poignancy to the queen's tortured cry when she can no longer bear her son's accusations:

Ham. 3. 4. 88

O Hamlet, speak no more:
Thou turn'st mine eyes into my very soul,
And there I see such black and grained spots
As will not leave their tinct.

It is in *Othello* that repugnance to sin and evil is aroused in us most consistently by its being thought of as foul, black, stained and filthy.

Iago keeps alive this repugnance as much as anyone, for he is fully conscious of, and indeed glories in, the foulness of his own deeds. When plotting his devilish handling of Desdemona and Cassio, playing on her pity and gaining his gratitude, he reflects,

> When devils will the blackest sins put on,   *Oth.* 2. 3. 356
> They do suggest at first with heavenly shows,
> As I do now,...
> So will I turn her virtue into pitch;   *2. 3. 365*

and when torturing Othello, appearing to minimise what he has suggested as Cassio's sin, he asks may not 'foul things' sometimes intrude into a palace, and 'uncleanly apprehensions' into the purest breast?

The stain and blackness of evil are suggested repeatedly through the play, as they are constantly in   *5. 1. 36; 1. 3.* Shakespeare, and the idea is brought out vividly in such   *65; 1. 3. 117;* pictures as Othello's pathetic lament,   *1. 2. 62, etc.*

> Her name, that was as fresh   *3. 3. 386*
> As Dian's visage, is now begrimed and black
> As mine own face,

or his unsuspecting sketch—in which is concentrated all the dramatic irony of the tragedy—of Iago as 'an honest man', who

> hates the slime   *5. 2. 148*
> That sticks on filthy deeds.

Shakespeare also thinks of evil as a sickness, an infection, a sore and an ulcer. This is very clear throughout *Macbeth* and *Hamlet* (as is also the idea of 'dirt', see pp. 316–18, 332), but it is there only a concentration and intensification of a picture Shakespeare has with him always.

All through the disturbances, murders and evil deeds which abound in the historical plays, the picture of the 'infection of the time', the distempered body of the kingdom, full of 'rank diseases', is constant.

K.J. 5. 2. 2
2 H. IV,
3. 1. 38–43

The idea also that one evil leads to another is ever present with Shakespeare:

Per. 1. 1. 137

> One sin, I know, another doth provoke;
> Murder's as near to lust as flame to smoke.

This conception is repeatedly conveyed through the image of infection, as in Salisbury's description of the state of England in *King John* (5. 2. 20–3).

A more subtle development of the same idea, that the quickly spreading and infectious quality of evil is so great that even the finest natures may be smirched or degraded by being connected with it, we find in the well-known image in *Hamlet* about the 'dram of eale'— corrupt though understandable—which clearly means that a small admixture of what is base may easily leaven a whole substance and change it to the baser character.

Ham. 1. 4. 36

The undoubted fact that the remedy hastily sought by those suffering from an evil may possibly do more harm than the original ill, which many have felt tempted to think is true of such measures as the 'dole' in England or 'prohibition' in America, is aptly pictured by Salisbury, also in *King John*, when he declares he is

K.J. 5. 2. 12

> not glad that such a sore of time
> Should seek a plaster by contemn'd revolt,
> And heal the inveterate canker of one wound
> By making many.

The conception of evil as a tumour or ulcer is also constant, as when Lear turns on Goneril, calling her 'a boil, a plague-sore, an embossed carbuncle' in his *K.L.* 2. 4. 226 'corrupted blood'. It lies also behind many of the metaphors dealing with sin, such as the duke's rebuke to Jaques, when he declares that he will

> Cleanse the foul body of the infected world, *A.Y.L.I.*
2. 7. 64–9

Richard's warning to Northumberland that foul sin is 'gathering head', or the description of John's fears and *R. II*, 5. 1. 57 anger, his passion which 'is so ripe, it needs must break', 'And when it breaks', says Pembroke,

> I fear will issue thence *K.J.* 4. 2. 79
> The foul corruption of a sweet child's death.

The sickening smell of evil is the natural outcome of its being thought of as dirt and foul disease, and on the whole, perhaps, it is through this sense that Shakespeare most vividly pictures the horror of it.

In discussing his acute sense of smell I have already (pp. 78–81) given several examples of this, but for the sake of completeness in presenting his conception of evil it is necessary to repeat some of these here.

The horror of sin as conveyed through its evil *K.J.* 4. 3. 111 smell is especially noticeable in *Othello* and *King John*. The climax of the revolt of the nobles from the evil of John (and what was practically Arthur's murder) is expressed by Salisbury with startling vividness purely as a physical revolt from a loathsome smell, when he cries,

> Away with me, all you whose souls abhor
> The uncleanly savours of a slaughter-house;
> For I am stifled with this smell of sin.

The evil smell of sin is in *Othello* as constantly kept before us as are its foulness and dirt. When Iago tentatively suggests to Othello that in choosing to marry him—a black man—Desdemona has already shown a perverted and unnatural taste, he exclaims:

Oth. 3. 3. 232
> Foh! one may smell in such a will most rank,
> Foul disproportion, thoughts unnatural.

Emilia, when she realises what Iago has done, cries,

5. 2. 190
> Villany, villany, villany!
> I think upon't: I think: I smell't: O villany!

and Othello brings out the horror of the contrast between the fair looks of Desdemona and what he believes her deeds entirely by means of smell, lamenting,

4. 2. 67
> O thou weed,
> Who art so lovely fair and smell'st so sweet
> That the sense aches at thee, would thou hadst ne'er been born!

and answering her piteous query,

> Alas, what ignorant sin have I committed?

with the agonised cry,

> What committed!
> Heaven stops the nose at it.

This conception of the evil smell of evil deeds lies behind many exclamations and descriptions by Shakespeare's characters:

Ham. 3. 3. 36
> O, my offence is rank, it smells to heaven,

3. 4. 148 cries Claudius; 'rank corruption', Hamlet tells his mother, 'mining all within, infects unseen'; Prospero assures his brother he forgives his 'rankest fault' and so on. Sometimes it gives great poignancy to the sense of horror at some special deed, as when Antony declares that the stabbing of Caesar is a 'foul deed' which

J.C. 3. 1. 274
> shall smell above the earth
> With carrion men, groaning for burial;

or Polixenes, aghast at the foul suspicions of Leontes, *W. T. 1. 2. 420*
pictures himself as a man emitting so loathsome an
odour that people flee before him.

The thought of evil as a blot or stain carries with it
the idea of washing or wiping it off, which is constant.
'This noble passion', cries Malcolm on listening to
Macduff's reproach and lament,

> hath from my soul   *Mac. 4. 3. 115*
>Wiped the black scruples.

This combines with the idea of bloodstains after a
murder, and the obvious picture of washing the blood
off guilty hands which occurs repeatedly. Macbeth's   *Ham. 3. 3. 43;*
 R. II, 3. 1. 5;
unforgettable cry, in which he first uses this image and   *5. 6. 50; R.III,*
 1. 4. 273, etc.
then reverses it, is a fine example of how the sheer   *Mac. 2. 2. 60–3*
force of Shakespeare's imagination enables him to take
a perfectly commonplace idea (compare how it appears
in *Much Ado*, 4. 1. 142–3), and transmute it, in a
moment of high tension, into magnificence.

The heavy weight of sin and evil is also a constant
thought, and, like the preceding image, is probably
Biblical in origin. Shakespeare uses it with great vividness to portray the hampering and depressing effects
of a sense of guilt. 'Confess thy treasons', says Boling-   *R. II, 1. 3. 199*
broke to Norfolk, and

> Since thou hast far to go, bear not along
> The clogging burthen of a guilty soul.

>Let us be lead within thy bosom, Richard,   *R. III,*
                  5. 3. 152

cry the ghosts of the two young princes,

> And weigh thee down to ruin, shame, and death!

So heavy is the weight of sin, or the sense of sin, that
it is pictured as having a physical effect:

> Be Mowbray's sins so heavy in his bosom,   *R. II, 1. 2. 50*
> That they may break his foaming courser's back,

cries the Duchess of Gloucester, and Iachimo, kneeling
to Posthumus, falters,

Cym. 5. 5. 413   ...my heavy conscience sinks my knee.

Sins are measured by their weight:

T. and C.   to persist
2. 2. 186   In doing wrong extenuates not wrong,
                   But makes it much more heavy,

says Hector, and the duke tells Juliet that her sin was
M. for M.   'of heavier kind' than Claudio's.
2. 3. 28
                   Another aspect of evil which specially interested
Shakespeare, and seemed to him its most dangerous
feature, was its power of disguising itself as good—

L.L.L.   Devils soonest tempt, resembling spirits of light.
4. 3. 256

This quality is pictured by him chiefly in terms of
clothing and painting, and is especially frequent in his
early work:

Luc. 93   Hiding base sin in plaits of majesty,

C. of E.   Apparel vice like virtue's harbinger,
3. 2. 12
R. III, 3. 5. 29   So smooth he daub'd his vice with show of virtue,

Luc. 1074   My sable ground of sin I will not paint,
                  To hide the truth.

Evil as a weed is a natural outcome of the running
imagery of the untended garden throughout the historical plays, where it occurs constantly, and much
penetrating thought is conveyed in these plays and
elsewhere through this image. Thus we are made to
realise the fact, for instance, that it is the richest nature
which has the greatest capacity for evil—as for good—
in Henry IV's remark on Prince Hal,

2 H. IV,   Most subject is the fattest soil to weeds,
4. 4. 54

that idleness and emptiness of mind are a fruitful source
of mischief, in Antony's exclamation,

> O then we bring forth weeds
>   When our quick minds lie still,

A. and C.
1. 2. 110

that indulgence in sin increases its growth with astound-
ing celerity, in Hamlet's exhortation to his mother,

> And do not spread the compost on the weeds,
>   To make them ranker,

Ham. 3. 4. 151

and that one evil quality in a member of a community
is a real danger to the rest, in Ulysses' reflection,

> the seeded pride
> That hath to this maturity blown up
> In rank Achilles must or now be cropp'd,
> Or, shedding, breed a nursery of like evil,
> To o'erbulk us all.

T. and C.
1. 3. 316

These ideas are all made vividly clear by this constant
analogy with the habits and characteristics of the growth
of weeds.

The personifications of evil are chiefly noticeable for
their tendency to take the form of animals rather than
persons: dogs chiefly, used with almost startling effect,
as when Hamlet pictures the king's guilt 'unkenneling' *Ham. 3. 2. 86*
itself as he watches the play, or when he sees John's
fears, following, as a dog, 'the steps of wrong'. Some- *K.J. 4. 2. 57*
times we have the image of other animals, as when
Henry V pictures, by means of the runaway horse, the
impossibility of restraining soldiers inflamed by war
from violent and destructive acts, and asks,

> What rein can hold licentious wickedness
> When down the hill he holds his fierce career?

H. V, 3. 3. 22

And sometimes only the type of animal is indicated, as

when Lucrece, in her vivid picture of the passions of
men, suggests wild beasts of prey,

Luc. 1249

> In men, as in a rough-grown grove, remain
> Cave-keeping evils that obscurely sleep.

Thus in these pictures as a whole, we see evil as
something corrupt, horrible and repugnant, which is
to the world as foulness and disease are to a body or rank
weeds to a garden; it is a condition, a growth, which,
if health or fruitfulness are to be attained, must at all
costs be expelled. But it carries with it no more 'sense
of sin' than would be experienced by a gardener looking
at an overgrown and choked-up garden or a doctor
treating a poisoned body. If we add what these pictures
tell us to Bradley's masterly summary of Shakespeare's
presentation of evil as revealed in the tragedies, it will
be seen that they support and reinforce it.

Mr Bradley points out that in the tragic plays evil
exhibits itself as something alien to the whole or ultimate order of the world, which order, nevertheless,
seems first to produce it, then to struggle with it, and
finally, with great loss and waste to itself, to expel it.
He argues, therefore, that this ultimate order or power,
which is antagonistic to evil, which is disturbed by evil
and reacts against it, must be akin to good, and is in
fact a 'moral' order.

In the pictures of dirt and foulness, and most
especially of sickness and disease we see this same conception of something produced by the body itself,
which is indeed in a sense part of it, against which, at
the same time, if it is to survive, it has to struggle and
fight; in which 'intestinal struggle', as Bradley rightly
calls it, it casts out, not only the poison or foulness
which is killing it, but also a precious part of its own

substance. In this consists tragedy, 'there is no tragedy in its expulsion of evil: the tragedy is that this involves the waste of good'.[1]

The rank weeds in field or garden carry out in slightly different terms the same idea; they are produced by the earth and form as much a part of it as do the wheat and flowers, but in their case the inevitable waste of vital force consists not in the act of weeding or expelling them, but rather in allowing them to flourish at all, and so to impoverish and, if unchecked, ultimately to ruin the ground.

[1] *Shakespearian Tragedy* by A. C. Bradley, 1904, p. 37.

CHAPTER IX

EVIDENCE IN THE IMAGES OF
SHAKESPEARE'S THOUGHT (*continued*)

SHAKESPEARE'S views about goodness are less easy to disentangle from his images than is his general attitude towards evil. That is, he has fewer pictures of goodness and these nearly all show it in its relation to evil.

One thing is clear, from his plays and images alike—that he is ever conscious of the strange mixture of both good and evil in our life and being, of the necessity for the presence of both to make up the fabric as we know it, for

All's Well,
4. 3. 75

The web of our life is of a mingled yarn, good and ill together.

Not only that, but the one actually produces or gives birth to the other, and too much goodness may even make it easier for evil to flourish and escape punishment, as when York, the 'loyal father of a treacherous son', is pictured as a pure and silver stream, from whence Aumerle

R. II, 5. 3. 62

through muddy passages
Hath held his current and defiled himself:

Bolingbroke tells York,

5. 3. 64

Thy overflow of good converts to bad,
And thy abundant goodness shall excuse
This deadly blot in thy digressing son:

to which York answers bitterly,

5. 3. 67

So shall my virtue be his vice's bawd.

On the other hand it is clear that evil continually
calls out good, affliction produces patience and other
virtues, war and danger are the trumpet calls to courage
and endurance, as Harry the king perceives so clearly
when, before Agincourt, he makes the rounds of his
camp and reflects on the 'soul of goodness in things   *H. V, 4. 1. 4*
evil'.

The contagion of goodness (and the fact that one
good deed leads to another) is felt very keenly by Shakespeare, though it is not so constantly dwelt on as the
'infection' of evil, and it may not be wholly chance
that it is women who seem chiefly conscious of the one
and men of the other:

> ...one good deed dying tongueless   *W.T. 1. 2. 92*
> Slaughters a thousand waiting upon that,

urges Hermione, when trying to spur Leontes to say
something pleasant to her. The far-reaching effects of
goodness have rarely been so vividly pictured as by
Portia when she sees the light in the hall flooding her
garden at the darkest moment before dawn, and turning
to Nerissa says,

> How far that little candle throws his beams!   *M. of V.*
> So shines a good deed in a naughty world.   *5. 1. 90*

Hermione emphasises the value of kindly words, and
it is a characteristically Shakespearian thought which
occurs again in a scene which bears many other such
marks of his authorship, when Henry VIII, apparently
responding to Wolsey's hope that he will 'yoke together' his 'doing well' with his 'well saying', answers,

> 'Tis well said again;   *H. VIII,*
> And 'tis a kind of good deed to say well.   *3. 2. 152*

The kindling and reverberating quality of goodness is more present in Shakespeare's mind in the later plays, the 'infection' of evil in the earlier. The former is discussed at greatest length in that most interesting conversation between Ulysses and Achilles, when Ulysses, stimulated by what he is reading, points out that any good in us has its existence only by virtue of its effect on others, for a man possesses it only by reflection,

T. and C.
3. 3. 100

> As when his virtues shining upon others
> Heat them, and they retort that heat again
> To the first giver.

This conception of the 'fructifying' quality of goodness, as well as the closely allied realisation that the only value of our good qualities lies in how far they affect, influence or delight others, is one which is much in Shakespeare's mind, especially during a certain group of years, probably from about 1602 to 1605, and he crystallises and preserves it after his habit in a succession of vivid pictures. 'No man', says Ulysses, 'is the lord of any thing'

> Till he communicate his parts to others

and beholds them

3. 3. 119

> formed in the applause
> Where they're extended; who, like an arch, reverberates
> The voice again; or, like a gate of steel
> Fronting the sun, receives and renders back
> His figure and his heat.

The duke expresses his view of it in the opening words of *Measure for Measure*:

M. for M.
1. 1. 33

> Heaven doth with us as we with torches do,
> Not light them for themselves.

And Timon, in his enthusiastic response to the expressed desire of his friends that he should use them, declares that if friends did not help each other they would 'resemble sweet instruments hung up in cases, that keep their sounds to themselves'. *Timon, 1. 2. 98*

Yet one more thought of Shakespeare's about goodness as expressed in his images may here be noted. We have seen that he pictures evil as something foul, as a sickness and poison, but it is a poison to a healthy nature or to what is on the whole a healthy state of things. On the other hand, as we see by other images, there are circumstances under which goodness can also be a poison and can appear foul and vile, and that is to the vicious man. In other words, Shakespeare has instinctively grasped for himself the old Platonic doctrine that the soul can perceive beauty only in so far as it is itself beautiful, and that consequently the debased nature will dislike and positively shrink from beauty and goodness.

So that if, as Ruskin affirms,[1] the whole science of aesthetics is, in the depth of it, summed up in the passage in *Faust* where Mephistopheles describes the angels' song as 'discord' and 'filthy jingling', so equally one may say, the truth that love of goodness depends entirely on the health and purity of the spirit is summed up in Wolsey's remark to Surrey,

> All goodness *H. VIII,*
> Is poison to thy stomach, *3. 2. 282*

or in Albany's bitter reproach to Goneril,

> Wisdom and goodness to the vile seem vile: *K.L. 4. 2. 38*
> Filths savour but themselves.

[1] *Aratra Pentelici*, Lecture I, par. 12.

Passing now to Shakespeare's conception of Time, we find that one of the most important of time's functions is as a revealer and disentangler of truth. His office is

Luc. 937

> To eat up errors by opinion bred;

his glory,

940

> To unmask falsehood and bring truth to light.

It is he who straightens out and resolves the problems and perplexities of life, in comedy and tragedy alike. Cordelia, listening with disgust to her sisters' false professions, is content to wait till

K.L. 1. 1. 283

> Time shall unfold what plaited cunning hides,

while Viola, surveying the troubles of her little world, in which every one appears intent on loving the wrong person, sighs in despair,

T.N. 2. 2. 41

> O time! thou must untangle this, not I;
> It is too hard a knot for me to untie!

Time is sometimes thought of as a fruit being ripened:

1 H. VI,
2. 4. 99
1 H. IV,
1. 3. 294
M. of V.
2. 8. 40

> Were growing time once ripen'd to my will;
> When time is ripe, which will be suddenly,
> But stay the very riping of the time,

and both ideas, of revealer of truth and of ripened fruit, are combined in Isabella's exasperated prayer, when the duke professes unbelief in her indictment of Angelo,

M. for M.
5. 1. 116

> Keep me in patience, and with ripen'd time
> Unfold the evil which is here wrapt up.

Time is also pictured as the sun, which ripens. 'The royal tree', says Gloucester of Edward,

R. III,
3. 7. 167

> hath left us royal fruit,
> Which, mellow'd by the stealing hours of time,
> Will well become the seat of majesty.

Closely connected with this life-giving, nourishing power is the conception of him as a nurse, breeder and begetter of good and ill alike.

> With news the time's with labour, and throes forth
> Each minute some,   *A. and C.*
>   *3. 7. 81*

cries Canidius, on the eve of defeat, having listened to conflicting reports and distracting decisions;

> Time is the nurse and breeder of all good,   *Two Gent.*
>   *3. 1. 243*

declares Proteus hopefully; and equally certainly Iago asserts, 'There are many events in the womb of time, *Oth. 1. 3. 378* which will be delivered'; Lennox tells of the prophecies of

>   confused events   *Mac. 2. 3. 62*
> New hatch'd to the woful time,

on the terrible night of Duncan's murder; and the son looking on the face of the father he has unawares killed in battle cries,

> O heavy times, begetting such events!   *3 H. VI, 2. 5.*
>   *63. See also*
>   *Titus, 4. 3. 30*

This conception of time's part in bringing to birth and maturing seeds or germs is most fully worked out and interestingly applied by Warwick to the development of character, when discussing with Henry IV the early indications of Northumberland's falseness:

>   a man may prophesy,   *2 H. IV, 3. 1.*
> With a near aim, of the main chance of things   *82–6, also 75–9*
> As yet not come to life, which in their seeds
> And weak beginnings lie intreasured.
> Such things become the hatch and brood of time.

So that time, like Janus, is two-faced; if he is the destroyer, he is also the medium, the necessary condition by the aid of which events, qualities, projects, ideas and thoughts are born into actual and material being.

T. and C.
1. 3. 312

> I have a young conception in my brain,

says Ulysses to Nestor,

> Be you my time to bring it to some shape,

that is, into actuality, out of the mind or spirit into definite tangible form.

This is a characteristic Shakespearian thought, found again and again. Agamemnon, complaining that during the long seven years' siege of Troy, all the designs projected in the minds of the besiegers when brought into action, went awry, describes these misfortunes thus:

1. 3. 13

> Sith every action that hath gone before,
> Whereof we have record, trial did draw
> Bias and thwart, not answering the aim
> *And that unbodied figure of the thought*
> *That gave't surmised shape.*

Similarly, the birth of poetry takes place

M.N.D.
5. 1. 14

> as imagination bodies forth
> The forms of things unknown, the poet's pen
> Turns them to shapes.

Sometimes, as here, imagination, human genius and time—for the working of genius necessitates time—seem to share the *shaping* or materialising function; sometimes imagination and time only, as when Hamlet declares he has more offences at his beck than he has

Ham. 3. 1. 126

'thoughts to put them in, imagination to give them shape, or time to act them in'.

On the other hand, time is the sole factor when

2 H. IV,
3. 2. 352

Falstaff cries, 'Let time shape, and there an end', as he reflects with some exasperation on what time has done for the foolish and empty-pated Shallow, and resolves in the near future to benefit by the 'lands and beefs' his old acquaintance has so undeservedly acquired.

The two characteristics of time which press chiefly on Shakespeare's consciousness, however, are the variations of his pace, and—much the more important—his destroying power.

The variable speed of time, dependent entirely on the emotional state of those experiencing it, is a theme which attracts Shakespeare all through his work, from Lucrece's rhetorical maledictions on Tarquin when she calls on time to

> Let him have time to mark how slow time goes   *Luc. 990*
> In time of sorrow, and how swift and short
> His time of folly and his time of sport,

to Troilus' passionate invective when Cressid is torn from him, and he denounces 'injurious time' who with a robber's haste

> Crams his rich thievery up.   *T. and C.*
> *4. 4. 42*

As Rosalind wittily expounds to Orlando, 'Time travels *A.Y.L.I.* in divers paces with divers persons'. For those who *3. 2. 317* love and have to part he moves with lightning speed; *M.N.D. 3. 2. 200; T. and C.* to those who are enjoying themselves he is 'swift and *4. 2. 11* short'; he is 'swift-footed' and 'never-resting' for him *Luc. 991–2; V. and A. 23, 842* who watches youth and beauty fading; and is in 'con- *Son. xix, v* tinual haste' for the lover fearing change; he gallops *Son. cxxiii* with the thief on his way to the gallows, and those who *A.Y.L.I.* are old discover that on their *3. 2. 336*

> quick'st decrees   *All's Well,*
> The inaudible and noiseless foot of Time   *5. 3. 40*

'steals ere' they 'can effect them'. On the other hand, *M. Ado, 2. 1. 361; A.Y.L.I.* for lovers parted who desire re-union he 'goes on *3. 2. 313* crutches'; to those in sorrow he 'seems long'; while to *Luc. 990*

the idler and lotus eater who 'fleet' him 'carelessly',
to those who watch, and to the man expecting reward
from kings, his hours creep slowly.

But whether his pace be swift or slow, time has one
constant characteristic, one constant function: he de-
stroys. Injurious, shifting, wasteful, a devourer, a
spoiler and a thief, he swallows up cities and defaces
proud buildings, is an eater of youth, 'feeds on the
rarities of nature's truth' and devours good deeds past
as fast as they are made, he steals minutes and hours,
wrecks and despoils beauty,

> And nothing stands but for his scythe to mow.

This, at least, is one mood—and the most constant—
in which Shakespeare sees time, and, like many of his
pictures of death, it is an entirely mediaeval conception
he has before him of the 'cormorant' devourer, the
'bloody tyrant', the all-powerful reaper with his scythe.
It is of this figure which Ulysses is thinking when he
declares that

> beauty, wit,
> High birth, vigour of bone, desert in service,
> Love, friendship, charity, are subjects all
> To envious and calumniating time.

But again, as in his vision of death, I believe in all this
Shakespeare was but giving his audience and readers
the figure he and they were accustomed to have presented to them. If we look closer, however, we shall
find a hint of Shakespeare's own conception, both in
the *Sonnets* and in that great play, *Troilus and Cressida*,
the philosophy of which centres round the power and
limitations of time.

In some of the *Sonnets* (c, cviii, cxvi, cxxiii), the
reputed might of time is doubted or assailed, by *Lucrece*

Marginal references:
A.Y.L.I. 2. 7.
112; Luc. 1575;
K.J. 3. 3. 31

Luc. 774; *Son.*
xv
L.L.L. 1. 1. 4
Luc. 927
T. and C. 4. 4.
42; *Son.* xix,
lx, lxv
T. and C.
3. 2. 191
Son. lxiv
Luc. 927
Son. lx
T. and C.
3. 3. 148
All's Well, 2. 1.
169; *R. III,* 3.
7. 168
Luc. 145; *Son.*
lxv, lxiii
Son. lx

T. and C.
3. 3. 171

he is assigned a definitely humble sphere, 'thou ceaseless *Luc.* 967
Son. CXV
lackey to eternity', and in one sonnet we are definitely
told that in spite of time's tyranny and his 'million'd
accidents', which

Creep in 'twixt vows, and change decrees of kings, CXV

there is one power immeasurably greater than he, for
it is of unplumbed worth, eternal, unshakable and unalterable. That power is love; not the love CXVI

Which alters when it alteration finds

but the 'ever-fixed mark'

That looks on tempests and is never shaken.

Everything seems to come under the dominion of time—
youth, beauty, strength, even life itself—[1] save only love,
which belongs to another sphere and is independent
of time:

... eternal love in love's fresh case CVIII
Weighs not the dust and injury of age,
Nor gives to necessary wrinkles place,
But makes antiquity for aye his page;

Love's not Time's fool, though rosy lips and cheeks CXVI
Within his bending sickle's compass come.

It might be argued that this is merely rhetorical, a
fitting climax to a series of ardent love poems, but
when we find the poet, in his fortieth year, writing a
tragic drama, full of deepest thought and experience,
aflame with passionate feeling, which embodies, as its
central theme, the realisation that the infinity of faithful
love is out of its element—cannot indeed continue to
exist—within the bounds of finite time, we tend to
believe that the experience and reflections of Troilus are
very nearly akin to those of his creator.

---

[1] 'But thought's the slave of life, and life's time's fool', cries the
wounded Hotspur (1 *Hen. IV*, 5. 4. 81).

The concept of time is ever present with Shakespeare in *Troilus and Cressida*, and the constant time imagery is unusual and magnificent, even for him, so that we find presented to us, by the different characters of the play, a series of the most varied and unforgettable aspects of time to be found in all his work.

We have Cressida's beautiful figure while swearing her love:

T. and C.
3. 2. 189–93

> When time is old and hath forgot itself,

a reminiscence of Whitney, but worth in itself, as poetry, the whole of his big book; Agamemnon's

4. 5. 166–71 greeting to Hector, when, sweeping away both past and future, he offers him immediate and present friendship and welcome; Hector's conception of time as

4. 5. 224–6 judge:

> The end crowns all,
> And that old common arbitrator, Time,
> Will one day end it;

3. 3. 145–74 Ulysses' tremendous speech, embodying in rapidly successive pictures, melting the one into the other, his cynical view of time the destroyer, the forgetter, and what we would call—curiously enough—the time-server; the beggar with

3. 3. 145

> a wallet at his back
> Wherein he puts alms for oblivion,

the 'great-sized monster of ingratitudes'; the rush of those who desire advancement in time, sweeping all before them, 'like to an enter'd tide', trampling down the foremost who have fallen in the race; the 'fashionable host',

3. 3. 165

> That slightly shakes his parting guest by the hand,
> And with his arms outstretch'd, as he would fly,
> Grasps in the comer,

all emphasising the shifting, changing, ruthless and destructive qualities of time. Above all we have Troilus' pictures: the witch night, who

> flies the grasps of love
> With wings more momentary-swift than thought,

T. and C.
4. 2. 11–14

the rough and heartless interferer who

> Puts back leave-taking, justles roughly by
> All time of pause,

4. 4. 34

the killer, who strangles lovers' vows 'even in the birth of' their 'own labouring breath', and the robber, who snatching

> As many farewells as be stars in heaven,

4. 4. 44

fumbles them up 'into a loose adieu'.

It is of course not only through the imagery that we sense in this play Shakespeare's conception of time. In the direct utterances of the characters also we find similar ideas. Thus, through and above all Troilus's invective, we feel that what he cannot forgive time is that it seems to hurt, change, diminish and even to destroy love. From the beginning he is half conscious this must be so, he doubts the possibility of love's permanence in a world of change, yet he recognises the supreme and permanent quality of his own experience:

> never did young man fancy
> With so eternal and so fix'd a soul.

5. 2. 164

From this apparent contradiction there emerges the implied conception, or even philosophy, of the reality of love as something greater, more spiritual, more delicate, and yet more durable than time himself, and precisely because of this, 'incapable of continued concrete embodiment in the difficult flux of events'.[1]

---

[1] This last sentence is quoted from the fine exposition of the philosophy of *Troilus and Cressida* by Mr G. Wilson Knight (*The Wheel of*

Love is apparently killed by time, only because it transcends time; and its spiritual and infinite essence cannot be confined within the limitations of a material and finite world:

T. and C.
3. 2. 160

                        to be wise and love
Exceeds man's might; that dwells with gods above.[1]

The way is thus left open for the possibility of a condition or a consciousness beyond the temporal, where love may survive in a timeless reality.

DEATH   We find in Shakespeare upwards of fifty images and personifications of death, and it is impossible to study all these without gaining some clue to his own attitude towards it.

There is, of course, much well-known and intensely suggestive discussion and reflection on death in his work, especially in those three closely related plays, *Hamlet*, *Measure for Measure* and *Timon of Athens*, but it is all strictly the outcome of the dramatic situation and the view of the character who speaks.

Hamlet's obsession with and revolt from the physical horror of death, his fears and doubts as to the death of the mind, and his final realisation that death not life is 'felicity'; the duke's arguments to prove that the best of life is sleep, and death itself no more; Claudio's natural horror of the unknown; Timon's certainty that for him the 'nothingness' of death is liberation and fulfil-

Fire, 1930, p. 74), where this and other themes are worked out at length, to which I owe suggestion here, and to which I would refer all readers who are interested.

[1] See also the chapter in *The Wheel of Fire* on *Timon of Athens*, a play which is an unfaltering exposition of the fact that love, unalloyed by practical wisdom, prudence and caution, is, in the world of actuality, amidst imperfect humanity, doomed to failure, 'For bounty, that makes gods, does still mar men'.

ment, all this and much more Shakespeare himself may have felt and believed, but we do not know that he did.

What we do know is that when he thought of death certain sets of pictures flashed into his mind, and these we can look at with him, and by virtue of his own genius, we can see them almost as vividly as he did.

These pictures reveal a highly sensitive imagination which realises to the full that 'cowards die many times *J.C.* 2. 2. 32 before their death', and that the sense of death 'is most *M. for M.* 3. 1. 78 in apprehension', yet which shrinks intensely from its physical side and the horrors of it, and in that mood sees death as a 'carrion monster', a 'rotten carcass' in *Cym.* 5. 3. 70 rags, an 'odoriferous stench'. *K.J.* 3. 4. 33; 2. 1. 456 3. 4. 26

This side of Shakespeare is very conscious of the greed and destructiveness of death, especially in war or tragic accident, as in *King John* and *Romeo and Juliet*, and pictures him as a warrior with jaws of steel 'mousing *2. 1. 352* the flesh of men', a skeleton feasting upon soldiers by the thousand, a 'carrion monster', a proud and mighty *5. 2. 176; 3. 4. 33* being, who to supply food for his feast strikes down kings, queens and princes 'at a shot'. To Romeo's *Ham.* 5. 2. 367 imagination the tomb is the 'womb of death' gorged with food. 'Thou detestable maw', he cries,

> thou womb of death, *R. and J.* 5. 3. 45
> Gorged with the dearest morsel of the earth,
> Thus I enforce thy rotten jaws to open,
> And in despite I'll cram thee with more food.

Viewed thus, as the destroyer of youth untimely, by accident or battle, death is frightful and repellent to look at, a

> Hard favour'd tyrant, ugly, meagre, lean,... *V. and A. 931*
> Grim-grinning ghost.

It is, however, sometimes suggested that what we see is not death as he really is, but a mummer or actor:

1 H. VI,
4. 7. 18
> Thou antic death which laugh'st us here to scorn;

a bogey masked to frighten children, as when the messenger after the battle of Shrewsbury cries,

2 H. IV,
1. 1. 66
> hateful death put on his ugliest mask
> To fright our party.

Yet we cannot feel that anything of Shakespeare's own hope or experience is expressed in the words of Northumberland in an earlier play,

R. II, 2. 1. 270
> even through the hollow eyes of death
> I spy life peering.

When death takes toll of youth and beauty he is thought of sometimes as a lover, especially in the case of Juliet:

R. and J.
4. 5. 38
> Death is my son-in-law, death is my heir;
> My daughter he hath wedded,

cries old Capulet: Romeo, gazing upon Juliet in the monument, declares that death, who has sucked the honey of her breath, has not yet touched her beauty. Can this be, he asks, because

5. 3. 103
> unsubstantial death is amorous,
> And that the lean abhorred monster keeps
> Thee here in dark to be his paramour?

A. and C. 1. 2.
145; 5. 2. 315
Enobarbus and Charmian both speak of death as Cleopatra's lover. 'Now boast thee, death,' cries Charmian,

> in thy possession lies
> A lass unparallel'd;

3. 13. 192
Antony resolves that the next time he fights he will make death love him, and Cleopatra herself, in dying, likens the stroke of death to

5. 2. 295
> a lover's pinch,
> Which hurts, and is desired.

Constance, in her grisly picture, greets him as husband *K.J. 3. 4. 25*
and lover; while Claudio in despair, Lear in his frenzy, *M. for M.*
3. 1. 84
and Antony in set determination, each resolves to greet *K.L. 4. 6. 203*
A. and C.
death bravely and with zest, as a bridegroom running *4. 14. 99*
to meet his bride.

The power of death, and man's helplessness in his
grip, are constantly kept before us, and Shakespeare
shows us death as a wrestler, a tilter, an antagonist
against whom we fight a losing game, and whom we can
at most hold 'awhile at the arm's end'; a hound dogging *A.Y.L.I.*
2. 6. 10
us at the heels, a hunter, a fowler and an archer, with *R. III, 4. 1. 40;*
All's Well, 3. 4.
an ebon dart; a fell sergeant, 'strict in his arrest'; a *15*
1 H. IV,
soldier, laying siege to the mind, pricking and wounding *5. 4. 107*
it; a king boldly keeping his court within the very *Per. 1. 1. 40*
V. and A. 948
confines of the crown of a mortal king; a jester scoffing *Ham. 5. 2. 339*
R. II,
and grinning at the pomp with which he humours a *3. 2. 160–70*
monarch's vanity, while, at his own time, with a little
pin he bores his castle wall and claims him for his own;
and life itself is seen but as death's fool or dupe, ever *M. for M.*
3. 1. 11
vainly trying to escape him, while ever irresistibly
drawn towards him.

These are, for the most part, aspects of death seen
under special circumstances, the terrible and hungry
feeder in war, the ravisher of youth, beauty and strength,
who mockingly plays with and dominates not only
kings and princes, but even life itself; and we realise
that Shakespeare is here merely presenting to his
audience the figure of the grim yet semi-jocular skeleton
with which he and they alike were familiar in medieval
jest and picture.

May we dare to conjecture from his many other
images something of Shakespeare's own view of death?
I believe we may.

Even a glance at his pictures of life gives us some clue to its opposite. Thus, life is a voyage, uncertain and bound in shallows and miseries, a journey, a pilgrimage; death is a journey's end, sometimes a shipwreck, but never a haven or harbour. Life is a fever, a dream; death is the sure physician and a sleep; life is merely a breath, and death the mirror which proves this to us; life is a light, a candle, a lamp, a fire, a spark; death the extinction of all these. Life is a spring flower, death a frost; life is a prison, death a release; life is a thread, a knot, death is the thread cut, decayed or cracked, and the knot untied.

In general it would seem Shakespeare does not rebel against death, but accepts it as a natural process, a debt we owe to God, the cancelling of the bond of life; he thinks of it fairly constantly as the end of all we know, sometimes coming abruptly and harshly, as the untimely frost on a flower, a winter that kills, an axe set to a tree, or more gradually, as a canker or over-ripeness; but on the whole, most often, in spite of Hamlet's questionings and Claudio's ravings, an end wholly peaceful, merciful and restful.

Most constantly of all he sees it as a sleep[1] when 'the long day's task is done', or it is a window closing, shutting out the daylight, a black veil, very often a cloud over the sun,[2] or, as I have said, the extinguishing of light, a burnt-out torch or candle, a spent lamp and the coming of night, when

the bright day is done,
And we are for the dark.

1 H. IV, 5. 1. 126; 1. 3. 185
2 H. IV, 3. 2. 247
R. III, 3. 2. 80
Cym. 5. 4. 27
R. and J. 4. 5. 28
H. VIII, 3. 2. 177
R. and J. 2. 3. 30
R. III, 4. 4. 2

R. and J. 4. 1. 101
3 H. VI, 5. 2. 16

A. and C. 4. 14. 46
4. 15. 85
5. 2. 193

---

[1] A. and C. 4. 14. 35; M. for M. 3. 1. 17; Mac. 3. 2. 23, 2. 2. 38, 2. 3. 81; Sonnet LXXIII; Cym. 2. 2. 31; 2 H. IV, 4. 5. 35.

[2] 3 H. VI, 2. 6. 62; R. III, 1. 3. 265, 1. 3. 267; 1 H. VI, 5. 4. 89; 2 H. VI, 3. 2. 54.

It is the key that unlocks the shackles of trouble and
disease by which we are held fast in this world, that *Cym.* 5. 4. 7
shuts up and makes an end of the day; but it is never *R. and J.*
the key that unlocks the door of a new life.   4. 1. 101

On the other hand, it is a way to freedom and liberty, *Cym.* 5. 4. 3–4
a gaoler releasing a prisoner to 'enlarge his confine', *A. and C.*
and the kind umpire of men's miseries, who 'with   3. 5. 13
sweet enlargement doth dismiss' them hence.   *I H. VI,*
                                                           2. 5. 29
Only once does Shakespeare in his own person seem
to tell us directly what he himself thinks about death,
and that is in the grave 146th sonnet, addressed to
the soul of man. Here we see the medieval picture
reversed, and the greedy feaster on the flesh of men
subdued and annihilated in his turn by the spirit of
man grown strong, and here Shakespeare points out to
us the way of life, and so of the defeat of death. This
way is to concentrate on the nurture of the soul or
spirit rather than the body, even at the expense of the
body, which is but the 'fading mansion' of the soul,
its servant and inferior; and here for the first and only
time we find a note of hope and triumph markedly
absent from all his other pictures of man in his relation
to 'that dark spirit':

> Then, soul, live thou upon thy servant's loss,
> And let that pine to aggravate thy store;
> Buy terms divine in selling hours of dross;
> Within be fed, without be rich no more:
> So shalt thou feed on Death, that feeds on men,
> And Death once dead, there's no more dying then.

CHAPTER X

ASSOCIATION OF IDEAS

SHAKESPEARE'S tendency to have a similar group of ideas called up by some one single word or idea is a very marked feature of his thought and imagination. He must have been perfectly aware of this tendency himself, and in the person of Salarino, he describes very accurately how inevitably such association works in the mind.

M. of V.
I. I. 23–34

My wind, cooling my broth,
Would blow me to an ague, when I thought
What harm a wind too great at sea might do.
I should not see the sandy hour-glass run,
But I should think of shallows and of flats,
And see my wealthy Andrew dock'd in sand.
...Should I go to church
And see the holy edifice of stone,
And not bethink me straight of dangerous rocks,
Which touching but my gentle vessel's side
Would scatter all her spices on the stream...

It is very interesting to trace these groups, and to note, for instance, in his early and late work, how his art develops and gains strength and freedom in the expression of them.

In this connection the two poems are full of material, full of the embryos, as it were, of thoughts, views, images, and clusters of ideas which later we find worked out in fuller detail in the plays. Thus, these lines in *Lucrece*,

Luc. 985

Let him have *time* a *beggar's orts* to crave,
And *time* to see one that by *alms* doth live
Disdain to him *disdained scraps* to give,

show exactly the same group of ideas which later are brought together again in the somewhat curious but very vivid personification of time in Ulysses' great speech in *Troilus and Cressida*. There we see time as a *T. and C.* beggar, with
3. 3. 145

> a wallet at his back
> Wherein he puts alms for oblivion,

> . . . . . .
> Those scraps are good deeds past, which are devour'd
> As fast as they are made.

Although the complete thought of the two passages is quite different, yet we can see that without doubt, when Shakespeare wrote the later one, the connection between time and a beggar, scraps and alms, had been sleeping in his imagination for at least five years (1594–9).

Another example, which also illustrates the development and growth of ease in his art, is the group of ideas which cluster round the house martin. Shakespeare only twice mentions the house martin or martlet, and its habits of nest building. The first time is when Arragon comes to woo and to choose his casket, and in his preliminary and lengthy reflections somewhat prosily introduces the simile of the martlet, who

> Builds in the weather on the outward wall,   *M. of V. 2. 9. 29*
> Even in the force and road of casualty,

as an example of the stupidity of the 'fool multitude', who choose by show,

> Not learning more than the fond eye doth teach;   *2. 9. 27*
> Which pries not to the interior,

pointing out that he, Arragon, will not be thus stupid, but will avoid gold which 'many men desire', and will choose silver which will give him 'as much as he deserves'; the whole scene being an ironical presentation of the deceptiveness of appearances.

Our minds at once fly to another scene in Shakespeare, the whole object of which is to emphasise the irony of the deceptiveness of appearances, which is brought out in a few lines by a master's hand with poignant dramatic force. Here we find the martlet again, only instead of its being rather dragged in as a simile, the whole little scene is built round the bird and its peculiar choice of a site for its nest. I mean, of course, the moment when Duncan with his lords arriving at Macbeth's castle, where he is to meet his doom, appreciates the beauty of its site and the mild sweetness of the air, while Banquo points out that

Mac. 1. 6. 4
> The temple-haunting martlet, does approve
> By his loved mansionry that the heaven's breath
> Smells wooingly here: no jutty, frieze,
> Buttress, nor coign of vantage, but this bird
> Hath made his pendant bed and procreant cradle.

We may notice, in addition to the main underlying idea, the number of subsidiary ideas in and connected with the two scenes which are the same, and which are clearly linked together in Shakespeare's mind with the house martin's habit of building 'in the weather on the outward wall'.[1]

In each case a guest arrives, Arragon or Duncan, a guest who is to be 'fooled' or deceived, Arragon to find a fool's head instead of his bride, Duncan to be foully murdered by his thane and kinsman. A possible reason for the connection in Shakespeare's mind between the house martin and someone who is fooled or duped is that in the sixteenth and seventeenth centuries a kind

---

[1] See note in Appendix VI.

of slang term for a 'dupe' was 'martin', and the word is so used by Greene and Fletcher (see *N.E.D.*).

In both these two scenes we have in mind a man aspiring to high dignity and honour who takes what he thinks will bring it him, and is disappointed—Arragon, who 'assumes desert', Macbeth with 'vaulting ambition'; both are embarked on a hazardous adventure, and with both we hear the reiterated cry of the fear of failure (six times altogether, Arragon twice, Portia once, Macbeth once, and Lady Macbeth twice). Arragon's reflection on a man presuming 'to wear an undeserved dignity', and his words,

> O, that estates, degrees and offices   *M. of V. 2. 9. 41*
> Were not derived corruptly, and that clean honour
> Were purchased by the merit of the wearer!

might well be uttered by Macbeth, who tells his wife he has 'bought golden opinions from all sorts of people', and who, though longing for the 'degrees and offices', yet shrinks from the 'horrid deed' by which he must gain them. In both cases too the honours are thought of as garments to be worn, for Macbeth is constantly represented symbolically as the wearer of robes not belonging to him.

There are also many minor verbal resemblances, both in the two scenes, and in the parts connected with the idea of disillusionment; some of which may be worth noting.

Arragon comes to woo, the air at Macbeth's castle 'smells wooingly'; when Arragon leaves, Portia heaves a sigh of relief and exclaims, 'Thus hath the candle singed the moth'; immediately after Duncan's arrival Banquo speaks of heaven's candles being all out; and

the rhyme which so rudely disillusions Arragon runs
on fools and shadows:

M. of V. 2. 9. 66

> Some there be that shadows kiss;
> Such have but a shadow's bliss:
> There be fools alive, I wis,
> Silver'd o'er; and so was this.

Macbeth, when he sees his shadow dagger, declares his
'eyes are made the fools o' the other senses', while at
the moment of his sorest stroke of misfortune and the
shattering of all his hopes, he cries aloud in his bitterness of 'fools', a 'candle', a 'walking shadow' and 'a tale
told by an idiot'.

There is another group of ideas, constantly repeated, which possibly throws light on Shakespeare's
own thoughts and experiences. It is noticeable how
continually he associates dreaming with kingship and
flattery, so much so that one might almost deduce that
he had often dreamed he was himself a king of men,
surrounded by homage and sweet flattering words, and
had awakened to find this but empty and vain imagining,
and that he was, after all, only Will, the poor player.

King Henry, before Agincourt, reflecting on the
hard condition of kingship, anxious and sleepless with
responsibility, asks what do kings get that lesser mortals
lack, save worthless ceremony and poisoned flattery,
and dismisses greatness as a 'proud dream' which
'play'st so subtly with a king's repose'. Richard II,
trying to comfort his queen, as she meets him on his
way to the Tower, urges her to learn

R. II, 5. 1. 18

> To think our former state a happy dream;
> From which awaked, the truth of what we are
> Shows us but this.

When Polixenes reveals himself in the shepherd's cottage, Perdita urges Florizel to leave her, saying,

>   this dream of mine,—   *W.T.* 4. 4. 453
> Being now awake, I'll queen it no inch farther,
> But milk my ewes and weep.

Queen Katharine, on her trial, says,

>   thinking that   *H. VIII,*
> We are a queen, or long have dream'd so.   2. 4. 70

Romeo, on two occasions, when he feels exhilarated, refers to the flattering sweetness of a dream, and fears to trust its reality. On leaving Juliet after their betrothal he cries,

> O blessed, blessed night! I am afeard,   *R. and J.*
> Being in night, all this is but a dream,   2. 2. 139
> Too flattering-sweet to be substantial.

And again, in Mantua, when, about to buy the poison for himself, he cries,

> If I may trust the flattering truth of sleep   5. 1. 1.
> My dreams presage some joyful news at hand;

he tells of a dream he has had, when

> I dreamt my lady came and found me dead   5. 1. 6
>   .   .   .   .   .   .
> And breathed such life with kisses in my lips,
> That I revived and was an emperor;

and the moving eighty-seventh sonnet of farewell and relinquishment, ends,

> Thus have I had thee, as a dream doth flatter,
> In sleep a king, but waking no such matter.

There are, of course, several other groups of ideas which recur together, but some of them—though they undoubtedly and definitely follow one another in Shakespeare's mind—are so apparently unrelated that it is difficult to trace more than a thread of meaning in them. Such a group is the association of death, cannon, eye-ball, eye-socket of skull (a hollow thing), tears, vault, mouth (sometimes teeth), womb, and back to death again. The association is so vivid that whenever Shakespeare speaks of death he seems immediately conscious of the hollows in the skull where the eyes have been:

K.J. 3. 4. 29

And I will kiss thy [Death's] detestable bones
And put my *eyeballs* in thy *vaulty* brows,

cries Constance in *King John*. In the Dauphin's speech to Salisbury about war (i.e. *death*), the whole series is seen: Salisbury has been moved to *tears*, and the Dauphin says,

5. 2. 49

But this effusion of such manly drops,
This shower, blown up [cannon?] by tempest of the
    soul,
Startles mine *eyes*, and makes me more amazed
Than had I seen the *vaulty* top of heaven
Figured quite o'er with burning meteors.

A curious early example of these linked ideas, used in quite a different connection, is the description of Pinch in the *Comedy of Errors*. What starts the train of thought, evidently, is that Pinch is imagined as a kind of picture of death, a

C. of E.
5. 1. 237–50

                    hungry lean-faced villain,
A mere anatomy, a mountebank,
A threadbare juggler, and a fortune-teller,
A needy *hollow-eyed*, sharp-looking wretch,
A living dead man: this pernicious slave,
Forsooth, took on him as a conjurer;
And, gazing in mine *eyes*, feeling my pulse,
And with no face, as 'twere, outfacing me,

Cries out, I was possessed. Then all together
They fell upon me, bound me, bore me thence,
And in a dark and dankish *vault* at home
There left me and my man, both bound together;
Till, gnawing with my *teeth* my bonds in sunder
I gain'd my freedom. . . .

Eyes, tears and vaults are often associated; which
explains a curious expression such as Timon's steward
uses in describing the bounty and hospitality of his
lord:

> when our *vaults* have *wept*
> With drunken spilth of wine.

Timon,
2. 2. *166*

So Romeo declares,

> I'll say yon grey is not the morning's *eye*
> .   .   .   .   .   .
> Nor that is not the lark, whose notes do beat
> The *vaulty* heaven so high above our heads,

R. and J.
3. 5. *19*

and Iachimo asks Imogen,

> What, are men mad? Hath nature given them *eyes*
> To see this *vaulted* arch and the rich crop
> Of sea and land?

Cym. 1. 6. 32

and the queen in *Henry VI* says,

> The pretty-*vaulting* sea refused to drown me,
> Knowing that thou wouldst have me drown'd on shore,
> With *tears* as salt as sea, through thy unkindness.

2 H.VI, 3. 2. 94

In *King Lear* we find the sequence, *tongues (mouth)*, *eyes*,
vault and *death*, when the old king cries,

> Howl, howl, howl, howl! O, you are men of stones:
> Had I your *tongues* and *eyes*, I'ld use them so
> That heaven's *vault* should crack. She's gone for ever!
> I know when one is *dead* and when one lives.

K.L. 5. 3. 257

The words of Prospero, too, show the same association, *sea* (*tears?*), *vault*, *war* (*death*), when he asserts,

Temp. 5. 1. 41
>   I have bedimm'd
> The noontide sun, call'd forth the mutinous winds,
> And 'twixt the green *sea* and the azured *vault*
> Set roaring *war*.

A constant attribute of death, brought out by the association with eye-socket, vault, mouth and womb, is *hollowness*:

R. II. 3. 2. 160
>   for within the *hollow* crown
> That rounds the mortal temples of a king
> Keeps Death his court.

The thought of death, the carrion feeder, strengthens
K.J. 2. 1. 457 the connection with *mouth*. 'Here's a large *mouth*, indeed', says the Bastard,

> That spits forth death and mountains, rocks and seas;

R. and J.
5. 3. 45 and Romeo cries, 'Thou detestable *maw*, thou *womb* of death'. A curious combination of this idea of hollow places when thinking of death comes out in Exeter's defiant words to the Dauphin when he says the English king sends to him 'scorn and defiance'...

H. V, 2. 4. 120
>   an if your father's highness
> Do not, in grant of all demands at large,
> Sweeten the bitter mock you sent his majesty,
> He'll call you to so hot an answer of it,
> That *caves* and *womby vaultages* of France
> Shall chide your trespass....

Here the connection of idea seems so far-fetched that it is difficult to see the reason for the threat until we remember how Shakespeare's imagination works.

By far the clearest and most striking example that I have met with of this tendency to group repeatedly a certain chain of ideas round some particular emotional or mental stimulus, is another group of ideas centring round an animal. This is so marked in its repetition that it has been noted by others—I mean the dog, licking, candy, melting group, called up inevitably by the thought of false friends or flatterers.

It is quite certain that one of the things which rouses Shakespeare's bitterest and deepest indignation is feigned love and affection assumed for a selfish end. He who values so intensely—above all else in human life —devoted and disinterested love, turns almost sick when he watches flatterers and sycophants bowing and cringing to the rich and powerful purely in order to get something out of them for themselves. It is as certain as anything can be, short of direct proof, that he had been hurt, directly or indirectly, in this particular way. No one who reads his words carefully can doubt that he had either watched someone, whose friendship he prized, being deceived by fawning flatterers, or that he himself had suffered from a false friend or friends, who, for their own ends, had drawn out his love while remaining 'themselves as stone'.

Now whenever the idea, which affects him emotionally, of false friends or flatterers occurs, we find a rather curious set of images which play round it. These are: a dog or spaniel, fawning and licking; candy, sugar or sweets, thawing or melting. So strong is the association of these ideas in Shakespeare's mind that it does not matter which of these items he starts with—dog or sugar or melting—it almost invariably, when used in this particular application, gives rise to the whole series.

The simplest example is that in *Julius Caesar*, which

starts with *thawing*. When Metellus Cimber prostrates himself before him, Caesar checks him, saying,

J.C. 3. 1. 39
> Be not fond,
> To think that Caesar bears such rebel blood
> That will be *thaw'd* from the true quality
> With that which *melteth* fools, I mean, *sweet* words,
> *Low-crooked court'sies* and *base spaniel-fawning.*
> Thy brother by decree is banished:
> If thou dost bend and pray and *fawn* for him,
> I spurn thee like *a cur* out of my way.

In *Hamlet* the image starts with *candy*. Hamlet tells Horatio he is the most just man he has ever known, and checks his friend's natural impulse to demur at this sudden and unlooked-for praise by saying, 'Nay, do not think I flatter', for what have I to gain from you?

Ham. 3. 2. 64
> Why should the poor be flatter'd?
> No, let the *candied tongue lick* absurd pomp,
> And *crook* the pregnant hinges of the knee
> Where thrift may follow *fawning.*

A touch of the idea recurs when Hotspur, speaking of Bolingbroke's attitude before he was king, cries,

1 H. IV. 1. 3.
251
> Why, what a *candy* deal of courtesy
> This *fawning greyhound* then did proffer me!

In *Antony and Cleopatra* the first item of the image is *dog*, and the underlying idea is again false flattery, when Antony, thinking himself betrayed and deserted by Cleopatra and her followers, cries,

A. and C. 4. 12.
20
> The hearts
> That *spaniel'd*[1] me *at heels*, to whom I gave
> Their wishes, do *discandy*, melt their *sweets*
> On blossoming Caesar.

---

[1] The Folio reading is 'pannelled'; Hanmer suggested 'spaniel'd'. The passage, being obscure, has given rise to much emendation, but no one seems to have noticed that it is but a repetition of a favourite Shakespearian image, and that 'spaniel'd' therefore *must* be right.

Fragments of the same image recur when the original chord of 'flatterers' is touched, as when Cassius tells Antony that his words

> *rob the Hybla bees,*   *J.C.* 5. 1. 34
> *And leave them honeyless,*

and Antony then rounds on both Brutus and Cassius, crying,   Villains, . . .

> You... *fawn'd like hounds,*   5. 1. 39
> And bow'd like bondmen, kissing Caesar's feet;
> Whilst damned Casca, *like a cur,* behind
> Struck Caesar on the neck. O, you *flatterers!*

Here we begin with 'sweets', and, with the exception of 'melting', the rest of the series follows.

The explanation of this curious and repeated sequence of ideas is, I think, very simple. It was the habit in Elizabethan times to have dogs, which were chiefly of the spaniel and greyhound type, at table, licking the hands of the guests, fawning and begging for sweet-meats with which they were fed, and of which, if they were like dogs today, they ate too many, dropping them in a semi-melting condition all over the place. Shakespeare, who was unusually fastidious, hated the habit, as he disliked all dirt and messiness, especially connected with food.

So there come to be linked in his mind two things he intensely dislikes, one in the physical everyday world, the other in the world of the mind and emotions: the fawning cupboard love of dogs, their greed and gluttony, with its sticky and disagreeable consequences, and the other fawning of insincere friends, bowing and flattering for what they hope to get, and turning their backs when they think no more is coming to them.

In one play, *Timon of Athens*, in which Shakespeare expressed some of his profoundest as well as his most bitter thoughts, we find that the whole subject is just this particular one about which he felt so acutely—a man betrayed by false friends and flatterers.

What do we find is the central image, the picture constantly before Shakespeare's eyes in this play? Dogs: dogs fawning and eating and lapping and licking, with 'gluttonous maws' devouring their lord's meat; hounds feasting on the blood of the animal they have killed; dogs being given food denied to men; dogs licking up remnants; dogs being stoned and spurned and kicked; a mangy dog, a sleeping dog, an unpeaceable dog, a beggar's dog.

Even Timon's imprecations are coloured by this
Timon, 4. 3. 23 picture, which is ever with him: 'Destruction *fang* mankind', he cries,

4. 3. 540   And may diseases *lick up* their false bloods!

and the thought of Flavius is likewise tinged with it. Why, he asks the servants of his ruined lord's creditors, did you not submit your bills,

3. 4. 50 When your false masters eat of my lord's meat?
Then they could smile and *fawn upon* his debts,
And take down the interest into their *gluttonous maws*.

This constant preoccupation with dog nature can be seen by anyone on turning over the pages of the play; I need only remind readers of the great central scene, practically every word of which I believe to be Shakespeare's, when Timon, found by Apemantus in the woods, rounds on the cynic and tells him he is but a rogue and a beggar who really scorns and envies those who are better off than he is, and had he ever had a chance he

would have rioted with the best. He then proceeds to
expound his own position in a passionate speech.

It opens with 'dog' and ends with 'flatter'd', but
had we not the key of the earlier group of images we
should scarcely realise that it also is shot through with
the picture of dogs licking sweets, and with their
mouths and tongues melting the iced sugar on cake or
sweetmeats:

> Thou [says Timon] art a slave whom Fortune's *Timon, 4. 3. 250*
>   tender arm
> With favour never clasp'd, but bred a *dog*;

and the associative picture starts again:

> Hadst thou, like us from our first swath, proceeded
> The *sweet* degrees that this brief world affords
> To such as may the passive drugs of it
> Freely command, thou wouldst have plunged thyself
> In general riot, *melted* down thy youth
> In different beds of lust, and never learn'd
> The *icy* precepts of respect, but follow'd
> The *sugar'd* game before thee. But myself,
> Who had the world as my *confectionary*,
> The *mouths*, the *tongues*, the eyes and hearts of men
> At duty,...I, to bear this,
> That never knew but better, is some burden:
> ...Why shouldst thou hate men?
> They never *flatter'd* thee:...Hence, be gone!

This curious group of images illustrates better, I think,
than any other, Shakespeare's strong and individual
tendency to return under similar emotional stimulus
to a similar picture or group of associated ideas, and
it is obvious at once that it forms an extraordinarily
reliable test of authorship.

CHAPTER XI

SHAKESPEARE THE MAN

He is a marvellous good neighbour, faith, and a very good bowler.
L.L.L. 5. 2. 584.

AS I have collected and examined these many
thousands of images, and have pondered over
them during the last nine or ten years, there
has gradually emerged before my eyes a very definite
figure of the man who was the author of them.

Naturally every student of Shakespeare gradually
forms some picture—more or less defined—of the man
himself behind the plays, but equally every student is
well aware of the danger and futility of trying, or even
of passively allowing himself, to deduce from Shakespeare's dramatic utterances what Shakespeare himself
thinks and feels; for it is study along this line which
has led industrious and well-meaning people to argue
and prove that he was a devout Christian like Isabella,
or a scoffing materialist like Macbeth, while others
prefer to see him rather with the philosophic Edgar
when he affirms, 'Ripeness is all'.

In and through these utterances Shakespeare himself
for ever eludes us, and the reason is, it would seem,
because he is with all his characters and feels with them
all; he debates and hesitates with Hamlet, and is all
impulse with Romeo; he prays to the God of battles
with King Harry, and rails on Heaven with Gloucester.
He was, in short, as all men of greatest imagination must
be, many-sided and of many moods, not set stiffly as
most of us are, running along certain well-used grooves,

but almost fluid in his swift adaptability and respon-
siveness both to what he saw and to what he imagined.
His mind, in this sense, it is clear, was, like Orsino's,
'a very opal', absorbing and reflecting its environment,
actual and imaginative. That is a poet's nature, of which
Keats, in his letters, has given us incidentally the most
enlightening and vivid account ever written. He tells
us, among other things, how he entered into the being
of a sparrow pecking outside his window, and explains
that a poet 'has no Identity—he is continually in for
and filling some other body'.[1]

But the recognition of this does not help us in our
human and natural desire to know a little more closely
and definitely what Shakespeare was like as a mere
mortal, in his habit as he lived. Not that we want to
know necessarily, or only, as Professor Raleigh scoff-
ingly says, how he wore his hat; we crave knowledge
of the more significant small things about him which
we know and love in those who are dear to us, such
as what in daily life thrilled him with pleasure, what
offended and revolted him, what were his chief personal tastes and interests and how did these change
or develop; what did he like to eat and drink, which
of his senses were the most acute, as well as what was
his own general attitude towards the universal things
which concern us all, life and love and death.

Some of these things we can guess at, and it may be
that it should be enough for us to know, as we do from
reading his book, that he was the most diversely minded,
as well as the sanest and most balanced of men, that
he had a free spirit and a rare judgment, and that his
wit, humour and imagination gave him a sympathetic

[1] Letter to Woodhouse, Oct. 27, 1818.

understanding of all varieties of human nature which has never been approached. All this, and of course much more, we learn indirectly from his plays.

I would submit, however, that we can add a little to our detailed knowledge of Shakespeare as a person by studying the data which he has left us, incidentally and by the way as it were, embedded in his images.

I propose therefore to make the bold attempt in this chapter to set down some of his characteristics as they strike me, or as they have been borne in upon me after long study of him from this particular angle. Naturally some of the characteristics which I point out have been suggested or surmised before. The interest of their appearance here is that they are confirmed from evidence never before systematically examined; evidence from Shakespeare's own lips, which is all the time being measured up against the same kind of unconscious self-revelation in a number of his contemporaries.

All I say, except in the last few paragraphs, is based on facts or impressions drawn from the images, and for nearly all the characteristics which I suggest, the evidence has been worked out in detail in the earlier chapters of this book.

The figure of Shakespeare which emerges is of a compactly well-built man, probably on the slight side, extraordinarily well co-ordinated, lithe and nimble of body, quick and accurate of eye, delighting in swift muscular movement. I suggest that he was probably fair-skinned and of a fresh colour, which in youth came and went easily, revealing his feelings and emotions. All his senses were abnormally acute, especially—probably—those of hearing and taste.

He was healthy in body as in mind,[1] clean and
fastidious in his habits, very sensitive to dirt and evil
smells. Apart from many indirect proofs of these facts
in the plays, no man could have written his images on
sickness, surfeit, gluttony, dirt and disease, who had not
naturally a strong feeling for healthy living, a liking
for fresh air and 'honest water', and who was not him- *Timon, 1. 2. 58*
self clean, temperate and healthy.

Of all the semi-legendary later remarks about Shakespeare, the one, to my mind, which rings with most
undoubted truth, and probably could not have been
written of any of his companions, is Aubrey's scratched-
out note which he deemed unworthy of inclusion in
the life:

the more to be admired q. (because) he was not a
company keeper lived in Shoreditch, wouldn't be de-
bauched, & if invited to writ; he was in paine.[2]

One of the first things we notice in his collected 'sickness' and 'food' images is how far ahead of his age he
is in his belief—implied and stated—that we bring
upon ourselves a great deal of our own bad health
by ill-regulated living, and especially by over-eating.

This physical alertness and well-being is but a part
of Shakespeare's intense vitality, which goes to make
him an almost incredibly sensitive and amazingly observant man. Probably he was a quiet one—he does not

---

[1] Goethe shows his usual acumen when he says that, whilst reading
Shakespeare, 'we receive the impression of a man thoroughly strong and
healthy, both in mind and body'. (*Conversations with Eckermann*, 1828,
Bohn's edition, p. 310.)

[2] It will be noted that John Ward's remark that Shakespeare died as
the result of a drinking bout, is, as regards this point, purely supposi-
titious: 'Shakespear, Drayton, and Ben Jhonson, had a merry meeting,
and *itt seems* drank too hard, for Shakespeare died of a feavour there
contracted'. The italics are mine.

like noise—though not, it would seem, a dreamer, but practical and watchful, all the time absorbing impressions and movements like a sponge, registering them like a sensitive plate.

We see he is a countryman through and through, that it is the sights and sounds of boyhood which chiefly remain with him, and that half a lifetime spent in the midst of a great city has never deflected by one iota his interest from the pageant of the English country-side to that of the streets, which latter, indeed, he seems, in comparison, scarcely to notice. What he does notice and rejoice in are the sky and clouds, the revolving seasons, the weather and its changes, rain, wind, sun and shadow, and of all the outdoor occupations what he loves most is to walk and saunter in his garden or orchard, and to note and study the flight and movements of the wild birds. This persistent preoccupation with country things bears out the probable truth of Aubrey's report: 'He was wont to goe to his native Country once a year'.

He was, one would judge, a competent rider, and loved horses, as indeed he did most animals, except spaniels and house dogs. These he disliked probably because his fastidious senses revolted from the dirty way they were kept and fed at table. He was almost certainly an expert archer (as probably were most able-bodied young men of his day) and enjoyed the sport. Of all games, bowls would seem to be the one he knew most intimately and played with keenest zest.

He had, in short, an excellent eye for a shot, with bowl or with arrow, and loved exercising it. He was, indeed, good at all kinds of athletic sport and exercise, walking, running, dancing, jumping, leaping and swimming. He had an extraordinarily sensitive ear for time, and what he seems to notice most about riding is the pace and rhythm of the horses' movement; plodding, tired, ambling, trotting and galloping, the peculiar ambling action of the countrywoman's horse going to market (*A.Y.L.I.* 3. 2. 100), or the rough uneven paces of the young untrained colt (*M.N.D.* 5. 1. 119).

He was deft and nimble with his hands, and loved using them, particularly in the carpenter's craft, and, contrary to our idea of most poets, he was probably a practical, neat and handy man about the house, as we know that he was a 'Johannes Factotum' about the stage.

Next to his delight in outdoor life, he was, one would gather from the images, most interested in the homely indoor occupations and routine, eating, drinking, sleeping, the body and its clothes, light, fire, candles and lamps, birth and death, sickness and medicine, parents and children; while that which, next to an orchard and garden, has registered itself most clearly and continuously upon his mind is the picture of a busy kitchen, and the women's work for ever going on in it, preparing food, cooking, washing up, scouring, dusting, knitting, darning and patching. We see that in that kitchen, he has enjoyed much, and has also suffered from many things, from smoky chimneys, stopped ovens, guttering evil-smelling candles and ill-trimmed lamps, as well as greasy badly cooked food and tainted or musty meat. In fact it is his acute sensitiveness to these things of which we are continually becoming aware to such an extent that it makes one wonder how he managed to survive the dirt and smells of Elizabethan England.

For the rest of him, the inner man, five words sum

up the essence of his quality and character as seen in
his images—sensitiveness, balance, courage, humour
and wholesomeness. We see, on the one hand, sensitiveness; on the other, balanced poise, amounting at
times almost to aloofness. His sensitiveness is quick
and abnormal, to a depth and degree rarely found
in any human being. It is this side of his nature,
revealed chiefly in those images bearing on sport and
animals, which enables him to enter into the hearts
of so many different characters. The other side of him,
calm, detached, even ironic, keeps him steady and
balanced in the midst of the whirlpool of passion he calls
into being. There is another salient quality, naturally not
to be seen in his images (except in some of Falstaff's),
which must be mentioned, for it is the salt and savour
of his whole being, and keeps it ever fresh and wholesome. This is his sense of humour. And above and
surrounding all these, we find one other constant
characteristic—his passion for health, for soundness,
cleanliness and wholesomeness in all realms of being,
physical, moral and spiritual. In this, as in humour, his
whole nature seems to be steeped. If it were anyone
but Shakespeare, I might use the words 'purity' and
'holiness', but for one so firmly rooted in things
material and concrete as he, the physical terms best fit
the facts.

These, then, as I see them, are the five outstanding
qualities of Shakespeare's nature—sensitiveness, poise,
courage, humour and wholesomeness—balancing, com-
plementing and supporting each other. If he is abnormally sensitive, he is also unusually courageous,
mentally and spiritually. The intense sensitiveness, the
vividness of the imagination, make the courage the more
remarkable. In his own outlook on life he is absolutely

clear-eyed, but rarely bitter. In looking at evil, he sees it, not in terms of sin or a sinner, nor does he attach blame to it, but he views it with concern and pity as a foul and corrupt condition or growth produced by the world order, yet alien to it, as disease is to a body; which, if health is to be attained, must at all costs be expelled. That which he prizes most in life is unselfish love, what he instinctively believes to be the greatest evil is fear; which, far more than money, is, in his view, the root of all evil. Fear drives out love, as love drives out fear. What most rouses his anger is hypocrisy and injustice, what he values supremely is kindliness and mercy.

He is indeed himself in many ways in character what one can only describe as Christ-like; that is, gentle, kindly, honest, brave and true, with deep understanding and quick sympathy for all living things. Yet he does not seem to have drawn any support from the forms and promises of conventional religion, nor does he show any sign of hope or belief in a future life. But he does show a passionate interest in this life, and a very strong belief in the importance of the way it is lived in relation to our fellows, so that we may gain the utmost from the ripening processes of experience and of love.

This last point, the relation of ourselves to our fellows, would seem to me to be the centre of Shakespeare's belief and the mainspring of his actions. There is one thought already referred to (p. 170), which we find recurring in his work in many forms all through his career, and it would seem, quite simply, to be this: that by, in and for ourselves, we are as nothing; we exist only just in so far as we touch our fellows, and receive back from them the warmth or light we have ourselves sent out. To befriend, to support, to help, to cheer and illuminate our fellow-men is the whole object

of our being, and if we fail to do this, we have failed
in that object, and are as empty husks, hollow and
meaningless. Only thus can we fulfil ourselves and be
in truth that which we are intended to be.

We find a first hint of this idea in *Venus and Adonis*:

V. and A. 163   Torches are made to light, jewels to wear,
Dainties to taste, fresh beauty for the use,
Herbs for their smell, and sappy plants to bear;
Things growing to themselves are growth's abuse.

In *Troilus and Cressida* Shakespeare's mind is full of it.
Ulysses, immersed in the book he is reading, declares
the writer proves

T. and C.   That no man is the lord of any thing,
3. 3. 115   Though in and of him there be much consisting,
Till he communicate his parts to others,

.   .   .   .   .   .

3. 3. 99–102   Nor feels not what he owes [owns], but by reflection;
As when his virtues shining upon others
Heat them, and they retort that heat again
To the first giver.

The thought is touched on by Timon, when he declares
that if friends did not help each other they would
Timon,   resemble 'sweet instruments hung up in cases, that
1. 2. 94–100   keep their sounds to themselves'.

But it is in *Measure for Measure*, that strange play
which holds so much of Shakespeare's deepest thought,
that we find the idea expounded most fully by the duke
in his opening exhortation to Angelo, in the course of
which he tells him,

M. for M.   Heaven doth with us as we with torches do,
1. 1. 33–7   Not light them for themselves; for if our virtues
Did not go forth of us, 'twere all alike
As if we had them not. Spirits are not finely touch'd
But to fine issues.

It is just because this thought is so often repeated, reaching us through so many different voices, wrapped in so many different images, that I suggest we are for once justified in assuming it to be Shakespeare's own conviction, and in believing that we have here the philosophy by which he instinctively guided his life and actions.

PART II

THE FUNCTION OF THE IMAGERY
AS BACKGROUND AND UNDERTONE
IN SHAKESPEARE'S ART

CHAPTER XII

LEADING MOTIVES IN THE HISTORIES

THERE is no question but that the most striking function of the imagery as background and under-tone in Shakespeare's art is the part played by *recurrent* images in raising and sustaining emotion, in providing atmosphere or in emphasising a theme.

By recurrent imagery I mean the repetition of an idea or picture in the images used in any one play. Thus in *Romeo and Juliet* the dominating image is light with its background of darkness, while in *Hamlet* there hovers all through the play in both words and word pictures the conception of disease, especially of a hidden cor-ruption infecting and destroying a wholesome body.

This secondary or symbolic imagery within imagery is a marked characteristic of Shakespeare's art, indeed it is, perhaps, his most individual way of expressing his imaginative vision.

In the earlier plays these dominating images are often rather obvious and of set design, such as that of war and weapons, arising out of the 'civil war of wits' in *Love's Labour's Lost*; in the later plays, and especially in the great tragedies, they are born of the emotions of the theme, and are, as in *Macbeth*, subtle, complex, varied, but intensely vivid and revealing; or, as in *King Lear*, so constant and all-pervading as to be reiterated, not only in the word pictures, but also in the single words themselves.

Any reader, of course, must be aware of certain recur-

rent symbolic imagery in Shakespeare, such as that of
the growth and destruction of a tree, which runs through
the English historical plays; he is conscious of the
imaginative effect of the animal imagery in *King Lear*,
or of the flash of explosives in *Romeo and Juliet*; but it
was not until the last few years, when, in the course of
this intensive study of Shakespeare's imagery, I had
listed and classified and counted every image in every
play thrice over, that the actual facts as to these dominating pictures stared me in the face.

I found, as I have already said, that there is a certain
range of images, and roughly a certain proportion of
these, to be expected in every play, and that certain
familiar categories, of nature, animals, and what one
may call 'every day' or 'domestic', easily come first.
But in addition to this normal grouping, I have found,
especially in the tragedies, certain groups of images,
which, as it were, stand out in each particular play and
immediately attract attention because they are peculiar
either in subject, or quantity, or both.

These appear to form the floating image or images in
Shakespeare's mind called forth by that particular play;
for it is clear that the theme he is handling raises in
his imagination as he writes some picture or symbol
which recurs again and again in the form of simile and
metaphor throughout the play. He was probably conscious of the picture in his mind, but the imagery it
evoked was, at any rate in the later plays, so entirely
spontaneous and so natural a creation that it is likely
he was himself unaware of how completely and repeatedly it revealed his symbolic vision.

It would seem that this habit of his partakes of the
nature of that creative imagery described by Coleridge

in a famous passage, in the first part of which he says
that images 'become proofs of original genius only as
far as they are modified by a predominant passion; or
by associated thoughts or images awakened by that
passion'. This 'predominant passion' is a marked
characteristic in the imagery of many of Shakespeare's
great passages of poetry; thus, as we have already seen
(pp. 54–5), certain movements, such as rushing, riding,
swaying or bending, are the central motives which
symbolise for him the meaning or emotion of a soliloquy, a description or a reflection, and these movements are therefore expressed and re-expressed in the
imagery.

The iterative imagery which runs, not only through
a passage, but all through a play, is a kind of extension
of this creative and modifying impulse, functioning
over a much larger area, and acting on our imaginations
with proportionately greater cumulative force and effect.

Such an undertone of running symbolic imagery is
to be found to some extent in almost every one of
Shakespeare's plays, contributing in various ways to
the richness and meaning of the play, and, in some
cases, profoundly influencing its effect upon us. Its
function and importance vary greatly according to the
type of play, and the profundity of thought or imaginative vision which informs it. In the histories as a whole,
such continuous symbolism as we find is of a very
elementary and obvious nature. There is a simple but
persistent running image through all the early histories
from the first part of *Henry VI* (where there are touches
of it only), culminating in *Richard II*. The two parts of
Henry IV are curiously free from any continuous imagery
of this kind, while *King John* is a very interesting

example of a most strong and individual symbolism, which powerfully affects us pictorially and emotionally.

In the comedies, this imagery contributes chiefly atmosphere and background, as well as sometimes emphasising or re-echoing certain qualities in the plays. In the later plays, the romances, this symbolism becomes, as we shall see, more subtle, and illustrates an idea rather than a concrete picture; while in the tragedies it is closely connected with the central theme, which it supplements and illuminates, sometimes with extraordinary force, as in *Hamlet* and *King Lear*, or with rare beauty, as in *Romeo and Juliet* and *Antony and Cleopatra*.

Let us now look first, in more detail, at the histories. They naturally do not yield so rich a field of interest or variety in the matter of running imagery.as do the great tragedies; yet they are well worth examining from this point of view, if only as a proof that this habit of mind is characteristic of Shakespeare, and is to be found in his work from the very beginning.

The most constant running metaphor and picture in Shakespeare's mind in the early historical plays as a whole (from 1 *Henry VI* to *Richard II* inclusive) is that of growth as seen in a garden and orchard, with the deterioration, decay and destruction brought about by ignorance and carelessness on the part of the gardener, as shown by untended weeds, pests, lack of pruning and manuring, or on the other hand by the rash and untimely cutting or lopping of fine trees.

We find it first in the scene in the Temple Gardens in 1 *Henry VI* (2. 4), with its continuous play, in true Shakespearian style, on white and red roses, thorns, blossoms, canker, plucking, cropping, rooting, withering, growing and ripening, which is carried over into

the following scene, where we have the vivid picture of
Mortimer as a withered vine, pithless and strengthless,
drooping 'his sapless branches to the ground', detained *1 H. VI,*
2. 5. 12
during his 'flowering youth' in a loathsome dungeon,
in consequence of an attempt to 'plant' him as the
rightful heir; while Richard Plantagenet is described
as 'sweet stem from York's great stock'. 2. 5. 41

The metaphor—which probably takes its rise very
simply from the badges of York and Lancaster, together
with the meaning of the name Plantagenet—clearly
pleases Shakespeare, and, having started it in the first
part of *Henry VI*, he carries it on in the second and
third parts, developing it considerably in *Richard III*, and
making it finally the central theme of *Richard II*. Thus,
in a scene undoubtedly written by him (2 *Henry VI*,
3. 1), Queen Margaret, warning the king against the
good Duke Humphrey, and urging his removal, uses
for the first time the metaphor of the untended garden:

> Now 'tis the spring, and weeds are shallow-rooted; *2 H. VI,*
3. 1. 31
> Suffer them now, and they'll o'ergrow the garden,
> And choke the herbs for want of husbandry.

Later the king ironically thanks his nobles, who are
eagerly supporting the queen and doing their utmost
to blacken the character of the duke, for the care they
take

> To mow down thorns that would annoy our foot; 3. 1. 67

and York carries on the picture when, on hearing the
bad news from France, he mutters,

> Thus are my blossoms blasted in the bud, 3. 1. 89
> And caterpillars eat my leaves away.

The idea of the royal house as a tree or branches or
slips of a tree is also present in this second part of the

play, as when Warwick describes York's two sons as

2 H. VI,
2. 2. 58
3. 2. 214 'fair slips of such a stock', or Suffolk accuses Warwick of being 'graft with crab-tree slip', and pictures Duke

2. 3. 45 Humphrey as a lofty pine, who droops 'and hangs his sprays'.

In 3 *Henry VI* the metaphor becomes more definite.

3 H. VI,
1. 1. 48 Warwick vows he will 'plant Plantagenet, root him up who dares'; and in dying he cries,

5. 2. 11   Thus yields the cedar to the axe's edge.

1. 3. 32 Clifford declares that until he *roots* out the accursed line of York, he lives in hell; Clarence tells Queen Margaret

2. 2. 163–8 they have *set the axe* to her *usurping root*, and will not leave till they have hewn her down; Richard reminds Edward that Clifford was

2. 6. 47   not contented that he lopp'd the branch
In hewing Rutland when his leaves put forth,
But set his murdering knife unto the root
From whence that tender spray did sweetly spring.

When Prince Edward shows signs of being trouble-
5. 5. 13 some, the king (Edward IV) says, 'What! Can so young a thorn begin to prick?' and, when a few minutes later he is stabbed to death by his cousins, his mother cries,

5. 5. 62 'How sweet a plant have you untimely cropp'd!'
Gloucester, when born, was an

5. 6. 51   indigested and deformed lump,
Not like the fruit of such a goodly tree;

3. 2. 156 he describes his shrunken arm as a 'wither'd shrub',
3. 2. 126 he trusts no 'hopeful branch' may spring from Edward, and at the end he mockingly greets his infant nephew, saying,

5. 7. 31   And, that I love the tree from whence thou sprang'st,
Witness the loving kiss I give the fruit.

In *Richard III* this metaphor is further developed, and the number of tree and garden images is unusual, even for Shakespeare. The royal house is definitely thought of as a tree, with the children and kinsfolk as branches, leaves, flowers or fruit, and the idea of this tree being planted, shaken by storms, grafted, rooted up and withered is constantly present.

The royal tree hath left us royal fruit,   *R. III, 3. 7. 167*

says Gloucester hypocritically, when pretending to refuse the invitation to take the crown himself,

Which, mellow'd by the stealing hours of time,
Will well become the seat of majesty.

Buckingham, referring to Edward IV's marriage, speaks of England's 'royal stock graft with ignoble plants',   *3. 7. 127*
and declares to Gloucester that his brother's son shall never reign,

But we will plant some other in the throne.   *3. 7. 216*

When Edward IV dies, his queen, lamenting, asks,

Why grow the branches now the root is wither'd?   *2. 2. 41*
Why wither not the leaves the sap being gone?

Herself and other parents whose children Richard has murdered, she calls 'old wither'd plants', and she be-   *4. 4. 394*
wails the little princes as her 'unblown flowers'.   *4. 4. 10*

This idea or picture of the garden, orchard or wood, is moreover kept ever before us by small touches. Thus one of the citizens, discussing the dangerous position after Edward's death, says, in a vivid image, revealing the countryman's observation, 'When great leaves fall,   *2. 3. 33*
the winter is at hand'. Rivers advises the widowed queen to think of her son,

And plant your joys in living Edward's throne;   *2. 2. 100* little York, on being told that he is almost outgrowing his elder brother, is not pleased about it as a child should be, but repeats what his uncle Gloucester said to him one night,

R. III, 2. 4. 13   Small herbs have grace, great weeds do grow apace; adding,

And since, methinks, I would not grow so fast,
Because sweet flowers are slow and weeds make haste.

The saying clearly made a great impression on the boy, for later, when most unwisely, but spiritedly, he is about to taunt and bait his uncle, he recalls to him his words

3. 1. 103 that 'idle weeds are fast in growth'. And Gloucester carries on the same picture, when, after talking to the elder prince and being much struck with his precocious wisdom, he mutters to himself with sinister meaning,

3. 1. 94   Short summers lightly have a forward spring.

Other examples of this same figure are when Clarence's murderer reminds him that he struck dead the young

1. 4. 221 Prince Edward, 'gallant-springing brave Plantagenet';
1. 2. 248 when Gloucester refers to himself as having 'cropp'd the golden prime' of Edward, and once more compares
3. 4. 70 his own shrunken arm to a 'blasted sapling, withered
1. 3. 123 up'; when he tells the queen that he was 'a weeder-out' of her husband's 'proud adversaries'; and when she, thinking of the dangers which surround a king, expresses her thought in terms of a tree growing in an exposed position, saying,

1. 3. 259   They that stand high have many blasts to shake them.

Thus the idea of trees and branches, plants and planting, ripeness, decay, weeds and flowers 'unblown' and withered, runs as an undertone throughout the play.

In *Richard II* this becomes still more marked. The

Duchess of Gloucester pictures Edward III's sons as 'seven fair branches springing from one root'. Some *R. II*, *1. 2. 13* of these have been cut 'by the Destinies', but one flourishing branch (her husband)

> Is hack'd down, and his summer leaves all faded,
> By envy's hand and murder's bloody axe.

Later, Gaunt cries bitterly to Richard not to spare him, nor to hesitate with his unkindness 'To crop at once *2. 1. 134* a too long withered flower'; and Richard, when he hears of Gaunt's death, comments complacently,

> The ripest fruit first falls, and so doth he. *2. 1. 153*

The repeated use of the verbs plant, pluck, crop, wither, as applied to kings and members of the commonwealth, shows how continually the picture of a garden is in Shakespeare's mind. Richard himself is a 'fair rose', and as he passes his queen on his way to the Tower, she cries to her ladies,

> But soft, but see, or rather do not see, *5. 1. 7*
> My fair rose wither: yet look up, behold,
> That you in pity may dissolve to dew,
> And wash him fresh again with true-love tears.

It is interesting to note how, at the thought of Richard, this metaphor recurs to Hotspur when later he reproaches Northumberland for his share in the fate of the unhappy king:

> To put down Richard, that sweet lovely rose, *1 H. IV*,
> And plant this thorn, this canker, Bolingbroke. *1. 3. 175*

The Bishop of Carlisle warns the nobles that if they depose Richard—the king who has been 'planted many years'—and crown Bolingbroke,

> The blood of English shall manure the ground. *R. II*, *4. 1. 137*

When Aumerle—Richard's friend—comes after the deposition to see his mother, she asks him who are those now in favour with Bolingbroke, and words her query thus:

R. II, 5. 2. 46
> Who are the violets now
> That strew the green lap of the new come spring?

He answers, showing where his sympathies lie,

5. 2. 48
> Madam, I know not, nor I greatly care not:
> God knows I had as lief be none as one.

Whereupon his father, deeply pledged to the new king, sharply reproves him, carrying on the metaphor:

5. 2. 50
> Well, bear you well in this new spring of time
> Lest you be cropp'd before you come to prime.

And so what has been but an undertone—at first faint, later clear and definite—in the earlier historical plays, here in *Richard II* gathers strength and volume, until it becomes the leading theme, which is, as it were, gathered up, focussed and pictorially presented near the middle of the play in the curious garden scene (3. 4), a kind of allegory, unlike anything else in Shakespeare, deliberately inserted at the cost of any likeness to nature, for no human gardeners ever discoursed like these.

They explain the whole position in detail with a heaviness of touch rare in Shakespeare, and we see that all the horrors suffered by England under the civil wars, shaken and frighted as she was by murders and battles, scheming and treachery, by the putting up and putting down of kings, by waste and misrule, have translated themselves into the pictorial imagination of the young country playwright as the despoiling of a fair 'sea-walled garden', full of fruit, flowers and healing herbs, which ignorance and lack of care have allowed to go to seed, to rot and decay; so that now in spring time, instead of all being in order and full of promise, the whole land is, as the under gardener says,

> full of weeds; her fairest flowers choked up,   *R. II, 3. 4. 44*
> Her fruit-trees all unpruned, her hedges ruin'd,
> Her knots disorder'd, and her wholesome herbs
> Swarming with caterpillars.

To the real gardener no picture could be more distressing, because he knows that this condition, which is a cumulative result of long-continued neglect, can be set right only by hard years of toil and expense, and the terrible mischief wrought seems out of all proportion to the small amount of skilled attention which would have prevented this deterioration.

The careless gardener, who has 'suffer'd this disorder'd spring', is in turn pictured as a tree, who

> Hath now himself met with the fall of leaf;   *3. 4. 49*

and the parasites of the realm—Richard's false friends—

> The weeds which his broad-spreading leaves did   *3. 4. 50*
>   shelter,
> That seem'd in eating him to hold him up,
> Are plucked up root and all by Bolingbroke.

'What pity is it', cries the head gardener, that Richard   *3. 4. 55* had 'not so trimm'd and dress'd his land as we this garden', keeping in check unruly members of the state who are apt to be 'over-proud in sap and blood', pruning them as fruit trees are pruned, of which the superfluous branches have to be lopped away so that 'bearing boughs may live'.   *3. 4. 64*

So Shakespeare likens the land he loves to that corner of it he knows and loves best, an orchard and garden, and he pictures its desolation in the homely terms which make the most poignant appeal to him and are the most completely understood, not only by him, but also by the great majority of his countrymen then and now.

I have assembled this imagery, which is of course perfectly obvious, and must be noticed—at any rate in part—by the most casual reader, chiefly for two reasons.

In view of the later development of this habit of continuous and dominant imagery, peculiar I believe to Shakespeare, and of the subtle yet important part it plays in the great tragedies and to a lesser extent in the comedies, it is of interest to trace the beginnings of it in so simple a form in this series of the early histories. The subject of this running imagery here chiefly serves to accentuate the place held in Shakespeare's love and imagination by the familiar country pursuit, so dear to him all his life, of the care of the fruit and flower garden. In the later plays, on the other hand, as we shall see, the running image becomes very often not only an index to his likes and dislikes, but also a means of throwing fresh light on the way he looked on the chief problem or problems of the play and his attitude towards them.

The other point of interest is the question of authorship. The fact that this metaphor is continuous, that it starts in 1 *Henry VI* and is developed in the two later parts, seems to me one of many proofs that the same mind and imagination has functioned through all five plays, and that the writer of *Richard III* and of *Richard II* had, therefore, at least a very great share in the authorship of 1, 2 and 3 *Henry VI*.

I cannot develop this subject here, but I hope to submit later, in another study, more close and detailed evidence as to the authorship of the histories, more especially as regards the *Henry VI* plays and *Henry VIII*.

Apart from this image of the fruit and flower garden in which these five early historical plays share, there are other subsidiary running images to be found in individual plays.

It seems to me that, even in 1 *Henry VI*, some indications of this peculiar habit of Shakespeare's can intermittently be traced.

Thus, in the first scene—the funeral of Henry V in Westminster Abbey—we are at once struck by the effect produced upon us by the contrast of a blaze of dazzling light—comets, planets, sun and stars—against a background of black and mourning, typifying the brilliance and glory of the dead king and the heavy gloom of his loss. The first line strikes the note of mourning:

Hung be the heavens with black, yield day to night;

and this is followed by the rapidly moving pictures of comets brandishing their crystal tresses and scourging the stars who have consented to Henry's death, of his flashing sword blinding men with its beams, his arms spread wider than a dragon's wings, and his sparkling eyes shooting fire, which

> More dazzled and drove back his enemies   *1 H. VI,*
> Than mid-day sun fierce bent against their faces.   *I. I. 13*

The mourning note is then revived, with the colour red added:

> We mourn in black: why mourn we not in blood?   *I. I. 17*

and the sense of contrast and conflicting emotions is maintained by the picture of the mourners following the wooden coffin

> Like captives bound to a triumphant car.   *I. I. 22*

The loss of Henry is so great that it is natural it should be the concern of the heavenly bodies themselves, and Exeter asks,

1 H. VI,
I. I. 23

> What! shall we curse the planets of mishap
> That plotted thus our glory's overthrow?

Bedford follows by bidding the gold-coated heralds to attend them to the altar draped in mourning, where, instead of gold, they offer up their arms, and he ends by invoking the dead king's spirit, begging him to prosper his realm, and to combat on its behalf with adverse planets in the heavens.

And the last picture he gives us of the great king is in keeping with the whole scene:

I. I. 55

> A far more glorious star thy soul will make
> Than Julius Caesar or bright ——

a cry which is rudely interrupted and the mourners brought with a shattering blow from heaven to earth by the succession of messengers rushing in with ill tidings of the loss, with 'slaughter and discomfiture', of the greater part of Henry's brilliant and hard-won conquests in France.

The imagery of the heavenly bodies is carried over into scene 2, which opens with the picture of the planet Mars and his uncertain or eccentric orbit, shining sometimes on the English, sometimes on the French side, and ends with Charles' apostrophe to Joan as

I. 2. 144

> Bright star of Venus, fall'n down on the earth.

The scene in the Temple Gardens, as already noted (p. 216), is full of play on the running imagery of growth, ripening and withering in Shakespeare's characteristic style.

There is also continuity in the imagery of the Talbot

scenes in the emphasis laid upon the way Talbot and *1 H. VI,*
his soldiers are surrounded, ensnared, entangled, walled 4. 2. 22
'from the liberty of flight', 'park'd and bounded in a 4. 2. 24
pale' like deer, 'girdled with a waist of iron', 'hemm'd 4. 2. 45
about with grim destruction', 'ring'd about with bold 4. 3. 20, 21
adversity'; there is continuity in the conception of death 4. 4. 14
as a foe confronting Lord Talbot, 'Triumphant death, 4. 2. 26
smear'd with captivity', 'antic death, which laugh'st 4. 7. 3
us here to scorn', and in the picture conjured up in 4. 7. 18
his desperate appeal to his dead son, to

> Brave death by speaking, whether he will or no; 4. 7. 25
> Imagine him a Frenchman and thy foe.

In 2 and 3 *Henry VI*, outside the symbol of the fruit
and flower garden, already noticed, there is the even
more obvious one of the butcher and slaughter-house,
slightly carried on in *Richard III*.

This figure is first used by Henry, when, in a long *2 H. VI,*
simile, he pictures the helplessness both of himself and 3. 1. 210–18
of the chief victim in the play, in the hands of their
enemies, and sees Duke Humphrey as a calf taken away
by the butcher, bound, beaten, and borne to 'the bloody
slaughter-house', while he, Henry,

> As the dam runs lowing up and down,
> Looking the way her harmless young one went.

The same image comes naturally to Warwick, when,
after the duke's murder, the queen asks him does he
suspect Suffolk, and he answers caustically, if you find
a 'heifer dead and bleeding fresh', and see 'fast by a 3. 2. 188
butcher with an axe', you will suspect ''twas he that
made the slaughter'. York also touches it again at the
end, when in his anger he declares he could spend his 5. 1. 26

fury on sheep and oxen. The image naturally recurs with Dick the butcher in Cade's rebellion, who is to *2 H. VI, 4. 2. 27* strike down sin like an ox, and cut iniquity's throat like a calf, and who is commended by his leader because *4. 3. 3* his enemies fell before him 'like sheep and oxen', and he behaved himself as if he had been in his own slaughter-house.

3 H. VI, 2. 2. 95
5. 5. 61
5. 5. 77
1. 1. 71

5. 4. 78

3. 2. 181

5. 6. 8

In 3 *Henry VI*, Clifford, Edward and Clarence are all called 'butchers', Richard is 'that devil's butcher', parliament is thought of as a 'shambles' and the realm as a 'slaughter-house', Gloucester sees himself hewing his way to the crown with a bloody axe, and Henry, when Gloucester comes to kill him, pictures himself very aptly as a sheep yielding his throat unto the butcher's knife.

In 2 *Henry VI* I see no other running symbol, except in Act 3, where there seems to be a somewhat continuous idea of the enemies or of the claimants to the crown and their treacherous ways being thought of in terms of snakes and scorpions.

2 H. VI, 3. 2. 86

3. 1. 228

The queen declares that on nearing the 'unkind shore' of England, the wind seemed to warn her not to seek 'a scorpion's nest'; she compares Gloucester and his effect on Henry to a snake 'with shining checker'd slough' which stings a child 'that for the beauty thinks it excellent'; and when the king turns his face away and answers her questions only by bemoaning Gloucester's death, she rounds on him with the angry words,

3. 2. 76

art thou, like the adder, waxen deaf?
Be poisonous too and kill thy forlorn queen.

York asserts that in sending him to Ireland with an

army, when troops are exactly what he needs for his
own ends, the nobles are but warming

> the starved snake,   *2 H. VI,*
> Who, cherish'd in your breasts, will sting your hearts.   *3.1.343*

Salisbury, in a long image, compares Suffolk to a serpent   *3. 2. 259*
with forked tongue slily gliding towards the king to
sting and kill him as he did Gloucester. Warwick seems
to have the same thought of him when he calls him

> Pernicious blood-sucker of sleeping men!   *3. 2. 226*

and Suffolk himself, in cursing his enemies, wishes that
their softest touch may 'smart as lizards' stings', and   *3. 2. 325*
their music be 'frightful as the serpent's hiss'.

Henry's enemies are also thought of occasionally as
wild beasts, ravening wolves, beating away the shepherd
(Duke Humphrey) from the lamb so that they may   *2. 2. 73;*
devour it, and in 3 *Henry VI*, lions, tigers, wolves and   *3. 1. 191*
bears completely take the place of the serpents in
symbolising the enemies or claimants to the crown.

Queen Margaret sees the king as a 'trembling lamb   *3 H. VI,*
environed with wolves', and when he is finally taken   *1. 1. 242*
prisoner, she calls Edward 'the wolf that makes this   *5. 4. 80*
spoil'. Henry also, when Gloucester comes to kill him,
and dismisses his guard, sees himself as a 'harmless   *5. 6. 7*
sheep' deserted by the shepherd when the wolf appears,
and elsewhere pictures the civil wars as the 'bloody   *2. 5. 74*
times',

> Whiles lions war and battle for their dens,
> Poor harmless lambs abide their enmity.

Young Rutland, shrinking with shut eyes from Clifford's
murderous stab when forced to face his murderer, cries,

> So looks the pent-up lion o'er the wretch   *1. 3. 12*
> That trembles under his devouring paws;

and Richard, when pursuing Clifford in battle, tells
Warwick to

3 H. VI, 2. 4. 12

> single out some other chase;
> For I myself will hunt this wolf to death.

2 H.VI, 2. 2. 73 York describes Duke Humphrey as 'the shepherd of
3 H. VI, 1. 4. 5 the flock', sees his own followers as 'lambs pursued by
hunger-starved wolves', and addresses Margaret as
1. 4. 111 'she-wolf of France', apostrophising her, in a famous
1. 4. 137 phrase, as a 'tiger's heart wrapp'd in a woman's hide!'
1. 4. 154 declaring, with justice, that she is more inhuman, 'ten
times more than tigers of Hyrcania'. And so on; I need
not particularise further; it is a somewhat wearisome
and very obvious symbolism.

There is also in 3 *Henry VI* an unusually large
number of pictures of the sea and ships, more than in
any other play. Thus King Henry, in a fine passage
already referred to, describes the battle of Towton
3 H.VI, 2. 5. 5 swaying like a mighty sea

> Forced by the tide to combat with the wind.

3. 2. 134 Gloucester, in a very vivid simile, dreaming of his
desire for the crown, sees himself standing on a promontory gazing at a far-off shore 'where he would
tread', and chiding

> the sea that sunders him from thence,
> Saying, he'll lade it dry to have his way,

the sea in this instance symbolising the king and all his
kinsmen who stand between Gloucester and the throne.
The picture of the wrecked ship is in King Henry's
mind, when, on entering York, the queen, pointing to
the head of the Duke of York set upon the gates, asks,
2. 2. 4 'Doth not the object cheer your heart, my lord?' and
he answers, 'Ay, as the rocks cheer them that fear their

wreck'. It is rather a peculiarity of this play that the
various characters are repeatedly thought of as ships
fighting the waves or borne before the wind. There are
two touches of the figure in 2 *Henry VI* (3. 2. 411,
4. 9. 31–3), but it is in the third part that it becomes
noticeable. Thus York describes his beaten soldiers as
flying 'like ships before the wind', Edward pictures   *3 H. VI, 1. 4. 4*
'calm Henry' being led into battle by the bloody-
minded queen

> As doth a sail, fill'd with a fretting gust,   *2. 6. 35*
> Command an argosy to stem the waves.

Margaret herself, in a moment of unwonted humility,
tells Lewis of France that she

> Must strike her sail and learn a while to serve   *3. 3. 5*
> Where kings command;

and when urged by Gloucester to kneel to Edward as
king, Warwick declares he would rather chop one hand
off and with the other fling it in Gloucester's face

> Than bear so low a sail, to strike to thee;   *5. 1. 52*

to which Edward answers,

> Sail how thou canst, have wind and tide thy friend,

but when your head is newly cut off, this sentence shall
be written in the dust with your blood,

> Wind-changing Warwick now can change no more.

The culmination of this figure occurs in an unusually
elaborate simile, thirty-four lines in length, in which,   *5. 4. 2–36*
after Henry has been carried off to the Tower, Queen
Margaret compares the condition of the king's army to
a ship in distress, near rocks and quicksands, her mast
blown overboard, her cable broken, her holding-anchor
lost, half her crew drowned, but with the young prince,
her pilot, still alive. Warwick she calls the anchor,

Montague the topmast, 'our slaughter'd friends the tackles'; these, she says, can be replaced, and she and the prince will keep their course

3H.VI,5.4.23   From shelves and rocks that threaten us with wreck.

Edward is the ruthless sea (to which indeed he has already likened himself in 4. 8. 55), Clarence a quick-sand of deceit ('false, fleeting, perjured Clarence'), Richard a 'ragged fatal rock', and there is no mercy to be hoped for from any of the three brothers

5. 4. 36   More than with ruthless waves, with sands and rocks.

In *Richard III* there is a very simple but quite con-tinuous and insistent animal symbolism, all centring on Richard, and bringing out the quality of ruthless cruelty in his character as it strikes those who come into contact with him.

By his womenkind, who hate and fear him, Richard is likened to everything most repulsive in the animal
R. III, 4. 4. 48 world; his mother calls him a 'hell-hound', a 'biting
1. 3. 290
1. 3. 242, 246 venom-toothed dog', 'a bottled spider', a 'poisonous
1. 3. 228   bunch-back'd toad', an 'elvish-mark'd abortive rooting hog'; Queen Elizabeth later, echoing his mother, calls
4. 4. 81 him 'toad' and 'spider', and bewails her gentle lambs
4. 4. 22 thrown in the entrails of the wolf; and Anne, in her first memorable interview with him, cries,

1. 2. 148   Never hung poison on a fouler toad,

and implies he is worse than a wild animal, for

1. 2. 71   No beast so fierce but knows some touch of pity.

Others—Hastings, Richmond, Derby—speak of him
4. 5. 2; 5. 2. 10 as a 'most bloody boar' and a 'foul swine':

5. 2. 7   The wretched, bloody, and usurping boar,

cries Richmond to his soldiers,

> That spoil'd your summer fields and fruitful vines,
> Swills your warm blood like wash, and makes his
>   trough
> In your embowell'd bosoms.

In *Richard II*, though the metaphor of the fruit and
flower garden is the most continuous, it is by no means
the only recurrent one. One of many noticeable things
about the play is the way in which our sympathy is
called out for the weak, vacillating king, who in action
is so selfish and indolent, but in speech is so eloquent.
We are made to feel to the full his charm of person and
his kingly dignity, and if we look closely, we see this
is done partly through metaphor. If he is the careless
gardener and the stricken tree, he is also the 'fair rose'
and the rising sun; and the loss of his glory is 'like *R. II, 2. 4. 19*
a shooting star' falling 'to the base earth from the
firmament'.

Shakespeare clearly conceived of Richard as good to
look at, probably following Holinshed's remark, 'he was
seemelie of shape and favor'; and he is depicted as fair
and of a high colour, easily yielding to pallor (2. 1. 118
and 3. 2. 75–9), a characteristic which may have been
the reason for his being likened both to a rose and—in
the English climate—to the sun. His dramatic entrance
on the walls of Flint Castle is prepared for by Bolingbroke's rhetorical assertion that he and the king should
meet

> With no less terror than the elements   *3. 3. 5*
> Of fire and water, when their thundering shock
> At meeting tears the cloudy cheeks of heaven.

Bolingbroke goes on to describe Richard's appearance,

with irony it is true, but still in terms of great magnificence:

R. II, 3. 3. 62–7

> See, see, King Richard doth himself appear,
> As doth the blushing discontented sun
> From out the fiery portal of the east.

This is reinforced by York's comment that his eye

> As bright as is the eagle's, lightens forth
> Controlling majesty.

Richard himself earlier, in a long and most elaborate 3. 2. 36–53 simile, compares himself to the 'searching eye of heaven', who, when

> He fires the proud tops of the eastern pines,

lays bare murders and treasons. So, he argues,

> when this thief, this traitor, Bolingbroke,
>
> .   .   .   .   .
>
> Shall see us rising in our throne, the east,
> His treasons will sit blushing in his face,
> Not able to endure the sight of day.

This is his own constant idea of himself, and the beauty and grandeur of it impress us; so that when he finally comes down from the walls of Flint to meet his adversary in the base court, the characteristically rhetorical picture he draws of that apparently simple descent seems in keeping with the royal splendour of his appearance earlier,

3. 3. 178

> Down, down I come; like glistering Phaeton,
> Wanting the manage of unruly jades.

And when the deposition is an accomplished fact, and he scans his face in the glass he has sent for, it is this dazzling brilliance which is the quality he most prizes and most regretfully loses—'Was this the face', 4. 1. 283 he asks, 'That, like the sun, did make beholders wink?'

> A brittle glory shineth in this face:
> As brittle as the glory is the face;

and he dashes the glass to the ground.

So that there is deep and poignant meaning in what are his real words of abdication, when the actual power and kingship have passed to Bolingbroke, and he transfers to his successor also the royal qualities of the sun, crying in his bitterness and anguish,

> O that I were a mockery king of snow,   *R. II, 4. 1. 260*
> Standing before the sun of Bolingbroke,
> To melt myself away in water-drops!

This conception of the king as sun is fairly constant with Shakespeare. Touches of it are to be found in many of the historical plays, both earlier and later than *Richard II*, where it is so fully developed. The first part of *Henry VI*, as we have seen, opens with the king being pictured as the midday sun, shining fiercely in his enemies' faces, dazzling and driving them back. In the second part York boasts that he will incite rebellion in England which will be subdued only when he becomes king, and describes it in terms of stirring up a 'black storm' of wind, which shall not cease to rage, 'until the golden circuit' on his head,

> Like to the glorious sun's transparent beams,   *2 H. VI,*
> Do calm the fury.   *3. 1. 349–54*

In 3 *Henry VI*, Edward, looking at the sunrise, suddenly exclaims that he is dazzled by 'three glorious suns'   *3 H. VI, 2. 1. 25* blazing and shining in the sky—himself and his two brothers—and urges that they should join their lights together 'and o'er-shine the earth', as the sun in the heavens shines over the world. Gloucester's well-known opening words in *Richard III* carry on the same image.

It reappears also in both parts of *Henry IV*. In part 1 it is interesting to compare Henry's rhetorical comparison of Richard on the walls of Flint, to the 'blushing discontented sun', with the picture he draws in retrospect when describing him to Prince Hal. He tells his son that he himself, by being seldom seen, could not stir

1 H. IV, 3. 2. 47

> But like a comet I was wonder'd at,

whereas Richard made himself so common that men's eyes were 'sick and blunted', and afforded him

3. 2. 78

> no extraordinary gaze,
> Such as is bent on sun-like majesty
> When it shines seldom in admiring eyes;
> But rather drowzed and hung their eyelids down,
> Slept in his face and render'd such aspect
> As cloudy men use to their adversaries.

The idea of 'sun-like majesty' is carried on in the person of Prince Hal, who is described by Vernon as

4. 1. 102

> gorgeous as the sun at midsummer,

and the prince himself, when in soliloquy he defends his idle madcap ways, proving he is his father's son in his deliberately planned action, compares himself to the sun who allows

1. 2. 208

> base contagious clouds
> To smother up his beauty from the world,

so that when he breaks through them he may be the more wondered at.

Harry Percy also, in his wife's eyes, shares some of the attributes of princes, when she describes how honour

2 H. IV,
2. 3. 18–21

> stuck upon him as the sun
> In the grey vault of heaven, and by his light
> Did all the chivalry of England move
> To do brave acts.

The thought of the king as sun naturally carries with it the idea of favourites of a prince ripening under his beams, as when Prince John, reproving York for his leadership of the rebels, points out that the man who

> sits within a monarch's heart,   *2 H. IV*, 4. 2. 11
> And ripens in the sunshine of his favour,

if he sets out to abuse the king's trust, may do untold mischief 'in shadow of such greatness'. Once also in a comedy, in *Much Ado*, we find this idea further developed to illustrate a too common sight in Tudor England: the courtier raised by the monarch to power and greatness, only to become in turn a menace to the throne. This is introduced by Hero in a charming picture, when she tells Margaret to bid Beatrice

> steal into the pleached bower,   *M. Ado*, 3. 1.
> Where honeysuckles, ripen'd by the sun,   7-11
> Forbid the sun to enter; like favourites,
> Made proud by princes, that advance their pride
> Against that power that bred it.

To return to the histories, we have a touch of the same 'sun' image in *Henry V*, when, conceiving of himself as the sun, the king sends his threat to the French prince:

> When I do rouse me in my throne of France,   *H. V*, 1. 2. 275
>
> . . . .
>
> ...I will rise there with so full a glory
> That I will dazzle all the eyes of France,
> Yea, strike the Dauphin blind to look on us.

Later, the special qualities of the sun, the power of generating fresh life and vigour, are ascribed to him in detail with great effect, as he makes his rounds, cheering and heartening his dispirited soldiers before the battle:

H. V, 4 Prol. 43

> A largess universal like the sun
> His liberal eye doth give to every one,
> Thawing cold fear, that mean and gentle all
> Behold, as may unworthiness define,
> A little touch of Harry in the night.

In *Henry VIII* also the same image reappears very
H. VIII, 1.1.6 definitely: the two kings, Henry and Francis, are 'suns of glory', 'two lights of men'; Wolsey, in disgrace, bidding Cromwell seek the king, ejaculates,

3. 2. 415

> That sun, I pray, may never set!

and other images in the play become completely clear only when this central idea of the king as sun is kept in mind. Thus, Buckingham contemptuously wonders
1.1.55 that such a 'keech'—such a lump of fat—as Wolsey, can take up the rays of the 'beneficial sun' and keep it from the earth, and later, as he turns away from his peers to go to the Tower, he pictures himself as shadowed from the source of life by this same obstructing enemy, and sighs,

1. 1. 224

> I am the shadow of poor Buckingham,
> Whose figure even this instant cloud puts on,
> By darkening [Bedarkening?] my clear sun.

So much for the 'sun-king' image, one of the most persistent in the historical plays. Returning to the study of the running images in *Richard II*, we find that the ideas of birth and generation, also of inheritance from father to son, are a good deal in Shakespeare's mind in this play, and the recurrence of these images undoubtedly increases the effect of Nemesis, of cause and effect, of tragedy as the inevitable result of deeds done and in no way to be avoided.

Gaunt, in his dying speech, first touches on this idea, as he does on various themes which recur during the play, such as music, jewels, sickness, and the 'setting sun'—which symbolises, as regards Richard, the end of the whole tragedy. England herself is thought of by Gaunt as *R. II, 2. 1. 12*

> This nurse, this teeming womb of royal kings, *2. 1. 51*
> Fear'd by their breed and famous by their birth;

and when the queen, after Richard's departure for Ireland, betrays her fear and anxiety to Bushy and Green, she expresses it almost wholly in this particular metaphor. She is depressed naturally in parting with the king, but this sensation, she declares, is something greater than that. She feels within her an unaccountable heaviness, the working of anguish which she believes is about to bring a great grief to birth:

> methinks, *2. 2. 10*
> Some unborn sorrow, ripe in fortune's womb,
> Is coming towards me.

Bushy assures her it is nothing but conceit (fancy, imagination). Even so, she answers, in one of those passages of involved word play dear to the young Shakespeare, there must be some foundation for it; either her real grief is born of nothing, or her imaginary grief takes its rise in reality; and she clothes the whole in the same metaphor which is still running in her mind:

> conceit is still derived *2. 2. 34*
> From some forefather grief; mine is not so,
> For nothing hath begot my something grief;
> Or something hath the nothing that I grieve:
> 'Tis in reversion that I do possess.

So that, when she stops speaking, and Green bursts

in upon them, bearing the bad news she has been dreading to hear, she naturally cries,

R. II, 2. 2. 62

> So, Green, thou art the midwife to my woe,
> And Bolingbroke my sorrow's dismal heir:
> Now hath my soul brought forth her prodigy,
> And I, a gasping new-deliver'd mother,
> Have woe to woe, sorrow to sorrow join'd.

The whole framework of Richard's last great monologue is built up on birth and generation. He is thinking how he may compare his prison to the world, which is so full of people,

5. 5. 4

> And here is not a creature but myself.

So he conceives of his brain and his soul as the mother and father,

5. 5. 7

> and these two beget
> A generation of still-breeding thoughts,
> And these same thoughts people this little world,
> In humours like the people of this world,
> For no thought is contented.

The idea of inheritance from father to son, constantly debated in the play (1. 2. 11, 2. 1. 104, 189–99, 2. 3. 118–36, 3. 3. 103–14, etc.), and repeated in the imagery, increases the feeling of the inevitable and foreordained, as also of the unlimited consequences of action. Repeated emphasis is laid on the unborn children doomed to suffer for their fathers' sins. 'God', says Richard to Northumberland,

3. 3. 86

> Is mustering in his clouds on our behalf
> Armies of pestilence; and they shall strike
> Your children yet unborn and unbegot,

and goes on to declare that Bolingbroke

> is come to open
> The purple testament of bleeding war,

that is, the inheritance he has taken on himself. And the deposition scene closes with the chant of the clergy as in chorus:

> A woeful pageant have we here beheld. *R. II, 4. 1. 321*
> The woe's to come; the children yet unborn
> Shall feel this day as sharp to them as thorn.

Later, Bolingbroke, in speaking of Aumerle's treason, sees the silver stream of York's loyalty defiled and muddied through his son, but the overflow of York's goodness is so abundant that it washes away this deadly blot. York, taking up the metaphor, answers bitterly,

> he shall spend mine honour with his shame, *5. 3. 68*
> As thriftless sons their scraping fathers' gold.

There is no question but that the whole brings out with unmistakable emphasis and repetition the idea which dominates not only *Richard II* but the entire series of early histories (*Henry VI* to *Richard II*)—of the terrible heritage of blood and strife, of *evil*, in character and in deeds, which is generated and bequeathed by civil war and all that it brings with it:

> What stratagems, how fell, how butcherly, *3 H. VI, 2. 5. 89*
> Erroneous, mutinous and unnatural,
> This deadly quarrel daily doth beget!

The touches of jewel imagery in *Richard II* should also be noticed, for they add beauty to the conception of the value of love, especially of love of country— a leading note in the play—and of the honour and devotion of her sons. Thus Mowbray assures the king that a spotless reputation is the purest treasure he can have:

> A jewel in a ten-times-barr'd-up chest *R. II, 1. 1. 180*
> Is a bold spirit in a loyal breast.

Richard, when he is alone in prison and hears the sound of music, blesses the heart that gives it him, for it is a sign of love, and love to Richard, he says,

R. II, 5. 5. 66   Is a strange brooch in this all-hating world.

He means it is a most precious but unfashionable thing; for the brooch, which was a large valuable ornament, seems to have been out of fashion in Shakespeare's time (compare *All's Well*, 1. 1. 166).

The setting of jewels interests Shakespeare, and he draws several well-known images from the way in which the beauty of a precious stone is enhanced by its background or foil, as when Prince Hal declares his earlier irresponsible behaviour will actually add value to his change of conduct later:

1 H. IV,   like bright metal on a sullen ground,
1. 2. 222   My reformation, glittering o'er my fault,
            Shall show more goodly and attract more eyes
            Than that which hath no foil to set it off.

The reverse process is illustrated when Richmond denounces Richard III as

R. III, 5. 3. 250   A base foul stone, made precious by the foil
            Of England's chair, where he is falsely set.

There are two such images in *Richard II*. One is when Gaunt, trying to reconcile his son to the thought of the weariness and pain of his long exile, bids him esteem it

R. II, 1. 3. 266   as foil wherein thou art to set
            The precious jewel of thy home return.

To which Bolingbroke replies,

            Nay, rather, every tedious stride I make
            Will but remember me what a deal of world
            I wander from the jewels that I love.

And one of the best-known lines in all Shakespeare is Gaunt's picture of England herself as a rare and loved jewel, enhanced in beauty and strength by the happy fortune of her setting:

> This precious stone set in the silver sea.   *R. II, 2. 1. 46*

Beyond what has already been noted, I see no running imagery in the first or second part of *Henry IV*. In *Henry V*, however, the opening words of the chorus— sighing for 'a Muse of fire' to 'ascend the brightest heaven of invention'—seem to give the key-note to the dominating atmosphere of the earlier and best part of the play, swift and soaring movement; and it is not mere chance, I think, that we find, through the play, an unusual number of images of the flight of birds, which for our forefathers symbolised the swiftest movement known to man. **HENRY V**

The desire adequately to convey to the audience this particular combination of intense swiftness and dignity, with the consciousness of the limitations of the rude and primitive theatre, dominates the opening prologue. Indeed, the urgent appeal to the onlookers to use their imaginations and piece out with their thoughts the imperfections of actors and stage, is the main theme of the vivid and stirring poetry of all five prologues.

The brilliant description of the fleet on its way from Southampton to Harfleur opens,

> Thus with imagined wing our swift scene flies   *H. V, 3 Prol. 1*
> In motion of no less celerity
> Than that of thought.

Later when, on the return journey, the king is crossing from Calais to Dover, the audience are urged to use their thoughts with the strength or swiftness of a bird's flight, to

> Heave him away upon your winged thoughts   *H. V, 5 Prol. 8*
> Athwart the sea.

Henry himself, when making ready for France, with all
the expedition possible, falls into the same simile:

H. V, *1. 2. 304*
     let our proportions for these wars
Be soon collected, and all things thought upon
That may with reasonable swiftness add
More feathers to our wings.

He measures emotion—its height and depth—by the
same picture of the flight of a bird; though the king's
4. 1. 106 affections, he tells his soldiers, are 'higher mounted'
than those of common folk, 'yet, when they stoop, they
stoop with the like wing'; and when arguing later with
them as to the king's responsibility for the fate of
individuals in battle, he points out that those of his
soldiers who have previously been evil-doers—thieves or
murderers—meet their deserts in war, though they may
4. 1. 173 have 'defeated the law and outrun native punishment,
though they can outstrip men, they have no wings to
fly from God: war is His beadle, war is His vengeance'.

 Finally, the Duke of York's moving cry, when he
finds his friend dead on the battle field, sums up, in
the last two words, with Shakespeare's characteristic
magic, the whole force of this favourite image:

4. 6. 15
       Tarry, dear cousin Suffolk!
My soul shall thine keep company to heaven;
Tarry, sweet soul, for mine, then fly abreast.

We may note, that, though birds are not mentioned in
any one of these images, yet the picture of their sure
and soaring flight, swift and strong, is in each intense
and vivid.

 The little scene of the Dauphin with his spirited
horse (3. 7) adds to this feeling of strong and soaring
motion, and coming where it does, just before the
description of the 'poor condemned English', sitting

by their camp-fires, patient and sad, lean and pale as H. V, 4 Prol. 22
ghosts, it points the contrast vividly between them and
the 'over-lusty' French. The Dauphin's horse bounds
from the earth like a tennis ball ('as if his entrails were
hairs'), he is 'le cheval volant, the Pegasus', 'he trots
the air', 'the earth sings when he touches it', 'he is
pure air and fire', and 'when I bestride him', declares
his master proudly, 'I soar, I am a hawk'. And the next
minute we are with 'Harry in the night', 'walking
from watch to watch, from tent to tent', cheering his
war-worn soldiers.

King John, from the point of view of imagery, stands KING JOHN
quite apart from the series of York and Lancaster plays.
The proportion of subjects of the images is markedly
different, and they seem to me to play as a whole a
much more dominating part in creating and sustaining
atmosphere, than is the case in any other 'history' play.

The images in themselves are in many ways remarkable, and noticeably vivid. The dominating symbol,
which out-dominates all others in the play, is the body
and bodily action. It is so in an entirely different and
infinitely more imaginative way than in *Coriolanus*,
where certain functions or persons in the state are rather
wearisomely and perfunctorily compared with various
parts of the body. Here one feels, on the contrary,
that the poet's imagination was intensely and brilliantly alive, dancing with fire and energy like Philip
Faulconbridge himself, and a great part of the extraordinary vigour and vividness of the images is due to
the fact that Shakespeare seems to have thought more
continuously and definitely than usual of certain outstanding emotions and themes in the play in terms of
a person with bodily characteristics and bodily move-

ment. It is not possible, especially in a play like *King John*, where Shakespeare's mind is full of a bodily symbol, entirely to separate images of body and bodily action from those of personification, for quite a number might equally well be classified under either heading. In such cases I usually put the image under 'Personification' when that seems the most striking aspect, and under 'Body' when the special movement appears accentuated.

For the only time in a play of Shakespeare's, images of nature or animals do not head, or almost head, the list, but take definitely the second and third place; by far the greatest number in *King John* are these personifications, reinforced by the large group coming under body or bodily action, making seventy-one listed images in all under these two headings (see Chart VI).

The two great protagonists, France and England, the fate that befalls them under the guises of fortune, war and death; the emotions and qualities called into play by the clash of their contending desires: grief, sorrow, melancholy, displeasure, amazement, commodity; the besieged city of Angiers; all these, and other entities or abstractions, are seen by Shakespeare— many of them repeatedly—as *persons*; angry, proud, contemptuous, saucy, indignant, smooth-faced, surly and wanton; sinning, suffering, repenting, kissing, winking, wrestling, resisting, whirling, hurrying, feasting, drinking, bragging, frowning and grinning. If one looks at it from this angle, one sees that Shakespeare has painted, as a kind of illumination or decorative marginal gloss to the play, a series of tiny allegorical pictures, dancing with life and movement, which, far from lessening the vigour of reality, as allegory sometimes does, increase its vividness and poignancy tenfold.

He sees England, here as elsewhere (cf. *R. II*, 3. 3. 96 and 2. 3. 92), as a pale-faced woman, with Neptune's arms clipping her about, or standing with *K.J. 5. 2. 33* her foot spurning back 'the ocean's roaring tides', the *2. 1. 23* mother of sons, who, in war, are reluctantly forced to 'march upon her gentle bosom' and 'fright her pale- *5. 2. 24* faced villages'. *R. II, 2. 3. 92*

France, on the other hand, in the eyes of Constance, is a 'bawd to Fortune and King John'; fortune, who *K.J. 3. 1. 60* joined with nature to make Arthur great, is corrupted, changed and sins with John, and has taken France with her golden hand and led her on 'to tread down fair respect and sovereignty'. The besieged city, the centre of their tussle in the early scenes, is thought of throughout as a *person*—a woman—engirdled with a waist of stones, whose brows, ribs, eyes, cheeks and bosom are referred to, and of whom the ad- *2. 1. 38, 215,* jectives resisting, contemptuous, winking and saucy *225, 384, 410* are used.

And war is dominant throughout, a wild and ruthless force, a mighty being with 'grappling vigour and rough *3. 1. 104* frown'. Little pictures like that of the dogs 'bristling' *4. 3. 145–50* and 'snarling' for the 'bare-pick'd bone of majesty', of the 'jolly troop of huntsmen', 'with purpled hands, *2. 1. 321* dyed in the dying slaughter of their foes', of the 'storm *5. 1. 17* of war' blown up by Pandulph's breath or the fire of war rekindled by it, of John being urged to go forth *5. 2. 83* 'and glister like the god of war', not to hide in his *5. 1. 54* palace, but to run

To meet displeasure farther from the doors, *5. 1. 59*
And grapple with him ere he come so nigh,

K.J. 5. 2. 74 enhance the consciousness of the ever present 'savage spirit of wild war' which broods over all.

Beside war stalks death, a terrible and gruesome figure, as seen by Faulconbridge, his dead chaps lined with steel, the swords of soldiers for his fangs, feasting *2. 1. 352* and 'mousing the flesh of men'. Or he appears as the skilful and ever victorious enemy, as Prince Henry sees him, who 'having prey'd upon the outward parts', directs his siege

5. 7. 17 Against the mind, the which he pricks and wounds
With many legions of strange fantasies.

To the distraught Constance he is a 'carrion monster', the embodiment of all that is most abhorrent and repulsive; yet such is her agony that he is to be longed for and fondled and greeted as a lover, so that she is moved to cry,

3. 4. 25–35   O amiable lovely death!
Thou odoriferous stench! sound rottenness!
Arise forth from the couch of lasting night,

. . . .

Come, grin on me, and I will think thou smilest,
And buss thee as thy wife.

It is worth noting that though fortune, war and death are thought of as persons, King John, who is England's greatest enemy, is always pictured as a *portion* of a body only, which seems in some strange way to create of him something specially sinister and horrible. Pandulph thinks of him as represented by the hand which clasps Philip's in seeming amity, and warns the French king that he may

3. 1. 258   hold a serpent by the tongue,
A chafed lion by the mortal paw,
A fasting tiger safer by the tooth,
Than keep in peace that hand which thou dost hold.

He sees that hand dipped in blood, and tells Lewis that when John hears of his approach, if Arthur be not already dead, the king will kill him, and then his people will revolt from him,

> And kiss the lips of unacquainted change,   *K.J. 3. 4. 166*
> And pick strong matter of revolt and wrath
> Out of the bloody fingers' ends of John.

John thinks of himself as a foot, which, wheresoe'er it treads, finds Arthur as a serpent in his way; and the most terrible and haunting image in the play, which indeed sums up its whole movement, is when his own followers revolt against him as Pandulph prophesied they would, and on the king's bidding them to his presence, Salisbury in their names angrily refuses to

> attend the foot   *4. 3. 25*
> That leaves the print of blood where'er it walks.

At the end too, when John gets his deserts, this same feeling of his being but a fragment—a mere counterfeit of humanity—is again emphasised, this time in his own bitter cry that his heart is cracked and burned, that all the shrouds wherewith his life should sail

> Are turned to one thread, *one little hair*,   *5. 7. 54*

and that all his faithful servant and his son are now looking at

> is but a clod   *5. 7. 57*
> And module of confounded royalty.

This presentation of King John is a good example of one of the varied ways in which Shakespeare—through imagery—often without our conscious recognition of his method, profoundly affects us.

Long before I noticed, in actual statistics, the unusual predominance in this play of images of personification and bodily action, I was generally aware—as
all readers must be—of a marked feeling of vigour, life
and energy radiating chiefly from Faulconbridge, and
of an overpowering feeling of repulsion for John,
hardly accounted for by the text. I now believe these
two impressions to be partly due to the subtle effect
of the curious but quite definite symbolism, which, in
a play crowded with pictures of dancing, wrestling,
whirling human figures, lets us see the king as a portion of a body only, and that portion at times steeped
in human blood.

Readers hardly need reminding how extraordinarily
vivid are many of the personifications of emotions, such
as Constance's two well-known descriptions of grief
(*K.J.* 3. 1. 68 and 3. 4. 93), the later one carrying with
it again the same contradictory attraction as in the case
of death:

> Grief fills the room up of my absent child,
> Lies in his bed, walks up and down with me,
>
> .   .   .   .   .   .
>
> Then have I reason to be fond of grief.

John's description of that 'surly spirit, melancholy'
and his action on the blood, and of 'that idiot, laughter'
when he is working Hubert to his purposes, is unusual
and arresting, as is indeed the whole speech, with its
five vivid personifications treading close on each other's
heels in the space of sixteen lines. So also Faulconbridge's account of the havoc and flurry wrought among
John's few remaining followers when they hear he has
yielded to the Pope is unsurpassed in terse pictorial
quality:

K.J.
3. 3. 31–46

And wild amazement hurries up and down
The little number of your doubtful friends.[1]

K. J. 5. 1. 35

John is very fond of personifications, but then so are many of the characters—Constance, Faulconbridge, Pandulph and Arthur—and this general tendency causes the strangest things to be visualised as persons—the cannon with their 'bowels full of wrath' spitting forth 'iron indignation'; the midnight bell, with 'iron tongue and brazen mouth'; even the insentient iron with which Hubert is to put out Arthur's eyes, and the fire which heats it, the 'burning coal' which has no malice in it and is now cold, but which, if revived, will 'glow with shame' for his proceedings.

2. 1. 210
3. 3. 37
4. 1. 61
4. 1. 106–12

Like *King Lear*, where the symbol of a body torn and shattered is so vivid that it overflows into the ordinary language—the verbs and adjectives of the play—so here, the consciousness of the aspect of a living person, a face, an eye, a brow, a hand, a finger, with characteristic gestures and actions, is almost continuous, and description takes naturally the form of which the following phrases, chosen at random, are a type. They might easily be multiplied two or threefold. 'The *coward hand* of France'; 'not a word of his But *buffets* better than a *fist* of France'; 'peace and *fair-faced* league'; 'the outward *eye* of fickle France'; 'move the *murmuring lips* of discontent'; 'the *gentle brow* Of true sincerity'; 'O, that my *tongue* were in the thunder's

2. 1. 158
2. 1. 464
2. 1. 417
2. 1. 583
4. 2. 53
3. 1. 247
3. 4. 38

---

[1] This type of personification is of course to be found in other Elizabethan writers; but nothing more emphasises Shakespeare's supreme quality than to take things in him which are of the nature of commonplaces and to put them beside others. Compare here, for instance, Dekker's

> Fantastic compliment stalks up and down,
> Tricked in outlandish feathers.

> (*Old Fortunatus*, 2. 2.)

K.J. 5. 1. 49 *mouth*!'; 'outface the *brow* Of *bragging* horror'; 'the
5. 6. 17 *black brow* of night'. It is not surprising therefore that
we find nearly all the chief emotional themes or moving
forces in the play summed up with unforgettable vividness in little vignettes of this type: the selfish motives
of the two kings in the Bastard's sketch of

2. 1. 573 That smooth-faced gentleman, tickling Commodity;

the terrible position Blanch finds herself in with a newly-wed husband in one army and her uncle in the other,
in her amazing and haunting picture of being torn
asunder in opposite directions:

3. 1. 327 Which is the side that I must go withal?
I am with both: each army hath a hand;
And in their rage, I having hold of both,
They whirl asunder and dismember me;

Constance's grief; Arthur's horror at the red-hot iron;
5. 1. 35 the bewilderment and uncertainty of John's followers;
John's own faithlessness and cruelty pictured in the
bloody finger tips and footprint; and his mental and
physical agony at the end, when, forsaken, defeated and
dying from a virulent poison which is burning him up
internally, making a hell within him, he cries, in answer
to his son's query, 'How fares your majesty?'

5. 7. 35 Poison'd,—ill fare—dead, forsook, cast off:
And none of you will bid the winter come
To thrust his icy fingers in my maw,
. . . nor entreat the north
To make his bleak winds kiss my parched lips
And comfort me with cold.

In *Henry VIII*, so far removed in treatment and spirit
from *King John*, the dominating image, curiously
enough, is again the body and bodily action (see Chart 6),
but used in an entirely different way and at a different

angle from that in the earlier play. The continuous picture or symbol in the poet's mind is not so much a person displaying certain emotions and characteristics, as a mere physical body in endlessly varied action. Thus I find only four 'personifications' in the play, whereas in *King John* I count no less than forty.

In a play like *Henry VIII*, a large part of which it has HENRY been generally decided on good critical grounds is not written by Shakespeare, the question which immediately presents itself is whether there is any evidence or not in the imagery that one mind has functioned throughout. For our present purpose, however, I suggest we leave this question aside, and look at the way the running symbol works out as a whole.

There are three aspects of the picture of a body in the mind of the writer of the play: the whole body and its limbs; the various parts, tongue, mouth and so on; and—much the most constant—bodily action of almost every kind: walking, stepping, marching, running and leaping; crawling, hobbling, falling, carrying, climbing and perspiring; swimming, diving, flinging and peeping; crushing, strangling, shaking, trembling, sleeping, stirring, and—especially and repeatedly—the picture of the body or back bent and weighed down under a heavy burden. Except for this last, I see no special symbolic reason for the lavish use of this image, other than the fact that it is a favourite one with Shakespeare, especially the aspect of bodily movement, and we find it in the imagery from various points of view in *King Lear*, *Hamlet*, *Coriolanus*, *King John*, and in a lesser degree, in *Henry V* and *Troilus and Cressida*.

The opening scene—a vivid description of the tourney on the Field of the Cloth of Gold when Henry and

Francis met—with its picture of bodily pomp and action, may possibly have started the image in the poet's mind, as it did in Buckingham's, when after listening to Norfolk's glowing words he asks,

H.VIII, 1.1.45

> Who did guide,
> I mean, who set the body and the limbs
> Of this great sport together...?

Norfolk, trying to restrain Buckingham's anger with the cardinal, says,

1. 1. 129

> Stay, my lord,
> ...to climb steep hills
> Requires slow pace at first...
>
>   .   .   .   .   .
>
> Be advised;
> ......we may outrun,
> By violent swiftness, that which we run at,
> And lose by over-running;

and the utter uselessness of the treaty which was the avowed object of the costly Cloth of Gold meeting is brought home by the amazingly vivid picture of a support or means of walking offered to the human body when no longer capable of any movement at all: the articles were ratified, says Buckingham, 'to as much *1. 1. 171* end as give a crutch to the dead'. At the end of the scene the original image returns, and the plot against the king is thought of as a body, so that when the nobles are arrested Buckingham exclaims,

1. 1. 220   These are the limbs o' the plot: no more, I hope.

We note as we read that many of the most vivid images in the play are those of movements of the body, *2. 2. 27* such as Norfolk's description of Wolsey diving into the king's soul, and there scattering dangers and doubts, Cranmer, crawling into the king's favour and strangling his language in tears, Anne's ejaculation about Katharine's deposition, and her divorce from the majesty and pomp of sovereignty, and Katharine's *H. VIII,* 5. 1. 156

> sufferance panging
> As soul and body's severing.

2. 3. 15

Wolsey thinks constantly in terms of body movement: among his images are those of a soldier marching in step with a 'file', a man scratched and torn by pressing through a thorny wood, or set on by thieves, bound, robbed and unloosed; and in his last great speeches, which, in spite of falling rhythm, I incline to believe are Shakespeare's, he speaks of having *trod* the ways of glory, sees Cromwell *carrying* peace in his right hand, urges him to *fling away* ambition, and pictures himself successively as a rash *swimmer* venturing far beyond his depth with the meretricious aid of a bladder, a man *falling* headlong from a great height like a meteor or like Lucifer, and finally, standing bare and *naked* at the mercy of his enemies.

1. 2. 42
1. 2. 75
2. 4. 146

3. 2. 435, 440, 445

3. 2. 358–61

3. 2. 223, 371
3. 2. 456

The image of the back bent under the load recurs five times, and is obviously and suitably symbolic of Wolsey's state, as well as of the heavy taxation. Wolsey complains that the question of the divorce was 'the weight that pulled him down', and after his dismissal, sees himself as a man with an unbearable burden suddenly lifted off him, assuring Cromwell that he thanks the king, who has cured him, 'and from these shoulders' taken 'a load would sink a navy',

3. 2. 407

3. 2. 381

> a burden
> Too heavy for a man that hopes for heaven!

The idea of a man falling from a great height is constant in the case of both Wolsey and Cranmer; and

the remonstrances made with their accusers are in each
case exactly alike:

H. *VIII*,
3. 2. 333   Press not a falling man too far;...

.   .   .   .

5. 3. 76   'tis a cruelty
    To load a falling man.

The queen draws on the same range of bodily
similes. She speaks of unmannerly language 'which
breaks the sides of loyalty', 'bold mouths' and 'tongues'
spitting their duties out, and her description of the
great cardinal, with the king's aid going swiftly and
2. 4. 111–15 easily over the shallow steps until mounted at the top
of the staircase of fame, is extraordinarily vivid.

The king also uses it with great force when relating
his mental and emotional suffering and the self ques-
tioning that followed on hearing the French ambassador
demand a 'respite' [an adjournment] in order to de-
termine whether the Princess Mary were legitimate,
thus raising the whole question of the divorce.

He draws a picture of the word 'respite' and its
effect on him as of a rough and hasty intruder rushing
noisily into a quiet and guarded place, shaking and
splitting it, forcing a way in so ruthlessly that with him
throng in also from outside many other unbidden
beings, pressing and pushing, dazed and puzzled with
the commotion and the place wherein they find themselves. 'This respite', he declares,

2. 4. 181   shook
    The bosom of my conscience, enter'd me,
    Yea, with a splitting power, and made to tremble
    The region of my breast; which forced such way
    That many mazed considerings did throng
    And press'd in with this caution.

A little later, as he tells the court how he sought counsel from his prelates, he, like Wolsey, pictures himself as a man almost unbearably burdened, groaning and sweating under his load, when he turns to the bishop with the query,

> my lord of Lincoln; you remember
> How under my oppression I did reek,
> When I first moved you.

H. VIII,
2. 4. 207

When we trace out in detail this series of images, we recognise that it is a good example of Shakespeare's peculiar habit of seeing emotional or mental situations throughout a play in a repeatedly recurring physical picture, in what might more correctly indeed be called a 'moving picture'; because having once, as here, visualised the human body in action, he sees it continuously, like Wolsey's 'strange postures' in every form of physical activity.

3. 2. 112–19

I must not, however, here be led into the question of authorship, beyond stating that the imagery of *Henry VIII* distinctly goes to prove that in addition to the generally accepted Shakespearian scenes (1. 1 and 2, 2. 3 and 4, the early part of 3. 2, and 5. 1), the whole of 3. 2 and of 5. 3 are also his, and that he at least gave some touches to 2. 2.[1]

It will be seen that on the whole this running imagery in the histories fulfils a somewhat different function from what it does in either tragedy or comedy. It is, as I have said, simpler and more obvious in kind, and although, as in *Richard II*, it sometimes emphasises a leading idea, it does not, as in *Hamlet* or *Macbeth*, shed

---

[1] For a fuller discussion of the authorship of *Henry VIII*, see my British Academy Shakespeare lecture for 1931, *Shakespeare's Iterative Imagery*, Oxford University Press, 1931, pp. 22, 23.

definite light on the central problem, because, with the exception perhaps of Falstaff, there are in the histories no problems of character.

In two of the histories we note that the image symbolism quite definitely—in the method of the comedies—contributes atmosphere and quality to the play. Thus in *Henry V* the feeling of swift and soaring movement is markedly emphasised, and in *King John*, which in treatment stands out from all the other histories, the very marked and consistent 'floating' image brings out the contrast between the surging vigorous life in most of the characters in the play, and the negation of life, which is evil, in the person of the cruel and craven king. It thus heightens immensely the imaginative and poetical effectiveness of the theme.

CHAPTER XIII

LEADING MOTIVES IN THE COMEDIES

AS far as there is any continuous symbolism in the imagery of the comedies, its function would seem to be, as I have said, to give atmosphere and background, as well as to emphasise or re-echo certain qualities in the plays.

Thus, in *A Midsummer Night's Dream*, we know that what we feel overpoweringly is the woodland beauty of the dreaming summer night, and it is only when we look closer that we realise in some measure how this sensation is brought about.

The influence and presence of the moon are felt throughout, largely through the imagery, from the opening lines when the noble lovers impatiently measure the days to their wedding by the waning of the old moon and the coming of the new,

> like to a silver bow *M.N.D. 1. 1. 9*
> New-bent in heaven,

to the end, when Puck tells us the 'wolf behowls the *5. 1. 369* moon', and that it is therefore the time of night for the fairies' frolic.

Time and movement are both measured by her, for mortals as well as for Puck and the fairies; the lovers make their tryst for the moment on the morrow,

> when Phoebe doth behold *1. 1. 209*
> Her silver visage in the watery glass;

the fairies compass the globe 'swifter than the wan-

M.N.D.   dering moon'. She is the 'governess of floods', and
4. 1 102   controls not only the weather, but also the fiery shafts
2. 1. 103
2. 1. 161   of love which at will she quenches in her 'chaste
            beams'; she symbolises the barren air of the cloister,
            where the sisters live

1.1.73   Chanting faint hymns to the cold fruitless moon;

            she serves, as does the sun, for an emblem of steadfast
            constancy; and Hermia cries she would as soon believe
3. 2. 52   a hole might be bored in the centre of the earth and
            the moon creep through it, as that Lysander should
            willingly have left her.

            The word 'moon' occurs twenty-eight times, three
            and a half times more often than in any other play,
            partly of course owing to the prominence of moonshine,
            often addressed as 'moon', as a character in the comedy
            of the 'homespuns'. 'Moonlight' naturally also occurs
            unusually often: indeed Shakespeare only mentions
            moonlight in his plays eight times altogether, and six
            of these are in *A Midsummer Night's Dream*, as is also
            his only reference to moonbeams. His single use of
            'starry' is also here, when Oberon tells Puck to cover
3. 2. 356   the 'starry welkin', and the sensation of starlight, which
2. 1. 29   is constant (the fairies dance by 'spangled starlight
3. 2. 407   sheen', Puck accuses Demetrius of 'bragging to the
            stars', if moonshine be gone Thisbe will find her lover
5. 1. 313   by starlight, and so on), is largely owing to the many
            comparisons to the stars which come naturally to those
            who are looking at them, as when Demetrius assures
            Hermia that though she has pierced his heart, and is
            a murderer, she looks

3. 2. 60   as bright, as clear,
                  As yonder Venus in her glimmering sphere,

and Lysander declares that Helena

> more engilds the night
> Than all yon fiery oes and eyes of light.

M.N.D.
3. 2. 187

This moonlit background, then, partly supplies the dreaming and enchanted quality in the play, which is reinforced by woodland beauty. This is drawn largely from two sources, closely allied and sometimes melting into one: the high proportion of poetical images— ninety-five out of a total of a hundred and fourteen— considerably higher than in any other comedy, and the very large number of nature images, including animals and birds. These Shakespeare always has, but their number here is unusual, for in addition to those listed under 'nature', there are many which have to be classified under other headings, which really, all the time, are calling up country pictures before us. Thus the 'green corn' which

> Hath rotted ere his youth attain'd a beard,

2. 1. 95

which is really a personification, brings to the mind above all else the sight of the fields at the end of many a wet English summer, just as the description of the way

> the spring, the summer,
> The childing autumn, angry winter, change
> Their wonted liveries,

2. 1. 111

which comes under 'clothes', really presents us with a pageant of the swift succession of the seasons in their many-coloured garb.

Even the measurement of time is made, not only by the moon, but also by the cock-crow, the 'middle summer's spring', and the 'lightning in the collied night', by the greening of the wheat and the coming of the hawthorn buds, by the mating of the birds and

2. 1. 82
1. 1. 145

the swimming powers of the leviathan, by dawn and sunrise, by a shadow and a sound.

And the birds too, whose song and sound are heard throughout, as it should be in an English woodland play, the dove, the nightingale, the rook, and the lark— these are, as with Shakespeare always, used as a measure of all kinds of activities and sense-values: of light movement, 'hop as light as bird from brier', of sweet sound, 'more tuneable than lark to shepherd's ear', of colour-sense,

M.N.D.
5. 1. 391
1. 1. 184

3. 2. 141

> high Taurus' snow,
> Fann'd with the eastern wind, turns to a crow
> When thou hold'st up thy hand,

or of headlong scattered flight, as when the wild geese or russet-pated choughs,

3. 2. 22

> Rising and cawing at the gun's report,
> Sever themselves and madly sweep the sky.

Even in the farce of the rustics we get—as it were by chance—a splash of nature-beauty flung by the way such as:

3. 1. 96

> Of colour like the red rose on triumphant brier,

and in the play as a whole the succession of imaginative pictures crystallising experiences, emotions, and sensations familiar to all English nature lovers has never been surpassed by Shakespeare himself. These are all well known, for they are among our greatest poetry, and a score of them could be named in this play alone, but two must suffice here.

We English all know that delightful mid-season of early autumn when the night frosts nip the late summer flowers, and through which the hardy monthly roses persist in gaily blooming, but it is Shakespeare who has painted the poet's picture of it for ever, with its exquisite mingling of sharp air and sweet scents, in the Fairy Queen's description of what was probably the experience of many a gardener at the end of the cold wet summer of 1594: we see

> The seasons alter: hoary-headed frosts
> Fall in the fresh lap of the crimson rose;
> And on old Hiems' thin and icy crown
> An odorous chaplet of sweet summer buds
> Is, as in mockery, set.

M.N.D.
2. 1. 106

We have most of us seen a summer's sunrise over the sea, but Shakespeare has immortalised the pageant for us in a riot of colour and beauty when we watch with Oberon,

> Even till the eastern gate, all fiery-red,
> Opening on Neptune with fair blessed beams,
> Turns into yellow gold his salt green streams.

3. 2. 391

No wonder Keats underscored this play in parts almost continuously, for sheer poetry, nature and moonlight were his loves, and he found them all here together to his hand, as nowhere else in literature, in rich and joyous abundance. And these, largely through the imagery we have been analysing, have stamped their special impress on the play, which leaves us, as it has left myriads, over nearly three and a half centuries, amazed and bewitched by beauty and the strange power of the poet's pen.

In *Much Ado* we step into an entirely different atmosphere, gay, sparkling, unsentimental, witty, and we notice at once what a number of lively images there are in this play, of light sound and swift movement, which sustain this atmosphere, dancing (a Scotch jig, a measure,

MUCH ADO

M.Ado, 2. 1. 74

M. Ado, 3.2.57
3.2.13
1.1.185
3.1.35
5.2.11
3.1.51
3.1.28

a cinque pace), music (the jesting spirit crept into a lute string, the clapper of a bell), song ('in what key shall a man take you, to go in the song?'), riding, galloping, ambling, shy swift birds (spirits 'coy and wild as haggerds of the rock'), the lightning-quick action of the hunting dog ('wit as quick as the greyhound's mouth'): these and others form a fitting accompaniment and setting for the gay and high-spirited girl born under a dancing star, in whose eyes 'disdain and scorn ride sparkling'.

Besides this note of gaiety, the dominant motive is English country life, but of a sort entirely different from the languorous moonlit atmosphere of the enchanted wood. It is a setting of active outdoor work and sport, at times contending against cold and storm, largely created indirectly through the imagery, in which the most noticeable and continuous idea is that of the country sports of bird-snaring and angling; both lovers being thought of as birds limed and caught in a net, or fish hooked by the 'treacherous bait'.

This atmosphere of outdoor sport is not imagination, but is supported by statistics. For the only time in Shakespeare's plays, the images from sport head the list, and are therefore more numerous than those of either nature or animals. They include many from bird-snaring, riding and fishing, as well as others from archery, shooting, tilting, hunting, fencing, bird-nesting, and bear-baiting. Others, such as wrestling and dancing (listed under Bodily Action), might legitimately be added.

As compared with some plays, there are not a great many nature similes, but at times they run almost continuously. Thus, in the charming little scene of only slightly over a hundred lines, in the orchard (3. 1), when Hero and Ursula bait their trap for Beatrice, we notice a succession of rural pictures—the pleached honeysuckle-bower, which, ripened by the sun, yet keeps it out; the lapwing running close to the ground, couched in the woodbine; the pleasant angling

> to see the fish
> Cut with her golden oars the silver stream;

M. Ado, 3. 1. 26

the young wild hawks, the vane 'blown with all winds', the 'covered fire' of weeds, the smoke of which so deliciously scents English gardens, the 'limed trap', and the wild bird being tamed—all of which stimulate and sustain in us the consciousness of the background of active outdoor country life.

This is augmented by the repeated use of weather and seasons for purposes of comparison, as when Beatrice so wounds Benedick's pride by telling him he was 'duller than a great thaw', or Don Pedro exclaims at his 'February face',

2. 1. 245
5. 4. 41

> So full of frost, of storm, and cloudiness,

as well as by touches like Dogberry's ewe that will not hear her lamb when it baas, the sound of Beatrice's dog barking at a crow, Don John's 'forward March-chick', or the secret of the rooting of crops, expounded by Conrade. To these may be added the many vivid country pictures drawn so easily and lightly by Benedick, such as the poor hurt fowl that creeps into the sedges, the melancholy lodge in a warren, the schoolboy who, overjoyed at finding a bird's nest, unwarily shows it to his companion, who steals it, the howling dog, or the honest drover who sells bullocks. All through, whatever the scene, the country outdoor atmosphere is

1. 3. 56

kept before us, as when Don Pedro rounds off the rite of hanging Hero's epitaph on her tomb in church, by his picture, in delicate classical vein, of the coming of an English dawn:

M. Ado, 5. 3. 25

look, the gentle day,
Before the wheels of Phoebus, round about
Dapples the drowsy east with spots of grey.

MERRY WIVES
    Atmosphere befitting its subject and tone is also given to the *Merry Wives* by the number of lively images in it of all kinds, many drawn from sport, games, ships in action or adventure, quaint or comic pictures: *M.W. 3. 5. 119* Falstaff hissing hot, cooling in the Thames like a *5. 5. 139* horseshoe, or asking has he laid his brain in the sun and dried it that it lacks matter to deal with his tormentors; Anne Page's asseveration that rather than marry Dr Caius she would

3. 4. 92

be set quick i' the earth,
And bowl'd to death with turnips!

1. 3. 26 Bardolph's filching, which was like an unskilful singer, for 'he kept not time', and the rogues who threw *3. 5. 9* Falstaff into the river 'with as little remorse as they would have drowned a blind bitch's puppies, fifteen i' the litter'. There are also many town and topical ones; *3. 3. 73* the smell at Bucklersbury (where the druggists' shops *3. 3. 81; 3. 5. 5* were) at simple time, the reek of a lime kiln, the barrow *1. 4. 20* of butcher's offal to be thrown in the Thames, Slender's *2. 1. 65* beard 'like a glover's paring-knife', the whale thrown ashore at Windsor, or a delicious touch, carrying with it the essence of youth and spring-time, such as the *3. 2. 66* Host's description of young Master Fenton, 'he speaks holiday, he smells April and May'.

TWO GENTLEMEN
    In the *Two Gentlemen*, likewise, the prevailing group of images—those taken from types and classes of

people—gives character to the play. Shakespeare is always fond of this kind of simile, and it is largely through it that we get so many little pictures of the populace of Elizabethan England. (See p. 142.) But the number of them here is remarkable, partly owing to Speed's mocking answer to Valentine's naïve query, 'Why, how know you that I am in love?', when he cites a whole list of characters or beings that his master resembles in some one particular which betrays his lovelorn condition: 'you have learned...to wreathe your arms like a male-content;...to walk alone, like one that had the pestilence; to sigh, like a schoolboy that had lost his A. B. C.; to weep, like a young wench that had buried her grandam; to fast, like one that takes diet', and so on. But apart from this amusing and vivid speech, these little 'characters' used for comparison seem to be a favourite method of simile with Shakespeare in this play, and for this purpose he draws, among others, upon a child, a babe, a nurse, a physician, a beggar, a pilgrim, a bankrupt, a beadsman, a soldier, a swarthy Ethiope, a herald, a mighty lord, as well as on prisoners, slaves, bastards and messengers.

Two Gent.
2. 1. 16

Three of his images of love exemplify very well his different ways of handling these: the simple statement, with an explanatory phrase:

> for Love is like a child,
> That longs for every thing that he can come by;

3. 1. 124

the vivid little picture of 'wayward' 'foolish' love,

> That, like a testy babe, will scratch the nurse,
> And presently, all humbled, kiss the rod!

1. 2. 58

and the longer, slower-moving metaphor of love pictured as a mighty lord who humbles and corrects his vassal.

2. 4. 136

There is probably no particular reason why there are
so many of this type of image, except perhaps that
Shakespeare was writing the play in a considerable
hurry, and got into the habit of it. For there is evidence,
I think, of haste of a kind we so rarely find in later
plays, in the many repetitions of images, such as the
comparison of the transitory nature of love by Proteus
to the thawing of a waxen image, and by the duke to
the melting of an ice figure; the references by both
Proteus and Julia to 'Love's wings' and their swift
flight, the comparison of the hardness of Julia's nature
to steel, and of the dog Crab's to a 'pebble stone'; and
the two uses of the chameleon, and of the spaniel.

Two Gent.
2. 4. 200
3. 2. 5
2.6. 42; 2. 7. 11
1. 1. 140
2. 3. 10
2. 1. 169; 2. 4. 23
3. 1. 270; 4. 2. 14

However this may be, the general effect of the many
'character' images in the play is undoubtedly to give
colour and decoration, variety and liveliness.

TWELFTH
NIGHT

In *Twelfth Night* the types of images reflect subtly
and accurately the rather peculiar mixture of tones in
the play, music, romance, sadness and beauty interwoven with wit, broad comedy, and quick-moving snap-
ping dialogue.

The first thing one notices is that out of a hundred
images there are only fourteen which can be called
poetical, but these are either peculiarly beautiful, and
very well known, such as the

Tw. N. 1. 1. 5

sweet sound,
That breathes upon a bank of violets,
Stealing and giving odour!

(needing no emendation to my mind); Viola's description of how she let

2. 4. 113

concealment, like a worm i' the bud,
Feed on her damask cheek,

Olivia's purging 'the air of pestilence', and the 'bab- *Tw. N. 1.1.20*
bling gossip of the air' crying out her name; or they *1. 5. 283*
are vivid and unforgettable, like Sir Andrew's hair
which 'hangs like flax on a distaff', and the duke's mind *1. 3. 103*
which is 'a very opal'; or inimitable pictures, such as *2. 4. 76*
Fabian's of Malvolio as a 'rare turkeycock' jetting *2. 5. 33*
'under his advanced plumes'; or his threat to Sir Toby,
that having sailed into the north of his lady's opinion *3. 2. 26*
he will hang there 'like an icicle on a Dutchman's
beard'.

Further, one remarks that this play has, even for a
comedy, an unusual number (sixteen) of 'topical' images,
amusing, quaint, ingenious and witty, mostly in the
prose parts and the Sir Toby scenes, such as his declara-
tion that 'he's a coward...that will not drink to my *1. 3. 42*
niece, till his brains turn o' the toe like a parish-top',
or his direction to Sir Andrew to scout for him 'at the *3. 4. 189*
corner of the orchard like a bum-baily', Viola's message
that she will stand at Olivia's door 'like a sheriff's post', *1. 5. 151*
Maria's well-known comparison of the lines in Mal- *3. 2. 83*
volio's face to the 'new map', the clown's comparison *3. 1. 13*
of a cheveril glove to a good wit, or Sir Toby's sheet
of paper 'big enough for the bed of Ware in England'. *3. 2. 48*
These and many more give a lightness and brilliance
to the play which must have delighted the early
audiences, and which keep alive the atmosphere of
repartee and topical fun which is one of the characteristics of this sophisticated and delicious comedy.

As an example of atmosphere, the constant presence MER-
of music in so much of the *Merchant of Venice* must not CHANT OF
VENICE
pass unnoticed here. Although one cannot say it is
given by images, yet it is much enhanced by them. The
two great moments of emotion and romance are in-

troduced and accompanied by music, and the sweetness
of its sound echoes through them, so that in the space
of forty-five lines we find it named more often than in
the whole of any other play. Although there are actually
only two similes drawn from it, it dominates both
scenes, and gives rise to a series of pictures in which
music is the central thought.

When Bassanio is about to make his choice, Portia
orders that music shall sound,

> Then, if he lose, he makes a swan-like end,
> Fading in music.

But if he win—there crowd upon her images of what
music then is,

> Even as the flourish when true subjects bow
> To a new-crowned monarch,

or
> those dulcet sounds in break of day
> That creep into the dreaming bridegroom's ear,
> And summon him to marriage.

And in the exquisite scene at the end when Lorenzo
and Jessica are awaiting the return of their mistress, 'the
sounds of music' again 'creep in our ears', 'to draw her
home'; Lorenzo, pointing to the stars, declares,

> There's not the smallest orb which thou behold'st
> But in his motion like an angel sings,

and he goes on to expound to Jessica, in the well-known
magical words, that the music of the spheres finds its
counterpart in the harmony 'in immortal souls'.

When she remarks she is never merry when she hears
sweet music, he explains that the reason is her 'spirits
are attentive', and compares the strange and magical
power of music in instantly taming and subduing so

wild a thing as a herd of young colts 'bellowing and neighing'; no wonder, he adds, is it that the poet

> Did feign that Orpheus drew trees, stones and floods;   *M. of V. 5. 1. 80*
> Since nought so stockish, hard and full of rage,
> But music for the time doth change his nature,

and he ends with the assertion of what is surely Shakespeare's own view (cf. Caesar's mistrust of Cassius, 'he hears no music', 'Such men...are...very dangerous'),   *J.C. 1.2.204–10* that the man 'that hath no music in himself' and is not   *M. of V. 5. 1. 83* moved by it should not be trusted.

Only in three of the comedies do we find slight traces of the running symbolical imagery, used as in the tragedies, to illustrate or underline a leading 'motive' in the action or plot of the play, and these three are *Love's Labour's Lost*, *Much Ado*, and *All's Well*. Thus in *Love's Labour's Lost*, apart from the   LOVE'S nature and animal images, the dominating series, as is   LABOUR'S LOST easily seen, is that of war and weapons, emphasising the chief interest and entertainment of the play, the 'civil war of wits', the whole being, in Armado's words,   *L.L.L. 2. 1. 226* little more than 'a quick venue of wit—snip, snap,   *5. 1. 58* quick and home!' The main underlying theme of the confounding and dispelling of the fog of false idealism by the light of the experience of real life, is presented through a series of brilliant encounters, when even the laughter 'stabs', the tongue is keen as 'the razor's edge   *5. 2. 256* invisible', and lets missiles fly to right and left—conceits having wings

> Fleeter than arrows, bullets, wind, thought, swifter   *5. 2. 260*
>   things,

and words being pictured throughout as rapier-like thrusts, arrows, bullets fired from a cannon or as combatants tilting with their spears at a tournament.

L.L.L. 2. 1. 49 Longaville's wit is described as a sharp-edged sword
3. 1. 63 handled by too blunt a will, Moth carries Armado's
message as a bullet from the gun, Boyet and Biron tilt
straight and merrily at each other, Boyet's eye wounding
5. 2. 480 'like a leaden sword', while the jesting Biron, at the
end, in despairing capitulation, stands in front of
Rosaline and cries,

> lady, dart thy skill at me;

. . . . . .

5. 2. 396
> Thrust thy sharp wit quite through my ignorance;
> Cut me to pieces with thy keen conceit.

In addition to this general 'civil war', we witness three
other kinds of combat, that of the little group of scholars
in their 'Academe', who, as the king rather prematurely
1. 1. 8 assures them in the opening lines, are 'brave con-
querors', warring against their own affections 'and
the huge army of the world's desires'; the war of the
men upon the women in the cause of love, headed by
the king when he cries,

4. 3. 365
> Saint Cupid, then! and, soldiers to the field!

and Biron who adds,

> Advance your standards, and upon them, lords;
> Pell-mell, down with them! but be first advised,
> In conflict that you get the sun of them;

the defence made by the women with their wits, incited
by Boyet:

5. 2. 82
> Arm, wenches, arm! encounters mounted are
> Against your peace: Love doth approach disguised,
> Armed in arguments; you'll be surprised:
> Muster your wits; stand in your own defence;

and their final victory with the enforcement of strict
terms of probation on their prisoners.

It is all, of course, very obvious running symbolism, but it is interesting to find, in Shakespeare's earliest play, even in this simple form, the tendency which in the great tragedies becomes so marked a feature, and plays in them a definite part—subtle but decisive—in expressing the poet's own conception of his theme, as well as in raising and sustaining the emotions of his audience.

In *Much Ado* also we find a slight touch of the same MUCH ADO underlying idea, the war of wits in love, and the weapons the mock fighters use. Benedick complains that Beatrice's handling of him made him feel like 'a man at a mark, *M. Ado*, 2. 1. 247 with a whole army shooting' at him, for 'she speaks poniards, and every word stabs'. Margaret tells him his wit is 'as blunt as the fencer's foils, which hit, but 5. 2. 13 hurt not', and this gives rise to the badinage which follows about swords and bucklers. Much, however, as Benedick shrinks from the 'quirks and remnants of 2. 3. 237 wit' which may be broken on him like rapiers, the jests which his friends break 'as braggarts do their blades', 5. 1. 188 he rallies his courage in the end and defies these 'paper 2. 3. 241 bullets of the brain' to awe him 'from the career of his humour', for 'if a man will be beaten with brains, a' 5. 4. 102 shall wear nothing handsome about him'.

Another touch of symbolic thought is to be found in ALL'S WELL *All's Well*, though not expressed continuously in imagery. Helena, in the first scene, sums up her position in an astronomical image,

> 'Twere all one *All's Well*, 1. 1. 92
> That I should love a bright particular star
> And think to wed it, he is so above me:
> In his bright radiance and collateral light
> Must I be comforted, not in his sphere.

And the idea—not of being stars—but of being born under good or evil stars, and so being subject to their influence, and to that extent the plaything of fortune, runs through a great part of the play.

Helena refers to herself and Parolles as

All's Well,
1. 1. 191

> the poorer born,
> Whose baser stars do shut us up in wishes,

declares her father's receipt shall for her legacy

1. 3. 250

> be sanctified
> By the luckiest stars in heaven,

and, when repudiated by Bertram, says she will ever seek with true observance

2. 5. 76

> to eke out that
> Wherein toward me my homely stars have fail'd
> To equal my great fortune.

She tells Parolles he was born under a charitable star, 1. 1. 199 under Mars, when he was retrograde, and Parolles himself, when taking leave of the young nobles off to the 2. 1. 48 war, cries, 'Mars dote on you for his novices', and 2. 1. 56 confides to Bertram that they 'move under the influence of the most received star'. So also the clown ungallantly declares to the countess that if a good woman were 1. 3. 89 born 'but one every blazing star' the world would do well. It may be pure chance, but many of Helena's sayings and images increase and carry on the suggestion or idea of stars and heavenly bodies moving in the firmament, as in her well-known speech beginning,

1. 1. 226

> Our remedies oft in ourselves do lie,
> Which we ascribe to heaven: the fated sky
> Gives us free scope; only doth backward pull
> Our slow designs when we ourselves are dull;

her assertion to the king that two days shall see him cured, which in good round rhetoric she phrases thus:

> Ere twice the horses of the sun shall bring
> Their fiery torcher his diurnal ring;

All's Well,
2. 1. 164

and her refusal to stay under Bertram's roof,

> no, no, although
> The air of paradise did fan the house.

3. 2. 127

Both *Love's Labour's Lost* and *As You Like It* are remarkable for having more images than any other one of the comedies, and in both plays these form a considerable part of the entertainment.

But this large number does not in *Love's Labour's Lost* denote, as it would in most other plays, a high percentage of sheer poetry, for the images chiefly go to form the tissue of verbal wit, puns and double meaning, of which the fabric is woven. In this the play also resembles *As You Like It*, but the wit is not nearly so easy or natural, while the poetical, romantic element is almost wholly absent. So that out of the hundred and sixty-four images in *Love's Labour's Lost*, I find only eleven which are really poetical, to which one may add a further eleven which, though graceful and decorative, are often artificial and far-fetched. Thus the play has an unusual number of nature images, actually the highest number of any of the comedies—the writer was not long from Stratford—but they are either very slight and general, as

> Such short-lived wits do wither as they grow,

L.L.L. 2. 1. 54

or they are fantastic and artificial, full of euphuistic verbal play, such as all seven images of the sun and moon, of which this is typical,

> Your wit makes wise things foolish: when we greet,
> With eyes best seeing, heaven's fiery eye,
> By light we lose light.

5. 2. 374

As You Like It fairly scintillates with wit, largely in
the form of images. Celia and Rosalind's dialogue is
full of tropes, as in the opening of Act 1, scene 3, and
the fun for the onlookers is to watch the two girls
catching the jests dexterously from each other, tossing
them to and fro like shuttlecocks.

Rosalind's gay, chaffing talk with Orlando is, similarly, a mass of verbal fireworks in metaphor and simile,
sometimes a kind of 'set piece' to amuse the audience,
A.Y.L.I.　like the comparison of time to an ambling, trotting or
　3. 2. 317　galloping nag, which covers some twenty-six lines, some-
4. 1. 162　times a quick bright shower of sparks, as in her retort,
'make the doors upon a woman's wit and it will out
at the casement; shut that and 'twill out at the key-
hole; stop that, 'twill fly with the smoke out at the
chimney'.

Jaques is one of the great simile makers in Shakespeare, and his long and formal 'set piece' of the seven
ages is probably the best known passage in the plays.
Touchstone's wit, too, scintillates with simile, reminding us at times of Lyly, by his delight in the mere
sound of a succession of comparisons, as when he
3. 3. 77　answers Jaques' query 'Will, you be married, motley?'
with the euphuistic refrain, 'As the ox hath his bow,
sir, the horse his curb and the falcon her bells, so man
hath his desires; and as pigeons bill, so wedlock would
be nibbling'. More often he is 'swift and sententious'
with deep meaning behind his words; as when, whimsi-
cally intrigued with the blank incomprehension of
Audrey, he plays to Jaques as audience, and, in the
form of a simile, makes the oblique reference, easily
recognised by his larger audience, to the death of
Marlowe by Ingram Frysar's dagger in the so-called

quarrel over 'le recknynge' in Eleanor Bull's house at Deptford:

When a man's verses cannot be understood, nor a man's good wit seconded with the forward child, understanding, it strikes a man more dead than a great reckoning in a little room.

A.Y.L.I.
3. 3. 12

The double allusion here, first to the facts of Marlowe's death, and secondly to his well-known line,

> Infinite riches in a little room,

makes the meaning of the reference a certainty, and is also entirely in keeping with Touchstone's subtle rapier-like wit.

This simile is perhaps the most interesting 'topical' allusion in the whole of Shakespeare, but the entire play is remarkable for an unusual number of what may be called 'topical' similes—similes, that is, which refer to things familiar to the Elizabethan audience, but not to us, or indeed in many cases to any but the people of that day. Such are Rosalind's threat that she will weep for nothing 'like Diana in the fountain', by which she may mean the fountain set up in Cheapside in 1596, described by Stowe, with the image of Diana with 'water prilling from her naked breast'; or Silvius description of the common executioner asking pardon from his victim before chopping off his head; or Orlando's retort to Jaques' taunting query as to whether he has not culled his 'pretty answers' out of the posies on rings, 'Not so; but I answer you right painted cloth, from whence you have studied your questions', referring to the familiar painted canvas hangings for rooms, which often had the words spoken by the characters written in above them, or issuing

4. 1. 154

3. 5. 3

3. 2. 283

from them in a balloon, as in eighteenth-century broad-sides.

Sometimes these topical allusions throw a sinister light on current customs or characters, as in Rosalind's description of the dark house and the whip meted out to madmen, and Celia's comparison of the oath of a lover to the word of a tapster, 'they are both the confirmer of false reckonings'.

All these topical similes seem to strike and re-echo the key and tune of the play, which, though set in the greenwood, where they 'fleet the time carelessly', is yet so clearly written to please a highly sophisticated town audience, which delights in bouts of sparkling wit 'made of Atalanta's heels', is ever alive to double meanings, and is quick as lightning to seize on and laugh at a local or topical allusion.

Finally, as in *A Midsummer Night's Dream*, the number of nature images is very high. Of nature and animals together there are more in *As You Like It* than in any other comedy and these play their part in the general atmosphere. It has been pointed out, that although there is, in the play, a peculiarly vivid feeling of outdoor country life, there is very little nature description, indeed only two short passages, one of the sheepcote 'fenced about with olive trees', and one of the oak 'whose boughs were mossed with age'. But although there is little set description, there are, as in *Much Ado*, continual touches which keep ever before the audience the background of nature, such as the opening scene in the orchard, the duke's references to winter's wind and trees and running brooks, the stag hunt, the shepherd's cot, Amiens' song, Orlando's verses, the meal under the shade of melancholy

A.Y.L.I.
3. 2. 411

3. 4. 30

1. 1. 123

3. 2. 285

boughs, Corin's shepherd's talk, the foresters and *A.Y.L.I.*
5. 3. *16–33*
their song, and the exquisite 'foolish song' at the
end, to which Touchstone counted it but time lost to
listen.

But a still more subtle and less obvious way of intensifying the country and open air feeling is through
simile and metaphor, and of this full use is made, such
as the picture of walking through a thorny wood, in *1. 3. 11*
the girls' jests about briers and burs; the charming
little glimpse, given by Silvius in his modesty, of *3. 5. 100*
gleaning the broken ears in the harvest field; or even
so tiny a touch as Celia's description of finding Orlando
'under a tree, like a dropped acorn'. *3. 2. 243*

We find an unusual number of animal similes, the
highest in any of the comedies, and these add greatly
to the life of the country pictures: the doe going to find *2. 7. 128*
her fawn to give it food, the weasel sucking eggs, *2.5.11; 2.7.30*
chanticleer crowing, the wild goose flying, pigeons *2.7.86; 1.2.92*
feeding, and such vivid glimpses of animal passion and
emotion as those given us by Rosalind, 'there was never *5. 2. 33*
anything so sudden but the fight of two rams', 'I will *4. 1. 150*
be more jealous of thee than a Barbary cock-pigeon
over his hen'.

We are constantly reminded of Shakespeare's favourite
haunts of garden and orchard in the many similes from
grafting, pruning and weeding, as in Rosalind's chaff with
Touchstone about 'graffing' with the medlar, Orlando's *3. 2. 120*
warning to Adam that in staying with him he prunes
'a rotten tree', Touchstone's metaphor of fruit ripening *2. 3. 63*
2. 7. 26
and rotting, or Jaques' suggestion that the duke should
weed his 'better judgments of all opinion that grows *2. 7. 45*
rank in them'; and it would be hard to say how strongly
and yet how subtly our feeling of being out of doors,

of wind and weather, is increased or reinforced by such
remarks as Adam's comparison of his age to

A.Y.L.I.
2. 3. 52

a lusty winter,
Frosty, but kindly;

Jaques' demand for

2. 7. 48

as large a charter as the wind,
To blow on whom I please;

Hymen's doggerel chant,

5. 4. 141

You and you are sure together,
As the winter to foul weather;

Rosalind's taunt to Silvius foolishly following Phoebe,

3. 5. 50

Like foggy south, puffing with wind and rain,

1. 147 or her gay defiance to Orlando, 'men are April when they
woo, December when they wed: maids are May when
they are maids, but the sky changes when they are wives'.

MER-
CHANT OF
VENICE As regards the *Merchant of Venice*, I have already
noticed, as an example of atmosphere, the constant
suggestion of music which pervades it (pp. 269-71).
It is also remarkable, like *A Midsummer Night's Dream*,
for its high proportion of poetical images, eighty out of
a total of a hundred and thirteen, some of them very
beautiful and among the best known in Shakespeare.

There are sensitive little nature pictures such as
M. of V.
4. 1. 77 Antonio's etching of the mountain pines 'fretten with
the gusts of heaven'; or more artificial and worked up
2. 6. 14 'pieces' like Gratiano's double image of the 'scarfed
bark' putting out from her native bay compared to a
prodigal and his return; highly imaginative and decorative beauties as when the 'floor of heaven' is likened
5. 1. 58-9 to a mosaic 'thick inlaid with patines of bright gold';
brilliantly vivid and unusual comparisons, as

3. 2. 83

cowards, whose hearts are all as false
As stairs of sand;

or, most unusual of all with Shakespeare, several detailed
glimpses of everyday life and experience in a city. Such
are the demeanour of the rich and haughty burghers   *M. of V.*
in London streets; the feelings of the prizewinner in   *1. 1. 9–14*
wrestling or some feat of strength, who, hearing the
shouts and applause of the populace, stops

> Giddy in spirit, still gazing in a doubt   *3. 2. 144*
> Whether those peals of praise be his or no,

which Bassanio uses with such effect to describe his
feelings when he realises he has won Portia; or the
wonderfully vivid description he gives later of the
'pleased buzzing' among the crowd after

> some oration fairly spoke   *3. 2. 179*
> By a beloved prince,

a little vignette surely drawn by an eyewitness of what
must often have happened in Elizabethan London and
its neighbourhood when the great queen was on her
progresses.

Bassanio uses the greatest number of images and
Portia runs him very close, so that between them they
are responsible for nearly half the images in the play.
Next to them, but at a long distance, comes the gay and
talkative Gratiano, who, though Bassanio thinks he
'speaks an infinite deal of nothing', possesses a lively
imagination and a pretty wit which result in such
delightful comparisons drawn from simple country
things as the unforgettable description of the

> sort of men, whose visages   *1. 1. 88*
> Do cream and mantle like a standing pond.

The distribution of images is unusual; it is very
uneven, varying with the tone and subject, and in no
other play, I believe, is this unevenness so marked,

though we get a touch of it in the *Comedy of Errors*, where the only three really poetical images in the play are crowded together at the end in Aegeon's appeal to his son, where emotion is deeply stirred. The high points of emotion in the *Merchant of Venice* are the third casket scene, when Bassanio makes his choice, the trial scene, and the preparation for the final gathering together of the pairs of lovers in the moonlit garden, and it is in the first and last named of these that the images are chiefly grouped.

C. of E.
5. 1. 307

It is worth while to note—as an indication of the difference of tone and feeling—the difference in the number and use of images in the three casket scenes. In the first (2.7), 79 lines in length, there are four images only, somewhat frigid and detached, used by Morocco, who rather pettishly describes Venice as the

M. of V.
2. 7. 44

> watery kingdom, whose ambitious head
> Spits in the face of heaven,

2. 7. 47 where Portia's suitors come 'as o'er a brook' to see her, and who has a play of words on a gem set in gold, and *2. 7. 54, 58* an 'angel in a golden bed'. In the second (2. 9), of 84 lines, we find three images, two used by Arragon, the martlet's nest, and the picking of seed from chaff (real merit from mere titles and dignities), finished off by Portia's dry and caustic summing up of the incident,

2. 9. 79

> Thus hath the candle singed the moth.

But when, immediately afterwards, the servant arrives to say that Bassanio's messenger is at the gate, he describes him with one of Shakespeare's most charming similes of spring:

2. 9. 93

> A day in April never came so sweet,

thus striking the note of beauty, romance and true love

which rings through the great scene when Bassanio makes his happy choice (3. 2).

It opens quietly, for Portia has herself well in hand, but when the actual moment of choice arrives, and the tension of emotion increases, images crowd thick and fast in the speech of both lovers, so that in eighteen lines spoken by Portia (3. 2. 44–62), no less than seven follow one another without a break, as she orders music to be played, and stands back, tense and excited, longing to give a hint, but loyally refraining, to watch the decision being made; while Bassanio, in thirty-two lines of anxious musing, tumbles out image after image, twelve of them, each fast on the heels of the other, each taking light from the one before it and in turn fading into the next.

M. of V.
3. 2. 75–107

The opening of the fifth act, so full of romance and glamour, is naturally full of images, though the decoration in the very beginning is given, not by images in the technical sense, but by the well-known exquisite series of direct pictures drawn from old romance and the great love stories of the world. It is not until Lorenzo and Jessica are sitting on the bank in the sleeping moonlight, awaiting the sounds of sweet music they have ordered, that the images proper begin (l. 54). Then they come with a rush, close together (ll. 54–113), so long as Lorenzo and Jessica, and later Portia and Nerissa are, or think themselves, alone in the garden listening to the music, but after they meet, and the music stops and the others come trooping in (l. 127), the glow of romance fades, and the tone changes to badinage and light comedy. On this note the play ends, so that in the remaining hundred and seventy lines, only four sparsely scattered images occur.

We find therefore that the images are chiefly grouped round these two high points of emotion. In addition, we get a good many in the opening scene where Antonio, Gratiano and Bassanio all speak at length, revealing the setting of the story and their own characteristics, one of which, as regards the speech of the two latter, is that they delight in simile and metaphor. So it is that 59 images—nearly half the total number in the play—are crowded into the space of 392 lines (1. 1; 3. 2. 24–148; 4. 1. 69–77; 5. 1. 53–126), while the remaining 77 are spread out over the other 2162 lines.

Naturally in the prose scenes, or the semi-comic ones, such as the talk between Launcelot and Gobbo (2. 2), or those chiefly occupied with practical affairs, such as Portia's preparations for departure, there are few images, or none; but it is surprising that the trial scene, where we are conscious of great tension of emotion, has so few. It is much the longest scene in the play—457 lines—and there are only ten images throughout the whole of it. Five of these are Antonio's, used under great stress of emotion, three of them to express the *M. of V.* futility of hoping to touch Shylock, and two in de-
4. 1. 71–7
4. 1. 114–16 spairing descriptions of himself; two are the duke's, two are Shylock's (when he likens Antonio to a serpent, and Portia to Daniel); while Portia, in her great opening speech and subsequent arguments and decision, makes use of one image only, which is perhaps the best known
4. 1. 184–6 one in the whole of Shakespeare.

The truth is, it would seem, that the tension and deep feeling of the trial scene are maintained chiefly through the quality of the plot itself, its fears, doubts, suspense and surprises: first the apparent hopelessness of Antonio's position and the obduracy of Shylock, then the

appearance of Portia and the continued obduracy of the
Jew, followed by the swift and dramatic turning of the
tables upon him, so that except at the moments when
Antonio is most exasperated or depressed, imagery is
not needed either as an outlet or expression of feeling.

There does not appear to be any continuous symbol
in the images, though there is an instance of a twice
repeated image giving the key to the whole action. This
occurs first in Antonio's earliest business interview with
Shylock, conducted on Antonio's side with a contemptuous coolness, detachment and assurance which
almost frighten the spectators, and is in strong contrast to Shylock's burning but suppressed emotion,
which rises as he details his grievances, and finally
bursts forth like an erupting volcano, when he turns on
Antonio and cries, 'You call me misbeliever, cut- *M. of V.*
throat dog', *1. 3. 111*
you say *1. 3. 116*

> 'Shylock, we would have moneys:' you say so;
> You, that did void your rheum upon my beard,
> And foot me as you spurn a stranger cur
> Over your threshold.

This is one of five images only in the whole scene of
181 lines, and it is clear from the way the Jew dwells
on it (5 times in 17 lines) that it is the outcome of
his deepest feeling, and sums up symbolically in itself
the real and sole reason for his whole action—bitter
rancour at the contemptuous treatment he has received,
and desire for revenge. When Antonio comes later to
ask him for mercy, he repeats it:

> Thou call'dst me dog before thou hadst a cause; *3. 3. 6*
> But, since I am a dog, beware my fangs;

and probably it is present in his mind when he tells the
duke that if his house be troubled with a rat, he is at

perfect liberty to give 10,000 ducats if he so pleases to have it poisoned.

The irony and force of the symbol are heightened by Shylock's description of the way Christians use their dogs, and by Gratiano's outburst of feeling against him in the court, when he feels 'inexecrable dog' to be too good and mild a name for him, and asserts that his

> currish spirit
> Govern'd a wolf, who hang'd for human slaughter,
> Even from the gallows did his fell soul fleet,
> And, whilst thou lay'st in thy unhallow'd dam,
> Infused itself in thee; for thy desires
> Are wolvish, bloody, starved and ravenous.

TAMING OF THE SHREW   The *Taming of the Shrew* has comparatively few images, but, rather contrary to what we should expect, a high proportion—nearly one half—of poetical ones, counterbalancing the farce and roughness of the play, with touches of beauty. These are largely due to Petruchio, who uses close on one half of all the images in the play (40 out of 92), for he is a young man of keen perceptions, and observation of nature, and, when he chooses, he speaks with a poet's tongue.

Some of them he uses of Kate in irony:

> Say that she frown; I'll say she looks as clear
> As morning roses newly wash'd with dew.

> Kate like the hazel-twig
> Is straight and slender, and as brown in hue
> As hazel-nuts and sweeter than the kernels.

Some are frankly farcical, as when he rhapsodises over Vincentio's 'heavenly face'; or braggadocio, as when he swears that so long as he can find a rich wife, he cares not

T. of Sh.
1. 2. 73, 95

> were she as rough
> As are the swelling Adriatic seas:
> ...though she chide as loud
> As thunder when the clouds in autumn crack.

Some are more formal and used of set purpose, throwing light on his attitude towards Kate, and the principle of his conduct, as when he speaks of her as a falcon which has to be starved before she can be tamed and trained, and who needs watching,

4. 1. 190

> as we watch these kites
> That bate and beat and will not be obedient.

Some are little country pictures, brought in on occasion with tremendous effect of contrast, as when he turns on Gremio, describing all the terrifying noises he has heard, lions roaring, the sea raging, cannon booming in the field, thunder in the skies,

1. 2. 208

> And do you tell me of a woman's tongue,
> That gives not half so great a blow to hear
> As will a chestnut in a farmer's fire?

Another gives a glimpse of what doubtless was a common sight in country towns, or in the London of the day, in his bland query, when he arrives for his wedding, arrayed like a broken-down tinker,

3. 2. 94

> And wherefore gaze this goodly company,
> As if they saw some wondrous monument,
> Some comet or unusual prodigy?

and some seem to be just his natural, gay, imaginative speech, as when he answers Hortensio's query as to 'what happy gale' blows him to Padua, with

1. 2. 50

> Such wind as scatters young men through the world,
> To seek their fortunes farther than at home.

Measure for Measure in several respects stands alone among Shakespeare's plays. There are two points which

MEASURE
FOR
MEASURE

strike one at once on examining its images. The first
is that we find among them, chiefly in the speech of
the duke, some of the most beautiful, as well as the
most thoughtful similes in the whole of Shakespeare,

M. for M.
1. 1. 27–44 such as the two in his exhortation to Angelo at the
3. 1. 8, 32 beginning, his descriptions of life, his comparison of
3. 1. 25 the rich man to the heavily laden ass unloaded by death,
as well as many of the most brilliant and unusual of
Shakespeare's pictures and personifications:

3. 2. 197   back-wounding calumny
        The whitest virtue strikes,

5. 1. 398   It was the swift celerity of his death,
        Which I did think with slower foot came on,
        That brain'd my purpose.

4. 1. 60   O, place and greatness, millions of false eyes
        Are stuck upon thee!

3. 1. 236 he, a marble to her tears, is washed with them, but
relents not.

The second remarkable point is that out of the
hundred and thirty-six images in the play, I feel I can
classify eighteen only as 'poetical', because by far the
largest group (twenty-seven in number) seem to fall
under another category which I can only call vivid,
quaint, or grotesque. It is this which is the most
noticeable feature about the quality of the images as a
whole. Often these latter ones are poetical as well, from
sheer force and brilliance, as in Isabella's outburst
against man, and her description of his 'glassy essence,

2. 2. 120 like an angry ape', playing

            such fantastic tricks before high heaven
        As make the angels weep;

but what strikes one first is the unusual pictures they
conjure up, and their touch of grimness, grotesqueness,

or a vividness so piercing as to give one a shock almost
as if from lightning.

Many of these are personifications, semi-comic, and
very arresting, such as 'liberty plucks justice by the
nose', 'bidding the law make court'sy to their will',
'make him bite the law by the nose'. Others are marked
by what is, even for Shakespeare, an unusually vivid
use of concrete verbs and adjectives applied to abstractions:

> Hooking both right and wrong to the appetite,
> To follow as it draws;

> Lent him our terror, dress'd him with our love;

>   a purpose
> More grave and wrinkled than the aims and ends
> Of burning youth.

Some are little pictures with a slightly comic touch,
such as

> The baby beats the nurse, and quite athwart
> Goes all decorum;

the forfeits in the barber's shop, death's fool, the scarecrow, and the fathers with the birch rods, and there is
one which, though frankly grotesque, is still amazingly
vivid—Lucio's summary of Claudio's unfortunate position, 'thy head stands so tickle on thy shoulders, that
a milkmaid, if she be in love, may sigh it off'.

Shakespeare seems to be torn in this play, as nowhere
else, save in *Troilus and Cressida*, and, to some extent,
in *Hamlet*, between deeply stirred idealistic thought and
reflection, and a tendency to cynical bitterness and grim
realism which delights in a certain violence and even
distortion of speech and figure, and sometimes of incident. Just as a man with gnawing toothache takes

M. for M.
1. 3. 29
2. 4. 175
3. 1. 109

2. 4. 176

1. 1. 20

1. 3. 4

1. 3. 30

5. 1. 323
3. 1. 11
2. 1. 1
1. 3. 23

1. 2. 171

pleasure in biting on the tooth, and thereby increasing the pain, so one feels in these plays that Shakespeare, whose deepest and purest feelings have somehow been sorely hurt, takes pleasure in hurting them still more by exposing all the horrible, revolting, perplexing and grotesque aspects of human nature.

Whatever experience it was that so deeply stirred him about this time (1602–4?), it led him to ponder much on a certain range of thoughts—the amazing contradictions in man, the strange and often horrible transmutations of physical matter, the meaning and nature of death, and what possibly may constitute the chief value in life; while, going along with these grave reflections, there is ample evidence of a shocked, disillusioned and suffering spirit, taking refuge in mocks and jeers and bitterness.

So these two qualities, for which the images as a whole in *Measure for Measure* are remarkable, thoughtful poetry and strange brilliance, with a touch of the bizarre, are curiously expressive of the peculiar character and mental atmosphere of the play, and help towards the impression left on us of majesty and squalor, of thoughtful gravity and jeering cynicism, of the strange contradictions in life and still stranger contradictions in human nature, with its unexpected flaws and weaknesses and strengths and heroisms. This character, in spite of the intolerable nature of the plot, goes far, so it seems to me, to make it, of all the plays, the one which bears in it most clearly and unmistakably the impress of Shakespeare's mind and outlook.

CHAPTER XIV

LEADING MOTIVES IN THE ROMANCES

As I have said, the symbolism of the imagery in the romances is more subtle and less concrete than in the earlier plays; and tends to illustrate and reiterate an idea rather than a concrete picture. This tendency is particularly marked in the latest plays of all, the *Tempest* and *Winter's Tale*.

Pericles alone of the romances has no sign of any running 'motive' or continuity of picture or thought in the imagery, a fact sufficient in itself to throw grave doubts on its authorship.

The proportion and subjects of the images in *Pericles* are, however, quite in keeping with Shakespeare's other plays: though as a whole they seem rather thin, and there is a very small proportion (eleven of the hundred and nine) of poetical images. A certain selection, though they fall under Shakespeare's usual headings, are flat, general, uninteresting and un-Shakespearian (e.g. the diamonds round a crown, spring and summer, the unplucked flower, 'groves, being topp'd', storm, snowball, 'pretty wrens', 'angel-eagle'). On the other hand, we find quite a fair number of images which are markedly 'Shakespearian' in quality.

Per. 2. 4. 52
1. 1. 12
4. 6. 44
1. 4. 9
4. 1. 20
4. 6. 146
4. 3. 22
4. 3. 46

In *Cymbeline* there are two chief strains, one of CYMBE-LINE atmosphere, and one of thought, brought out in the imagery. The country atmosphere of the play is very marked, and this is as true of the scenes laid in Rome or the king's palace in Britain as of those in the moun-

tains of Wales. This atmosphere is largely created and
sustained by the very large proportion of country images,
unusually large even for Shakespeare, amounting to
about forty per cent. of the total number.

We are conscious especially of the background of
trees, the fragrance of flowers and the presence of birds,
for all these are much drawn upon. There are many
well-known and beautiful images and pictures of trees,
and several of the characters are very definitely thought
of as trees, or their characteristics are symbolised by
trees of different kinds, or by the winds affecting trees.
Cym. 5. 5. 453 Thus Cymbeline, as the soothsayer explains, is a stately
cedar, and his two lost sons lopped branches, revived
after many years, joined to the old stock and grown
afresh; and Belarius, describing how he fell suddenly
from high favour into his king's displeasure, pictures
himself dramatically as a fruit tree stripped bare by the
winds or by thieves; when Cymbeline loved him, he
says, and counted him among his bravest soldiers,

3. 3. 60
> then was I as a tree
> Whose boughs did bend with fruit: but in one night,
> A storm, or robbery, call it what you will,
> Shook down my mellow hangings, nay, my leaves,
> And left me bare to weather.

The characters of the two princely boys, kindly, yet on
occasion fierce, are painted by their proud foster-father
in a charming woodland picture of the wind and flowers
and trees:

4. 2. 171
> they are as gentle
> As zephyrs blowing below the violet,
> Not wagging his sweet head; and yet as rough,
> Their royal blood enchafed, as the rudest wind
> That by the top doth take the mountain pine
> And make him stoop to the vale.

The tactless intrusion of Cymbeline on the parting of the
lovers is similarly described by Imogen as the action
of the rough spring winds on the fruit trees:

Cym. 1. 3. 35

ere I could
Give him that parting kiss,...
.........comes in my father,
And, like the tyrannous breathing of the north,
Shakes all our buds from growing.

So also the outstanding characteristics of Imogen herself
as noted by the two boys, grief and patience, are
pictured as the growth of the hateful elder tree and
the fruitful vine, mingling 'their spurs together', and
Arviragus, wishing her better fortune, cries,

4. 2. 58

Grow, patience!
And let the stinking elder, grief, untwine
His perishing root with the increasing vine!

In the dirge, the conception that to the dead all earthly
differences are as nought, is tersely expressed in em-
blematic form,

4. 2. 267

To thee the reed is as the oak,

and one of the most vivid and moving images in Shakespeare, summing up in itself all we long to know of
the remorse and real feeling and (we hope) passionate
devotion of Posthumus, ten words which do more than
anything else in the whole play to bring him in weight
and value a little nearer to Imogen, this again is the
picture of a fruit tree, when, with her arms thrown round
him in an ecstasy of love and forgiveness, he murmurs,

5. 5. 263

Hang there like fruit, my soul,
Till the tree die!

Flowers and their special qualities are called upon
to aid in the description of the fair and delicate beauty

Cym. 2. 2. 15
4. 2. 201
4. 2. 221–3 of Imogen, by the two boys who love her, as well as by Iachimo when evilly gloating over her. She is fair and fresh and fragrant as the lily, pale as the primrose, 2. 2. 38 her veins are the tint of the azured harebell, her mole spotted as the centre of the cowslip, and her breath sweet as is the eglantine.

And the play is alive with the movement and sound of birds, for, even for Shakespeare, there is in it an unusual number of bird similes. In his characteristic way they are used continually for all sorts of purposes and comparisons, for they are ever in his mind and before his eyes. We find them as units of measurement; of size,

4. 2. 303
> but if there be
> Yet left in heaven as small a drop of pity
> As a wren's eye;

of distance; ere you ceased waving farewell to Posthumus, cries Imogen to Pisanio,

1. 3. 14
> thou shouldst have made him
> As little as a crow, or less,

and Belarius, starting the boys up the mountain, gives them instructions for reflection,

3. 3. 12
> When you above perceive me like a crow.

Birds symbolise liberty and wideness of range, as when Belarius, vainly trying to reconcile the spirited young princes to a quiet country life, assures them that

3. 3. 20
> often...shall we find
> The sharded beetle in a safer hold
> Than is the full-wing'd eagle.

They naturally symbolise also swiftness of movement, such as Imogen's, when, as the queen suggests,

3. 5. 61
> wing'd with fervour of her love, she's flown
> To her desired Posthumus.

Sometimes the point of view of the bird is used as a measure of something desired, as it is by Arviragus, who assures Imogen that 'the night to the owl and morn to the lark' is less welcome than her presence to him; or the habits of birds help to form a picture of what may happen in human life, as when Iachimo warns Posthumus that 'strange fowl light upon neighbouring ponds'.

Cym. 3. 6. 94

1. 4. 94

They are used constantly as a swift means of characterisation; the imperial Caesar is a 'princely eagle', Cloten is a crowing cock, the Britons are crows which peck the Romans:

5. 5. 473

2. 1. 24
5. 3. 93

> Forthwith they fly
> Chickens, the way which they stoop'd eagles,

5. 3. 41

says Posthumus, describing the soldiers in battle;

> I chose an eagle,
> And did avoid a puttock,

1. 1. 139

proudly retorts Imogen, when her father tells her she might have had Cloten instead of Posthumus; and Posthumus himself is described by Iachimo, when speaking of a little group of Romans, as 'the best feather of our wing'.

1. 6. 186

The boys, lamenting their inexperience, compare themselves to unfledged birds, who 'have never wing'd from view o' the nest'.

3. 3. 27

'Our cage', says Arviragus,

> We make a quire, as doth the prison'd bird,
> And sing our bondage freely.

3. 3. 42

When he finds Imogen, as he thinks, dead, he calls her a bird. Iachimo on first sight of her compares her to the fabulous phoenix and mutters, 'She is alone the Arabian bird'. When told she must leave her country,

4. 2. 197

1. 6. 17

Imogen agrees, quickly characterising in half a line the smallness of that country compared with the rest of the world and its peculiar homely cosy qualities,

Cym. 3. 4. 140

> I' the world's volume
> Our Britain seems as of it, but not in't;
> In a great pool a swan's nest.

By these and similar images, then,[1] the atmosphere of a woodland country is given and maintained; but there is as well to be traced in the imagery another very different set of ideas or interests in the poet's mind which persists throughout the play. This is the theme of buying and selling, value and exchange, every kind of payment, debts, bills and wages.

It is possible that the two central motives of the plot, the wager, and the Roman claim for tribute, may have suggested this; or it may just have been, for some reason unknown to us, a subject much in Shakespeare's mind at the time.[2] I incline to this latter view, because the idea seems so constantly with him that he almost drags it in at times, even in places where as a metaphor it is both far-fetched and awkward.

For instance, when the queen reflects complacently, as doubtless many other wives have done, that whenever she angers the king, he, in repentance, is doubly nice

---

[1] Such as the fog (3. 2. 81), the dew (5. 5. 351), the summer lightning (5. 5. 394), the unsunned snow (2. 5. 13), the paled-in park (3. 1. 19), the cattle grazing (5. 4. 2) and the hunting of the deer (2. 3. 74, 3. 4. 112).

[2] It seems to me quite permissible to surmise that Shakespeare's images might be influenced by some experience of daily life which was forcing itself upon his attention. It can hardly be doubted, for example, that the images from building and construction, in 2 *H. IV*, 1. 3. 41 and 1. 3. 56, about drawing the plans of a house, and then if it is too costly, cutting down the expenses, are connected with some personal experience, when we remember that Shakespeare was occupied in buying New Place in 1597, the same year in which he probably wrote 2 *H. IV*.

to her afterwards in order to be friends again, she words
it in this obscure way:

> I never do him wrong   *Cym.* 1. 1. 104
> But he does buy my injuries, to be friends;
> Pays dear for my offences;

when Iachimo invents the description of how Imogen
gave him her bracelet, he adds,

> Her pretty action did outsell her gift,   2. 4. 102
> And yet enrich'd it too;

and when Imogen boldly tells her father that Posthumus
is of so much greater value than she, that in marrying
her he gets nothing in return for the greater part of
what he gives, she uses the same somewhat involved
language; 'he is', she says,

> A man worth any woman, overbuys me   1. 1. 146
> Almost the sum he pays.

On the other hand this metaphor is sometimes in such
perfect keeping with the subject that we scarcely notice
it, as when Belarius reminds the boys that Cloten was   4. 2. 246
'paid' for his actions, or when in the dirge they sing,

> Thou thy worldly task hast done,   4. 2. 260
> Home art gone and ta'en thy wages.

The idea of the relative value of the two lovers
themselves is constantly in the minds of both, each
avowing that the other has lost heavily in the exchange.
Posthumus, putting on the ring Imogen gives him in
parting, says,

> And, sweetest, fairest,   1. 1. 118
> As I my poor self did exchange for you
> To your so infinite loss, so in our trifles
> I still win of you,

and he clasps a bracelet on her arm.

Imogen, when she first meets the two boys, wishes they might have been her brothers, for so she would not have been heir to a throne,

Cym. 3. 6. 77
       then had my prize
  Been less, and so more equal ballasting
  To thee, Posthumus.

Iachimo, discussing Posthumus with his friends, and saying that his marriage to the king's daughter has probably fictitiously enhanced the report of his parts and prowess, expresses his thought in the same metaphor of weights and values:

1. 4. 14 This matter of marrying his king's daughter, wherein he must be weighed rather by her value than his own, words him, I doubt not, a great deal from the matter.

When Posthumus, at the end, offers to the gods his life in exchange for Imogen's, he plays at length on the theme of debts, value, weight and exchange:

5. 4. 18 I know [he cries] you are more clement than vile men,
  Who of their broken debtors take a third,
  A sixth, a tenth, letting them thrive again
  On their abatement: that's not my desire:
  For Imogen's dear life take mine; and though
  'Tis not so dear, yet 'tis a life; you coin'd it:
  'Tween man and man they weigh not every stamp;
  Though light, take pieces for the figure's sake:
  You rather mine, being yours: and so, great powers,
  If you will take this audit, take this life,
  And cancel these cold bonds.

So also, when his gaolers return to take him to be hanged, the talk is again of the same theme, bills, debts and weight, and the gaoler offers curious comfort to the condemned man by reminding him that he is going
5. 4. 159 where he will 'be called to no more payments, fear no more tavern-bills', taverns, whence he will emerge with

'purse and brain both empty, the brain the heavier for
being too light, the purse too light, being drawn of
heaviness', and so on.

In all kinds of ways, sometimes, one would think,
unsuitable, these ideas of purchase, payment, weight
and value are introduced and dwelt upon. Thus, when
Guiderius tells Imogen he loves her, he immediately
translates it into weight:

> I love thee; I have spoke it: *Cym.* 4. 2. 16
> How much the quantity, the weight as much,
> As I do love my father.

The settling of the wager, naturally, gives an opening
for many such figures; Iachimo suggests to Posthumus
that his ring is of greater value than his wife, to which
Posthumus indignantly answers that his ring may be   *1. 4. 75*
bought or given, but that Imogen is not for sale, and
only the gift of the gods; then follows the discussion
of the terms of the wager, the value of Iachimo's estate
compared to the ring, his taunt that Posthumus is
'buying ladies' flesh at a million a dram', the final   *1. 4. 142*
agreement on the sum of 10,000 ducats and the ring,
which Iachimo hastens to get ratified in legal form,
'lest the bargain should catch cold and starve'.   *1. 4. 175*

Cloten, about to tip one of Imogen's waiting women,
startles us by speaking suddenly for a moment with
the voice of Timon,

> 'Tis gold   *2. 3. 71*
> Which buys admittance; oft it doth;
> ...and 'tis gold
> Which makes the true man kill'd and saves the thief;
> Nay, sometime hangs both thief and true man: what
> Can it not do and undo?

When he finally buys his way in to her presence, he is

given but a cold reception by Imogen, who greets him
by saying,

Cym. 2. 3. 91

> You lay out too much pains
> For purchasing but trouble.

Imogen herself later offers the boys money for her food,
which is angrily rejected, and Arviragus cries, in what
undoubtedly is, in some moods, the voice of his creator

3. 6. 54

> All gold and silver rather turn to dirt!
> As 'tis no better reckon'd, but of those
> Who worship dirty gods.

THE TEMPEST

The dominant image in the *Tempest* is, as I have said,
something more subtle than we have yet encountered,
in that it is not expressed through any one single group
of images which fall easily under one heading, but
rather through the action itself and the background,
reinforced by a number of images taken from many
groups, all illustrating or emphasising one single sensation. This sensation is in itself the physical expression
as well as the symbol of the whole theme.

It is the sense of *sound* which is thus emphasised,
for the play itself is an absolute symphony of sound,
and it is through sound that its contrasts and movement
are expressed, from the clashing discords of the opening
to the serene harmony of the close.

We hear, as we visit different parts of the island, the
singing of the winds and the roaring of the waters, the
cries of the drowning men, the reverberation of the
thunder; our ears are assailed by the hollow bellowing

Temp. 2. 1. 314

of wild beasts making 'a din to fright a monster's ear',
chattering apes and hissing adders, the drunken shouts
and catches of Caliban and his companions, the hal-
looing of hunters and dogs, and other 'strange, hollow,
confused' and nerve-shaking noises; while on the other

hand we catch the homely reassuring English sounds
of the owl's cry, the cock's crow and the dog's bark,
we hear the humming of 'a thousand twangling instru- *Temp. 3. 2. 144*
ments', we enjoy the contrast of sweet songs and airs,
delicate and bewitching, the charm of Ariel's tabor and
pipe and the fairy knell of the sea-nymphs, and through
it all the continually recurrent strains of music, 'mar- *3. 3. 19*
vellous sweet', soft and solemn, by the aid of which
the rough magic is lifted, and the whole is finally
resolved into peace.

This emphasis upon sound in the *Tempest* is but one
of many instances of Shakespeare's almost uncanny
instinct for divining or selecting salient and characteristic truth. Very probably he had heard sailors discussing their experiences on strange islands in tropical
seas, over their sack in a riverside tavern, and had caught
a hint which sufficed him; but however that may be,
in emphasising sound he certainly hit upon the truth,
for I have heard from one who knows well just such a
small sub-tropical isle as that on which Alonso's ship
foundered, that the most noticeable thing about it is the
many noises.

Wherever you wander, I am told, not only on the
shore, but inland through the woods, even in comparatively calm weather, the roar of the surf is ever in
your ears, diversified by the harsh rustling and rattling
of the wind through the palms and palmettos, and its
sighing and moaning through the pines; while in Ber-
muda itself, in addition, the singing of the wind through
the oleander hedges is so strange as to be almost
alarming; all of which, in a storm, rises and swells into
a strange wild medley of sound and a roar as of thunder.

Let us look at the play a little more closely, and note

how our sense of hearing is called upon throughout. The little opening scene is perhaps the most condensed and brilliant representation in literature of a confused and clattering din of noises, by means of which we can, even from the printed page, visualise the action in its full vividness. We can hear the boatswain yelling orders and heartening his men; the shrill whistle of the ship's master, urged to blow till he bursts his wind, the passengers shrieking their questions or lamenting so loudly that they outcry even the elements and the hoarse shouts of the seamen, ending in the chant of prayers punctuated with screams of terror and farewell; and through and over it all sound the 'tempestuous noise of thunder' and the roaring of the angry seas.

The clamour and din of the elements run as an overtone through the five acts; we are reminded of them in the imagery by the effect on Miranda of the 'roar'
Temp. 1. 2. 2 of 'the wild waters' and the cry of the shipwrecked man, which knocked against her very heart; by Prospero's description of his brother's treachery in leaving them at the mercy of 'the sea that roar'd to us';

1. 2. 149   to sigh
To the winds, whose pity, sighing back again,
Did us but loving wrong;

by Ariel's report of his action on the ship, the flames,
1. 2. 203 'the fire and cracks of sulphurous roaring', which he
1. 2. 201 likens to   Jove's lightnings, the precursors
O' the dreadful thunder-claps;

by the boatswain's account of how they were awaked

5. 1. 232   with strange and several noises
Of roaring, shrieking, howling, jingling chains,
And mo diversity of sounds, all horrible;

and by Prospero's summary of his magic when he

call'd forth the mutinous winds,   *Temp. 5. 1. 42*
And 'twixt the green sea and the azured vault
Set roaring war.

This consciousness of the noise of warring elements is accentuated also by the repeated claps of thunder and flashes of lightning in which Ariel appears and vanishes.

Storm, and the rage of sea and wind, are also kept before us by such images as Ferdinand's when describing Ariel's song,

This music crept by me upon the waters,   *1. 2. 391*
Allaying both their fury and my passion
With its sweet air;

Antonio's way of describing how the magical sleep overcame his companions,

They dropp'd, as by a thunder-stroke;   *2. 1. 204*

Trinculo's certainty that another storm is brewing, because 'Yond...black cloud' looks 'like a foul bom-   *2. 2. 20* bard that would shed his liquor'; Ariel's boast to the 'three men of sin' that he is invulnerable; that the   *3. 3. 66* elements, of which their swords are tempered,

may as well   *3. 3. 62*
Wound the loud winds, or with bemock'd-at stabs
Kill the still-closing waters; as diminish
One dowle that's in my plume;

and Alonso's dazed recollection of Ariel's accusation, which has in it the very movement and rhythm of the storm itself, blending with the strains of that music which is in the end to rescue them from it:

O, it is monstrous, monstrous!   *3. 3. 95*
Methought the billows spoke, and told me of it;
The winds did sing it to me; and the thunder,
That deep and dreadful organ-pipe,...
. . . . .did bass my trespass.

Our sense of hearing is further called upon by images such as Prospero's picture of his treacherous brother, who

Temp. 1. 2. 83
<blockquote>
having both the key
Of officer and office, set all hearts i' the state
To what tune pleased his ear,
</blockquote>

1. 2. 281 Ariel venting his groans 'as fast as mill-wheels strike', and so loudly that they made wolves howl, Alonso's *2. 1. 106* complaint that Gonzalo crams his words into his ears, or Prospero's threat to Ariel that he will peg him in an *1. 2. 296* oak till he has 'howl'd away twelve winters', and to Caliban that he will rack him with cramps and make him *1. 2. 371* roar 'that beasts shall tremble at thy din'. And through it all, like the glinting of a bright pattern on a dark woof, we hear ever and anon the strains of delicious song and sweet airs, exquisite, enchanted, gay and soft, solemn and strange, until finally these gather strength as Prospero abjures his magic, and deliberately calls *5. 1. 52* upon the aid of 'heavenly music' to resolve the discords, to charm the senses of his hearers, and to comfort and restore them to peace and harmony.[1]

Thus the roaring of winds and waters is quieted, the *5. 1. 65* thunder peals are past, 'and as the morning steals upon the night, melting the darkness', the ignorant human beings see their errors in their true light, are forgiven and released, so that at the close they, like ourselves, are 'not afeard' and remember only that though 'the *3. 2. 142* isle is full of noises' these are in truth but

<blockquote>
Sounds and sweet airs, that give delight, and hurt not.
</blockquote>

---

[1] It is worth noting, if we are tracing out the deeper symbolism of the play, which is not our immediate concern here, that at the end, when Prospero speaks in his own person and asks for release by the audience, the 'heavenly music' of the play becomes in the Epilogue

<blockquote>
prayer,
Which pierces so, that it assaults
Mercy itself, and frees all faults.
</blockquote>

In looking at the images in the *Winter's Tale* I do not see any one symbol occurring clearly and repeatedly, as I do for instance in *King Lear* or in *Hamlet*; but it does seem to me that—as in the *Tempest*—I become conscious of something more indirect and subtle, not a picture, but an *idea*, dominant in the poet's mind, and expressed recurrently through the imagery under many different aspects. It may well be that I see this partly because I have just been reading Sir James Jeans' wonderful and thought-provoking book, *The Mysterious Universe*, in which I find the following, 'The tendency of modern physics is to resolve the whole material universe into waves, and nothing but waves'. But be that as it may, I record my notes for what they may be worth.

The thought constantly in Shakespeare's mind in this play, or perhaps more correctly the idea in his imagination, seems to me to be the common flow of life through all things, in nature and man alike, seen in the sap rising in the tree, the habits and character of flowers, the result of the marriage of base and noble stock, whether it be of roses or human beings, the emotions of birds, animals and men, the working of the poison of disease alike in mind and in body, the curative power, the tonic 'medicine' of a gay or honest presence, and, above all, the oneness of rhythm, of law of movement, in the human body and human emotions with the great fundamental rhythmical movements of nature herself.

Much of this analogy between things human and natural is of course to be found all through Shakespeare's imagery; indeed without it imagery itself would have no meaning or existence.

The likeness in the life of a tree and of a human
W.T. 1. 1. 23 being, brought out here in the roots of affection in
4. 4. 570 youth which branch in age, the 'sap' or life essence in
2. 3. 88 human counsel, the source of poison in a rotten root, is, as we have seen, worked on continually in the historical plays; the likeness of the sickness of body and
1. 2. 296 mind, emphasised here (Leontes' 'diseased opinion',
2. 3. 36 Paulina's 'medicinal' words and so on), is constantly found elsewhere, as in *Macbeth* or *Hamlet*, as is also the similarity in human and animal life and emotion,
1. 2. 67 here illustrated by the children like lambs frisking and
4. 4. 154 bleating in the sun, or the constant love of turtle doves; but I have never noticed elsewhere so much insistence—and this in the most imaginative similes—on the likeness between human and natural processes and characteristics, and on the oneness of rhythmical movement and law.

The art of grafting and what it achieves is touched upon elsewhere, but it is discussed here at length by Polixenes and Perdita in language which today we might apply to eugenics:

4. 4. 92 we marry
A gentler scion to the wildest stock,
And make conceive a bark of baser kind
By bud of nobler race;

and flowers—the marigold, primrose and oxlip—are here more markedly than anywhere else endowed with human characteristics and emotions.

The great natural movements seem the normal mode of expression and comparison; so the old shepherd, seeking to convey to Polixenes the force of Florizel's love for Perdita and her attraction for him, does so most successfully when he says:

> for never gazed the moon
> Upon the water, as he'll stand and read
> As 'twere my daughter's eyes.

W.T. 4. 4. 172

In the same vein is the ardour of Leontes' greeting to Florizel, 'Welcome hither, as is the spring to the earth'; so also is Florizel's answer to the query as to whether he is married, when in his despair at achieving his wish, he cites in old ballad fashion the most unlikely event in nature:

5. 1. 151

> We are not, sir, nor are we like to be;
> The stars, I see, will kiss the valleys first.

5. 1. 205

More in this play than anywhere else is the ebb and flow of emotion exquisitely mirrored in the ebb and flow of blood in the face, obeying, as it does, the same laws, and responding to the same inner stimulus. 'I'll blush you thanks', cries Perdita to Camillo; and the many other touches reminding us of the fluctuating colour in her face and Florizel's we have already noticed (pp. 59–60).

4. 4. 589

So also the immutability of the laws of nature, working alike in the human and in the natural world, is in the poet's mind when he makes Camillo cry,

> you may as well
> Forbid the sea for to obey the moon

1. 2. 426

as hope by threat or counsel to move the stubborn human will, based upon what is a genuine even though it be a false belief.

And as the human will can be immovable and unchangeable as is the moon's influence on the tides, so also the influx and withdrawal of energy in these same tides of the sea come and go as do the tides of fluctuation of human emotion itself. This then is naturally the metaphor Paulina uses when, moved to anger on hearing the unknown Perdita praised as

W.T. 5. 1. 94

> the most peerless piece of earth...
> That e'er the sun shone bright on,

she turns on the unwitting courtier, reminding him curtly that in time past, when his emotions ran high about her beloved queen, Hermione, just so did he speak and write about her:

5. 1. 100

> 'She had not been,
> Nor was not to be equall'd'; thus your verse
> Flow'd with her beauty once; 'tis shrewdly ebb'd,
> To say you have seen a better.

And, above all, it is perfectly and exquisitely in keeping with this central imaginative idea, that Florizel, in the height of his emotion and adoration of the beauty and wild natural grace of Perdita, should see the poetry of the motion of her young body as a part of the ordered and rhythmic flow of nature herself in the movement of the tides, and would have her stay for ever part of that larger movement, so that he cries in ecstasy,

4. 4. 140

> when you do dance, I wish you
> A wave o' the sea, that you might ever do
> Nothing but that.

CHAPTER XV

LEADING MOTIVES IN THE
TRAGEDIES

IT is a curious thing that the part played by recurrent images in raising, developing, sustaining and repeating emotion in the tragedies has not, so far as I know, ever yet been noticed. It is a part somewhat analogous to the action of a recurrent theme or 'motif' in a musical fugue or sonata, or in one of Wagner's operas.

Perhaps, however, a more exact analogy to the function of Shakespeare's images in the tragedies is the unique work of another great artist, of the peculiar quality of which they constantly remind one, that is, Blake's illustrations to his prophetic books. These are not, for the most part, illustrations in the ordinary sense of the term, the translation by the artist of some incident in the narrative into a visual picture; they are rather a running accompaniment to the words in another medium, sometimes symbolically emphasising or interpreting certain aspects of the thought, sometimes supplying frankly only decoration or atmosphere, sometimes grotesque and even repellent, vivid, strange, arresting, sometimes drawn with an almost unearthly beauty of form and colour. Thus, as the leaping tongues of flame which illuminate the pages of *The Marriage of Heaven and Hell* show the visual form which Blake's thought evoked in his mind, and symbolise for us the purity, the beauty and the two-edged quality of life and danger in his words, so the recurrent images in *Macbeth* or *Hamlet* reveal the dominant picture or sensation—and for Shakespeare the two are identical—in terms of which he sees and feels the main problem or theme of the play, thus giving us an unerring clue to the way he looked at it, as well as a direct glimpse into the working of his mind and imagination.

In *Romeo and Juliet* the beauty and ardour of young love are seen by Shakespeare as the irradiating glory of sunlight and starlight in a dark world. The dominating image is *light*, every form and manifestation of it: the sun, moon, stars, fire, lightning, the flash of gunpowder, and the reflected light of beauty and of love; while by contrast we have night, darkness, clouds, rain, mist and smoke.

Each of the lovers thinks of the other as light; Romeo's overpowering impression when he first catches sight of Juliet on the fateful evening at the Capulets' ball is seen in his exclamation,

R. and J.
1. 5. 45

> O, she doth teach the torches to burn bright!
> It seems she hangs upon the cheek of night
> Like a rich jewel in an Ethiop's ear.

3. 2. 17 To Juliet, Romeo is 'day in night'; to Romeo, Juliet *2. 2. 3* is the sun rising from the east, and when they soar to *2. 2. 13–22* love's ecstasy, each alike pictures the other as stars in *3. 2. 21* heaven, shedding such brightness as puts to shame the heavenly bodies themselves.

The intensity of feeling in both lovers purges even the most highly affected and euphuistic conceits of their artificiality, and transforms them into the exquisite and passionate expression of love's rhapsody.

Thus Romeo plays with the old conceit that two of the fairest stars in heaven, having some business on earth, have entreated Juliet's eyes to take their place till they return, and he conjectures,

What if her eyes were there, they in her head?

If so,

> The brightness of her cheek would shame those stars, *R. and J.*
> As daylight doth a lamp; *2. 2. 19*

and then comes the rush of feeling, the overpowering realisation and immortal expression of the transforming glory of love:

> her eyes in heaven *2. 2. 20*
> Would through the airy region stream so bright
> That birds would sing and think it were not night.

And Juliet, in her invocation to night, using an even more extravagant conceit, such as Cowley or Cleveland at his wildest never exceeded, transmutes it into the perfect and natural expression of a girl whose lover to her not only radiates light, but is, indeed, very light itself:

> Give me my Romeo; and, when he shall die, *3. 2. 21*
> Take him and cut him out in little stars,
> And he will make the face of heaven so fine,
> That all the world will be in love with night,
> And pay no worship to the garish sun.

Love is described by Romeo, before he knows what it really is, as

> a smoke raised with the fume of sighs; *1. 1. 189*
> Being purged, a fire sparkling in lovers' eyes;

and the messengers of love are pictured by Juliet, when she is chafing under the nurse's delay, as one of the most exquisite effects in nature, seen especially on the English hills in spring—the swift, magical, transforming power of light:

> love's heralds [she cries] should be thoughts, *2. 5. 4*
> Which ten times faster glide than the sun's beams,
> Driving back shadows over louring hills.

The irradiating quality of the beauty of love is noticed by both lovers; by Juliet, in her first ecstasy, when she *R. and J.* declares that lovers' 'own beauties' are sufficient light *3. 2. 8* for them to see by, and, at the end, by Romeo, when, thinking her dead, he gazes on her and cries,

5. 3. 85   her beauty makes
This vault a feasting presence full of light.

There can be no question, I think, that Shakespeare saw the story, in its swift and tragic beauty, as an almost blinding flash of light, suddenly ignited, and as swiftly quenched. He quite deliberately compresses the action from over nine months to the almost incredibly short period of five days; so that the lovers meet on Sunday, are wedded on Monday, part at dawn on Tuesday and are reunited in death on the night of Thursday. The sensation of swiftness and brilliance, accompanied by danger and destruction, is accentuated again and again; by Juliet, when she avows their betrothal

2. 2. 118   is too rash, too unadvised, too sudden,
Too like the lightning, which doth cease to be
Ere one can say 'It lightens';

and by Romeo and the friar, who instinctively make repeated use of the image of the quick destructive flash *3. 3. 103,* of gunpowder. Indeed the friar, in his well-known *132; 5. 1. 63* answer to Romeo's prayer for instant marriage, succinctly, in the last nine words, sums up the whole movement of the play:

2. 6. 9   These violent delights have violent ends,
And in their triumph die; like fire and powder
Which as they kiss consume.

Even old Capulet, whom one does not think of as a poetical person, though he uses many images—some of great beauty—carries on the idea of light to represent love and youth and beauty, and of the clouding of the sun for grief and sorrow. He promises Paris that on the evening of the ball he shall see at his house

> Earth-treading stars that make dark heaven light;   *R. and J.*
> *I. 2. 25*

and when he encounters Juliet weeping, as he thinks, for her cousin Tybalt's death, he clothes his comment in similar nature imagery of light quenched in darkness:

> When the sun sets, the air doth drizzle dew;   *3. 5. 127*
> But for the sunset of my brother's son
> It rains downright.

In addition to this more definite symbolic imagery, we find that radiant light, sunshine, starlight, moonbeams, sunrise and sunset, the sparkle of fire, a meteor, candles, torches, quick-coming darkness, clouds, mist, rain and night, form a pictorial background, or running accompaniment, to the play, which augments unconsciously in us this same sensation.

We meet it at once in the prince's description of the attitude of the rival houses

> That quench the fire of your pernicious rage   *I. I. 83*
> With purple fountains issuing from your veins;

and later, in the talk of Benvolio and Montague about the rising sun, the dew and clouds, followed by Romeo's definition of love, Capulet's words just quoted, Benvolio's riming proverb about fire, the talk of Romeo and Mercutio about torches, candles, lights and lamps, the flashing lights and torches of the ball, four times accentuated, Romeo's conception of Juliet as a 'bright angel',

I. I. 117–18, 130–6
I. I. 189–90
I. 2. 46
I. 4. 35–45
I. 5. 28, 45, 88, 126
2. 2. 27

> As glorious to this night,....
> As is a winged messenger of heaven;

R. and J. 2. 2   in the moonlight in the orchard, the sunrise Friar Law-
2. 3. 1–6   rence watches from his cell, the sun clearing from heaven
2. 3. 73   Romeo's sighs, the exquisite light and shadow swiftly
2. 5. 4   chasing over Juliet's words in the orchard, the 'black
3. 1. 121   fate' of the day on which Mercutio was killed, the
3. 1. 126   'fire-eyed fury' which leads Romeo to challenge Tybalt,
3. 1. 174   their fight, to which they go 'like lightning', the sunset
                   which Juliet so ardently desires to be swift 'and bring
3. 2. 4   in cloudy night immediately', the exquisite play of
                   quivering light from darkness through dawn, till

3. 5. 9   jocund day
                   Stands tiptoe on the misty mountain tops,

which forms the theme of the lovers' parting song;
and, at the last, in Romeo's anguished reply to Juliet,
pointing the contrast between the coming day and their
own great sorrow:

3. 5. 36   More light and light: more dark and dark our woes!

5. 3   And then, at the end, we see the darkness of the church-
yard, lit by the glittering torch of Paris, quickly
quenched; Romeo's arrival with his torch, the swift
fight and death, the dark vault, which is not a grave
but a lantern irradiated by Juliet's beauty, Romeo's
grim jest on the 'lightning before death', followed immediately by the self-slaughter of the 'star-crossed'
lovers, the gathering together of the stricken mourners
as the day breaks, and the 'glooming' peace of the
overcast morning when

5. 3. 306   The sun for sorrow will not show his head.

Shakespeare's extraordinary susceptibility to suggestion and readiness to borrow are well exemplified in this
running imagery. He took the idea from the last place
we should expect, from the wooden doggerel of Arthur

Brooke, and the germ of it is in the sing-song line in which Brooke describes the attitude of the lovers:

For each of them to other is as to the world the sun.

Their mutual feeling and the feud of the families are constantly referred to by Brooke as 'fire' or 'flame'; in the beginning, he speaks of the feud as a 'mighty fire'; the families 'bathe in blood of smarting wounds', and the prince hopes he may 'quench the sparks that burned within their breast'. These three images are combined and unified by Shakespeare in the two lines *R. and J.* *1. 1. 83–4* already quoted (p. 313).

Other suggestions also come from Brooke, such as the emphasis on the bright light of the torches at the ball; Romeo's first sight of Juliet, which is a 'sudden kindled fire'; her first impression of him, when he

in her sight did seem to pass the rest as far
As Phoebus' shining beams do pass the brightness
    of a star;

and his description in his first talk to her, of the

            quick sparks and glowing furious glead
...from your beauty's pleasant eyne, Love causéd
    to proceed
Which have so set on fire each feeling part of mine
That lo, my mind doth melt away, my outward parts
    do pine,

which is transmuted by Shakespeare to the delightful image of the stars which have changed places with her *2. 2. 15–22* eyes.

But although Shakespeare took the idea from his original, it scarcely needs saying that in taking it, he has transformed a few conventional and obvious similes of little poetic worth into a continuous and consistent running image of exquisite beauty, building up a definite picture and atmosphere of brilliance swiftly quenched, which powerfully affects the imagination of the reader.

HAMLET   In *Hamlet*, naturally, we find ourselves in an entirely different atmosphere. If we look closely we see this is partly due to the number of images of sickness, disease or blemish of the body, in the play (see Chart vii), and we discover that the idea of an ulcer or tumour, as descriptive of the unwholesome condition of Denmark morally, is, on the whole, the dominating one.

Ham. 3. 4. 43   Hamlet speaks of his mother's sin as a blister on the 'fair forehead of an innocent love', she speaks of her
4. 5. 17   'sick soul', and as in *King Lear* the emotion is so strong and the picture so vivid, that the metaphor overflows into the verbs and adjectives: heaven's face, he tells her,
3. 4. 51   is *thought-sick* at the act; her husband is a *mildew'd ear*,
3. 4. 64–5   *blasting* his *wholesome* brother; to have married him,
3. 4. 73, 80   her sense must be not only *sickly*, but *apoplex'd*. Finally, at the end of that terrific scene (3. 4), he implores her not to soothe herself with the belief that his father's apparition is due to her son's madness, and not to her own guilt, for that

3. 4. 147   will but skin and film the ulcerous place,
Whiles rank corruption, mining all within,
Infects unseen.

So also, later, he compares the unnecessary fighting between Norway and Poland to a kind of tumour which
4. 4. 27   grows out of too much prosperity. He sees the country and the people in it alike in terms of a sick body needing medicine or the surgeon's knife. When he surprises Claudius at his prayers, he exclaims,

3. 3. 96   This physic but prolongs thy sickly days;
and he describes the action of conscience in the un-
3. 1. 84   forgettable picture of the healthy, ruddy countenance

turning pale with sickness. A mote in the eye, a
'vicious mole', a galled chilblain, a probed wound and
purgation, are also among Hamlet's images; and the
mind of Claudius runs equally on the same theme.

When he hears of the murder of Polonius, he declares
that his weakness in not sooner having had Hamlet shut
up was comparable to the cowardly action of a man
with a 'foul disease' who

> To keep it from divulging, let it feed
> Even on the pith of life;

and later, when arranging to send Hamlet to England
and to his death, he justifies it by the proverbial tag:

> diseases desperate grown
> By desperate appliance are relieved,
> Or not at all;

and adjures the English king to carry out his behest,
in the words of a fever patient seeking a sedative:

> For like the hectic in my blood he rages,
> And thou must cure me.

When working on Laertes, so that he will easily fall
in with the design for the fencing match, his speech
is full of the same underlying thought of a body sick,
or ill at ease:

> goodness, growing to a plurisy,
> Dies in his own too much;

and finally, he sums up the essence of the position and
its urgency with lightning vividness in a short medical
phrase:

> But, to the quick o' the ulcer:
> Hamlet comes back.

In marked contrast to *King Lear*, though bodily
disease is emphasised, bodily action and strain are little

drawn upon; indeed, only in Hamlet's great speech are they brought before us at all (*to be shot at* with slings and arrows, *to take arms against* troubles and *oppose* them, *to suffer* shocks, *to bear* the lash of whips, and *endure* pangs, *to grunt* and *sweat* under burdens, and so on), and here, as in *King Lear*, they serve to intensify the feeling of mental anguish. In *Hamlet*, however, anguish is not the dominating thought, but *rottenness*, disease, corruption, the result of *dirt*; the people are 'muddied',

> Thick and unwholesome in their thoughts and whispers;

and this corruption is, in the words of Claudius, 'rank' and 'smells to heaven', so that the state of things in Denmark which shocks, paralyses and finally over-whelms Hamlet, is as the foul tumour breaking in-wardly and poisoning the whole body, while showing

> no cause without
> Why the man dies.

This image pictures and reflects not only the out-ward condition which causes Hamlet's spiritual illness, but also his own state. Indeed, the shock of the dis-covery of his father's murder and the sight of his mother's conduct have been such that when the play opens Hamlet has already begun to die, to die internally; because all the springs of life—love, laughter, joy, hope, belief in others—are becoming frozen at their source, are being gradually infected by the disease of the spirit which is—unknown to him—killing him.

To Shakespeare's pictorial imagination, therefore, the problem in *Hamlet* is not predominantly that of will and reason, of a mind too philosophic or a nature temperamentally unfitted to act quickly; he sees it pictorially *not as the problem of an individual at all,* but as something greater and even more mysterious, as a *condition* for which the individual himself is apparently not responsible, any more than the sick man is to blame for the infection which strikes and devours him, but which, nevertheless, in its course and development, impartially and relentlessly, annihilates him and others, innocent and guilty alike. That is the tragedy of *Hamlet,* as it is perhaps the chief tragic mystery of life.

It is hardly necessary to point out, in a play so well known, and of such rich imaginative quality, how the ugliness of the dominating image (disease, ulcer) is counteracted, and the whole lighted up by flashes of sheer beauty in the imagery; beauty of picture, of sound and association, more particularly in the classical group and in the personifications. Thus, the tragic, murky atmosphere of Hamlet's interview with his mother, with its ever-repeated insistence on physical sickness and revolting disease, is illumined by the glow of his description of his father's portrait, the associations of beauty called up by Hyperion, Jove and Mars, or the exquisite picture evoked by the contemplation of the grace of his father's poise:

> like the herald Mercury
> New-lighted on a heaven-kissing hill.

Ham. 3. 4. 58

These beauties are specially noticeable in the many personifications, as when, with Horatio, we see 'the morn, in russet mantle clad', as she 'walks o'er the dew of yon high eastward hill', or, with Hamlet, watch Laertes leaping into Ophelia's grave, and ask,

1. 1. 166

> Whose phrase of sorrow
> Conjures the wandering stars and makes them stand
> Like wonder-wounded hearers?

5. 1. 267

Ham. 5. 2. 41;
1. 2. 149
Peace, with her wheaten garland, Niobe all tears,

4. 7. 182 Ophelia's garments 'heavy with their drink', which pull her from her 'melodious lay' to muddy death, or the magnificent picture of the two sides of the queen's nature at war, as seen by the elder Hamlet:

3. 4. 112
> But look, amazement on thy mother sits:
> O, step between her and her fighting soul;

these, and many more, are the unforgettable and radiant touches of beauty in a play which has, as images, much that is sombre and unpleasant.

TROILUS
AND
CRESSIDA
Troilus and Cressida and *Hamlet* are very closely connected in their imagery (see Chart 7). Did we not know it for other reasons, we could be sure from the similarity and continuity of symbolism in the two plays that they were written near together, and at a time when the author was suffering from a disillusionment, revulsion and perturbation of nature, such as we feel nowhere else with the same intensity.

The same two groups of images run through and dominate both plays, disease and food; in *Hamlet* the first is predominant, and in *Troilus and Cressida* the second (see Chart 7).

The main emotional theme in *Troilus and Cressida*—passionate, idealistic love, followed by disillusion and despair—is pictured with overwhelming vividness, through physical taste: the exquisite anticipation by a sensitive palate of delicious food and wine, and the sick revolt and disgust on finding on one's tongue only 'greasy relics' or rotting fruit.

The disgust at woman's wantonness seems to express itself instinctively to Shakespeare, especially in these two plays and in *Antony and Cleopatra*, in terms of

physical appetite and food. 'Heaven and earth!' cries
Hamlet,

> she would hang on him,   *Ham. 1. 2. 143*
> As if increase of appetite had grown
> By what it fed on: and yet, within a month—
> Let me not think on't.

So lust, says the elder Hamlet, 'though to a radiant   *1. 5. 55*
angel link'd', will 'prey on garbage'.

Cleopatra, like Cressid, is thought of as a tempting
and delicious piece of food, 'a dish for the gods':

> other women cloy   *A. and C.*
> The appetites they feed, but she makes hungry   *2. 2. 239*
> Where most she satisfies;

and in moments of revulsion, both alike become a cold
and greasy remnant; 'I found you', says Antony,

> as a morsel cold upon   *3. 13. 116*
> Dead Caesar's trencher.

In like manner, before Troilus has been undeceived, he
thinks of his sweet love as 'food for fortune's tooth',   *T. and C.*
and when the revulsion of disgust follows her treachery,   *4. 5. 293*
he cries bitterly,

> The fractions of her faith, orts of her love,   *5. 2. 157*
> The fragments, scraps, the bits and greasy relics
> Of her o'er-eaten faith, are bound to Diomed.

In that amazing image of the anticipation of her love,
it is the sense of taste which comes naturally to Troilus'
lips as the means of expressing it:

> I am giddy; expectation whirls me round.   *3. 2. 17*
> The imaginary relish is so sweet
> That it enchants my sense: what will it be,
> When that the watery palates taste indeed
> Love's thrice repured nectar?

It is an image drawn from the same sense, as applied to 'the poor creature, small beer', which Cressida uses, when Pandarus urges her to moderate her emotion at the thought of parting from Troilus:

T. and C. 4. 4. 5

> how can I moderate it?
> If I could temporise with my affection,
> Or brew it to a weak and colder palate,
> The like allayment could I give my grief.

Troilus, in the vivid, passionate speeches, the metaphors *2. 2. 37–50,*
61–96 of which throw so much light on his character, twice draws upon food to make his thought more clear. Thus, for instance, when he is fulminating against his brothers' prudent counsels, based on reason, to let Helen go, he uses a curious metaphor from a jugged or stuffed hare, which is clearly an associative one. He scorns their timidity, and, in true Shakespearian fashion, he expresses the quality by the concrete example of the most timid animal of the fields in England, turning it into an adjective; this, in turn, calls up the memory of the succulent dish still a favourite one with English country folk, and he applies the process of the larding and cooking of it (which he clearly knows well) to the dulling of men's minds and the sapping of their fiery manhood with overmuch reason and caution:

2. 2. 46

> Nay, if we talk of reason,
> Let's shut our gates, and sleep: manhood and honour
> Should have hare hearts, would they but fat their
> thoughts
> With this cramm'd reason.

And a little later, when he is again urging them to stand firm by honour, though it may not be the easiest way, or suit them at the moment, he takes an example from ordinary, thrifty household management to illustrate this:

> nor the remainder viands
> We do not throw in unrespective sieve,
> Because we now are full.

T. and C.
2. 2. 69

The force of this dominating symbol is so great that we find that fourteen of the characters make use of images of food, taste or cooking, and that there are no less than forty-four such images in the play: seething, stewing, mincing, baking, larding, stuffing, broiling, basting, brewing, frying, kneading, boiling and stirring the ingredients for a pudding, are among the various kinds of cooking described or referred to, sometimes at considerable length, as in the metaphors on grinding the wheat, bolting, leavening, kneading, making the cake, heating the oven, baking and cooling, carried on with expert knowledge by Pandarus and complete understanding by Troilus in the opening of the play (1. 1. 14–26).

A 'crusty batch' (of bread), cheese served for a digestive, or mouse-eaten and dry, an addled egg, mincemeat seasoned with spice and salt and baked in a pie, porridge after meat, a dish of fool (stewed fruit crushed with cream), a fusty nut, a hard sailor's biscuit, fair fruit rotting untasted in an unwholesome dish, and greasy remnants of food, are, in addition, all pressed into service; as are also hunger, appetite, ravenous eating, digestion, fasting, feeding, tasting, drinking up the lees and dregs of wine, tossing off a toast, sauce, flavouring, salt, sweet and sour.

Indeed, images of cooking seem so constantly with the speakers that they cannot refrain from using them even in the most far-fetched way; as when Pandarus describes how, when Helen was playing with Troilus, Queen Hecuba laughed, so that her eyes ran o'er, and Cassandra laughed, to which Cressida quickly retorts,

T. and C.
1. 2. 151   But there was more temperate fire under the pot of her eyes: did her eyes run o'er too?

2. 3. 186 or when Ulysses refers to Achilles as the proud lord

That bastes his arrogance with his own seam [lard],

and declares that if, as had been suggested, Ajax went to him,

2. 3. 197   That were to enlard his fat-already pride.

MACBETH   The imagery in *Macbeth* appears to me to be more rich and varied, more highly imaginative, more unapproachable by any other writer, than that of any other single play. It is particularly so, I think, in the continuous use made of the simplest, humblest, everyday things, drawn from the daily life in a small house, as a vehicle for sublime poetry. But that is beside our point here.

The ideas in the imagery are in themselves more imaginative, more subtle and complex than in other plays, and there are a greater number of them, interwoven the one with the other, recurring and repeating. There are at least four of these main ideas, and many subsidiary ones.

One is the picture of Macbeth himself.

Few simple things—harmless in themselves—have such a curiously humiliating and degrading effect as the spectacle of a notably small man enveloped in a coat far too big for him. Comic actors know this well— Charlie Chaplin, for instance—and it is by means of this homely picture that Shakespeare shows us his imaginative view of the hero, and expresses the fact that the honours for which the murders were committed are, after all, of very little worth to him.

The idea constantly recurs that Macbeth's new honours sit ill upon him, like a loose and badly fitting garment, belonging to someone else. Macbeth himself first expresses it, quite early in the play, when, immediately following the first appearance of the witches and their prophecies, Ross arrives from the king, and greets him as thane of Cawdor, to which Macbeth quickly replies,

> The thane of Cawdor lives: why do you dress me *Mac. 1. 3. 108*
> In borrow'd robes?

And a few minutes later, when he is rapt in ambitious thoughts suggested by the confirmation of two out of the three 'prophetic greetings', Banquo, watching him, murmurs,

> New honours come upon him, *1. 3. 144*
> Like our strange garments, cleave not to their mould
> But with the aid of use.

When Duncan is safely in the castle, Macbeth's better nature for a moment asserts itself, and, in debate with himself, he revolts from the contemplated deed for a threefold reason: because of its incalculable results, the treachery of such action from one who is both kinsman and host, and Duncan's own virtues and greatness as king.

When his wife joins him, his repugnance to the deed is as great, but it is significant that he gives three quite different reasons for not going ahead with it, reasons which he hopes may appeal to her, for he knows the others would not. So he urges that he has been lately honoured by the king, people think well of him, and therefore he should reap the reward of these things at once, and not upset everything by this murder which they have planned.

There is irony in the fact that to express the position he uses the same metaphor of clothes:

Mac. 1. 7. 32
> I have bought
> Golden opinions from all sorts of people,
> Which would be worn now in their newest gloss,
> Not cast aside so soon.

To which Lady Macbeth, quite unmoved, retorts contemptuously:

1. 7. 36
> Was the hope drunk
> Wherein you dress'd yourself?

After the murder, when Ross says he is going to Scone for Macbeth's coronation, Macduff uses the same simile:

2. 4. 37
> Well, may you see things well done there: adieu!
> Lest our old robes sit easier than our new!

And, at the end, when the tyrant is at bay at Dunsinane, and the English troops are advancing, the Scottish lords still have this image in their minds. Caithness sees him as a man vainly trying to fasten a large garment on him with too small a belt:

5. 2. 15
> He cannot buckle his distemper'd cause
> Within the belt of rule;

while Angus, in a similar image, vividly sums up the essence of what they all have been thinking ever since Macbeth's accession to power:

5. 2. 20
> now does he feel his title
> Hang loose about him, like a giant's robe
> Upon a dwarfish thief.

This imaginative picture of a small, ignoble man encumbered and degraded by garments unsuited to him, should be put against the view emphasised by some critics (notably Coleridge and Bradley) of the likeness between Macbeth and Milton's Satan in grandeur and sublimity.

Undoubtedly Macbeth is built on great lines and in heroic proportions, with great possibilities—there could be no tragedy else. He is great, magnificently great, in courage, in passionate, indomitable ambition, in imagination and capacity to feel. But he could never be put beside, say Hamlet or Othello, in nobility of nature; and there *is* an aspect in which he is but a poor, vain, cruel, treacherous creature, snatching ruthlessly over the dead bodies of kinsman and friend at place and power he is utterly unfitted to possess. It is worth remembering that it is thus that Shakespeare, with his unshrinking clarity of vision, repeatedly *sees* him.

Another image or idea which runs through *Macbeth* is the reverberation of sound echoing over vast regions, even into the limitless spaces beyond the confines of the world. Echoing sound, as also reflected light, always interested Shakespeare; he is very quick to notice it, and in the earlier plays he records it often, quite simply and directly, as in the reverberating roll of drums in *King John*, the smack of Petruchio's kiss resounding through the church, Juliet's delicate picture of Echo with her airy tongue repeating 'Romeo', Viola's assertion that were she Orsino, she would make the

> babbling gossip of the air
> Cry out 'Olivia!'

Tw. N.
1. 5. 283

or her more fanciful remark to the duke that the tune he likes

> gives a very echo to the seat
> Where love is throned.

2. 4. 21

He specially loves, and describes repeatedly (in *A Midsummer Night's Dream*, *Titus Andronicus* and the *Taming of the Shrew*), the re-echoing sound of hounds and horn,

M.N.D.
4. 1. 115

> the musical confusion
> Of hounds and echo in conjunction;

its doubling and mocking quality attracts him:

Titus, 2. 3. 17

> the babbling echo mocks the hounds,
> Replying shrilly to the well-tuned horns,
> As if a double hunt were heard at once;

and it is this quality which Warwick applies most appositely when, having been roused in the small hours to soothe the sleepless and fretful king, he finally loses patience with Henry's fears that the revolutionaries must be fifty thousand strong, and retorts, somewhat tartly,

2 H. IV, 3. 1. 96

> It cannot be, my lord;
> Rumour doth double, like the voice and echo,
> The numbers of the fear'd. Please it your grace
> To go to bed.

It is not until after 1600, and most noticeably in *Troilus and Cressida*, that Shakespeare uses this same idea of reverberation and reflection to illustrate subtle and philosophic thought. Ulysses' mind is full of it, and he applies it constantly; Kent, in *King Lear*, seizes

K. L. 1. 1. 155

on an analogous natural fact to point the truth that noise and protestation do not necessarily indicate deep feeling; while in *Macbeth*, the peculiar quality of echoing and re-echoing sound is used to emphasise, in the most highly imaginative and impressive way, a thought constantly present with Shakespeare in his middle years, the incalculable and boundless effects of evil in the nature of one man.

Macbeth himself, like Hamlet, is fully conscious of

how impossible it is to 'trammel up the consequence' *Mac.* 1. 7. 3
of his deed, and by his magnificent images of angels
pleading trumpet-tongued,

> And pity, like a naked, new-born babe,
> Striding the blast, or heaven's cherubin horsed 1. 7. 21
> Upon the sightless couriers of the air,

who

> Shall blow the horrid deed in every eye, 1. 7. 24
> That tears shall drown the wind,

he fills our imagination with the picture of its being
broadcast through great spaces with reverberating
sound.

This is taken up again by Macduff, when he cries,

>   each new morn 4. 3. 4
> New widows howl, new orphans cry, new sorrows
> Strike heaven on the face, that it resounds
> As if it felt with Scotland and yell'd out
> Like syllable of dolour;

and again by Ross, when he is trying to break the
terrible news of Macbeth's latest murders to Macduff—
the destruction of his own wife and children—

>   I have words 4. 3. 193
> That would be howl'd out in the desert air,
> Where hearing should not latch them.

One can scarcely conceive a more vivid picture of the
vastnesses of space than this, and of the overwhelming
and unending nature of the consequences or reverbera-
tions of the evil deed.

Another constant idea in the play arises out of the
symbolism that light stands for life, virtue, goodness;
and darkness for evil and death. 'Angels are bright', 4. 3. 22
the witches are 'secret, black and midnight hags', and, 4. 1. 48
as Dowden says, the movement of the whole play might

Mac. 3. 2. 52 be summed up in the words, 'good things of day begin to droop and drowse'.

This is, of course, very obvious, but out of it develops the further thought which is assumed throughout, that the evil which is being done is so horrible that it would blast the sight to look on it; so that darkness, or partial blinding, is necessary to carry it out.

Like so much in the play it is ironic that it should be Duncan who first starts this simile, the idea of which turns into a leading motive in the tragedy. When he is conferring the new honour on his son, he is careful to say that others, kinsmen and thanes, will also be rewarded:

1. 4. 41
> signs of nobleness, like stars, shall shine
> On all deservers.

No sooner has the king spoken, than Macbeth realises that Malcolm, now a prince of the realm, is an added obstacle in his path, and suddenly, shrinking from the blazing horror of the murderous thought which follows, he cries to himself,

1. 4. 50
> Stars, hide your fires;
> Let not light see my black and deep desires.

From now on, the idea that only in darkness can such evil deeds be done is ever present with both Macbeth and his wife, as is seen in their two different and most characteristic invocations to darkness: her blood-curdling cry,

1. 5. 51
> Come, thick night,
> And pall thee in the dunnest smoke of hell,

which takes added force when we hear later the poignant

5. 1. 23 words, 'She has light by her continually'; and his more gentle appeal in the language of falconry,

3. 2. 46
> Come, seeling night,
> Scarf up the tender eye of pitiful day.

And when Banquo, sleepless, uneasy, with heart heavy as lead, crosses the courtyard on the fateful night, with Fleance holding the flaring torch before him, and, looking up to the dark sky, mutters,

> There's husbandry in heaven, *Mac.* 2. 1. 4
> Their candles are all out,

we know the scene is set for treachery and murder.

So it is fitting that on the day following, 'dark night 2. 4. 7 strangles the travelling lamp', and

> darkness does the face of earth entomb, 2. 4. 9
> When living light should kiss it.

The idea of deeds which are too terrible for human eyes to look on is also constant; Lady Macbeth scoffs it— 'the sleeping and the dead', she argues, 'are but as 2. 2. 53 pictures':

> 'tis the eye of childhood
> That fears a painted devil;

but Macduff, having seen the slain king, rushes out, and cries to Lennox,

> Approach the chamber, and destroy your sight 2. 3. 76
> With a new Gorgon.

Macbeth boldly asserts he dare look on that 'which 3. 4. 60 might appal the devil', and the bitterness of defeat he realises on seeing one 'too like the spirit of Banquo' in the procession of kings, is expressed in his agonised cry,

> Thy crown does sear mine eye-balls; 4. 1. 113

while in his bitter and beautiful words at the close, the dominant thoughts and images are the quenching of light and the empty reverberation of sound and fury, 'signifying nothing'. 5. 5. 28

The fourth of the chief symbolic ideas in the play is one which is very constant with Shakespeare, and is

to be found all through his work, that sin is a disease—
Scotland is sick.

So Macbeth, while repudiating physic for himself,
turns to the doctor and says if he could, by analysis,
find Scotland's disease

Mac. 5. 3. 52

> And purge it to a sound and pristine health,
> I would applaud thee to the very echo,
> That should applaud again...
> What rhubarb, senna, or what purgative drug,
> Would scour these English hence?

Malcolm speaks of his country as weeping, bleeding
and wounded, and later urges Macduff to

4. 3. 214

> make us medicines of our great revenge,
> To cure this deadly grief;

5. 2. 27 while Caithness calls Malcolm himself the 'medicine
of the sickly weal', 'the country's purge'.

It is worth noting that all Macbeth's images of sickness are remedial or soothing in character: balm for
a sore, sleep after fever, a purge, physic for pain, a

5. 3. 43 'sweet oblivious antidote'; thus intensifying to the
reader or audience his passionate and constant longing
for well-being, rest, and, above all, peace of mind.

Other subsidiary motives in the imagery, which work
in and out through the play, insensibly but deeply affect
the reader's imagination. One of these is the idea of
the *unnaturalness* of Macbeth's crime, that it is a convulsion of nature. This is brought out repeatedly and
emphasised by imagery, as are also the terrible results
of going against nature.

Macbeth himself says that Duncan's wounds

2. 3. 118

> look'd like a breach in nature
> For ruin's wasteful entrance,

2. 3. 71 and Macduff speaks of his murder as the sacrilege of

breaking open the Lord's anointed temple. The events which accompany and follow it are terrible because unnatural; an owl kills a falcon, horses eat each other, the earth was feverous and did shake, day becomes night; all this, says the old man, is unnatural,

> Even like the deed that's done. *Mac. 2. 4. 10*

Macbeth's greatest trouble is the unnatural one that he has murdered sleep, and the whole feeling of dis- *2. 2. 36* location is increased by such images as 'let the frame *3. 2. 16* of things disjoint', or by Macbeth's conjuration to the witches with the terrible list of the convulsions of nature which may result from their answering him. Indeed, if from one angle the movement of the play may be summed up in Macbeth's words,

> Good things of day begin to droop and drowse, *3. 2. 52*

from another it is completely described by the doctor in his diagnosis of the doomed queen's malady as 'a great perturbation in nature'. *5. 1. 10*

In addition to these running images symbolising or expressing an idea, there are groups of others which might be called atmospheric in their effect, that is, they raise or increase certain feelings and emotions.

Such is the action of rapid riding, which contributes and emphasises a certain sense of rushing, relentless and goaded motion, of which we are very conscious in the play. This is symbolised externally by the rapid ride of the messenger to Lady Macbeth, arriving 'almost *1. 5. 37* dead for breath', ahead of Macbeth, who himself has outridden Duncan. The king remarks in unconscious irony, *he rides well*, *1. 6. 22*

> And his great love, sharp as his spur, hath holp him
> To his home before us.

It is noticeable what a large part riding plays in the images which crowd on Macbeth's heated brain when *Mac. 1. 7. 1–28* he is weighing the *pros* and *cons* of his plan: the new-born babe 'striding the blast', heaven's cherubin horsed

1. 7. 23   Upon the sightless couriers of the air,

and finally, the vision of his 'intent', his aim, as a horse lacking sufficient spur to action, which melts into the picture of his ambition as a rider vaulting into the saddle with such energy that it 'o'erleaps itself', and falls on the further side.

The feeling of fear, horror and pain is increased by the constant and recurring images of blood; these are very marked, and have been noticed by others, especially by Bradley, the most terrible being Macbeth's descrip-*3. 5. 136* tion of himself wading in a river of blood, while the most stirring to the imagination, perhaps in the whole of Shakespeare, is the picture of him gazing, rigid with *2. 2. 60* horror, at his own blood-stained hand and watching it dye the whole green ocean red.

The images of animals also, nearly all predatory, unpleasant or fierce, add to this same feeling; such are a nest of scorpions, a venomous serpent and a snake, a 'hell-kite' eating chickens, a devouring vulture, a swarm of insects, a tiger, rhinoceros and bear, the tiny wren fighting the owl for the life of her young, small birds with the fear of the net, lime, pitfall or gin, used with such bitter ironic effect by Lady Macduff and her boy just before they are murdered, the shrieking owl, and the bear tied to a stake fighting savagely to the end.

Enough has been said, I think, to indicate how complex and varied is the symbolism in the imagery of

Macbeth, and to make it clear that an appreciable part of the emotions we feel throughout of pity, fear and horror, is due to the subtle but definite and repeated action of this imagery upon our minds, of which, in our preoccupation with the main theme, we remain often largely unconscious.

The main image in *Othello* is that of animals in action, preying upon one another, mischievous, lascivious, cruel or suffering, and through these, the general sense of pain and unpleasantness is much increased and kept constantly before us.

More than half the animal images in the play are Iago's, and all these are contemptuous or repellent: a plague of flies, a quarrelsome dog, the recurrent image of bird-snaring, leading asses by the nose, a spider catching a fly, beating an offenceless dog, wild cats, wolves, goats and monkeys.

To these, Othello adds his pictures of foul toads breeding in a cistern, summer flies in the shambles, the ill-boding raven over the infected house, a toad in a dungeon, the monster 'too hideous to be shown', bird-snaring again, aspics' tongues, crocodiles' tears, and his reiteration of 'goats and monkeys'. In addition, Lodovico very suitably calls Iago 'that viper', and the green-eyed monster 'begot upon itself, born on itself', is described or referred to by Iago, Emilia and Desdemona.

It is interesting to compare the animal imagery in *Othello* with that in *King Lear*. The plays have certain likenesses; they were written near together (*Othello* probably in 1604, *King Lear* about 1605), they are the most painful of the great tragedies, and they are both studies of torture. But the torture in *King Lear*

OTHELLO

Oth. 3. 3. *107*

3. 3. *403*; 4. *1.*
265

3. 3. *166*; 3. *4.*
161, 163

is on so vast and so inhuman a scale, the cruelty of child to parent in the doubly repeated plot is so relentless and ferocious, that the jealous and petty malignity of Iago shrinks beside it.

This difference in scale is expressed in the animal imagery. In *Othello* we see a low type of life, insects and reptiles, swarming and preying on each other, not out of special ferocity, but just in accordance with their natural instincts, mischievous and irresponsible wild cats, goats and monkeys, or the harmless, innocent animal trapped or beaten. This reflects and repeats the spectacle of the wanton torture of one human being by another, which we witness in the tragedy, the human spider and his fly; whereas in *King Lear* our imagination is filled with the accumulated pictures of active ferocity, of wolf, tiger, wild boar, vulture, serpent and sea-monster, all animals of a certain dignity and grandeur, though seen here only when their desires

M. of V.
4. 1. 137

Are wolvish, bloody, starved and ravenous.

This represents the terrific scale of the suffering in *King Lear*, which makes us feel—as we never do in *Othello*—that the vileness of humanity is so great, so unchecked and universal that if the gods do not intervene, the end of such horrors must come and

K.L. 4. 2. 49

Humanity must perforce prey on itself,
Like monsters of the deep.

But the gods, who 'keep this dreadful pother', do not intervene, and the most terrible lines in Shakespeare

4. 1. 37

are those breathed by Gloucester in his agony, when he attributes to the gods themselves in their dealings with men, not only indifference and callousness, but the sheer wanton delight in torture, which, in *Othello*, we see exercised only by one human being on another.

If animals in action symbolise the main motive in *Othello*, there is another recurrent image which gives atmosphere and background. As is fitting, with a setting of two famous seaports, the sea, its images and language, play an important part throughout.

Iago, as the soldier of a city which owed its dominance to sea-power, uses sea imagery easily; when complaining that Othello had passed him over for Cassio, he describes himself as 'be-lee'd and calm'd'; he knows *Oth. 1. 1. 30* the state has not another of Othello's 'fathom'; he says *1. 1. 153* he must 'show out a flag and sign of love'; that *1. 1. 157* Brabantio will take action against Othello to whatever extent the law 'will give him cable'; later, he coarsely *1. 2. 17* describes his general's marriage in the terms of a pirate taking a prize galleon; he declares to Roderigo he is knit to his deserving 'with cables of perdurable tough- *1. 3. 343* ness'; and when he sees his plots shaping well, he murmurs with satisfaction,

My boat sails freely, both with wind and stream. *2. 3. 63*

The opening of Act 2, when those in Cyprus are anxiously awaiting the arrival of Desdemona and of Othello, is full of sea pictures and personifications, the ruffian wind upon the sea, the 'chidden billow', and the 'wind-shaked surge', so that it is well in keeping with the setting and atmosphere when Cassio, in high rhetorical terms, pictures the seas and rocks as traitors concealed to waylay the ship, who, on catching sight of the beauty of Desdemona, 'do omit their mortal natures', and let her go safely by.

Othello's use of sea images is noteworthy; they come naturally, for on each occasion they mark a moment of intense emotion. The first, at the height of his happiness, when he rejoins Desdemona, is an exclamation which to us, who know what lies before them, is, in its opening, one of the most poignant and moving in the play:

Oth. 2. 1. 186
     O my soul's joy!
If after every tempest come such calms,
May the winds blow till they have waken'd death!

The next is at the height of his torture, when, having been shown the handkerchief, suspicion becomes certainty and he vows vengeance. To clinch this, Iago urges patience, and suggests that perhaps his mind may change; to which Othello instantly reacts as his torturer intends, and affirms the unalterable quality of his resolve by comparing it to the 'icy current and compulsive 3. 3. 453 course' of the ebbless Pontic Sea.

And at the end, when he has carried out his resolve, and has suffered and realised all, again it is in sea language that he expresses his equally set determination to follow Desdemona:

5. 2. 267
  Here is my journey's end, here is my butt
  And very sea-mark of my utmost sail.

KING LEAR The intensity of feeling and emotion in *King Lear* and the sharpness of its focus are revealed by the fact that in Shakespeare's imagination there runs throughout only one overpowering and dominating continuous image. So compelling is this that even well-marked different and subsidiary images are pressed into its service, and used to augment and emphasise it.

In the play we are conscious all through of the atmosphere of buffeting, strain and strife, and, at moments, of bodily tension to the point of agony. So naturally does this flow from the circumstances of the drama and the mental sufferings of Lear, that we scarcely realise how greatly this sensation in us is increased by the general 'floating' image, kept constantly before us, chiefly by means of the verbs used, but also in metaphor, of a human body in anguished movement, tugged, wrenched, beaten, pierced, stung, scourged, dislocated, flayed, gashed, scalded, tortured and finally broken on the rack.

One can scarcely open a page of the play without being struck by these images and verbs, for every kind of bodily movement, generally involving pain, is used to express mental and abstract, as well as physical facts. I will name only a few of them. Lear, in his agonised remorse, pictures himself as a man *wrenched* and tortured by an 'engine', beating at the gate (his head) that let his folly in. Goneril has power to *shake* his manhood; he complains that she has *struck* him with her tongue; the hot tears *break* from him; his heart, he says, *will break into a hundred thousand flaws*. Albany wonders how far Goneril's eyes may *pierce*. Gloucester's '*flaw'd heart*' is cracked, and finally it '*burst* smilingly'. Kent longs *to tread* Oswald into mortar, and in his heated description of the steward's character, he evokes images of rats *biting* cords, weathercocks *turning*, dogs *following* and geese being *driven*. '*'Tis worse than murder*', cries Lear, this *violent outrage* of putting Kent in the stocks, and his emotion on witnessing it *swells* and *climbs*, while the fool adds the picture of a man being dragged along by *holding on* when a great wheel *runs down hill*, and *letting go* only in time to save his *neck being broken*.

So also in scenes not directly concerned with Lear, such as Gloucester's conversations with Edmund, we find the same characteristic. When Edmund, having roused his father's anger against the unwitting Edgar, desires to restrain him from immediate action until he has furnished further proof of the latter's wickedness, he words his argument thus: If you will suspend your indignation until you have 'better testimony of his intent, you should *run a certain course*; where, if you *violently proceed against* him, mistaking his purpose, it would *make a great gap* in your own honour and *shake in pieces the heart* of his obedience!' And a little later, Gloucester being indeed shaken to the heart by Edmund's revelations, in the course of ten lines uses these verbs and nouns: *scourged, cools, falls off, divide, cracked, falls from bias, follow disquietly, mutinies, discord, machinations, hollowness, ruinous disorders.*

This use of verbs and images of bodily and generally anguished motion is almost continuous, and it is reinforced by similar words used in direct description, as in the treatment of Gloucester; he is *bound* to a chair, *plucked* by the beard, his hairs are *ravished* from his chin, he is *tied to a stake*, like a bear to *stand the course*, and with his eyes blinded and bleeding, he is *thrust out* of the gates to *smell his way* to Dover.

All through the play, the simplest abstract things are described in similar terms. Even in a scene, pleasant in itself, such as the gentleman's ornate but delightful description of Cordelia's reception of his news (4. 3), this sense of bodily movement and strain is constant. The letters *pierced* her to a demonstration of grief, her passion

K.L. 4. 3. 15

> most rebel-like
> Sought to be king o'er her;

it *moved* her, patience and sorrow *strove*, she *heaved* the name of 'father' *pantingly forth*, as if it *press'd her heart*;

she *shook* the tears from her eyes, and away she *started*

To deal with grief alone. *K.L.* 4. 3. 33

Look at the six lines which follow, in which Kent, having declared that Lear will not *yield* to see his daughter, describes his master's mental and emotional suffering in a series of pictures of physical buffeting, pain and opposition, which, in addition to the two images of brutal dogs and poisonous serpents, have a cumulative and almost overwhelming effect on the mind:

A sovereign shame so *elbows him*: his own unkindness 4. 3. 43–8
That *stripp'd* her from his benediction, *turn'd* her
To foreign casualties, . . .
. . . . these things *sting*
His mind so venomously, that *burning* shame
Detains him from Cordelia.

The idea of unnatural horrors, of human beings *preying on themselves* 'like monsters of the deep', or like wolves and tigers tearing one another's flesh, is also constantly before us. Lear is sure that Regan, when she hears how he has been mistreated, with 'her nails' will *flay* Goneril's *wolfish visage*; filial ingratitude is as if *the mouth should tear the hand*

For lifting food to't. 3. 4. 16

Gloucester boldly avows to Regan he has sent Lear to Dover because

I would not see *thy cruel nails* 3. 7. 56
Pluck out his *poor old eyes*, nor thy *fierce sister*
In his anointed flesh stick boarish fangs;

and Albany, crying to Goneril that she and Regan are 'tigers', not daughters, declares if he followed his inclination he would *dislocate* and *tear her flesh and bones*.

The large number of animal images, and their effect
in the play, have often been noticed (notably by Bradley,
Shakespearian Tragedy, pp. 266 ff.). I would only point
out here that in addition to the feeling they give us that
'humanity' is 'reeling back into the beast', they also,
because portrayed chiefly in angry or anguished action,
very distinctly augment the sensation of horror and
bodily pain. In addition to savage wolves, tigers and
other animals, there are *darting* serpents, a *sharp-toothed*
vulture and *detested* kite, *stinging* adders and insects,
gnawing rats, the *baited* bear, as well as *whipped*,
whining, *barking*, *mad* and *biting* dogs. All this helps
to create and increase an unparalleled atmosphere of
rapine, cruelty and bodily pain.

To this is added an overtone running through the
crisis of the tragedy, the fury of the elements, described,
be it remarked, wholly in terms of the human body.
They are *wild, fretful, unquiet*; the wind and rain are
to and fro conflicting; with these, the old king, with his
heart-struck injuries, is contending, tearing his white hair

K.L. 3. 1. 8
> Which the *impetuous* blasts, with *eyeless rage*,
> *Catch* in their *fury*;

and bidding the winds to blow and *crack their cheeks*,
until, at the height of his half-demented passion, he
3. 2. 7 commands the *all-shaking* thunder to '*smite flat* the
thick rotundity o' the world'. This last amazing image
is one of several in Shakespeare, notably in *Antony and
Cleopatra*, which evoke the spectacle of devastating
bodily action on so stupendous a scale that the emotions
which give rise to it are lifted to a similar terrific and
vast intensity. So the picture which follows here, of
the great gods, through the bursts of thunder and
groans of roaring wind and rain, remorselessly seeking

and finding out their enemies, while 'close *pent-up* guilts' *rive* their concealing continents, and *cry*

> These dreadful summoners grace, *K.L.* 3. 2. 59

seems natural and only in keeping with the feeling aroused in the imagination of a being or a force mighty enough to remould the shape of the globe with one resounding blow.

The sense of bodily torture continues to the end. Gloucester catches the recurrent theme of the tragedy, and crystallises it for ever in the terrible picture of men being torn limb from limb by the gods in sport, to whom they are but as 'flies to wanton boys'. Lear tells 4. 1. 37 Cordelia he is bound

> Upon a wheel of fire, that mine own tears 4. 7. 46
> Do scald like molten lead;

Edgar sees the gods making instruments of torture with which to plague men; and, at the close, when Kent, who loves him, breathes the only valediction possible over his dead master's body, it is still the same metaphor which rises to his lips:

> O, let him pass! he hates him 5. 3. 313
> That would upon the rack of this tough world
> Stretch him out longer.

The effect made upon us by studying the images in TIMON OF ATHENS *Timon of Athens* is as confusing and unsatisfactory as that of the play as a whole. They fall into approximately the usual proportions, and, with some marked exceptions, every single one of them is as clearly and characteristically Shakespeare's as if he had signed his name after each. Yet there is something strange and contradictory about their effect upon us when studied in a group.

This may be partly owing to the fact that side by side with some of the most 'sophisticated' images in Shakespeare we find a number of animal images crude and rough in style like those which have been supposed to be inserted by Greene or others in the early histories (such as 1 *H. VI*, 1. 5. 23–6, 30–2, 2. 2. 30; possibly 2. 4. 11–14); and these mostly occur in a scene (4. 3) practically the whole of which it is certain was written by Shakespeare, and from the continuity of the sense of the passage (4. 3. 327–53) it would seem that these must also be his. On the other hand, we find undoubted Shakespearian images in scenes, and even in passages, which it is impossible to believe were written entirely by him as they stand. So that the whole thing is a puzzle and leaves a confused effect upon the mind.

I will examine this question of authorship in detail elsewhere, merely stating here that my evidence leads me to assign to Shakespeare a much larger part of this incoherent and unsatisfactory play than has hitherto generally been attributed to him.

Our concern is now with the dominating image.

A recent critic,[1] in a most profound and suggestive essay on *Timon of Athens*, has said that 'gold-symbolism' is persistent, and, he suggests, dominant, throughout the play. This is a good example of how misleading it may be in a study of this sort to trust to the impression rather than to the fact. Undoubtedly gold is constantly spoken of and kept before our minds; in one scene alone (4. 3) the word is repeated twenty times, considerably more than in the whole of any other one play, there is a number of images (ten to be exact) of which gold is *Timon, 4. 3. 388, 390* the subject, such as 'delicate wooer', 'visible god',

[1] G. Wilson Knight in *The Wheel of Fire*, 1930, p. 256.

'touch of hearts', 'yellow slave', 'strong thief', and so on; the metal symbols, 'base metal', 'iron heart', 'flinty mankind', all hard and valueless, are clearly used in contrast to the idea of the precious quality of pure gold; *but there is only one image from gold throughout the play.* This is at the end of the first scene, when the richness and brilliance of Timon's surroundings are pictured to us with the flash of jewels and the beauty of art, culminating in the description of his bounty: *Timon,4.3.393, 32, 45; 3.3. 6; 3.4.84; 4.3.492*

> He pours it out; Plutus, the god of gold, *1.1.275*
> Is but his steward;

which leaves us with a vision of an endless stream of gold issuing from his hands in unmeasured abundance.

But gold, however much it may be emphasised, was not the *picture* which was constantly before Shakespeare's eyes as he threw himself into this story of man's greed and ingratitude. It was a quite different picture, but an extraordinarily characteristic one. I have already described it in detail (pp. 198–9). It is the imaginative picture always linked in Shakespeare's mind with the theme of false friends and flatterers, which is the subject of this play: dogs, fawning and eating and lapping, with 'gluttonous maws' devouring their 'lord's meat', eating remnants, licking sweets and melting the sugar. This is the picture which runs as an undertone throughout the whole play, in the way I have described it in pp. 198–9. *3.4.52*

The difference in imagery in the three Roman plays is arresting, and very indicative of the difference in mood and temper in which they were written. All three owe much to North's *Plutarch*, but the difference in the way the material is handled well repays close study.

JULIUS
CAESAR

Julius Caesar is straightforward, slow-moving, restrained, almost bare in style; it has relatively few images (less than half those in *Coriolanus*, and less than one-third those in *Antony and Cleopatra*), and a characteristic of these is that they are clear, definite, and worked out in a full and leisurely way.

Antony's comparison of Lepidus to the ass turned out to graze is a good example of the peculiar amplification and slow movement of these similes:

J.C. 4. 1. 19

And though we lay these honours on this man,
To ease ourselves of divers slanderous loads,
He shall but bear them as the ass bears gold,
To groan and sweat under the business,
Either led or driven, as we point the way;
And having brought our treasure where we will,
Then take we down his load and turn him off,
Like to the empty ass, to shake his ears
And graze in commons.

2. 1. 21
2. 1. 66
1. 3. 107
4. 2. 22
3. 1. 204
5. 3. 60
4. 3. 216
3. 1. 60

Others of like nature are the ladder of ambition, the state and kingdom of man, the bonfire, the likeness of 'hollow men' and prancing mettlesome horses, the stricken deer, the setting sun, the turn of the tide and the northern star.

There is no leading or floating image in the play; one feels it was not written under the particular stress of emotion or excitement which gives rise to a dominating image. There is, however, a certain persistence in the comparison of the characters to animals: Caesar is a wolf, a lion, a falcon, a serpent's egg, an adder, a stricken deer; the Romans are sheep and hinds and bees; the conspirators are apes and hounds; Brutus is a lamb; Lepidus is an ass, a horse; Metellus and Casca are curs; Cassius is a showy, mettlesome steed which fails at the moment of trial; and Octavius and Antony are bears tied to the stake. But this animal imagery is not nearly so marked as in either *King Lear* or *Othello*, and entirely lacks consistency of character, so that it fails to produce the cumulative effect so strongly felt in both those plays.

Coriolanus, however, has a central symbol, and a very CORIO-
LANUS definite one, but it is significant that this has not been born out of the creator's feeling of the tragedy; it has just been taken over by him wholesale, with much else, from North's *Plutarch*.

It is the old tale, with which the play opens, expounded by Menenius, of the rebellion of the various members of the body, the citizens, against the belly, the senate, which they accuse of being idle while they do all the work, and the belly's answer, somewhat developed by Shakespeare, that, on the contrary, it is the 'storehouse and the shop of the whole body', *Cor. 1. 1. 136* sending out, through rivers of blood, sustenance to all.

The images arising out of this central theme of the body and sickness are many, nearly one-fifth of the whole; and by means of them this idea is played upon throughout, though in a somewhat languid and artificial way.

The king, statesman, soldier, horse and trumpeter are compared to the head, eye and heart, arm, leg and tongue, and Menenius laughingly taunts one of the basest of the citizens with being the great toe of the rebellion. The people are the hands, the tribunes are the 'tongues o' the common mouth', or they are the *3. 1. 21* mouths themselves, as when Coriolanus, turning on them, asks,

You being their mouths, why rule you not their teeth? *3. 1. 36*

This conception is constantly with Coriolanus, as when he speaks of the 'navel' of the state, or asks,

Cor. 3. 1. 131   How shall this bosom multiplied digest
The senate's courtesy?

and goes on to tell the tribunes they are risking the giving of a dangerous drug to a body 'that's sure of death without it', recommending them at once to pluck out

3. 1. 156   The multitudinous tongue; let them not lick
The sweet which is their poison.

His action towards Rome is described by his mother as
5. 3. 102   'tearing his country's bowels out', and a similar image of hurt to the vitals of a body is used by Aufidius, when, after welcoming Coriolanus, he pictures the Volscians

4. 5. 132   pouring war
Into the bowels of ungrateful Rome.

Coriolanus refers to the people as
                                                  measles,
3. 1. 78   Which we disdain should tetter us, yet sought
The very way to catch them;

and their discontent is as self-made sores on the body,
1. 1. 168   brought about by 'rubbing the poor itch' of their opinion, and so making themselves scabs.
Coriolanus himself is represented by the tribunes as
3. 1. 222, 295,   a 'violent' disease, which spreads infection, and must be
310   cut away, whereas Menenius argues that he is a limb

3. 1. 296   that has but a disease,
Mortal, to cut it off; to cure it, easy;

and to Brutus's remark that when Coriolanus loved his country it honoured him, he answers drily,

3. 1. 306   The service of the foot
Being once gangrened, is not then respected
For what before it was.

The condition of the time is a 'violent fit' that craves *Cor.* 3. 2. 33 3. 1. 235 physic, a sore which needs a physician, for it cannot be cured by self-probing, and so on; it is wearisome to pursue the metaphor further, for it is a very obvious, and rather laboured and overworked one at best.

It obtrudes itself throughout the play; anyone on a first reading will notice and remember it, whereas it might be possible to know *King Lear* or *Macbeth* very well without consciously realising the dominating symbolic motives in these plays. That is because in them the symbols are the outcome of the imagination at white heat, and thus become one with the movement and characters and could be no other than they are.

So one feels, for example, that Coriolanus is called a diseased limb or a gangrened foot because it fits in with a preconceived design, whereas Kent, in his agonised grief, sees the death of Lear as the release of a tortured body from the rack, not because bodily struggle or torture has been the dominating symbol throughout, but because, after the experience of burning through

the fierce dispute
Betwixt damnation and impassion'd clay,

there was no other possible way to see it.

Keats's Sonnet On sitting down to read King Lear once again.

In *Antony and Cleopatra* we find ourselves emotionally in another world, in an entirely different atmosphere from that of the other two Roman plays. The difference in poetic fire between *Coriolanus* and *Antony and Cleopatra* is as if, in the one case, the poet's imagination had caught alight three or four times only, and in burning had scattered sparks in the neighbourhood, while, in the other, it is a pure flame driving throughout, fanned by emotion, whose heat purifies, fuses and transmutes into gold all kinds of material, and it is this fierce

ANTONY AND CLEOPATRA

atmospheric heat which creates the pictures, dominating and directing them.

The group of images in *Antony and Cleopatra* which, on analysis, immediately attracts attention as peculiar to this play, consists of images of the world, the firmament, the ocean and vastness generally. That is the dominating note in the play, magnificence and grandeur, expressed in many ways, and pictured by continually stimulating our imaginations to see the colossal figure of Antony, *A. and C. 1. 5.* 'demi-Atlas of this earth', 'triple pillar of the world', *23; 1. 1. 12* built on so vast a scale that the whole habitable globe is but a toy to him, as it were a ball or apple which he *3. 11. 64* quarters with his sword, playing with 'half the bulk of it' as he pleases, 'making and marring fortunes'.

Antony himself touches this note at once in his royal love-making, when he tells Cleopatra that if she would put a bourn to the measure of his love, she must *1. 1. 17* 'needs find out new heaven, new earth'.

Indeed, nothing short of the whole universe suffices for comparison with Antony, and in Cleopatra's lyrical elegies, wherein is concentrated all the passion and poetry of the most passionate and poetical of the plays, she likens him to one whose face was as the heavens,

5. 2. 79
                                        and therein stuck
A sun and moon, which kept their course and lighted
The little O, the earth.

In these soaring love laments she sees him and makes *4. 15. 63* us see him as a stupendous super-being, the 'crown o' *5. 2. 81* the earth', whose 'legs bestrid the ocean', whose 'rear'd arm crested the world', and whose qualities can be compared only to the vast elemental forces of nature; his voice, to friends, was propertied

A. and C.
5. 2. 83

As all the tuned spheres,...
But when he meant to quail and shake the orb,
He was as rattling thunder.

Even the verbs used of his aspect are such as are applicable to the sun and planets; when he smiles, he would *shine* on those

That make their looks by his; 1. 5. 56

and Alexas, lately come from him, is *gilded* with his *tinct*. 1. 5. 37
The perennial seasons themselves, with their wealth of association, become as mere adjectives to express the magnificence and scale of his bounty:

There was no winter in't; an autumn 'twas 5. 2. 87
That grew the more by reaping.

When, mortally wounded, he is borne aloft to her, Cleopatra calls on the sun to burn up the sphere in which it is fixed and so plunge the earth in darkness, and, when he dies, she knows there is

nothing left remarkable 4. 15. 67
Beneath the visiting moon.

Not only Cleopatra thinks of him thus; by a common instinct all who know him compare him to great natural phenomena. He is a 'mine of bounty', says Enobarbus; 4. 6. 32
in temper, reports Alexas,

Like to the time o' the year between the extremes 1. 5. 51
Of hot and cold, he was nor sad nor merry;

his faults in him, cries Lepidus,

seem as the spots of heaven, 1. 4. 12
More fiery by night's blackness;

and his messenger, Euphronius, is so conscious of his inferiority to his master, that he avows he was

A. and C.
3. 12. 8

> of late as petty to his ends
> As is the morn-dew on the myrtle-leaf
> To his grand sea.

When the battle goes against him, Scarus remarks,

3. 10. 6

> The greater cantle of the world is lost,
> ......we have kissed away
> Kingdoms and provinces;

and when he dies, so great a convulsion of nature is it that Caesar declares,

5. 1. 15

> the round world
> Should have shook lions into civil streets,
> And citizens to their dens. The death of Antony
> Is not a single doom; in the name lay
> A moiety of the world.

This vastness of scale is kept constantly before us by the use of the word 'world', which occurs forty-two times, nearly double, or more than double, as often as in most other plays,[1] and it is continually employed in a way which increases the sense of grandeur, power and space, and which fills the imagination with the conception of beings so great that physical size is annihilated and the whole habitable globe shrinks in comparison with them. Caesar, lamenting his differences with Antony, cries,

2. 2. 115

> if I knew
> What hoop should hold us stanch, from edge to edge
> O' the world I would pursue it;

and Octavia declares that wars between these two mighty ones, her husband and her brother, would be

3. 4. 31

> As if the world should cleave, and that slain men
> Should solder up the rift.

---

[1] In *Julius Caesar* 'world' occurs 17 times; in *Lear*, 18; in *Coriolanus*, 19; in *Othello*, 23; in *Hamlet*, 29.

The emotional effect of such a simile as this is incalculable, with its amazing picture of the gigantic gaping fissures in the round globe packed tight with the bodies of the dead. Were the feeling in it not so intense, it would verge on the grotesque, as do some others among these vast world images. Such, for instance, is the kind of huge gargoyle depicted by the saturnine Enobarbus when he hears that Caesar has deposed Lepidus, thus leaving only Antony and himself in power. He imagines them as the two mighty jaws in the world's face, grinding and destroying everything that comes between them, and exclaims,

> Then, world, thou hast a pair of chaps, no more; *A. and C.*
> And throw between them all the food thou hast, 3. 5. 14
> They'll grind the one the other.

Antony's imagination moves on this same vast plane, and the pictures that he draws stimulate our vision and keep us ever conscious of the puny size of even the greatest of worldly princes, powers and spaces compared to his stupendous force. Especially is this so when power is slipping from him, when the old lion is dying, and the tragedy is thus increased by contrast. With what a sublime sweep of simple words he sums up his earlier activities:

> I, that with my sword 4. 14. 57
> Quarter'd the world, and o'er green Neptune's back
> With ships made cities;

and how vivid is the picture of the kings of the earth starting forth at his call, like small boys in a scramble, crying out to know what is his will! When he is angry, the insolent magnificence of his images surpasses that of all others in Shakespeare. Thus, after his defeat at sea, when, furious with Caesar's messenger, he has him soundly whipped and bids him get back to his master,

he gives a characteristic picture in style and scale of
the reason why it is particularly easy just then to anger
him, for his 'good stars' that were his 'former guides'

A. and C.
3. 13. 143–7

Have empty left their orbs and shot their fires
Into the abysm of hell;

and when earlier, Cleopatra mischievously suggests that
Caesar has sent for him, the thunder of his reply in
majestic sweep and cadence still comes echoing down
the centuries:

I. I. 33

Let Rome in Tiber melt, and the wide arch
Of the ranged empire fall! Here is my space.

Through all the tragedies I have now traced the
recurring images which serve as 'motifs' in the plays.
My analysis is perhaps sufficient to show how definite
and how potent are these images within images, and
how profoundly we are influenced by the emotional
background which they call into being. No other
writer, so far as I know, certainly no other dramatist,
makes such continual use of the running and recurrent
symbol as does Shakespeare. Shelley, in his *Prometheus
Unbound*, perhaps comes nearest to it,[1] when he brings
out and emphasises, by means of his nature imagery,
certain philosophical and ethical thoughts; but the
Prometheus, though nominally a drama, is really a lyrical
poem in a single mood, which lends itself far more
readily to such continuity of symbolism than do Shakespeare's varied and tremendous dramas.

This method of working by way of suggestion,
springing from a succession of vivid pictures and concrete details, is, of course, of the very essence of
'romantic' art; and, in the case of Shakespeare, the

---

[1] See an article by me, 'De l'emploi du symbole dans la Poésie de
Shelley', in *La Revue Germanique*, Juillet–Août, 1912, p. 426.

poet's mind, unlike the dyer's hand, subdues to itself what it works in, and colours with its dominating emotion all the varied material which comes its way, colours it so subtly and so delicately that for the most part we are unconscious of what is happening, and know only the total result of the effect on our imaginative sensibility.

Hence it seems to me that a study of Shakespeare's imagery from the angle from which we have been looking at it in the latter part of this book helps us to realise a little more fully and accurately one of the many ways by which he so magically stirs our emotions and excites our imagination. I believe it not only does this, but sometimes even throws a fresh ray of light on the significance of the play concerned, and—most important of all—on the way Shakespeare himself saw it.

APPENDICES

APPENDIX I

Difficulties connected with the counting and classifying of images

T H E difficulties and problems connected with the counting and classifying of images could hardly be believed by one who has not experienced them. Probably no two people would entirely agree as to the number of images to be found in any one play. First, there is the question as to whether what we are considering is an 'image' at all, or not? Secondly, is it one image, or two, or three? Thirdly, is it one image with a subsidiary idea, and if this, how should it be classified?

As I worked, it soon became clear that some images, although they form only one image, must be entered, for purposes of reference, under two headings, one main heading and one subsidiary, the subsidiary one being called a 'cross-reference'. Thus

> The caterpillars of the commonwealth, *R. II, 2. 3. 166*
> Which I have sworn to weed and pluck away

has as a main heading, 'insects, caterpillars', and as a subsidiary heading or cross-reference, 'gardening, weeding'. But in the count of images in the play as a whole (in the charts or in tables) it is reckoned as one image only, under the heading of 'insects'. At the same time, in examining the 'leading motives' in the images, I have made full use of these 'cross-references'. For example, in *Hamlet*, I have quoted as showing Shakespeare's imaginative interest in disease or sickness, images such as

> O, my offence is rank, it smells to heaven, *Ham. 3. 3. 36*

which is really classified under 'senses, smell'; or

> diseases desperate grown *4. 3. 9*
> By desperate appliance are relieved
> Or not at all,

which has, as a main heading, 'proverbial'.

There are, however, some cases in which, when the image divides into two parts, it is difficult to say which, if either, is the more important. In these cases, I have arbitrarily chosen one element, generally the first named, and have listed it under that. Thus the following,

Per. 2. 3. 36

> To me he seems like *diamond* to *glass*,

is entered, as a main heading, under 'jewels, diamonds', and cross-referenced under 'substances, glass'.

Some images are, of course, very complicated as to the different elements contained in them; such is Lady Macbeth's query,

Mac. 1. 7. 35

> Was the hope drunk
> Wherein you dress'd yourself? hath it slept since?
> And wakes it now, to look so green and pale
> At what it did so freely?

This falls under the main heading of 'personification', and is so entered, but is cross-referenced under 'drunkenness', 'clothes', 'sleep' and 'turning pale'.

I can only explain as clearly as possible the method I have followed, with the reminder that the counting of images is an elusive and intangible task, differing entirely from the counting of concrete objects, and submit for what they may be worth the following figures as the result of my own personal count. It must be remembered that any count of this kind, however carefully done, must to some extent be an approximate one, dependent on the literary judgment and methods of the person who has compiled it. The safeguard of this particular count is that it has all been done by the same person and on the same method. So, on the whole, we may assume that the results and general proportions are sound.

APPENDIX II

The total number of images in each of Shakespeare's plays

SHAKESPEARE'S plays in approximate chronological order, showing the total number of images in each:

	No. of images	No. of lines in play[1]
Love's Labour's Lost	204	2651
Two Gentlemen	102	2193
Comedy of Errors	60	1753
Romeo and Juliet	204	2989
1 Henry VI	152	2676
2 Henry VI	185	3069
3 Henry VI	200	2904
Richard III	234	3600
Richard II	247	2755
Titus Andronicus	151	2522
The Merchant of Venice	136	2554
King John	248	2570
A Midsummer Night's Dream	133	2102
All's Well	151	2738
Taming of the Shrew	92	2552
1 Henry IV	207	2968
2 Henry IV	235	3180
Merry Wives	103	2634
Henry V	224	3166
Much Ado	164	2535
As You Like It	180	2608
Twelfth Night	131	2429
Julius Caesar	83	2450
Hamlet	279	3762
Troilus and Cressida	339[2]	3329
Othello	192	3229
Measure for Measure	136	2660

[1] Taken from Hart's count from Cambridge ed. 1863–6, in *Review of English Studies*, Jan. 1932, p. 21.

[2] The largest number in any one play.

	No. of images	No. of lines in play
Macbeth	208	2084
King Lear	193	3205
Timon of Athens	139	2299
Pericles	118	2331
Antony and Cleopatra	266	3016
Coriolanus	189	3279
Cymbeline	187	3264
Winter's Tale	155	2925
Tempest	103	2015
Henry VIII	182	2807
Sonnets	296	
Venus and Adonis	229	
Lucrece	305	

APPENDIX III

The works of the twelve contemporary dramatists which have been examined and from which the images have been assembled, classified and compared with Shakespeare:

MARLOWE (Clarendon Press. Ed. Tucker Brooke. To conform with the Shakespearian text, I have modernised the spelling)

The first and second parts of *Tamburlaine*.
Edward II.
Hero and Leander.
The Jew of Malta (omitting all prose).
Faustus (omitting all prose).
Dido (the better authenticated parts).
The Massacre at Paris (only the long opening speech of Guise).

KYD (Temple edition. Clarendon Press)

The Spanish Tragedy.   *Soliman and Perseda.*

LYLY (Clarendon Press. Ed. Warwick Bond)
  The Woman in the Moon.   *Endimion.*
  Midas.

GREENE (Clarendon Press. Ed. Collins)
  James IV.   *Alphonsus King of Arragon.*
  Friar Bacon and Friar Bungay.   *Orlando Furioso.*

PEELE (1–3, Routledge. 4, Malone Society)
  The Arraignment of Paris.   *David and Bethsabe.*
  The Old Wives Tale.   *Edward the First.*

DEKKER (Mermaid edition)
  The Shoemaker's Holiday.
  Old Fortunatus.
  The Honest Whore, parts I and II.
  The Witch of Edmonton.

BEN JONSON (Mermaid edition)
  Every Man in his Humour.   *Sejanus.*
  Every Man out of his Humour.   *Cynthia's Revels.*
  Volpone.

HEYWOOD (Mermaid edition)
  A Woman Killed with Kindness.   *The English Traveller.*
  The Fair Maid of the West.   *Lucrece.*
  The Wise Woman of Hogsden.

CHAPMAN (Mermaid edition)
  Bussy D'Ambois.   *Byron's Tragedy.*
  The Revenge of Bussy.   *All Fools.*
  Byron's Conspiracy.

BEAUMONT AND FLETCHER (Mermaid edition)
  Philaster.   *Valentinian.*
  The Maid's Tragedy.   *The Faithful Shepherdess.*
  Bonduca.

MASSINGER (Mermaid edition)
  The Duke of Florence.   *The Fatal Dowry.*
  The Duke of Milan.   *The Guardian.*
  The Roman Actor.

APPENDIX IV

A detailed analysis of the subject-matter of the images in *Romeo and Juliet* and *Hamlet*

I THINK it may be of interest to give the detailed analysis of the subject-matter of the images in two of the plays I am discussing (*Romeo and Juliet* and *Hamlet*), as these serve as samples of the kind of way each play has been analysed.

It will be noticed that in each play, as in nearly all Shakespeare's, the images from 'nature' and 'animals' are very high in number (animals generally come second in this respect, but are displaced in *Romeo and Juliet* by the large number of personifications, many of them of 'light and darkness'). In *Hamlet* 'sickness and medicine' furnish the large number of twenty (in *Romeo and Juliet* eight). In *Romeo and Juliet* the images from 'fire and light' come next in number to 'animals'.

ROMEO AND JULIET. 204 IMAGES

NATURE 39:

Gardening 11: canker 3 (canker'd with peace, bud bit by envious worm, the canker death), buds 2 (fresh female buds, bud of love), rose, flower, ripeness, medlars, thorn, mandrake.

Sea 9: love a sea, boundless and deep as the sea, more inexorable, steer ship, adventure for merchandise, top-gallant, ship in storm, bark on rocks, see into the bottom.

Weather 7: lightning 2, clouds and dew, wind-swift, storm, mist, frost on flower.

Celestial bodies 7: stars 3 (earth-treading, fairest stars in heaven, cut him out in little stars), sunrise, sunbeams, meteor, sunset and dew.

Elements 3: deep as a well, springs, thin of substance as the air.

Seasons 1: April after winter.

Farming 1: scarecrow (crow-keeper).

PERSONIFICATION 23 (note how many are of 'light and darkness'): winds hissing in scorn, *sun peering from the window of the east*, love sees without eyes, masks kissing ladies' brows, wind wooing the frozen north, desire on his death-bed, echo's airy tongue, *grey-eyed morn smiles on the frowning night, darkness like a drunkard, sun's eye*, care keeping watch, night a sober-suited matron, happiness in her best array, jocund day stands tiptoe, dry sorrow drinks our blood, death a lover 3, heart the bosom's lord, woe delights in fellowship, *sun hiding head*, that word 'banished' hath slain ten thousand Tybalts, sun and envious moon.

ANIMALS 21:

> Birds 10: swan and crow, dove trooping with crows, cockerel, wild goose, bird on a string, raven 2, eagle, love's wings, borrow Cupid's wings.
>
> Four-footed 4: lamb 2, beast, tigers.
>
> Insects 3: gossamer, carrion-flies, flies.
>
> Fabulous 2: dragon, cockatrice.
>
> Reptiles 2: toad, serpent.

FIRE AND LIGHT 12:

> A fire sparkling, quench fire with fountains, love a smoke, ashes 2, lovers see by their own beauties, lamps by day, daylight shames a lamp, night's candles, lantern, eyes stream with light, 'Romeo...thou day in night'.

FOOD AND COOKING 11:

> Gall, preserving sweet, sweet and gall, sweet and sour, dried herring, hare in pie, honey, milk, beat as addle as an egg, gorge and cram, season with salt.

CLASSES AND TYPES 11:

> Prisoner 2 (in twisted gyves, 'to prison, eyes'), heretics, pilgrims, idiot (drivelling love like a great natural), fool, madman, usurer, sinners, heralds, executioner.

WAR AND WEAPONS 10:

> Siege 2 (of loving terms, of grief), opposing camps, general, ensign, fire and powder, gun, powder in a skilless soldier's flask, cannon, dart.

SICKNESS AND MEDICINE 8:

Blindness 2, love a madness, cure one grief with another,
infection and poison, wound ('he jests at scars'), stab and
shoot, poison.

DOMESTIC 7:

Scales, bench, curtain, wash, dish-clout, window, door.

SPORT AND GAMES 7:

Archery 2, fishing (steal love's bait from fearful hooks), falconry 2 (lure this tassel-gentle, hood my unmann'd blood),
bird-nesting, tennis (as swift a motion as a ball...bandy
her to my sweet love).

BODY AND BODILY ACTION 5:

Action 4: burden 2 (sink under, pack of blessings), shake off
yoke, they stumble that run fast.
Parts of Body 1: seal mouth.

PROVERBIAL 5:

Fire burns out fire, turn backwards to cure giddiness, they
are beggars that can count their worth, as full as an egg
with meat, sharp sauce to sweet goose.

RELIGION AND SUPERSTITION 5:

Angel (winged messenger of heaven), fiend angelical, fiend
in mortal paradise, wide as a church door, round worm
pricked from the lazy finger of a maid.

CLASSICAL 4:

Cupid, Aurora, Phoebus and Phaeton, Venus.

HUMAN RELATIONS 4:

Schoolboys, child that hath new robes, childhood, marriage
(wedded to calamity).

BOOKS AND READING 4:

Volume of young Paris' face, read by rote, vile book fairly
bound, writ in sour misfortune's book.

LAW 3:   sign deed 2, fee-simple.

BUILDINGS 3:   mansion 2 (I have bought the mansion of a love, sack the hateful mansion), deceit in gorgeous palace.

SUBSTANCES 3:   wax, lead 2 (soul of lead, heavy...as lead).

CLOTHES 3:   night's cloak, a wit of cheveril (gloves?), pale as any clout.

JEWELS 2:   agate-stone, rich jewel in an Ethiop's ear.

MUSIC 2:   lovers' tongues like softest music, ballad of King Cophetua.

THEATRE 2:   prologue and prompter, mask of night.

INDOOR GAMES 2:   dun in the mire, gambling (lose a winning match played for a pair of stainless maidenhoods).

ONE EACH 8:
Birth: earth nature's mother, etc.
Death: knell.
Royalty: honour crowned sole monarch.
Science: centre (turn back, dull earth, and find thy centre out).
Topical: conduit.
Facts from Books: Laura a kitchen-wench, Dido a dowdy, etc.
Money: tribute.
Emblem: Cupid with bow.

HAMLET. 279 IMAGES

NATURE 32:

Gardening 11:   weeds 2 (unweeded garden, 'do not spread the compost on the weeds to make them ranker'), violet, rose, canker 2, thorns ('prick and sting'), inoculate old stock, shake fruit from tree ('like fruit unripe sticks to the tree but fall unshaken when they mellow be'), palm tree, cut off in blossoms.

Weather 8:   wind 2 (whirlwind, wind of blame), clouds and sun, sky, rain, frost, snow, ice.

Sea 4:   'post haste and romage', draw into a gulf, 'ocean eats not the flats with more impetuous haste', quick sail.

Celestial bodies 2:   stars 2.

Seasons 2:   'it must follow as the night the day', 'flush as May'.

Elements 2: currents turn awry, 'it is as the air invulnerable!'
Shadow 1: 'a shadow's shadow'.
Farming 1: 'mildewed ear'.
Natural features 1: 'a sterile promontory'.

ANIMALS 27:

Birds 11: pelican, dove, chough, lapwing, hawk and heron, eyases, brood and hatch, new hatched and unfledged, moult, wing 2 (hot love on the wing, wings as swift as meditation, etc.).

Four-footed 9: dogs 2 (tarre them to controversy, fawning), porcupine, mole, donkey, ape, Hyrcanian tiger, tether, feed on moor.

Reptiles 2: serpent, adders.

Insects 2: flies ('buzzers to infect his ear'), water-fly.

Fish 2: crab, shark.

Fabulous 1: mermaid-like.

SPORT AND GAMES 22:

Archery 3 (shot mine arrow o'er the house, arrows too slightly timbered, 'as level to your judgement pierce'), hunting 4 (cries on havoc, cry counter, recover the wind, hunts the trail of policy), riding (crack the wind), fencing ('fell incensed points'), fishing 2 (angle, bait), coursing ('coted'), bird-snaring 3 (springes to catch woodcocks, limed soul, 'as a woodcock to mine own springe'), falconry 3 (checking at, pitch, French falconers), wrestling, football, bowls 2 (rub, assays of bias).

BODY, SENSES AND SLEEP 21:

Action 9: tear a passion to tatters, shove, cleave and throw away, bear burden, cry, peep, climbing (steep and thorny road to heaven), walking 2 (sweep way, beaten way).

Parts 7: 'make milch the burning eyes of heaven', head and hand, teeth and forehead of our faults, womb of earth, brow of woe, body and soul, soul and limbs ('brevity is the soul of wit').

Senses 3: smell 2 (offence is rank...smells to heaven, perfume), sound (grating harshly).

Sleep 2: sleep of death...what dreams may come, dream.

SICKNESS AND MEDICINE 20:

Contagious blastments, tent, purgation, physic, apoplexy, ulcer 2 ('skin and film the ulcerous place', 'the quick o' the ulcer'), foul disease, imposthume that inward breaks, cicatrice, pleurisy, hectic in the blood, wounded name, blister on forehead, vicious mole, mote to trouble the mind's eye, galled chilblain, stitch (spend-thrift sigh), 'sicklied o'er with the pale cast of thought', poison of deep grief.

(See also under other headings, Ossa like a wart (Classical), desperate diseases (Proverbial), thoughtsick (Personification), offence is rank (Senses).)

FOOD AND DRINK 18:

Appetite, distill'd to jelly, dram of eale, sate and prey on garbage, curdle milk, caviare, sallets, gall, sugar over, suck honey, stew, roast, bake, digest, carve, fruit to feast, wholesome as sweet, fermenting beer ('a kind of yeasty collection').

CLASSES AND TYPES 13:

Prisoner 3 (a prison, put fetters round, take prisoner), beggars, slave, mutines in the bilboes, thief (cutpurse), soldiers, sergeant, watchman, journeyman, emperor, harbingers.

WAR, WEAPONS AND EXPLOSIVES 12:

Siege 2, single spies, armour. Daggers 2, slings and arrows. Shooting, cannon 2, trigger, 'the engineer hoist with his own petard'.

PERSONIFICATION 12:

Morn in russet mantle clad, sepulchre oped his jaws, the monster Custom, Amazement, Sea and Wind contending, Heaven blushing and Earth thought-sick, Ophelia's garments heavy with their drink, stars like wonder-wounded hearers, Death feasting, Peace with wheaten garland, Guilt unkennelling itself, Woes treading on each other's heels.

CLASSICAL 12:

'Hyperion to a Satyr', 'Niobe all tears', Hercules, Nemean lion, Lethe wharf, Cyclops and Mars, Vulcan's stithy, Hyperion and Jove, Mars, 'the herald Mercury', Pelion and Olympus, Ossa.

DOMESTIC 11:

Scales 2 (turn the beam, equal scales), mirror 2 (glass of fashion, hold the mirror up to nature), washing (wring), dirt 3 (the people muddied, 'soil nor cautel', 'slight sullies'), spill, lock and key, bar door.

SUBSTANCES AND METALS 7:

Sponge 2, wax. Metal 3 (unimproved metal, metal more attractive, ore among base metals), quicksilver.

HUMAN RELATIONS 7:

Baby 3, harlot, drab, bawds, woman's love.

CRAFTS AND TOOLS 7:

Out of frame, hoop with steel, varnish, rough hew, dyeing, dull edge, whet.

RELIGION, BIBLICAL AND SUPERSTITION 6:

Hell 2 (black as hell, loosed from hell to speak of horrors), temple, Jephthah, wheel bowled down hill 2.

LAW 6:

Seal 3, audit, summons, brokers.

MUSIC 6:

Keep time, pipe 2 (pipe for fortune's finger, play upon me know my stops), tune, trumpet, sweet bells jangled.

FIRE AND LIGHT 5:

Blazes, false fire, sprinkle water on, dout, snuff.

THEATRE 4:

Prologue 2, audience, vice.

MONEY 4:

Tenders not sterling, stamp, cracked in the ring, purse is empty.

ROADS AND TRAVEL 4:

Posting, undiscovered country, whips 2.

ART 3:

heraldry (total gules), painted cloth, painting of a sorrow.

SCIENCE 3:

star out of sphere, 'out of thy star', geometry.

PROVERBIAL 3:

false as dicers' oaths, galled jade, desperate diseases need desperate remedies.

CLOTHES 2:
  button in cap, ribbon in cap.
INDOOR GAMES 2:
  blindman's buff, gambling
JEWELS 2:
  brooch, carbuncles.
BOOKS 2:
  table of my memory, comma.
ONE EACH 6:
  Topical: 'the spring that turneth wood to stone'.
  Life: 'my bedded hair, like life in excrements'.
  Death: 'black as death'.
  Buildings: roof.
  Facts from books: the famous ape.
  Town life: gates and alleys.

APPENDIX V

Notes on the Charts

CHARTS I, II and III are intended to be looked at together. They have been drawn in order to show the reader in a quickly grasped visual form the outstanding difference in the subjects and interests which came most readily to the minds and imaginations of Shakespeare, Marlowe and Bacon. In order to bring the work of the three writers more nearly into proportion, the subject-matter of the images from five only of Shakespeare's plays has been compared with that from the whole of Marlowe's work, and practically the whole of Bacon's. Notice the different proportion of images drawn by Shakespeare and Marlowe from such subjects as 'Classical', 'Sport and Games', 'Sickness', 'Jewels', 'Plants and Growing Things', 'Birds' and so on. Also the difference between Shakespeare and Bacon as to the amount they draw on 'Animals' (especially 'Birds'), 'Science', 'Food', 'Classes and Types of People'. When one remembers that Bacon's work is in prose, his small number of 'Imaginative' images is easily understood.

CHART IV is drawn in order to show the different proportions of interests in the minds of Shakespeare and five contemporary dramatists as seen in one special small group of images: those listed under 'Daily Life'. The five plays of Shakespeare of which the images are here examined are *Romeo and Juliet*, *Macbeth*, *As You Like It*, *A Winter's Tale*, and *Richard III*; the images from other dramatists are drawn from their plays listed on pp. 360–1 above. Under the heading of 'Daily Life' come:

1. *Sport and Games*, which include images from bird-snaring (traps, lime and nets), rabbit-snaring, falconry, hunting, fishing, bear-baiting, tilting, wrestling, fencing, archery (when it seems to be the sport of aiming and hitting the mark rather than the use of the bow and arrow in war), riding and outdoor games.

2. *Classes and Types*. This includes images drawn from various classes and types of human beings, such as pedlars, gypsies and beggars, slaves, prisoners and thieves, orators, ambassadors and preachers, sinners, fools and traitors, soldiers and sailors. This is a favourite kind of image with most of the Elizabethan dramatists and often a very effective one, as when Hastings in his bitter disillusionment likens the man who trusts in Gloucester's fair looks to

R. III, 3. 4. 101

> a drunken sailor on a mast,
> Ready, with every nod, to tumble down
> Into the fatal bowels of the deep.

R. and J.
1. 5. 96

or Romeo describes his lips as 'two blushing pilgrims' and Juliet declares she would have him go no further from her than a wanton's bird on a string,

2. 2. 180

> Like a poor prisoner in his twisted gyves.

3. *Trades and Crafts*, as distinct from 'Classes' (tinker, tailor, smith, etc.), represent, on the whole, images which refer to a process or characteristic of some special occupation or craft;

All's Well,
4. 3. 75
W. T. 4. 4. 387

such as 'the web of our life is of a mingled yarn, good and ill together', 'by the pattern of mine own thoughts I cut out the purity of his'.

4. *War and Weapons*. Under this heading fall the large number of images of a siege (the siege of love, the siege 'of battering days', the 'siege of grief'), of a breach in a fortification, of troops and soldiers on a battlefield, of prisoners of war,

sentinels, spies, of barricades and defences, of ambushes, of forts and fortifications, of flags and standards, and of all kinds of weapons, arrows, battering rams, daggers, spears, lances, swords, etc., of armour, of explosives, cannon, mines, bullets and gunpowder.

5. *Substances* are images which refer to an object from the point of view of its quality, consistency or texture: crystal, wax, sponge, straw, marble, and the like. This is also, and especially in Shakespeare's hands, a common and very effective type of image, 'my kingdom stands on brittle glass', 'hearts as false as stairs of sand', 'this hand as soft as dove's down', etc.

R. III, 4. 2. 63
M. of V. 3. 2. 83
W. T. 4. 4. 368

6. *Money and Merchandise.*

7. *Topical* and (11) *Town Life* are, of course, closely allied. Generally speaking, under 'Topical' I have grouped references to some local or contemporary event, place, custom or person, which would be known to an Elizabethan audience. Such are monsters painted on a pole, the smell of Bucklersbury, the forfeits in a barber's shop and so on. It will be noticed that Ben Jonson has the greatest number of 'Topical' images, Dekker and Shakespeare come next, while the other four playwrights have none at all.

8. *Roads and Travel.* This heading covers all things which might be seen or experienced on the road or in travelling; a highway, dust blown in the face, posting, harness, whips and curbs, losing the way, and so on.

9. *Buildings.*

10. *State and Royalty.*

11. *Town Life.* Under this heading come things more specially to be seen in the streets, such as shop-windows, crowds and throngs of people, signs, taverns and alehouses.

CHART V. The range and subjects of Shakespeare's images. The grouping, on the whole, I think, explains itself. There are certain points which may strike the reader as strange, such as 'War' under 'Daily Life'. 'War' includes 'weapons'; and, as 'daggers' or 'arrows' appear to form part of an Elizabethan's daily life, there seemed no more suitable place to put it— except possibly under 'Arts', which, in other ways, would be misleading.

APPENDIX VI

Note on the 'martlet' image

THE 'martlet' or swallow image is a good example of the way in which an examination of the images may conceivably lead us on to the discovery, not only of ideas working in Shakespeare's mind, but also of facts and incidents of his life. Let me just tell the story of the swallows. From my experience of Shakespeare's methods I was convinced that the vivid picture of the masses of swallows' nests on the outer walls of Macbeth's castle was not purely imagination on his part, but that he had somewhere *seen* such nests on a castle's walls, and that they had called up in his mind reflections on the contrast between the bird and his fragile nest and the massive walls of the castle fortress he had so boldly and trustingly chosen for his home. I began therefore to look about for such a castle that he could easily have seen in his youth. I tried both Kenilworth and Warwick with no success; no swallows build on either of them, nor is there any tradition that they have ever done so. I then thought of another castle, not so very far from Stratford, which Shakespeare gives unmistakable evidence that he had seen and noticed.

This is Berkeley Castle in Gloucestershire. Holinshed, in his history of Richard II, has but passing references to the 'castell of Berkelie' where the Duke of York stayed to receive the king on his way back through Wales from Ireland. Shakespeare, in his play, deliberately lays a scene in the 'wilds of Gloucestershire' (*R. II*, 2. 3), through which Bolingbroke and Northumberland with their soldiers make their way from the north towards Berkeley Castle. The road and landscape are described, the 'high wild hills and rough uneven ways', and presently Northumber-

R. II, 2. 3. 51 land asks 'How far is it to Berkeley?' to which Harry Percy answers 'There stands the castle, by yon tuft of trees', clearly showing that Shakespeare knew the aspect of the castle as it appears when viewed from a road coming towards Berkeley from the north 'from Ravenspurgh to Cotswold' (*R. II*, 2. 3. 9). The 'tuft of trees' is to this day a landmark of the site of the castle. (See photograph opposite.)

It would seem almost certain from the Gloucestershire scenes in 2 *Henry IV*, that Shakespeare was familiar with the neighbourhood of Berkeley, for he speaks of 'William Visor of Woncot' (Woodmancote) and 'Clement Perkes o' the Hill' (as Stinchcombe Hill is called locally). Vizor or Vizard is the name of a local family, and on Stinchcombe Hill there is a site of a house formerly belonging to a family called 'Purchase' or 'Perkes'. (For fuller detail of all this see *The Diary of Master William Silence* by Madden, 1897, pp. 86–7 and 372–4, Note vii, 'Shakespeare and Gloucestershire'. Also *A Glossary of the Cotswold (Gloucestershire) Dialect* by Richard Webster-Huntley, 1868, Note, pp. 22–3.) It is certainly interesting that one of the most persistent beliefs concerning Shakespeare is the local tradition that he passed some part of his early life—probably with cousins—in Dursley, which is a small town about five miles from Berkeley on the further side of Stinchcombe Hill (see Madden, p. 88). Quite a body of evidence has been collected bearing on Shakespeare's connection with and knowledge of Gloucestershire, which is summarised by Madden (pp. 372–4), and there would undoubtedly seem to be good ground for believing that he had seen Berkeley Castle and was familiar with its surroundings.

Having come to this conclusion, I next enquired at Berkeley Castle itself from the present Lord Berkeley's private secretary, Mr O'Flynn, whether swallows built their nests on the front of the castle. He replied that they did not, nor was there any tradition that they had done so. So I felt discouraged, and yet all the time I had a strong feeling that Berkeley was the place I was looking for. In the meantime I explained to Mr O'Flynn my reason for the query, and he was much interested. In a few weeks' time he wrote to me again, and said he happened to have been reading the life of Edward Jenner, the great doctor and discoverer of the system of inoculation; and in that life he had found a reference to an entry in the *Note Books* of Jenner, in which, on a visit to Berkeley, he notes on June 9th, 1787, examining the martins' nests on the castle, and records that they 'exhibit every variety with regard to the forwardness of eggs'. Edward Jenner, who was a native of Berkeley, of which place his father was Vicar, was a scientist and a keen observer of birds (it was he who reported to the Royal Society in 1787 the murderous activities of the young cuckoo in the nest), so we may take this entry of his about the martins' nests as reliable evidence that as late as 1787, at any rate, there were large numbers of martin's nests on the castle walls. In view of this testimony I returned, therefore, with renewed enthusiasm, to my theory that Shakespeare had visited Berkeley Castle, and had there been struck by the masses of martins' or swallows' nests on its walls.

As to the reason of his going there, many suppositions suggest themselves. Henry, the Lord Berkeley of Shakespeare's day, was a very great lord, who lived at his magnificent castle in great state and feudal style. He maintained an imposing retinue, travelled with a hundred and fifty servants, and three hundred persons dined daily at the castle. He had a park of fine red deer, and was passionately fond of fox hunting, deer hunting and hawking. He was also fond of the drama, and kept a company of players, 'Lord Berkeley's Men', who played in different parts of the country, once in London in 1581, and at Bristol, Bath and Barnstaple. They also played at Stratford-on-Avon in 1580-1, and again in 1582-3[1], when Shakespeare was between sixteen and seventeen, and eighteen and nineteen years old. Berkeley is only about fifty miles by road from Stratford, quite an easy ride or a possible walk for a young and active man. It will be noticed that the time of the second visit of Lord Berkeley's players to Stratford coincides with the year of Shakespeare's marriage and the year after it, when he may well have been troubled about some means of a livelihood, and have been feeling restless and discontented. It seems not impossible that he may have accompanied the players back to Berkeley, and have stayed there for a time. The state and magnificence of the life at Berkeley Castle would fully furnish the experience of a great house, a patron and cultivated society which is looked for by

[1] See *The Elizabethan Stage* by E. K. Chambers, vol. II, pp. 103-4.

biographers of Shakespeare. (See, for instance, Mr Gray's arguments in favour of Shakespeare having been a page in the household of Sir Henry Goodere at Polesworth. *A Chapter in the Early Life of Shakespeare*, by Arthur Gray, Cambridge University Press, 1926.) All this is, of course, the merest supposition and conjecture, based on the frail evidence of swallows' nests, but it seems to me a likely possibility, and to have nothing serious against it.

I had hoped to have the opportunity myself to examine the household records which are still in existence at Berkeley Castle, but unfortunately I have not been able to obtain permission to do this, so I have to leave the matter in an inconclusive state.

APPENDIX VII

Note on images as a revelation of character in the dramas

THERE are, of course, other ways (besides by their purely aesthetic qualities) in which the images, considered from the point of view of their subject-matter only, add in tone and quality to the richness and the meaning of Shakespeare's plays, but the 'leading motive', emphasised by the repetition of certain kinds of images, is so very much the most important that I have given all my space to the description of it.

Other interesting functions of the images which I may just note here are (1) their cumulative effect in conveying emotion or tension, which I touch upon in speaking of the grouping of the images in the *Merchant of Venice* (pp. 280–4); (2) their aid to the revelation of the temperament and character of the person using them. This is most interesting, and might well be developed further. For instance, take Falstaff's images in the two parts of *Henry IV*. I do not think it is fanciful when I say that they distinctly indicate a change in the character of the fat knight.

In the first part of *Henry IV* one might argue, only from the images he uses, that Falstaff is a man of parts, of wit, sweet

temper and charm, and of some reading and culture. One rarely
finds facts from books or drama referred to by Shakespeare in
his imagery, yet four of such images, out of a total of five in
this play, are Falstaff's. He calls Mistress Quickly 'Dame
Partlet the hen' (from either Reynard the Fox or Chaucer),
compares himself to Turk Gregory (probably from Fox's *History*,
or possibly from an old tragedy), and speaks in 'King Cambyses'
vein' (alluding to the old play of Preston's *Cambyses*, 1570).
He has some knowledge too of the romances, for his name for
Bardolph, 'the Knight of the Burning Lamp' is a skit (like the
Knight of the Burning Pestle later) on the heroes of the old
romances, he refers to the Knight of the Sun in a Spanish
romance (1 *H. IV*, 1. 2. 16) and in his jesting recommendation to
the prince that when he is king, 'let not us that are squires of
the night's body be called thieves of the day's beauty: let us be
Diana's foresters, gentlemen of the shades, minions of the moon',
he reveals, not only a feeling for and knowledge of chivalry and
pageantry, but also a very charming gift of poetical expression.
He has some acquaintance with the classics, and declares that he
is as 'valiant as Hercules'. Apart from his image drawn from
Pharaoh's lean kine, it is certain from his language that he knows
his Bible well (1 *H. IV*, 2. 4. 456, etc.). He clearly also knows
his Lyly and enjoys the humour of the far-fetched comparisons,
which he copies (1 *H. IV*, 2. 4. 427, 439); he appreciates the
'drone of a Lincolnshire bagpipe' (1 *H. IV*, 1. 2. 82); he also
notices pictures, a trait rare on the whole in Shakespeare, and
refers, evidently with intimate knowledge, to Lazarus in the
painted cloth, and to Dives, who lived in purple, burning in his
robes. His, too, are the only images from heraldry in the play,
honour is a 'mere scutcheon', and his soldier's half shirt is 'two
napkins tacked together and thrown over the shoulders like a
herald's coat without sleeves'.

We notice in both parts of *Henry IV* in Falstaff's images the
signs of the sportsman and lover of animals, sensitive to their
feelings and conscious of their point of view, the knowledge of
the ways of the timorous wild duck (1 *H. IV*, 2. 2. 104) and the
'struck fowl' who fear the report of the gun (1 *H. IV*, 4. 2. 19),

Marginal references (left column):

1 H. IV, 3. 3. 57

5. 3. 46

2. 4. 413

3. 3. 30

1. 2. 26

2. 4. 290

5. 1. 142
4. 2. 45

the driven flock of wild geese (1 *H. IV*, 2. 4. 148) and their tendency to get together (2 *H. IV*, 5. 1. 75), the young dace which serves as bait for the old pike (2 *H. IV*, 3. 2. 350), the ways of a Barbary hen (2 *H. IV*, 2. 4. 104), the love of a cat for cream (1 *H. IV*, 4. 2. 61) and the gentleness and charm of a puppy greyhound (2 *H. IV*, 2. 4. 103).

I do not think it is mere chance that Falstaff's images in the second part of the play show less trace of genuine feeling, cultivation and reading, and partake more of grotesqueness and ribaldry than in the first part. Witty they always are, for else Falstaff would no longer be Falstaff, but I believe that, in the course of the two plays, Shakespeare definitely pictured a certain deterioration of spirit in the fat knight which is subtly reflected in his images.

One may compare, for instance, the charm of tone of his jesting reference to romance and the moon (1 *H. IV*, 1. 2. 26) already quoted, with the roughness of his semi-satirical threat later to Prince John, that if his valour be not recognised he will have a ballad made to commemorate his deeds 'with mine own picture on the top on't, Coleville kissing my foot: to the which course if I be enforced, if you do not all show like gilt twopences to me, and I in the clear sky of fame o'ershine you as much as the full moon doth the cinders of the element, which show like pins' heads to her, believe not the word of the noble' (2 *H. IV*, 4. 3. 49).

As in the first part, the only two biblical images in the play are his (a comparison with Job and with the glutton in hell) and he alludes to Shallow as a 'Vice's dagger', but otherwise, with the exception of his calling his tailor 'a whoreson Achitophel', we find in his images in 2 *H. IV* no references to books or drama, chivalry or painting.

On the other hand, there is quite a number of grotesque—and if not 'unsavoury' (1 *H. IV*, 1. 2. 85) then of rough and somewhat coarse—similes, as in his anger with his tailor, who, instead of sending him satin, has the nerve to demand 'security', which calls forth Falstaff's curse 'Let him be damned like the glutton, pray God his tongue be hotter!' and later his

2 *H. IV*, 3. 2. 337

1. 2. 39

1. 2. 38

double-edged description of how he may 'sleep in security'
(2 *H. IV*, 1. 2. 50). His pungent pictures of Shallow's temperament and appearance and of Bardolph's face (2 *H. IV*, 2. 4.
350) are also of this nature.

The brilliant flashes of wit which light up a whole scene are
in the second as well as the first part, as when he describes him-
2 H. IV, *1. 2. 13* self walking in front of his diminutive page 'like a sow that hath
overwhelmed all her litter but one', or selects Shadow as the
3. 2. 280 ideal soldier because 'the foeman may with as great aim level at
the edge of a pen knife'; also his inimitable touches of vivid
5. 1. 91 description, as of Prince Hal, who laughs 'till his face be like
a wet cloak ill laid up'; but there is no sustained, good-humoured,
sweet-flavoured wit of the quality of the immortal scene in the
Boar's Head Tavern when in King Cambyses' vein he plays the
part of the king reproving his erring son.

In like manner, an examination of the images used by other
characters reveals much of their individuality and tastes, and
their use of them must, of course, unconsciously, subtly affect
our impression of their personalities. In this respect, the images
of Macbeth, of Lady Macbeth and of Hamlet are especially
interesting.

APPENDIX VIII

Bell-ringing

I HAVE said that the man-made noises in a mediaeval city (and
London was only just emerging from this state) must have been
negligible compared to what they are in a modern city to-day, with
the excruciating steel drill and the horns and brakes of motor
traffic, but there was present at the earlier date a particular
clamour of sound, almost continuous and very insistent, which
we are now happily almost entirely spared, and that was the
ringing of bells.

One interesting point about this constant bell-ringing is that
it is symbolic of a fundamental attitude of mind, which, as

Spengler has pointed out[1], is one of the root differences between the classical and the modern man's outlook on the world, and that is the keen and ever present consciousness of Time, of past and future.

This sense—so deep in the older civilisations of Egypt and Babylonia—modern western man, from the early middle ages on, has strongly developed, symbolising it by the bell and later by the clock and watch.

The Greek, on the contrary, seems to have been without this sense, or deliberately to have turned aside from it; he lived in the moment, no time reckoning or recurrent commemoration, no preservation of the past or economic action for the future, seem to have entered into his daily life, and the form of his drama—a single situation or crisis at a special moment—as also his conception of tragedy—a blind stroke of Fate—are the natural outcome of this attitude.

Our drama, on the other hand, and the Shakespearian especially, is concerned above all else with the development or deterioration of a soul, the life history of a man or of a nation, while the sense of the passing of Time, and of its irreversibility, is the constant tragic theme of the poets from the Renaissance onwards.

This keen consciousness of Time, which to-day is regulated by clocks and punctuated by the catching of trains and the keeping of appointments, was in Shakespeare's London—as in mediaeval Europe generally, but most especially in England—outwardly expressed by the ringing of bells.

To the Elizabethan therefore, their sound was a constant reminder of the passage of time and all which that connotes. It aroused also many other associations and emotions, for the toll of the bell permeated the daily life of the people in a way very hard for us to realise to-day.

It marked not only the regular passing of the hours, but events of every sort, many of which led the mind unconsciously to dwell on past and future.

The bells rang, as to-day, as a summons to worship and prayer,

---

[1] In a very suggestive chapter, Destiny and Causality, in *The Decline of the West* (translated by Atkinson, 1926), especially pp. 131-4.

as a fire alarm and a wedding peal; but they rang also as a warning
of peril, a signal for action and a call to rebellion, as a protection
against storm, tempest and plague, and to summon the citizens
together (as in *Othello*, 2. 3. 159–60, 173–4); they ushered in
massacres and proclaimed victories, they rang for anniversaries
and memorials and coronations, for hangings and proclamations
and sermons, for the sick, the dying and the dead.

Everyday practical life in town and country was regulated by
their sound, the 'harvest', the 'seeding' and the 'gleaning'
bells directed labour, the lord's oven was declared ready for use
and the butter market open, the children were summoned to
school, and the night watchman announced his presence by the
ringing of a bell. The reverberation of chimes, and ringing and
tolling were thus continually in a Londoner's ear, for it was a city
of a hundred and fourteen churches, full of towers and spires and
belfries, some of which were probably always ringing (cp. *Per.*
2. 1. 45). We are told that this continual 'jangling' of bells gave
great offence to the sick, and in September 1592 'extraordinary
ringing' was forbidden. 'In the day time', writes the author of
Lachrymae Londinenses, 'what else have we almost but the Bells
ringing of knells? and in the night season (when we should take
our rest) we are interrupted by the Continual tolling of Passing
Bells, and anon the ringing out of the sunne.'

We naturally find references to this nerve-racking noise in the
dramatists, as in *The Silent Woman*, i, i, and also similes drawn
from it, as when Volpone, in torture from Lady Politick's 'hail
of words', cries:

Volpone, 3. 2   The bells, in time of pestilence, ne'er made
            Like noise, or were in that perpetual motion!

Sh. Hol. 3. 1 and Hodge, in the *Shoemaker's Holiday*, declares that the coins
jingle in his pocket 'like St Mary Overy's bells'.

It is strange, in view of Shakespeare's sensitive ear, that we
find nothing, except perhaps the reference in *Pericles* (2. 1. 45),
which can be interpreted as a complaint about this noise, and it is
interesting to note that out of all these various bell sounds on
occasions grave and gay, it is the passing bell and the funeral

knell that has chiefly impressed his imagination and remained in his memory.

He mentions bells knolling to church (*A.Y.L.I.* 2. 7. 114), and the bells of St Bennet (*Tw. N.* 5. 1. 37), he twice draws a simile from discordant bells, Ophelia's description of Hamlet's 'noble and most sovereign reason',

> Like sweet bells jangled, out of tune and harsh, *Ham. 3. 1. 163*

and the mimicry of Patroclus, who when he speaks,

> 'Tis like a chime a-mending; *T. and C. 1. 3. 159*

he refers several times to the 'midnight bell' who,

> with his iron tongue and brazen mouth *K. J. 3. 3. 37*
> sounds   on into the drowsy ear of night; *and cp. also A. and C. 3. 13. 185*

but nearly all his other references are to the passing or to the funeral bell. It is clear that its slow sound and sorrowful association has profoundly impressed him, and all the force of the peculiar emotional effect of its heavy saddening reiteration is summed up in the adjective 'sullen' (adopted later by Milton for the curfew), by which he thrice describes it. The knell symbolises for him sorrow, irrevocability, doom. *M.N.D. 5. 1. 370* *2 H. IV, 3. 2. 224*

He hears it in the tone of stern sad finality of the words of Coriolanus, in the mourning grief of Timon's faithful servants, and in the hopeless sorrow of the father who has killed his son in civil war, when he cries *Cor. 5. 4. 21* *Timon, 4. 2. 25*

> My sighing breast shall be thy funeral bell. *3 H. VI, 2. 5. 117*

Leontes, in his mad jealousy, pictures himself driven to his grave by disgrace, 'contempt and clamour' sounding his knell, Bertram's too tardy expression of love is heard by the king as 'sweet Helen's knell', and Chatillon, sent back to France with the English king's message of defiance is imagined by John to be at one and the same time the trumpet of his wrath and his own passing bell, the 'sullen presage' of his 'own decay'. *W.T. 1. 2. 189* *All's Well 5. 3. 67* *K.J. 1. 1. 27*

The sound of it echoes through Shakespeare's earliest poems,

> And now his grief may be compared well *V. and A. 701*
> To one sore sick that hears the passing-bell;
> For sorrow, like a heavy-hanging bell *Luc. 1493*
> Once set on ringing, with his own weight goes;
> Then little strength rings out the doleful knell;

it forms the lyric stimulus which gives rise to the emotion of the beautiful seventy-first Sonnet,

> No longer mourn for me when I am dead
> Than you shall hear the surly sullen bell
> Give warning to the world that I am fled,

in his first history (in a scene undoubtedly his) it strikes an ominous and dramatic note,

1 H.VI, 4. 2. 39

> Hark! hark! the Dauphin's drum, a warning bell,
> Sings heavy music to thy timorous soul,

and in his earliest tragedy the bell stands for a symbol of sorrow and death, 'turn our instruments', cries old Capulet, 'to melancholy bells', 'this sight of death', says Lady Capulet,

R. and J. 4. 5. 86; 5. 3. 206

> is as a bell
> That warns my old age to a sepulchre.

Perhaps the most vivid as well as most closely accurate use of it as a simile is Northumberland's comparison to it of the bringer of unwelcome news, whose tongue

2 H. IV, 1. 1. 102

> Sounds ever after as a sullen bell
> Remember'd tolling a departing friend,

and the most dramatic use of it is the moment when Macbeth, hearing Lady Macbeth's bell, goes to murder his kinsman and king, muttering,

Mac. 2. 1. 62

> I go, and it is done: the bell invites me.
> Hear it not, Duncan, for it is a knell
> That summons thee to heaven, or to hell.

One may well ask—was it just chance or an extraordinary sense of fitness which led Thomas Hardy to select the moment of the tolling of Shakespeare's own passing bell in Stratford town for the setting of his delightful poem, 'To Shakespeare after 300 years', published in *A Book of Homage to Shakespeare*, 1916?

INDEX

All entries, except those in which an author's name is given, refer to Shakespeare. The more important entries are given in heavy type and the less important ones are in a light type.

Titles of Shakespeare's works are given in the shortened forms (see p. xvi).

IMAGES OF WILLIAM SHAKESPEARE (cont.)

SHAKESPEARE, WILLIAM (*cont.*)

Mind and Imagination

SHAKESPEARE, WILLIAM (cont.)

working, 249, 354–5; objective in his dramatic characters, 4, 200; poetry, greatest, expressed in simplest metaphor, 15; style and method of imagery, 51, 52, 55; subjects which chiefly occupy his, 44, 45; suggestion, use of, 58–9, 62, 67, 69, 83; symbolic vision revealed in the floating images of each play, 214; tendency to return to a group of associated ideas, 186, 190, 199; theme of his drama, 381

imagination:
captivated by Ptolemaic system, 21, 22–3; *imaginative conception of:* Antony, 350–4; *Ham.,* the problem in, 318–19; King John, 248–50; Macbeth, 324, 326–7; Richard II, 233–4; Richard III, 232–3; *R. and J.,* 312; 'martlet' imagery, events of life possibly deduced from, 374–7; *mind,* his, revealed in his imagery, 43, 44, 146, qualities of his, 200–1; troubled mind revealed through imagery in *T. and C.,* and *Ham.,* 320; working of his, as seen in the tragedies. 310; qualities of his imagination, 67, 200–1, Murry, J. Middleton, on, 8; state of, when writing *K.J.,* 245, *M. for M.,* 289–90

ideas:
on physical phenomena:
colour, 57–69, food, 83–5, 117–24, 320–4; music, 69–70, 74–5, 271; reflection and reverberation, 328; sickness, 134–7, 203; silence and stillness, 74, 78; sound, 74–8; sunset and sunrise, 63; 'tempest' idea, 24–5; war, 28–9, 76–7
on abstract themes:
action, consequences of, 238, 240; birth and generation, 238–9, 240; death, 180–5, own view of, 183–5; evil, 79–80, 89, 158–67, 171, 328–9, own view of, 207, 328–9; fear, 154–6, 158, 207, own view of, 154–5; flattery, 195–9; friendship, 171, 195, 223; goodness, 168–71; hate, 153–4; heaven and hell, 78; human life and

action, 19, 25, 56, 86, 87–90, own view of, 206–7; inheritance, 238, 240–1; kingship, 217–21, 225–6, 235–8; love, 18, 146, 147–8, 149–53, own view of, 152, (false) 195, 207; lust, 70, 120–1, 147, 321; man, his nature, 19, 86, his position in human society, 75–6, his relation to his fellow-men, 207–9; pain, 107, 135, 335–6; temperance, 132–3, 136; time, 28, 172–80, own view of, 176, 177, 178–80; vastness, 350–4
central belief and philosophy, 207–9

imagery:
characteristics of, 213, 214, 215, 224, 225, 273, 288–9; contrasting, his use of, 58, 60, 62, 63–5, 66–8, 310–14, 319–20; events of life and experiences possibly seen in, 96, 99, 296 *n.* 2, 374; examples of effects of, 9–11; favourite (of the body and its actions), 253 (*see under* body *and under* movement *for details*); habits and character of, seen in his, 202, 203, 206; infinity of certain qualities in, 151–2; number of images in plays and poems, 361–2; omissions in range of, 45; outstanding characteristic of, 50; proportions of, compared with Bacon and Marlowe, 371
recurrent imagery, a habit of his, 224, 225 (*see under* images, recurrent); study of, and its results, 146, 202, 355
subject-matter of, 13, 43, 44–5, 377, charts, I, V; examples of analysis of, 364–71; two main groups of, 44; *see under* images, subject-matter; value and suggestiveness of, 5–6

Comparison with contemporary writers:
with Bacon, 16–29, 371; summary, 28–9
with Chapman, 30, 32, 38, 39, 95–6, 116–17
with Dekker, 30, 34–5, 38, 39, 40–1, 116, 251 *n.* 1

with Jonson, 30, 31-2, 34, 37-8,
49-50, 94-5, 111, 373
with Marlowe, 13-15, 113, 371
with Massinger, 41
with twelve dramatists (works of),
362-3
with various dramatists, 94-6
See also Elizabethan dramatists;
and individual dramatists by
name
Shakespeare's England
(vol. II), 32 n. 2, 69
Sharp, William
Life and Letters of Joseph Severn,
56 n. 1
Shelley, Percy Bysshe
quoted, on images and analogy, 7
Prometheus Unbound, nature imagery
of, 354
works, Defence of Poetry, A, 7
Ships
See under Sea
Sickness and medicine
interest in, and images from, 129-36,
366, 369, charts, I, V, VII
specific subjects:
counter-irritation, 153; inoculation, 135; plague, 130-2; poison,
medicinal use of, 153; surfeit,
cause of ill-health, 132-3; tumour or ulcer, 79, 134, 159-60,
161, 316, 318
used in plays:
in Cor., 134, 347-9; in Ham., 79,
133-4, 316-18, 320, 369; in Mac.,
331-2; in T. and C., 134, 320;
in W.T., 306
mind, influence of the, on health of
body, 136-7
Silence and Stillness
images of and attitude towards, 74-5,
78
Sin
ideas and images of, 79-80, 161-2,
331-2
See also Evil
Smell
acuteness of sense of, and images from,
78-81, 112
specific images:
bad smells, 78, 80; flowers, 80-1;
perfume, 81; rank smell of evil
(flowers and weeds), 79-80,
161-3; town smells, 78, 81

Snails
knowledge of, and images from, 107-8
Sonnets
birds, song of, in, 73
colour, use of, in, 68-9
death, views on, in Son. CXLVI, 185
ideas of time and love in, 176-7
passages referred to: V, 175; VII, 63;
VIII, 74; XII, 69; XV, 87, 176;
XVIII, 88; XIX, 175, 176; XXII,
137; XXIX, 73; XXXIII, 62; LIV,
80; LVI, 147; LX, 176; LXIII, 176;
LXIV, 176; LXV, 145, 176; LXIX,
81; LXXI, 384; LXXIII, 69, 73,
184 n. 1; LXXV, 117, 147; LXXXV,
145; LXXXVII, 191; XC, 15; XCIV,
81; XCVII, 73; XCIX, 69; C, 176;
CII, 73; CVIII, 176, 177; CXIV,
151; CXV, 148, 177; CXVI, 155,
176, 177; CXVIII, 80, 123, 135,
147; CXXIII, 175, 176; CXXV,
118; CXXXII, 62; CXLIII, 138;
CXLVI, 185
Sound
interest in, and images from, 74-8,
(in Temp.) 75, 300-4
specific subjects:
bells, passing or funeral, 73,
383-4; elements, clamour of,
302-4; reverberation over vast
regions, 73, 327, 328-9, 331;
three classes of sound in images,
73
See also Birds, song of; Music; Noise;
Voice, human
Spengler, Oswald
Decline of the West, The, quoted, 381
Sport
knowledge of, and images from, 26-7,
30-3, 44, 264, 266, 366, 368; subject-matter of, 372, charts, I, V
used by contemporary writers:
used by Bacon, 26-7; used by
Elizabethan dramatists, 30-3
See also Games, and sports by name
Stillness
See Silence
Stowe, John
Survey of London, A, 111, 277
**Substances, appearance and
texture of**
interest in, and images from, 36-7,
82-3, 367, 370, 373, charts,
I, V

Substances, appearance and texture of (*cont.*)
specific subject:
skin, human, colour of, 66, texture of, 82
used by other Elizabethan dramatists, 36-8, 39
See also Metals

Suggestion
colours indicated by, 58-9, 62, 67, 69
use of, in *Mac.*, 83, 334

Sun
observation of, and images from, 61-3, 235-8
specific subjects:
human face, compared with, 61-2; king seen under form of the sun, 235-8, 239, favourites of king seen as sun-beams, 237-8; rising sun (changing colours of), 58, 263, significance of, 63; setting sun, significance of, 63, 239

Svartengren, T. H.
Intensifying Similes in English, 9 *n.* 1

Swimming
knowledge of, and images from, 99

Sympathy
of Shakespeare, with people and animals; *see under* **Shakespeare**, characteristics
of writers, contemporary: of Bacon, 27; of Dekker, *see under* Dekker; of Elizabethan dramatists, 32-3

Taming of the Shrew, The
Petruchio's character and images in, 286-7
passages referred to: 73, 88, 111, 118, 120, 122, 124, 286, 287

Temperance
ideas on, 133, 136, 203

Tempest, The
dominating action and atmosphere of sound expressed in groups of images, 300-4; use of sound in, 75
special forms:
clamour of elements, 302-4; island sounds, 300-1; symphony of sound, 300
passages referred to: 5, 46, 55, 70 *n.* 1, 71, 75, 89, 103, 115, 124, 125, 138, 162, 194, 300, 301, 302, 303, 304

Tennis
knowledge of, and images from, 27, 110
used by Bacon, 27

Theatre
images from the, 45, 367, 370

Tilting
knowledge of, and images from, 110, 264

Time
ideas on, and images about, 28, 70, 172-80, 187; in *T. and C.*, 176, 177-80
specific functions and aspects:
destroying power, 175, 176-7, 178-9; effect of time on human life, 172; love not under the dominion of, 152, 177-80; nurse and breeder, 173-4; revealer of truth, 28, 172; ripening process of, 172; shaping function of, 174-5; two outstanding characteristics of, 175; variable pace of, 175-6
those used by Bacon, 28
measurement of, in *M.N.D.*, 259-60, 261-2
passing of, indicated by bells, 381-2

Timon of Athens
authorship of, 343-4
dominating image of dogs, licking and candy, in, 198-9, 345
gold and metals, symbolism in, 344-5
hate, emotion of, in, 154
idea of false friends and flatterers, in, 198-9, 345
images from animals, 344; qualities of, 343-4
love, aspect of, in, 180 *n.* 1
passages referred to: 25, 28, 76, 121, 126, 144, 154, 171, 180, 180 *n.* 1, 193, 198, 199, 203, 208, 344-5, 383

Titus Andronicus
passages referred to: 10, 62, 74, 82, 93, 102, 104, 112, 126, 137, 173, 328

Tools
knowledge of, and images from, 126, 128-9

Topical images
subject-matter of, 373, charts, I, V
used in plays:
in *A.Y.L.I.*, 277-8; in *M.W.*, 266; in *Tw. N.*, 269
used by Elizabethan dramatists, 373

CHARTS

I

CHART SHOWING THE RANGE AND SUBJECTS OF IMAGES IN FIVE OF SHAKESPEARE'S PLAYS

ROMEO AND JULIET, RICHARD III, AS YOU LIKE IT, MACBETH, A WINTER'S TALE

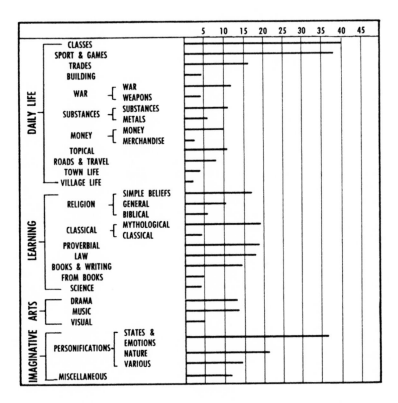

With Marlowe, learning (chiefly classical) leads, and nature (chiefly celestial bodies) and animals come second, whereas with Shakespeare, nature and animals lead, and learning takes fourth place only. With Marlowe, imaginative (chiefly personifications) is a larger section than the images drawn from daily life, whereas with Shakespeare, the daily life images are more than double the imaginative group.

II

CHART SHOWING THE RANGE AND SUBJECTS OF MARLOWE'S IMAGES IN THEIR EXACT PROPORTION

690 IMAGES ARE HERE REPRESENTED, TAKEN FROM *TAMBURLAINE I & II, EDWARD II, HERO AND LEANDER,* AND THE BETTER AUTHENTICATED PARTS OF *DR. FAUSTUS, THE JEW OF MALTA, THE MASSACRE OF PARIS,* AND *DIDO*

No. of Images	10	20	30	40	50	60	70	80	90	100	110	120	130

NATURE
- CELESTIAL BODIES
- WEATHER
- PLANTS
- ELEMENTS
- SEA
- FARMING
- GARDENING
- SEASONS

ANIMALS
- FOUR-FOOTED
- BIRDS
- FABULOUS
- FISH
- INSECTS

DOMESTIC
- FIRE & LIGHT
- HOUSE
- JEWELS
- CLOTHES
- BIRTH & DEATH
- CHILDREN
- GAMES

BODY
- BODY & ACTION
- FOOD
- SICKNESS

DAILY LIFE
- SUBSTANCES
- WAR
- CLASSES
- SPORTS
- TRADES
- MONEY

LEARNING
- CLASSICAL
- FROM BOOKS
- RELIGION
- SCIENCE
- BOOKS
- LAW

ARTS
- MUSIC
- DRAMA
- ART

IMAGINATIVE
- PERSONIFICATIONS
- FANTASTIC
- IMAGINATIVE

CHART SHOWING THE RANGE AND SUBJECTS OF BACON'S IMAGES

ESSAYS, NEW ATLANTIS, HENRY VII, AND ADVANCEMENT OF LEARNING

		5	10	15	20	25	30	35	40	45

NATURE
- SEA & SHIPS
- GROWING THINGS
- WEATHER
- GARDENING
- ELEMENTS
- FARMING
- NATURAL FEATURES
- CELESTIAL BODIES

ANIMALS
- BIRDS
- FABULOUS
- INSECTS

DOMESTIC
- LIGHT
- FIRE
- TEXTILES
- MISCELLANEOUS

BODY
- SICKNESS
- BODY & ACTION
- FOOD

DAILY LIFE
- SPORT & GAMES
- TRADES
- WAR
- SUBSTANCES
- ROADS
- COMMERCE
- CLASSES
- MISCELLANEOUS

LEARNING
- SCIENCE
- RELIGION
- CLASSICS
- FROM BOOKS

ARTS
- MUSIC
- THEATRE
- ART

IMAGINATIVE
- IMAGINATIVE

IV

A DETAILED CHART OF THE IMAGES GROUPED UNDER 'DAILY LIFE' IN SHAKESPEARE AND FIVE CONTEMPORARY DRAMATISTS: SHOWING THEIR PROPORTION AND DISTRIBUTION

	No. of Images	1	5	10	15	20	25	30	35	40	45	50

SHAKESPEARE
- SPORT
- CLASSES
- TRADES
- WAR
- SUBSTANCES
- MONEY
- TOPICAL
- ROADS
- BUILDINGS
- STATE
- TOWN LIFE

MARLOWE
- SPORT
- CLASSES
- TRADES
- WAR
- SUBSTANCES
- MONEY
- TOPICAL
- ROADS
- BUILDINGS
- STATE
- TOWN LIFE

BEN JONSON
- SPORT
- CLASSES
- TRADES
- WAR
- SUBSTANCES
- MONEY
- TOPICAL
- ROADS
- BUILDINGS
- STATE
- TOWN LIFE

CHAPMAN
- SPORT
- CLASSES
- TRADES
- WAR
- SUBSTANCES
- MONEY
- TOPICAL
- ROADS
- BUILDINGS
- STATE
- TOWN LIFE

		1	5	10	15	20	25	30	35	40	45	50
DEKKER	SPORT											
	CLASSES											
	TRADES											
	WAR											
	SUBSTANCES											
	MONEY											
	TOPICAL											
	ROADS											
	BUILDINGS											
	STATE											
	TOWN LIFE											
MASSINGER	SPORT											
	CLASSES											
	TRADES											
	WAR											
	SUBSTANCES											
	MONEY											
	TOPICAL											
	ROADS											
	BUILDINGS											
	STATE											
	TOWN LIFE											

In each case, except Marlowe, the images are taken from five selected
plays. The Marlowe images are from the whole of his work: i.e.
Tamburlaine I & II, Edward II, Hero and Leander, and the better
authenticated parts of four other plays.

CHART SHOWING THE RANGE AND SUBJECTS OF SHAKESPEARE'S IMAGES IN THEIR EXACT PROPORTION

No. of Images — 20 40 60 80 100 120 140 160 180 200 220 240 260

NATURE

GROWING THINGS — FLOWERS, TREES, PLANTS, FRUIT, WEEDS

WEATHER — COLD, STORM, WIND, RAIN, CLOUD, MIST, CHANGES

SEA & SHIPS — SHIPS & SEAFARING, SEA

CELESTIAL BODIES — SUN, STARS, SHADOW, MOON

ELEMENTS — WATER, RIVER, EARTH

GARDENING — VARIOUS, GRAFTING, RIPENESS, GROWTH

SEASONS — SPRING, NIGHT & DAY, WINTER, SUMMER

FARMING

NATURAL FEATURES

ANIMALS

FOUR-FOOTED — DOMESTIC, DOGS, WILD, LIONS, VARIOUS

BIRDS — SINGLE KINDS, GENERAL, WINGS & FLIGHT, FALCONRY, SNARING

INSECTS — VARIOUS, BEES, FLIES, SPIDERS, GENERAL, MOLLUSC

REPTILES

FABULOUS

FISH

DOMESTIC

HOUSE — INDOOR, OUT

TEXTILES — CLOTHES, TEXTILES

FIRE & LIGHT — FIRE, LIGHT &, DARKNESS

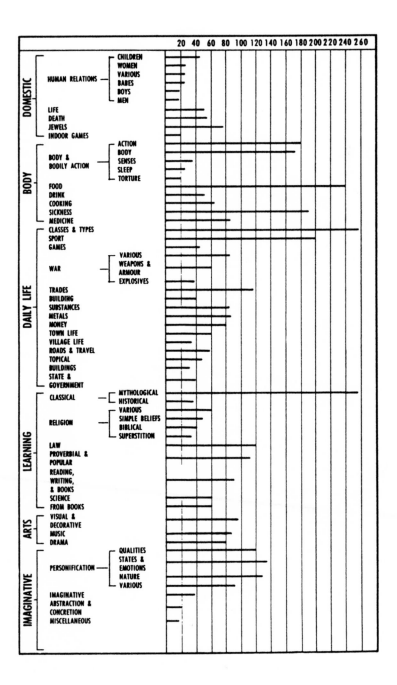

VI

A PICTORIAL STATEMENT OF THE DOMINATING IMAGES IN <u>KING JOHN</u> AND <u>HENRY VIII</u>

BODY & BODILY ACTION ════════
PERSONIFICATIONS ────────

Sh's Age	Date		No. of Images	5	10	15	20	25	30	35	40
27	1591	LOVE'S LABOURS									
		TWO GENTLEMEN									
28	1592	COMEDY OF ERRORS									
		I HENRY VI									
		II HENRY VI									
		III HENRY VI									
	1592-6	ROMEO & JULIET									
29	1593	RICHARD III									
		RICHARD II									
		TITUS									
30	1594-5	MIDSUMMER NIGHT									
	1594-6	MERCHANT OF VENICE									
31	1595	ALL'S WELL									
		TAMING OF THE SHREW									
	1595-6	KING JOHN									
33	1597	I HENRY IV									
		II HENRY IV									
		MERRY WIVES									
34	1598	HENRY V									
35	1599	MUCH ADO									
		AS YOU LIKE IT									
36	1600	TWELFTH NIGHT									
37	1601	JULIUS CAESAR									
38	1602	HAMLET									

Sh's Age	Date		No. of Images	5	10	15	20	25	30	35	40
39	1603	TROILUS & CRESSIDA									
40	1604	MEASURE FOR MEASURE									
41	1604-5	OTHELLO									
42	1606	MACBETH									
43	1607	KING LEAR									
44	1608	TIMON OF ATHENS									
		ANTONY & CLEOPATRA									
		PERICLES									
45	1609	CORIOLANUS									
46	1610	CYMBELINE									
47	1611	WINTER'S TALE									
		THE TEMPEST									
49	1613	HENRY VIII									

CHART VI

The outstanding point here is the extraordinary number of personifications in *King John*. It is the only case in the whole of the plays, in which
images of Nature or Animals are outnumbered by any other class. *King
John* has also a larger number of 'body' images than any other play
except *Henry VIII*, and these two groups together, amounting in all to
71 images, help to give the intense feeling of vivid life and movement so
characteristic of the play.

It is not possible entirely to separate images of body and bodily action
and personification, for quite a number might equally well be classified
under either heading. This is especially true of a play like *King John*.
In such cases my general practice is to put the image under 'Personification' when that seems the most striking aspect, and under 'Body' when
the special movement appears accentuated. Thus I class 'Confronts your
city's eyes, your winking gates' under the latter, and

> 'the hearts
> Of all his people shall revolt from him
> And kiss the lips of unacquainted change'

under the former. But although in *King John* and some other plays these
two classes of images touch and even overlap, yet in *Romeo and Juliet*,
where naturally—as it is highly poetical—personifications are many,
bodily movement is not specially emphasised, although these are, on the
other hand, eight personifications of light and darkness.

The great number of images from bodily action in *Henry VIII* is also
seen here, though in this case the imaginative impetus entirely differs
from that in *King John*, and personifications are very few.

The high number of body images in *Hamlet* is closely connected with
the leading 'motive' of disease, as also in *Troilus and Cressida*. In *King
Lear* and *Coriolanus* also they are connected with the dominating imaginative motives of torture and parts of the body respectively.

Apart from these plays, it is interesting to note how much higher is
this class of image (bodily action and personification) in the histories
generally than in the other plays.

Signs of its presence appear in the last 2 parts of *Henry VI*, in the two
Richards it is strong, culminating in *King John*, carried on in 2 *Henry IV*
and *Henry V*, and culminating again in a different way and in one group
only in *Henry VIII*.

It would seem as if the practical vigour, movement and action of a
historical drama called forth from the poet naturally an abundance of
this type of image.

CHART VII

Note the extraordinary number of food and cooking images in *Troilus,* which dwarfs all others of their kind throughout the plays, showing how much the poet's imagination ran on this subject in this play, as also in *Hamlet.*

The apparent number of food images in *Romeo and Juliet* is misleading, for they are chiefly of contrasting taste—sweet and sour, gall and sweet, carrying out the idea of sharp and sudden contrast which is symbolised throughout the play.

The number of sickness images in *Hamlet* is greater than in any other play, and the number of them in *Troilus* is only surpassed (after *Hamlet*) by those in *Coriolanus,* where they arise out of the general dominating image of the body and its members.

Food and sickness images are fairly constant in Shakespeare's work all through, and it is worth noting that where the number of one or both falls markedly below the average, it is either in a play with relatively few images (*Comedy of Errors* and *Julius Caesar*) or a doubtful play (3 parts of *Henry VI, Taming of the Shrew, Pericles*).

Though, however, these images are constant, they change considerably in character. The food images in the earlier plays, i.e. the 3 parts of *Henry VI,* and the early comedies are much more crude and simple than the very varied and sophisticated ones in the later plays. Surfeit, hunger, feasting, fasting and drinking, are the chief subjects of the early images, whereas later there is much individual mention of various kinds of food, while in *Troilus and Cressida* no less than twelve different processes of cooking are alluded to or described.

So also with the sickness images. The early ones are chiefly of corrosive or balm applied to wounds, broken limbs and bruises or light references to plague and pestilence. Only in the later ones comes the feeling of horror and disgust at foul disease, and in *Hamlet* we are almost startled at the constant conception of a corrupt and hidden tumour or cancer, which is the central imaginative symbol of the tragedy.

The dates of the plays are, of course, only approximate. The chart was drawn up before Sir E. K. Chambers's book appeared, or I should have adhered to his dates.

VII

A PICTORIAL STATEMENT OF THE DOMINATING IMAGES IN <u>HAMLET</u> AND <u>TROILUS</u> AND <u>CRESSIDA</u>

FOOD, DRINK, & COOKING ▭▭▭▭
SICKNESS, DISEASE, & MEDICINE ▬▬▬▬▬

Sh's Age	Date	No. of Images	5	10	15	20	25	30	35	40
27	1591	LOVE'S LABOURS								
		TWO GENTLEMEN								
28	1592	COMEDY OF ERRORS								
		I HENRY VI								
		II HENRY VI								
		III HENRY VI								
	1592-6	ROMEO & JULIET								
29	1593	RICHARD III								
		RICHARD II								
		TITUS								
30	1594-5	MIDSUMMER NIGHT								
	1594-6	MERCHANT OF VENICE								
31	1595	ALL'S WELL								
		TAMING OF THE SHREW								
	1595-6	KING JOHN								
33	1597	I HENRY IV								
		II HENRY IV								
		MERRY WIVES								
34	1598	HENRY V								
35	1599	MUCH ADO								
		AS YOU LIKE IT								
36	1600	TWELFTH NIGHT								
37	1601	JULIUS CAESAR								
38	1602	HAMLET								

			5	10	15	20	25	30	35	40
39	1603	TROILUS & CRESSIDA								
40	1604	MEASURE FOR MEASURE								
41	1604-5	OTHELLO								
42	1606	MACBETH								
43	1607	KING LEAR								
44	1608	TIMON OF ATHENS								
		ANTONY & CLEOPATRA								
		PERICLES								
45	1609	CORIOLANUS								
46	1610	CYMBELINE								
47	1611	WINTER'S TALE								
		THE TEMPEST								
49	1613	HENRY VIII								

Printed in the United States
136274LV00002B/24/P